SAN FRANCISCO
& NORTHERN CALIFORNIA

POWELL
AND
MARKET

9

"Meet me
at the
St. Francis"

HYDE to BEACH
FISHERMANS
WHARF

LONDON, NEW YORK,
MELBOURNE, MUNICH AND DELHI
www.dk.com

Produced by Pardoe Blacker Publishing Limited (UK)
PROJECT EDITOR Linda Williams
ART EDITOR Kelvin Barratt
EDITORS Jo Bourne, Irena Hoare, Esther Labi, Molly Lodge
DESIGNERS Jon Eland, Nick Raven, Steve Rowling
PICTURE RESEARCH Jill DeCet, Lindsay Kefauvre
CONSULTANT Don George
MAIN CONTRIBUTORS Jamie Jensen, Barry Parr
CONTRIBUTORS Dawn Douglas, Shirley Streshinsky

PHOTOGRAPHERS
Neil Lukas, Andrew McKinney

ILLUSTRATORS
Arcana Studios, Dean Entwhistle, Nick Lipscombe

Reproduced by Colourscan, Singapore
Printed and bound by L. Rex Printing Company Limited, China

First American Edition, 1994
10 11 12 13 10 9 8 7 6 5 4 3 2

Published in the United States by DK Publishing, 375 Hudson Street,
New York, New York 10014

**Reprinted with revisions 1997 (twice), 1999, 2000, 2001,
2002, 2003, 2004, 2005, 2006, 2008, 2009, 2010**

Copyright © 1994, 2010 Dorling Kindersley Limited, London

Published in Great Britain by Dorling Kindersley Limited.

A CATALOGING IN PUBLICATION RECORD IS AVAILABLE FROM THE
LIBRARY OF CONGRESS.

ISSN 1542-1554
ISBN 978-0-75666-153-3

*Front cover main image: Golden Gate Bridge and skyline,
view from Marin Headlands*

◁ Golden Gate Bridge in fog

CONTENTS

**Early cartoon of gold
prospector (1848)**

INTRODUCING
SAN FRANCISCO

**Ghirardelli Square,
Fisherman's Wharf**

A view of Mendocino in Northern California

Palace of Fine Arts, Presidio

A Dungeness crab

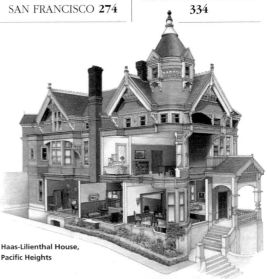
Haas-Lilienthal House, Pacific Heights

HOW TO USE THIS GUIDE

This Eyewitness Travel Guide helps you get the most from your stay in San Francisco with the minimum of difficulty. The opening section, *Introducing San Francisco*, locates the city geographically, sets modern San Francisco in its historical context and describes events through the entire year. *San Francisco at a Glance* is an overview of the city's main attractions. Section two, *San Francisco Area by Area*, starts on page 52. This

Planning the day's itinerary in San Francisco

covers the important city sights, with photographs, maps and illustrations. The *Northern California* section features recommended places of interest in the region plus two suggested excursions. Tips for restaurants, shopping, hotels, entertainment, sports and children's activities are found in the section on *Travelers' Needs*. The final section, *Survival Guide*, contains practical advice on everything from personal security to using public transportation.

FINDING YOUR WAY AROUND THE SIGHTSEEING SECTION

Each of the eight sightseeing areas in the city is color-coded for easy reference. Every chapter opens with an introduction to the part of San Francisco it covers, describing its history and character, followed by a Street-by-

Street map illustrating the heart of the area. Finding your way around each chapter is made simple by the numbering system used throughout. The most important sights are covered in detail on two or more full pages.

Each area has color-coded thumb tabs.

Locator map

A locator map shows where you are in relation to other areas in the city center.

A suggested route takes in the most interesting and attractive streets in the area.

1 Introduction to the area
For easy reference, the sights in each area are numbered and plotted on an area map. To help the visitor, this map also shows BART stations, cable car turntables, and parking areas. Key sights are listed by category: Churches and Temples; Museums and Galleries; Historic Streets and Buildings; Shopping Streets; and Parks and Gardens.

The area shaded pink is shown in greater detail on the Street-by-Street map on the following pages.

2 Street-by-Street map
This gives a bird's-eye view of the most important parts of each sightseeing area. The numbering of the sights ties in with the area map and the fuller descriptions on the pages that follow.

The list of star sights recommends the places that no visitor should miss.

SAN FRANCISCO AREA MAP

The colored areas shown on this map *(see inside front cover)* are the eight main sightseeing areas – each covered by a full chapter in *San Francisco Area by Area (pp52–181)*. They are highlighted on other maps throughout the book. In *San Francisco at a Glance (pp34–47)*, for example, they help locate the top sights. The area map is also used to show some of the top shopping areas *(pp246–7)* and entertainment venues *(pp260–1)*.

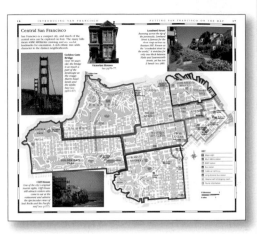

Façades of important buildings are often shown to help you recognize them quickly.

Practical information lists all the information you need to visit every sight, including a map reference to the *Street Finder (pp302–313)*.

Numbers refer to each sight's position on the area map and its place in the chapter.

The visitors' checklist provides all the practical information needed to plan your visit.

3 Detailed information on each sight

All the important sights in San Francisco are described individually. They are listed in order, following the numbering on the area map. Practical information on opening hours, telephone numbers, admission charges and facilities available is given for each sight. The key to the symbols used can be found on the back flap.

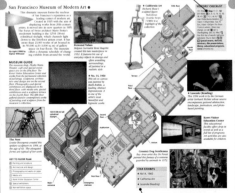

4 San Francisco's major sights

Museums and galleries have color-coded floor plans to help you find important exhibits; and historic buildings are dissected to reveal their interiors.

Stars indicate the features no visitor should miss.

INTRODUCING
SAN FRANCISCO

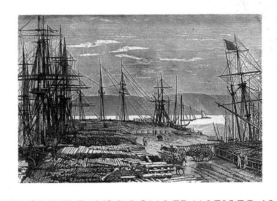

FOUR GREAT DAYS IN SAN FRANCISCO

Rhino sculpture – Asian Arts Museum

Set on steep, wooded hills and almost surrounded by a vast bay, this jewel of a city is, above all, photogenic. Equip yourself with a camera, a map and good walking shoes, and set off to discover its historic sights, cultural treasures, and vibrant neighborhoods. Follow, or pick and choose from these self-guided tours to see the city from four different points of view. Important sights have page references so you can check for more details. The price guides include cost of travel, food and admission charges.

Rodin's *Thinker* at the Legion of Honor

ART, OLD AND NEW

- See masterpieces at the Legion of Honor
- Contemporary art at SFMOMA
- Treasures and tea at the Asian Art Museum
- Shopping in Hayes Valley

TWO ADULTS allow at least $122

Morning
Start the day with 4,000 years of ancient and European art at the **Legion of Honor** in Lincoln Park (see pp156–7). From the wooded setting, enjoy the bay views, then take the Muni streetcar to the Latino **Mission District** (see p131) to see flamboyant outdoor murals and browse avant-garde galleries and shops. For a quick lunch, munch on *tacos* at **La Taqueria** (see p236).

Afternoon
Take a Muni to Mario Botta-designed, modernist **SFMOMA** (see pp118–21) to commune with Warhol, Picasso, and more modern masters. Walk to Civic Center Plaza and the **Asian Art Museum** (see p126),

one of the largest museums in the world devoted to Asian art. Relax over tea in its café. Cross the plaza to the Beaux Arts-style, gilt rotunda of the **City Hall** (see p127). Head to **Hayes Valley** (see p128) admiring as you walk by, the glass-walled **Davies Symphony Hall** (see p126) and the **War Memorial Opera House** (see p127). Enjoy shopping in upscale fashion boutiques and bookshops around Hayes Valley and end the day with an aperitif at the **Absinthe Brasserie and Bar** (see p235).

JUST FOR KIDS

- Playtime at Yerba Buena Gardens
- A picnic lunch
- Fun at Fisherman's Wharf
- Old ships at Hyde Street Pier

FAMILY OF 4 allow at least $111

Morning
Start with pancakes and jukebox tunes at **Mel's Drive-In** (see p243). Walk a half block to **Yerba Buena Gardens** (see pp114–15) and run up the ramps to the space-age

Rooftop playground and 360-degree city views. Watch skaters in the ice skating rink or toss a few balls in the bowling center. Drop teenagers off at Zeum for performing arts activities, while little ones can spin on the 1906 Charles Looff carousel. Grab a take-out at one of the outdoor cafés and relax in the gardens.

Afternoon
Walk to the **Embarcadero Center** (see p110) and along the waterfront, or take a streetcar to **Fisherman's Wharf** (see pp79–81). At Pier 45, feed quarters into the 200 antique arcade games at Musée Méchanique. Watch street performers at **Pier 39** (see p82), a sprawling seaside complex of shops, eateries, and entertainments. There's a Venetian carousel, sharks in Underwater World and video games at Riptide Arcade; not forgetting the sea lions on K Dock. End up at Hyde Street Pier – board a schooner then pop into the **Maritime Historical Park** (see p83).

Fun for kids – bungee-jumping at Fisherman's Wharf

Houses overlooking Ocean Beach, a magnificent sweep of sand with fine views

A DAY OUTDOORS

- **Sea views at Ocean Beach**
- **Golden Gate Park**
- **Walk Golden Gate Bridge**
- **Chocolate galore**
- **Cable car ride to Nob Hill**

TWO ADULTS allow at least $100

Morning
Start with breakfast at the Beach Chalet (1000 Great Highway), **Ocean Beach** *(see p153)*. View the Depression-era murals, then set off into **Golden Gate Park** *(see pp144–5)*, past gardens, lakes, meadows, and playing fields to the **Conservatory of Flowers** *(see p152)*, a restored Victorian glass-house filled with exotic flora. Stroll in the **Japanese Tea Garden** *(see p147)*, rent a bike or a row boat, or visit the Botanical Garden **Strybing Arboretum** *(see p152)*. Just outside the park, have a fresh sushi lunch at Japanese restaurant **Ebisu** *(see p237)*.

Afternoon
Take Muni to the **Golden Gate Bridge** *(see pp64–7)* for a windy walk across and back. Walk under the bridge to pre-Civil War-era **Fort Point** *(see p62)* and follow the bayfront trail to **Crissy Field** *(see p62)*, to watch boats and windsurfers. Have a hot drink here at the Warming Hut Café. The young at heart will enjoy an hour or two at the science and technology playhouse (Exploratorium) in the **Palace of Fine Arts** *(see pp60–1)*. Walk to **Ghirardelli Square** *(see p83)*, where you'll find shops, eateries, an old-fashioned soda fountain, and a chocolate factory. At the cable car turnaround, hop onto a cable car and ride to the top of **Nob Hill** *(see p101)*. After a wander here, amble down to the bustling streets of **Chinatown** *(see pp94–100)*.

ALONG THE WATERFRONT

- **Home of the Giants**
- **Gourmet treats**
- **A walk in Levi's Plaza Park**
- **Sail around the bay or pay a visit to Alcatraz**

TWO ADULTS allow at least $102

Morning
Start your expedition with a coffee at **Caffè Roma II** *(see p242)*, then head to **AT&T Park** *(see p272)*, home of the San Francisco Giants. Stroll around the perimeter of the ball park for fabulous views. Proceed to the tall **Ferry Building** *(see p112)*, where in the glass-enclosed marketplace you can buy artisan cheeses, rare teas, pastries, and locally grown produce. Across the street, **Embarcadero Center** *(see p110)* is a six block, high-rise complex of shops and restaurants topped by tree-lined, sky-high terraces. From here, walk out onto the waterfront to hobnob with fishermen, perch on a bench, watch passing ships and snap the **Transamerica Pyramid** *(see p111)* on the skyline. Walk to **Levi's Plaza** *(see p93)*, a grassy area with a backdrop of vintage houses on Telegraph Hill, topped by **Coit Tower** *(see p93)*. For lunch, try a burger or ribs with a sea view in 1930s-style, chrome and neon **Fog City Diner** *(see p230)*.

Afternoon
Jump onto a vintage streetcar, or walk to Pier 41 at **Fisherman's Wharf** *(see pp80–1)* and take an hour-long Blue and Gold Fleet sightseeing trip around the bay and under the bridge. You can also cruise to the notorious prison island **Alcatraz** *(see pp84–7)* for a guided tour. Back at the wharf, look into the **Wax Museum** *(see p82)*. Finally, amble to **Fort Mason** *(see pp74–5)* to watch the sun set over the harbor.

Fog City Diner, a 1930s-style restaurant

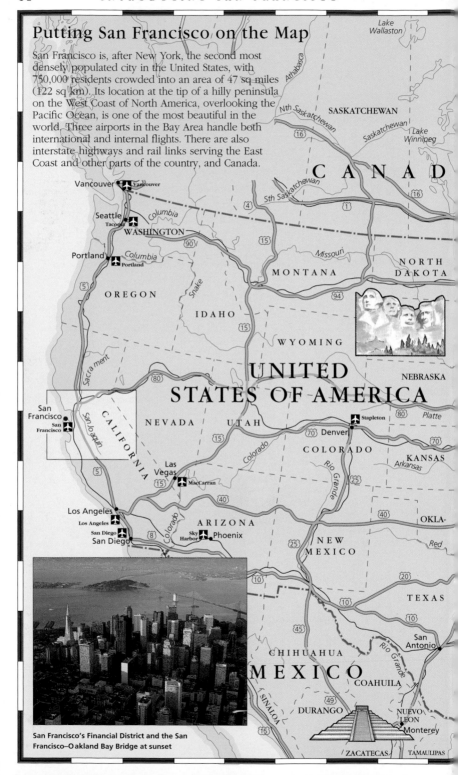

Putting San Francisco on the Map

San Francisco is, after New York, the second most densely populated city in the United States, with 750,000 residents crowded into an area of 47 sq miles (122 sq km). Its location at the tip of a hilly peninsula on the West Coast of North America, overlooking the Pacific Ocean, is one of the most beautiful in the world. Three airports in the Bay Area handle both international and internal flights. There are also interstate highways and rail links serving the East Coast and other parts of the country, and Canada.

San Francisco's Financial District and the San Francisco–Oakland Bay Bridge at sunset

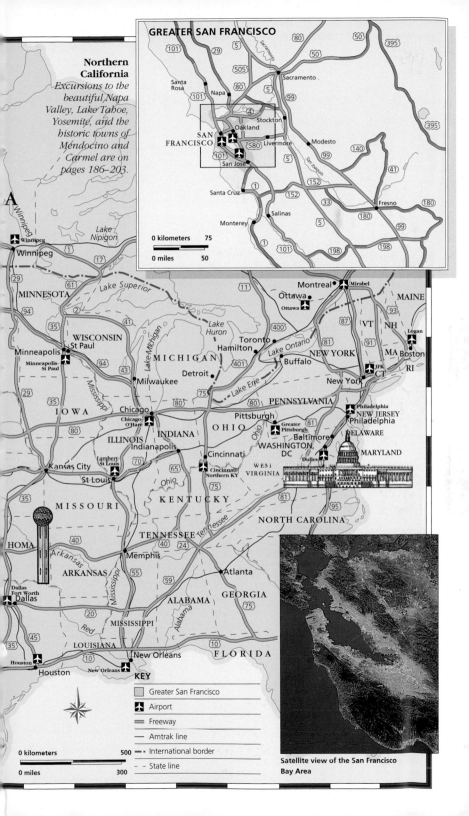

GREATER SAN FRANCISCO

Sacramento
Santa Rosa
Napa
Stockton
Oakland
SAN FRANCISCO
Livermore
San Jose
Modesto
Santa Cruz
Fresno
Monterey
Salinas

0 kilometers 75

0 miles 50

Northern California

Excursions to the beautiful Napa Valley, Lake Tahoe, Yosemite, and the historic towns of Mendocino and Carmel are on pages 186–203.

A

Winnipeg
Lake Nipigon
Winnipeg

MINNESOTA
Lake Superior
Montreal
Mirabel
Ottawa
Ottawa
MAINE
VT
NH
Logan

WISCONSIN
St Paul
Lake Huron
Toronto
Hamilton
Lake Ontario
NEW YORK
MA
Boston

Minneapolis
Minneapolis-St Paul
MICHIGAN
Buffalo
CT
RI

Detroit
Lake Erie
New York

Milwaukee
PENNSYLVANIA
JFK

IOWA
Chicago
Chicago O'Hare
Pittsburgh
Philadelphia
NEW JERSEY
Philadelphia

ILLINOIS
INDIANA
OHIO
Greater Pittsburgh
DELAWARE

Indianapolis
Cincinnati
WASHINGTON, DC
Baltimore
MARYLAND

Kansas City
Lambert-St Louis
WEST VIRGINIA
Dulles

St Louis
Cincinnati/Northern KY

MISSOURI
KENTUCKY
NORTH CAROLINA

HOMA
Arkansas
TENNESSEE
Tennessee

Memphis

Dallas Fort Worth
Dallas
ARKANSAS
Atlanta
GEORGIA

ALABAMA
Alabama

MISSISSIPPI
Red

LOUISIANA
FLORIDA

Houston
Houston
New Orleans
New Orleans

KEY

Greater San Francisco
✈ Airport
Freeway
Amtrak line
International border
State line

0 kilometers 500

0 miles 300

Satellite view of the San Francisco Bay Area

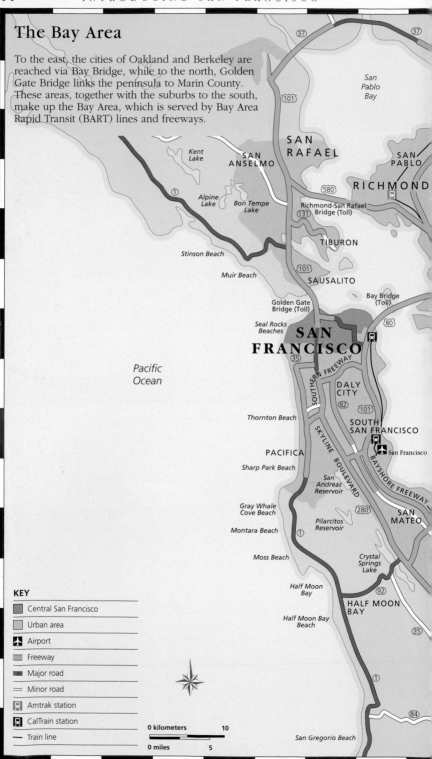

The Bay Area

To the east, the cities of Oakland and Berkeley are reached via Bay Bridge, while to the north, Golden Gate Bridge links the peninsula to Marin County. These areas, together with the suburbs to the south, make up the Bay Area, which is served by Bay Area Rapid Transit (BART) lines and freeways.

San Pablo Bay

Kent Lake

SAN ANSELMO

SAN RAFAEL

SAN PABLO

RICHMOND

Alpine Lake

Bon Tempe Lake

Richmond-San Rafael Bridge (Toll)

TIBURON

Stinson Beach

Muir Beach

SAUSALITO

Golden Gate Bridge (Toll)

Bay Bridge (Toll)

Seal Rocks Beaches

SAN FRANCISCO

Pacific Ocean

SOUTHERN FREEWAY

DALY CITY

Thornton Beach

SOUTH SAN FRANCISCO

PACIFICA

Sharp Park Beach

San Francisco

San Andreas Reservoir

SKYLINE BOULEVARD

BAYSHORE FREEWAY

Gray Whale Cove Beach

Montara Beach

Pilarcitos Reservoir

SAN MATEO

Moss Beach

Crystal Springs Lake

Half Moon Bay

HALF MOON BAY

Half Moon Bay Beach

KEY

- ▇ Central San Francisco
- ▢ Urban area
- ✈ Airport
- ▬ Freeway
- ▬ Major road
- — Minor road
- ▣ Amtrak station
- ▣ CalTrain station
- — Train line

0 kilometers   10

0 miles   5

San Gregorio Beach

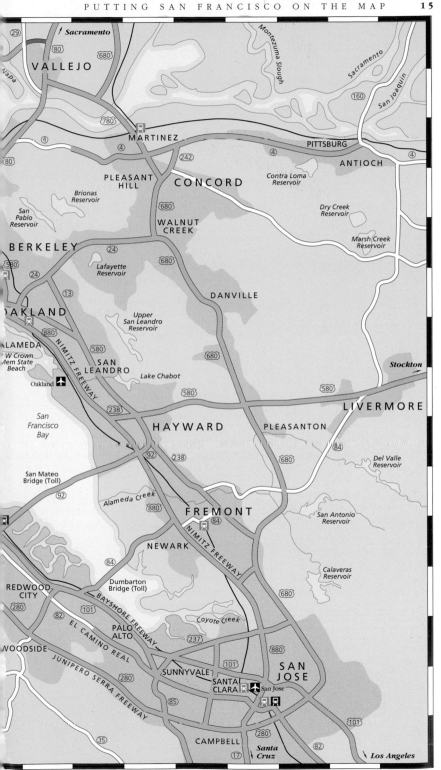

Central San Francisco

San Francisco is a compact city, and much of the central area can be explored on foot. The many hills mean some strenuous climbing and are useful landmarks for orientation. A rich ethnic mix adds character to the distinct neighborhoods.

Victorian Houses
See pp76–77.

Golden Gate Bridge

Over 50 years old, the bridge is as much a part of the landscape as the craggy Marin headlands and the idyllic bay (see pp64–67).

Cliff House

One of the city's original tourist sights, Cliff House still attracts visitors who come to eat at the restaurant and admire the spectacular views of Seal Rocks and the Pacific surf (see p157).

Lombard Street
Running across the tip of the peninsula, Lombard Street is famous for the short steep section on Russian Hill. Known as the "crookedest street in the world," it stretches for only one block between Hyde and Leavenworth streets, yet has ten Z bends (see p88).

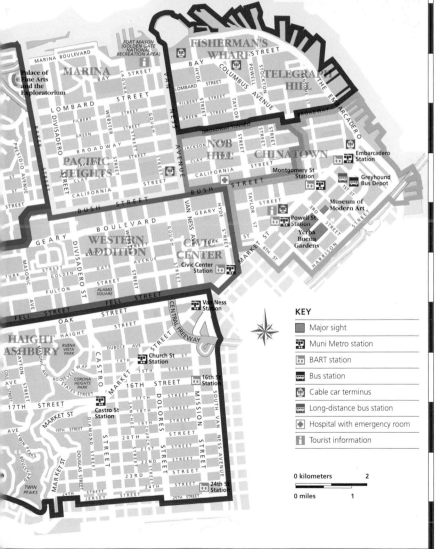

KEY

▨	Major sight
Ⓜ	Muni Metro station
⓫	BART station
🚌	Bus station
🚋	Cable car terminus
🚍	Long-distance bus station
✚	Hospital with emergency room
ℹ	Tourist information

0 kilometers   2

0 miles   1

San Francisco's Earthquakes

San Francisco lies on the San Andreas Fault and is under constant threat of earthquakes. The Loma Prieta earthquake of October 17, 1989, named after the hill close to its epicenter in the Santa Cruz Mountains, was the worst to hit the area since 1906 *(see pp28–9)*. Many buildings are now being strengthened to withstand tremors, and shelters like the one at the Moscone Center *(see pp114–15)* are stocked as emergency relief sites. In addition, most hotels have their own evacuation procedures, and the local telephone directory has four pages of advice.

The 1989 earthquake *measured 7.1 on the Richter scale. It caused some of the houses that were built on landfill in the Marina District to shift off their foundations.*

Berkeley

The San Andreas Fault *is a major fracture in the Earth's crust. It extends almost the full length of California, some 600 miles (965 km).*

San Francisco lies near the northern end of the fault.

PACIFIC PLATE MEETS NORTH AMERICAN PLATE

The San Andreas Fault is the result of friction where two major plates of the Earth's crust meet – the eastern Pacific and the North American plates.

San Andreas Fault

North American plate

L (long) waves travel across the surface.

Epicenter (point on the surface above the focus of an earthquake)

Hypocenter (the focus of an earthquake)

S (secondary) waves travel through solid parts of the crust.

P (primary) waves travel through the Earth's core.

Pacific plate

Hypocenter

Earthquake energy vibrations *travel like waves through the Earth's crust. The interval between the arrival of the P and S waves tells scientists how far away the epicenter of the earthquake is.*

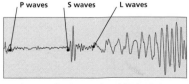

P waves   S waves   L waves

A seismograph printout *shows the intensity of earthquake vibrations graphically. Inside the seismograph a pen traces P (primary), S (secondary) and L (long) waves on a rotating drum.*

Scientists monitor *the movement of the San Andreas Fault by bouncing laser beams off a network of reflectors. The system can pick up movements of less than 0.025 inch (0.6 mm) over a distance of 4 miles (6 km), enabling seismologists to predict when earthquakes are likely to occur.*

The hills and coastal ranges of the Bay Area are pressure ridges formed by hundreds of fault movements compressing and uplifting the land.

In Oakland, 42 people were killed in 1989 when an elevated highway section collapsed and 44 slabs of concrete, each weighing 661 tons, fell onto the cars.

Hayward Fault

Calaveras Fault

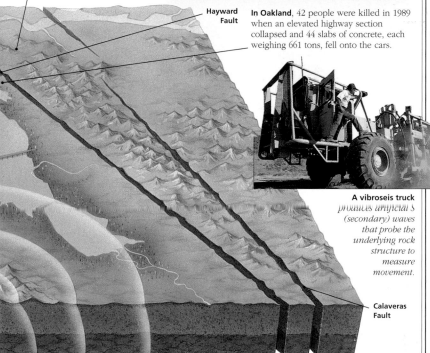

A vibroseis truck *produces artificial S (secondary) waves that probe the underlying rock structure to measure movement.*

TIMELINE

1769 Members of Portolá's expedition are first Europeans to experience an earthquake in California

1865 City suffers its first major earthquake on October 9, followed by second quake on October 23

1872 Earthquake demolishes town of Lone Pine and Sierra Nevadas rise 13 ft (4 m)

1890 Pronounced earth tremor

1989 Loma Prieta earthquake strikes city and Bay Area, killing 67 and making 1,800 homeless. Worst quake since 1906

1750　　1800　　1850　　1900　　1950

Don Gaspar de Portolá

1857 Strong earth tremor followed by smaller tremors in Bay Area

1868 Strong tremor in Hayward Fault

1906 earthquake damage

1957 Strong tremor in Bay Area

1977 8 earth tremors occur

1906 Strongest earthquake ever; 3-day fire destroys much of city leaving 3,000 dead and 250,000 homeless. 52 small tremors shake region over following two days

THE HISTORY OF
SAN FRANCISCO

Even by the standards of the New World, San Francisco remained *terra incognita* a surprisingly long time. A few early European explorers, including Portuguese-born João Cabrilho and England's Sir Francis Drake, sailed up and down the length of the California coast in the 16th century, but all of them sailed past the Golden Gate without noticing the bay that lay beyond it. It was not until 1769 that the first nonnatives laid eyes on what is now San Francisco; thereafter the area was colonized swiftly by the Spanish, who established both missions and *presidios* (forts). In 1821, when Mexico declared independence from Spain, it became Mexican territory.

Seal of the city and county
of San Francisco

the world, leading to the Gold Rush of 1849 (the prospectors of this time were known as '49ers). This coincided with the United States' takeover of the West Coast and, by 1869, San Francisco had grown into an international city renowned both for its wild "Barbary Coast," stretching west from the waterfront, and for the fortunes that were made speculating on the newfound riches of the American frontier.

THE GROWING CITY

The first significant boost to growth occurred in 1848, when gold was discovered at Sutter's Mill in the Sierra Nevada foothills near Sacramento. Hundreds of thousands of prospectors were attracted to California from all over

EARTHQUAKE AND RECOVERY

As the population increased, the city grew westward to fill the narrow peninsula: cable cars were invented to conquer the steep hills, and blocks of ornate Victorian houses were built. The great earthquake and fire of 1906 destroyed most of the city but not its spirit, and reconstruction was soon underway. Throughout all of this, San Francisco retained its unique character and seemingly limitless energy. The following pages illustrate significant periods in the city's history.

Telegraph Hill and North Beach at the time of the Gold Rush

◁ An 1873 print of the city looking south, with Market Street running from the center of the waterfront

Early San Francisco

The first inhabitants of the area around San Francisco Bay were American Indians, grouped into two main tribes, the Coast Miwok in the north and the Ohlone in the south. By the mid-1500s, European ships were exploring the California coast, but no contact was made with the Indians until Sir Francis Drake anchored off Point Reyes and claimed it for Queen Elizabeth I. The bay remained undiscovered until 1769, and in 1776 Spain established a small *presidio* (fort) and a mission, named in honor of the founder of the Franciscan order, *San Francisco de Asis.*

Miwok seed beater

EXTENT OF THE CITY

☐ Today ■ 1800
■ Land reclaimed since 1800

Tcholovoni Indians
Various tribes, including these Tcholovoni Indians, hunted and settled in small villages on the shores of San Francisco Bay.

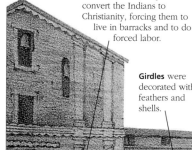

Missionaries from Spain tried to convert the Indians to Christianity, forcing them to live in barracks and to do forced labor.

Girdles were decorated with feathers and shells.

Drake Lands at Point Reyes *(1579)*
It is thought that Sir Francis Drake landed at what is now called Drake's Bay; he was greeted by Miwok Indians.

TIMELINE

10,000 BC First Indians migrate to the Bay area	**AD 1542** Portuguese-born explorer João Cabrilho sights the Farallon Islands off the coast of San Francisco	**1602** Sebastian Vizcaino visits Point Reyes, but also fails to find the bay. His glowing reports encourage the later expedition that discovers San Francisco Bay
10,000 BC	**AD 1550**	**1600** **1650**

João Cabrilho (died 1543)

1579 Sir Francis Drake lands near Point Reyes for ship repairs

1595 Spanish trading ship *San Augustin* sinks off Point Reyes

1666 *map showing California as an island*

Kule Loklo Indians
These early Bay Area inhabitants were depicted by Anton Refregier in his mural in the foyer of the Rincon Center Annex (see p113).

WHERE TO SEE EARLY SAN FRANCISCO
Early American Indian tools are at the California Academy of Sciences *(pp150–51)*, while Mission Dolores *(p137)* and Oakland Museum *(pp166–7)* have Mission-era artifacts.

The Missions
Under the direction of Father Narciso Duran, the mission of San Jose was the largest and most prosperous in the Bay Area.

A spear was an important dance accessory.

Male dancers painted their bodies with red, black and white pigments.

17th-century icon *of Saint Peter, carved in Mexico and carried to California, is now in Oakland Museum (p166).*

DANCE AT MISSION DOLORES
The Russian artist Ludovic Choris (1795–1828) drew this picture of Indians dancing outside Mission Dolores in 1816. They decorated their bodies, performing for the missionaries every Sunday.

1701 Father Kino crosses the Colorado River proving that Baja California is a peninsula, not an island

Portolá's 1769 expedition

1776 Juan De Anza leads the first party of settlers overland to San Francisco, arriving on March 28

1816 Russian traders arrive on the ship *Rurik* and are disturbed by the high mortality rate of American Indians

1700   **1750**   **1800**

1769 Don Gaspar de Portolá, leading a party of explorers overland, discovers the bay in November 1769

1797 Mission San Jose founded

1775 Spanish ship *San Carlos*, captained by Lt Juan Manuel de Ayala, is the first to enter San Francisco Bay

Indians gambling

The Gold Rush

Having broken away from Spain in 1821, Mexico opened California to foreign trade for the first time. Whaling vessels and traders anchored in San Francisco Bay, and a small village began to grow. In 1848, with the discovery of gold in the Sierra Nevada foothills, and the US annexation of California, everything changed. In two years, 100,000 prospectors passed through the Golden Gate, turning San Francisco into a wild frontier city.

Gold nuggets

EXTENT OF THE CITY

☐ Today ▧ 1853

Vallejo's Goblet
This elegant goblet reveals the gracious way of life of General Vallejo, the last Mexican governor of California.

Sam Brannan set up the city's first newspaper in 1847.

Firemen pulling firefighting rig

San Francisco Captured from Mexico
On July 9, 1846 the USS Portsmouth *took control of the undefended bay, and 70 US sailors and marines marched ashore, raising the Stars and Stripes in the central plaza.*

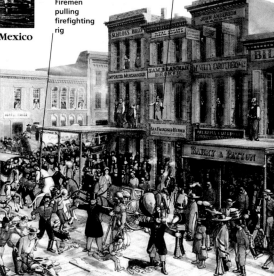

Gambling
Fortunes and lives were won or lost on the turn of a card; gambling was a way of life.

TIMELINE

1820 Whaling ships use Sausalito as main base of operations	**1823** Mission San Francisco de Solano founded at Sonoma	**1828** Fur trapper Jedediah Smith arrives at Presidio after making the first crossing of the rugged coastal mountains	**1834** Missions close, and their assets are divided among Mexican landowners

1820   **1830**

1822 The Mexican Revolution ends Spanish rule over California

Richardson's hand-drawn map of Yerba Buena (San Francisco) in 1835

1835 William Richardson founds Yerba Buena, later renamed San Francisco

Scales used by Wells Fargo

WHERE TO SEE GOLD RUSH SAN FRANCISCO

Little remains of the Gold Rush city, but you can get a feel for this era at the Wells Fargo History Museum *(see p110)*, the Bank of California's Museum of Money in the American West *(p112)*, or the Oakland Museum *(see pp166–7)*.

Ragged Gold Miner
A weary prospector endures the long trek to the gold fields; many returned empty-handed.

Burlesque theater was a popular entertainment in the growing city.

Wells Fargo administrators

Tall ships brought gold seekers from all over the world.

News of Gold Reaches New York
Confirmed by President Polk on December 5, 1848, the gold find inspired thousands to head west.

Panning for Gold
In 1849, more than 90,000 "Forty-Niners" passed through San Francisco. They faced long, hard hours panning for gold in the streams of the Sacramento Valley and Sierra Nevadas.

MONTGOMERY STREET IN 1852
This street was the business center. Here Wells Fargo, whose stagecoaches brought goods to the miners and carried back gold, built the city's first brick building.

1836 Juan Batista Alvarado marches on Monterey and declares California a "free sovereign state" within the Mexican republic

1846 Bear Flag Revolt is led by explorer John Fremont and settlers in May. US troops occupy state capital (Monterey) on July 7 and take Yerba Buena on July 9

1851 Clipper *Flying Cloud* takes 89 days to reach San Francisco from New York

1840	1850

John Fremont 1813–90

1847 Village of Yerba Buena is officially renamed San Francisco. City now comprises 200 buildings with 800 inhabitants

1850 California admitted to United States

1848 Gold discovered by John Marshall in Sierra Nevada foothills, starting the Gold Rush of 1849

The Victorian Years

The city's real boom years occurred during the second half of the 19th century, when some San Franciscans made huge fortunes from the silver mines of Nevada's Comstock Lode, and from the transcontinental railroad, completed in 1869. Saloons and brothels abounded along the waterfront in the legendary Barbary Coast district, while the wealthy built palaces at the top of Nob Hill. As the city expanded, its streets were lined by ornate Victorian houses, and by the turn of the century, the population topped 300,000, making it the largest city west of Chicago.

EXTENT OF THE CITY

	Today		1870

Transcontinental train

Bathroom with original bathtub and tiles

The dining room was used for family meals and formal dinners.

Silver Urn
Presented to Senator Edward Baker in 1860, this urn celebrated future San Francisco business projects, particularly the transcontinental railroad.

Barbary Coast Saloon
Gambling and prostitution were rife in the Barbary Coast, and drunken men were often pressed into naval service.

Supper room in basement

The second parlor was a private sitting room for the family.

The front parlor was used only for entertaining.

TIMELINE

1856 Increasing lawlessness: vigilantes hang four men

1862 First telegraph connection between New York and San Francisco

1869 Transcontinental railroad completed, making fortunes for the infamous "Big Four" *(see p102)*

1873 Levi Strauss patents process for making riveted jeans *(see p135)*

1850	1860	1870

Emperor Norton (died 1880)

1854 Local eccentric, Joshua Norton, proclaims himself Emperor of the United States and Protector of Mexico, issuing his own currency

1863 Ground is broken in Sacramento for the Central Pacific Railroad; thousands of Chinese are hired to build it

1873 First San Francisco cable car is tested on Clay Street

Union Pacific Railroad

In 1869, the Union Pacific met the San Francisco-based Central Pacific in Utah at Promontory Point to form the first transcontinental railroad.

WHERE TO SEE THE VICTORIAN CITY

Well-preserved Victorian buildings can be seen all over San Francisco, but only Haas-Lilienthal House (*see p72*) and Octagon House (*p75*) are open to the public on a regular basis. Jackson Square Historical District (*p110*) is the best place to see what remains of the Barbary Coast.

Gothic Revival birdcage from the 19th century at Oakland Museum (*pp166–7*)

HAAS-LILIENTHAL HOUSE

Wholesale grocer William Haas built this elaborate Queen Anne style house in 1886, one of many in the Victorian-era suburbs. Today it is a museum and shows how a well-to-do family would have lived at the turn of the century.

Sutro Baths

These public baths, which stood until the 1960s, were built by philanthropist and one-time mayor Adolph Sutro in 1896.

The sitting room was originally the master bedroom.

Comstock Lode Silver

Between 1859 and the mid-1880s, $400 million was extracted from the mines.

Porch

Hall, with Victorian corner sofa

1886 10,000 trade unionists take part in the biggest labor parade to date in San Francisco

1896 Adolph Sutro opens the world's largest public baths north of Cliff House

1901 Power broker Abe Ruef runs San Francisco

1880

1900

1887 Scottish gardener John McLaren is hired to tend Golden Gate Park. He stays for 50 years (*see p146*)

1899 Frank Norris writes the classic novel, *McTeague: A Story of San Francisco*

1900 Fisherman's Wharf is built

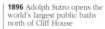

Adolph Sutro 1830–98

The 1906 Earthquake and Fire

The massive earthquake that hit San Francisco just after 5am on April 18, 1906 caused one of the worst disasters in US history. The tremor, many times more powerful than any other to hit the city before or since, instantly collapsed hundreds of buildings, and subsequent fires engulfed the city center. More than 6 sq miles (15 sq km) were reduced to rubble, and estimated death tolls ranged from an official 700 to a more credible 3,000, while as many as 250,000 people were made homeless. Since most property owners were insured against damage by fire, the city was able to rebuild quickly, and by the end of the decade business had returned to normal.

City Hall after the earthquake

EXTENT OF THE CITY

☐ Today   ■ 1906

Powell Street cable cars were back in service within two years. The rest of the system, much reduced, was operational by 1915.

The House of Mirth
In the summer of 1906 more than 100,000 residents had to make their homes in refugee camps.

The Ferry Building was saved from destruction by fireboats spraying water from the bay.

Chinatown burned completely to the ground.

Spirit of San Francisco
Cartoonists were quick to see the funny side of their changed lives; scarcity of water provoked some ironic comment.

TIMELINE

Fairmont Hotel

1905 Architect Daniel Burnham submits radical plans to improve the city center

1907 Fairmont Hotel re-opens exactly one year after the earthquake

1909 Jack London writes *Martin Eden*, a thinly veiled autobiography

1905	1906	1907	1908	1909

Burnham Plan

1906 Earthquake, measuring 8.25 on the Richter scale, and 3-day fire, reduce the city to rubble; tremors continue for 2 days

1907 Abe "Boss" Ruef pleads guilty to extortion

Jack London 1876–1916

Feeding the Homeless in Union Square

The US Army took responsibility for providing food and shelter for the thousands of victims who lost members of their family, their homes and possessions.

WHERE TO SEE THE 1906 EARTHQUAKE

Artifacts and exhibits pertaining to the 1906 disaster are found all over the city. Information on the quake can be viewed in the foyer of the Sheraton Palace Hotel and at www.sfmuseum.org.

South of Market District, built on unstable soil, was one of the hardest-hit areas in the earthquake.

The Fairmont Hotel burned, but was rebuilt inside the original façade.

The Flood Mansion's stone frame survived the quake; it can be seen today as the Pacific-Union Club.

Cups and saucers *fused by the heat of the fire are among artifacts on display at the Oakland Museum (pp166–7).*

THE DESTRUCTION

Traveling at 7,000 mph (11,265 km), the earthquake overwhelmed the city center. Flames erupted from burst gas mains and, in 3 days, destroyed 28,000 buildings: prime city property valued at $400 million.

The Homeless
Many people salvaged what they could and moved away for good.

Nob Hill's wooden mansions burned like kindling.

Clearing Up
As soon as the flames had abated, buildings were torn down and cleared for restoration.

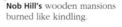

Mayor "Sunny Jim" Rolph 1869–1948

Plans for San Francisco, the Exposition City

1913 Last horse-drawn streetcar withdrawn from service

1914 Stockton Street tunnel opens

1910	1911	1912	1913	1914

1911 "Sunny Jim" Rolph is elected mayor; serves until 1930

1912 San Francisco named as official site of 1915 Panama–Pacific Exposition

1913 Congress controversially approves dam that floods the Hetch Hetchy Valley, 150 miles (240 km) east of the city

The Golden Age

Poster publicizing the Pan–Pacific Exposition

Neither World War I in Europe nor the beginning of Prohibition in the US could dampen the city's renewed energy after 1906. The 1920s saw the creation of major museums, theaters and other civic buildings. Even the Great Depression was not as painful as it was elsewhere in the US – many of the city's monuments, including Coit Tower and both bay bridges, were built during these years. World War II brought industrial investment in the form of shipyards at Richmond and Sausalito. Fort Mason was the main supply base for the Pacific theater, and shipped out more than 1.5 million soldiers.

EXTENT OF THE CITY

☐ Today   ■ 1920

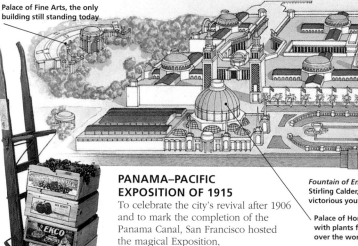

Palace of Fine Arts, the only building still standing today

Tower of Jewels, decorated with 102,000 cut-glass "gems"

Fountain of Energy by A. Stirling Calder, depicting victorious youth

Palace of Horticulture with plants from all over the world

PANAMA–PACIFIC EXPOSITION OF 1915

To celebrate the city's revival after 1906 and to mark the completion of the Panama Canal, San Francisco hosted the magical Exposition, which attracted 20 million visitors over 10 months (see p72).

Land of Plenty
California's farm-land became the most productive in the US in the 1920s.

King Oliver's Creole Band
Catching the mood of the 1920s, King Oliver's jazz band became the hottest combo of the decade.

TIMELINE

1915	1920	1925	1930

Pan–Pacific commemorative medal

1917 Crissy Field Airfield at Presidio opens

1921 de Young Museum opens

1924 California Palace of the Legion of Honor opens

1929 Stock exchange crash precipitates depression

1917 Main Public Library opens at Civic Center

1920 Prohibition begins

1924 First air mail flight lands at Crissy Field

1927 Mills Field airfield, now the site of San Francisco International Airport, opens

1915 Pan–Pacific Exposition runs from February 20 to December 4

1923 President Warren G. Harding dies at the Palace Hotel

Pan American Clippers Arrive
San Francisco Bay was the starting point for flights across the Pacific.

Defying Prohibition
Although Prohibition was not stringently enforced in the city, drinkers still had to be discreet.

WHERE TO SEE THE GOLDEN YEARS

The only survivor of the 1915 Exposition is the landmark Palace of Fine Arts *(see pp60–61)*. The Old US Mint *(p117)* and the History Room of the Main Library *(p125)* both have extensive displays of objects from this era.

Ticket for Treasure Island World's Fair

Festival Hall, the musical center of the Exposition, seated 3,500.

McLaren's Hedge, a wall of grass

Longshoreman's Strike
On "Bloody Thursday," July 5, 1934, police opened fire on dockers striking for better conditions, killing two.

Sausalito Shipyard
Workers at this shipyard completed one ship a day during the World War II period.

Hetch Hetchy Dam	**1939** World War II in Europe. Opening of World's Fair on Treasure Island	**1941** Japan attacks US at Pearl Harbor	**1942** Japanese-American internment begins	**1945** End of World War II	
	1937 Golden Gate Bridge opens				

1935		**1940**		**1945**	

1933 Prohibition ends	**1936** Bay Bridge opens. Pan American Clippers arrive in the city		**1945** UN Peace Conference held at San Francisco April 25– June 25 to found the United Nations
1934 Hetch Hetchy Dam project completed. Three-day general strike in sympathy with dockers	*Signing of the United Nations Charter in the city in 1945*		

Postwar San Francisco

Since World War II, San Francisco has seen both good times and bad. Site of the founding of the United Nations in 1945, the city was home to the Beats of the 1950s and the scene of "Love-ins" and "Be-ins" in the Flower Power 1960s. At the same time, the Bay Area was the scene of angry antiwar and civil rights demonstrations. One of the wealthiest parts of the US, the area was hit hard by AIDS, homelessness and a devastating earthquake in 1989.

1970s Leader of the Oakland-based Black Panthers, Huey Newton (on the right) gains widespread sympathy on college campuses during the turbulent '60s and '70s

1969 American Indian Movement occupies Alcatraz to publicize Indian grievances

1969 San Francisco blues and soul star Janis Joplin develops alcoholism and drug problems. She dies in 1970 from a heroin overdose

1978 Mayor George Moscone is assassinated at City Hall by a former policeman Dan White, who also kills popular gay politician Harvey Milk

Neal Cassady and Jack Kerouac

1950s Jack Kerouac, Neal Cassady, Allen Ginsberg and others strike chords of dissatisfaction and creativity to initiate the "Beat" movement and the "politics of dissent" and free love

George Moscone

1945	1950	1955	1960	1965	1970	1975	1980
1945	1950	1955	1960	1965	1970	1975	1980

August 15, 1945 Riotous celebrations break out across San Francisco at the end of World War II. Thousands of troops return to the US through the Golden Gate

1954 The new San Francisco International Airport opens at former Mills Field airfield

1965 Ground is broken for the Dragon Gateway on Grant Avenue

1973 Transamerica Pyramid is completed and given mixed reviews by San Francisco critics

1978 Apple Computer, which grows into one of the Bay Area's largest businesses, designs and produces its first personal computer

1958 The New York Giants baseball team moves to San Francisco, bringing major league professional sport to the West Coast

1967 First Be-in attracts 25,000 hippies and others to Golden Gate Park for a day of music. The Monterey Pop Festival features such talents as Jimi Hendrix, Otis Redding and The Who

1951 Six years after the fighting stopped between the US and Japan, the treaty ending the war was signed in the San Francisco War Memorial Opera House

San Francisco Giant Willie Mays

1992 Fires blaze across Oakland hills killing 26 people and burning 3,000 houses

1995 Candlestick Park renamed 3Com Park

2007 Residents experience an earthquake measuring 4.2 on the Richter scale

2000 Opening game played at new Pacific Bell Park (now AT&T Park)

1985	1990	1995	2000	2005	2010	2015	2020

1985	1990	1995	2000	2005	2010	2015	2020

2008 The Contemporary Jewish Museum, designed by Daniel Libeskind, opens

1994 Presidio Army Base turned over to the National Park Service

2006 San Francisco congresswoman Nancy Pelosi is the first woman to become elected speaker of the United States House of Representatives

1989 Major earthquake hits San Francisco during World Series baseball game between Bay Area rivals: freeways collapse, killing dozens

1999 After 15 years as the speaker of the California Assembly, Democrat Willie Brown is sworn in as San Francisco's first black mayor

SAN FRANCISCO AT A GLANCE

More than 200 places of interest are described in the *Area by Area* section of this book. They range from the bustling alleys, shops and restaurants of Chinatown to the verdant expanses of Golden Gate Park, and from ornate Victorian houses to soaring city center skyscrapers.

The following 12 pages are a time-saving guide to the best San Francisco has to offer visitors. Museums and architecture each have a section, and there is a guide to the diverse cultures that have given the city its unique character. Below are the top attractions that no tourist should miss.

SAN FRANCISCO'S TOP   TOURIST ATTRACTIONS

California Academy of Sciences
See pp148–51

Coit Tower
See p93

Ghirardelli Square
See p83

Golden Gate Bridge
See pp64–7

Golden Gate Park
See pp142–53

Grant Avenue
See p99

Cable Cars
See pp104–5

Union Square
See p116

Alcatraz Island
See pp84–7

Japan Center
See p128

◁ Celebrating on a motorized cable car tour *(see p279)*

San Francisco's Best: Museums and Galleries

Museums and galleries in the city range from the Legion of Honor and the de Young Museum to the contemporary art of the Museum of Modern Art and the Yerba Buena Center for the Arts. There are several excellent science museums, including the Exploratorium and the California Academy of Sciences. Other museums celebrate San Francisco's heritage and the people and events that made the city what it is today. More details on the area's museums and galleries are given on pages 38 and 39.

The Exploratorium
Visitors experiment with Sun Painting, a feast of light and color at this leading US science museum.

Legion of Honor
Sailboat on the Seine (c.1874) by Monet is part of a collection of European art from medieval times to the 19th century.

Presidio

de Young Museum
This landmark art museum showcases collections of art from the Americas, Africa, and the Pacific, as well as an astounding collection of textiles, photography, sculptures, crafts, and modern and contemporary art.

Golden Gate Park and Land's End

0 kilometers 2
0 miles 1

Haight Ashbury and the Mission

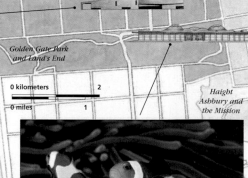

California Academy of Sciences
Re-opened in 2008 after an extensive re-build, the California Academy of Sciences is integrated more sensitively into the natural environment of Golden Gate Park.

Chinese Historical Society
This magnificent dragon's head belongs to the Society which administers one of the city's smallest museums. Within is a unique collection that tells the story of California's Chinese communities.

Fort Mason Museums
Muto *by Mimo Paladino (1985) is in one of the ethnic culture museums.*

Wells Fargo History Museum
This bronze stagecoach (1984) is by M. Casper. The small gallery in which this is situated illustrates the colorful history of California, from the early days of the Gold Rush.

Fisherman's Wharf and North Beach

Chinatown and Nob Hill

Pacific Heights and the Marina

Financial District and Union Square

Civic Center

San Francisco Museum of Modern Art
Back View *by Philip Guston (1977) can be found in this highly regarded museum. In 1995 the museum moved to premises, designed by architect Mario Botta.*

Yerba Buena Center for the Arts
This gallery at Yerba Buena Gardens displays contemporary art in rotating exhibits: there is no permanent collection.

Asian Art Museum
This museum is located in the Civic Center, a lovely 1917 Beaux Arts building.

Exploring San Francisco's Museums and Galleries

San Francisco boasts a number of established and respectable collections of paintings, sculpture, photography, artifacts and design. In addition, high-profile projects, such as the building of a new home for the Museum of Modern Art, and the renovation of the California Palace of the Legion of Honor, assure that the city will retain its identity as the US West Coast's center of art and culture. Other Bay Area treasures are the many science and technology museums.

Clay pot by Clayton Bailey, Craft and Folk Art Museum

Saint John the Baptist Preaching (c.1660) by Mattia Preti at the Legion of Honor

PAINTING AND SCULPTURE

Two renowned art museums, the **Legion of Honor** and the **de Young Museum** are impressive showcases for a comprehensive collection of European and American painting and sculpture. The Legion of Honor focuses on French art of the late 19th and early 20th centuries, with works by Renoir, Monet and Degas as well as more than 70 sculptures by Rodin. The famous collection of graphic works owned by the Achenback Foundation is also on display here.

The **Asian Art Museum** is located in its permanent home at the Old Main Library. It has Far Eastern paintings, sculpture, artifacts and fine jade figurines.

The most dynamic of the art museums in San Francisco is the **Museum of Modern Art**, with its vast array of

20th-century painting and sculpture. The SFMOMA holds works by Picasso and Matisse as well as an extensive holding of drawings and paintings by Paul Klee. Abstract Expressionists, particularly Mark Rothko and Clyfford Still, and California artists represented by Sam Francis and Richard Diebenkorn, are also included in this notable collection.

Another vibrant showcase for contemporary artists, the **Yerba Buena Center for the Arts** is well worth a visit. The same is true of the commercial **John Berggruen Gallery**, with its wide variety of works on display by both emerging artists and more mature, well-established artists.

Outside the city limits, the **Stanford University** Museum of Art has excellent Rodin sculptures, while both the **UC Berkeley** Art Museum and the **Oakland Museum** have valuable art collections.

Fletcher Benton's 'M' sculpture outside the Oakland Museum

DESIGN

Many of the larger, more prestigious museums in the San Francisco area have worthwhile holdings of design and applied art. Major collections of architectural models and drawings are held at the **Museum of Modern Art**.

You can see Mission-style and turn-of-the-century Arts and Crafts pieces at the **Oakland Museum**.

There is also a small, but interesting, collection of late 18th-century artifacts and furniture on display inside the **Octagon House**, itself a fine, and unique, example of Victorian architectural house design *(see pp76–7)*.

The **California Historical Society** *(see p113)* has an eclectic collection of fine and decorative arts as well as the largest single public collection of 19th century California prints and photography.

PHOTOGRAPHY AND PRINTS

Photography is a field in which San Francisco's museums excel, with world-class examples of most periods and styles. The **Museum of Modern Art**'s collection ranges from the earliest form of daguerreotypes to classic images by modern masters such as Helen Levitt, Robert Frank and Richard Avedon.

Oakland Museum displays rolling exhibitions by Bay Area-based photographers such as Ansel Adams and Imogen Cunningham and holds documentary collections including an impressive array of photographs by iconic American photographers such as Dorothea Lange. The commercial **Vision** and **Fraenkel** galleries are both excellent, while for prints, the Achenbach Foundation for Graphic Arts in the **Legion of Honor** has more than 100,000 works.

After the Earthquake (1906) photograph, Mission Dolores museum

HISTORY AND LOCAL INTEREST

No single museum is devoted to the city's entire history, although several collections cover different aspects of San Francisco's past. A small museum at **Mission Dolores** gives insight into the city's founding and early period. The **Wells Fargo History Museum** has a display on the Gold Rush, the small museum at the **Presidio Visitor Center** traces the area's military history, and the California Historical Society offers fertile ground for researchers and history buffs.

Well worth a visit are the **Chinese Historical Society Museum** and the African-American Historical and Cultural Society Museum at **Fort Mason**, which document the respective histories of the Chinese and African-American communities in San Francisco.

SCIENCE AND TECHNOLOGY

One of the preeminent hands-on technological museums in the world, the **Exploratorium** has hundreds of interactive displays that explore the science behind everyday events. This is one of San Francisco's most popular museums, and it is especially fascinating for children.

Across the bay, the Lawrence Hall of Science at **UC Berkeley** plays an equally important role in promoting interest in science. South of the city, San Jose's growing **Tech Museum of Innovation** tells the inside story of computers, developed largely in surrounding Silicon Valley, and also has exciting hands-on displays.

NATURAL HISTORY

An extensive natural history collection is displayed at the **California Academy of Sciences** *(see p113)*. This features such exhibitions as the evolution of species, plate tectonics (with a vibrating platform that simulates an earthquake), and gems and minerals. There is also a large planetarium, and a Fish Roundabout, where visitors cross a ramp surrounded by a tank of sharks and other sea life. The **Oakland Museum** has an entire floor devoted to the varied eco-systems of California, which are reconstructed through a series of realistic dioramas.

Octopus in the Oakland Museum

ART FROM OTHER CULTURES

Art and artifacts from California's native cultures are on display in the Hearst Museum of Anthropology at **UC Berkeley**. Exhibitions are drawn from the museum's collection. The **Albers Gallery of Inuit Art** on Market Street also stages shows by Inuit artists.

Fort Mason has a wealth of art from other cultures: ethnic and American art can

Tile mural (1940–45) by Alfredo Ramos Martínez, Mexican Museum

be seen at the African American Historical and Cultural Society and the San Francisco Craft and Folk Art Museum; Italian-American works of the 20th century are displayed at the Museo ItaloAmericano.

LIBRARIES

San Francisco has extensive general libraries including the **Main Library**, which has a special research collection comprising hundreds of books and thousands of photographs focusing on city history. The area's two main universities, **UC Berkeley** and **Stanford**, have extensive collections including historical holdings.

Exploring San Francisco's Many Cultures

Half the population of San Francisco is either foreign-born or first-generation American. Spanish and Mexican pioneers who arrived in the 18th and early 19th centuries established the foundations of today's city, and the Gold Rush *(see pp24–5)* attracted fortune-seekers from all over the globe. Those who stayed built new communities and some, such as the Italians and the Chinese, have continued to maintain their own traditions.

Mission District mural commemorating the cease-fire in El Salvador

THE HISPANIC-AMERICANS

You cannot go far in San Francisco without coming across signs of the Hispanic heritage of a city that was once the northernmost outpost of Spanish America, then Mexico. After the American takeover in 1846 *(see pp24–5)* Mexican landowners were displaced by incoming prospectors and settlers, and most were left homeless. However, many stayed in the Bay Area and the Hispanic population has remained stable (about 10 per-cent of the total) ever since.

Wandering among the *taquerias* (snack bars) and *mercados* (shops) of the Mission District, it is easy to imagine you are somewhere far south of the border.

THE CHINESE

Since the gold rush days in the late 1840s, when an estimated 25,000 people fled from the chaos of China to work in the California mines, the Chinese have maintained a significant presence in San Francisco. A second wave of immigrants, almost exclusively from Canton, arrived to work on the transcontinental railroad in the 1860s. By the 1870s, the Chinese formed the largest of the city's minority groups, with 40,000 people living in poor conditions in and around Chinatown. At this time, the Chinese men outnumbered the Chinese women by 20 to one. In the decades that

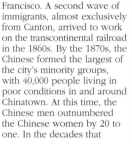

A young San Franciscan woman wearing Chinese costume

followed, the population of the Chinese community shrank due to the Exclusion Laws. In the 1960s, immigration controls were relaxed by President Kennedy, and opponents of the Mao regime living in Hong Kong were given permission to emigrate to the US. The population has now risen to over 100,000 – approximately one in five San Franciscans.

Chinatown *(see pp96–100)* is still the city's most populated sector, and the heart of the Chinese community. Banks, schools and newspapers testify to its autonomy, which is as powerful today as it was when the first settlers arrived more than 150 years ago.

THE IRISH

In the late 1800s, thousands of Irish immigrants came to San Francisco and took what jobs they could find. Many worked as laborers on the huge steam shovels used to fill in the bayfront mudflats, while others joined the police and fire departments and rose to positions of authority. By the turn of the century, Irish labor leaders had become an effective force in the city. There is no readily identifiable Irish section of San Francisco, but Sunset and Richmond districts are packed with Irish bars, and the annual St. Patrick's Day parade *(see p48)* still draws a considerable crowd.

THE ITALIANS

The original Italians in San Francisco depended on fishing for their livelihood. Today's thriving North Beach is inhabited by descendants of the southern Italian fishermen who came to settle here in the late 1800s. The early immigrants to the area were mostly from the city of Genoa, the birthplace of

Christopher Columbus, after whom North Beach's main avenue is named.

By the turn of the century, the Sicilians had become the major force in the area. In the 1940s, Italians were the predominant foreign-born group in the city, with some 60,000 living and working in the lively North Beach area alone.

Descendants of the families who owned and operated the fleet at Fisherman's Wharf set up shops and small businesses here. The businesses prospered after World War II, and many families moved to the suburbs in the 1950s and '60s. However they often return to "Little Italy" to patronize the excellent Italian cafés and restaurants that still flourish in the area.

Sign outside a Russian shop in the Richmond District

An Afro-Caribbean street stall selling sweet potatoes and yams

THE AFRICAN-AMERICANS

Although black people have played an important role throughout San Francisco's history, the city's large African-American community is a relatively recent phenomenon. In the 1930s, fewer than 5,000 blacks lived in San Francisco. Thousands more came to work in the factories and shipyards during World War II, increasing the black population tenfold. Some settled in areas made available by the relocation of Japanese-Americans to internment camps, others in newer communities near the shipyards in Hunters Point.

THE RUSSIANS

The first trappers and fur traders from Russia visited the bay during the early 1800s. Russian Hill is named after a

party of Siberian sailors thought to be buried there. Russians established a successful though short-lived colony at Fort Ross *(see p189)* 100 miles (160 km) north of the city, and many still live in San Francisco. Since 1921, five editions a week of the *Russian Times* have been published for the 25,000 Russians now concentrated in the Richmond District around the Orthodox Holy Virgin Cathedral *(see p63)*.

THE JAPANESE

Japanese businesses were active during the 1980s property boom, buying and building many prestigious city center offices and hotels. Generally, however, the 15,000-strong Japanese community in San Francisco keeps a low profile. The exception is at the Japan Center *(see p128)*, a prominent cultural and shopping complex on Geary Boulevard. In the late 1930s, this area extended over 40 blocks. During World War II, the Japanese along the US West Coast were relocated to internment camps in the nation's interior. After the war, they drifted back to the area, but now the community occupies only six blocks.

THE MELTING POT

Other cultures are also represented in the city, but they are not as distinctly defined. Compared with New York or Los Angeles, the Jewish community in San Francisco is very small, but Jews have still wielded tremendous influence throughout the city's history.

Far Eastern cultures have also formed identifiable communities. Groups of Vietnamese and Cambodians live in the Tenderloin neighborhood, and significant populations of Koreans and Thais are scattered throughout the city.

Indians and Pakistanis have settled in the Bay Area of San Francisco, particularly in Berkeley and the "Silicon Valley" computer industry heartland of the South Bay.

A police *koban* (booth) in Japantown

Gay San Francisco: A History

The history of the Lesbian, Gay, Bisexual and Transgender (LGBT) community in San Francisco is in some ways the story of the gay movement itself. The city has been a mecca for gay people for much of its existence, and social and political gains made here have had reverberations across the globe. The community is now more diverse than ever, spread out across the entire city, not just the Castro (see p136), and you can hold hands with your same-sex partner anywhere from the Financial District to Pacific Heights. This sense of freedom was a hard-won battle fought in the political arena of San Francisco.

The bohemian Black Cat Café, Montgomery Street, opened in 1933

THE EARLY DAYS: 1849–1960

The California Gold Rush of 1849 drew scores of adventurers to the Bay Area, and its rough-and-tumble atmosphere helped establish its reputation for sexual license. Life along the Barbary Coast offered freedom from the conservative mores of the rest of the country, and by the beginning of the 20th century the city was already being called "Sodom by the Sea."

During World War II, the city's gay population positively exploded. San Francisco was a main point of deployment and re-entry for troops, and gay soldiers had numerous "off-limits" bars and private gatherings to choose from. Also, for the first time in the military's history, homosexuals were being sought out and dishonorably discharged, and many of these men chose to settle in San Francisco rather than risk stigmatization back home.

The 1950s, however, heralded the real beginnings of a gay social consciousness, with the founding of several "homophile" organizations, which emphasized emotional rather than sexual components of same-gender coupling and advised assimilation within heterosexual society. Foremost among these groups were the Mattachine Society, which first advanced the idea of gay people as an oppressed minority, and the Daughters of Bilitis, the first lesbian socio-political organization in the United States.

GETTING ORGANIZED: 1960s–1970s

In the 1960s, police raids of gay gatherings were common, often resulting in public exposure of the arrested and affecting livelihoods. In 1961, José Sarria, a drag performer at the Black Cat Café, made history by running for the Board of Supervisors as an openly gay man. Although he wasn't elected, he proved there was a "gay vote" and inspired the founding of the Tavern Guild, the country's first gay business association.

Guests at the 1965 fundraising ball for the Council on Religion and the Homosexual (CRH) were harassed and photographed by police as they entered. The American Civil Liberties Union intervened, ultimately helping gays win legal support including a community police liaison officer.

Another pivotal event was New York's Stonewall riots in 1969. Once gay people had stood up to police, they were no longer content with mere acceptance. "Liberation" and "pride" became the move-

The colorful Gay Pride Parade celebrates the city's gay history, culture and community

TIMELINE

1930	1940	1950	1960	1970	1980	1990	2000	2010

1948 Alfred Kinsey's groundbreaking Sexual Behaviour in the Human Male is published

Alfred Kinsey

1955 Daughters of Bilitis, the nation's first lesbian group, is formed

1970 First San Francisco Gay Pride Parade, called "Gay-In"

1974 First Castro Street Fair

2002 First purpose-built LGBT center opens

2008 The California Supreme Court overturns state's ban on same-sex marriage

1930s First gay bars appear, including artists' hangout, the Black Cat Café, and Mona's, a lesbian bar

1964 *Life* magazine article "Homosexuality in America" names San Francisco "the capital of the gay world"

1981 First case of Kaposi's sarcoma (AIDS-related cancer)

1969 Police raid the Stonewall Inn in New York. Ensuing riots signal the start of the modern gay liberation movement

2004 Mayor Newson allows same-sex marriages but these are later annulled

ment's watchwords. Gays wanted not just equal treatment but also gay events, businesses, and organizations to thrive.

With the establishment of the Castro as a gay area, the community gained political force. In 1977, local shop owner Harvey Milk was elected to the Board of Supervisors, becoming the nation's first openly gay elected official. His tenure was cut short in 1978 when he and Mayor George Moscone were shot at City Hall by Dan White. This further fueled the political movement – when White was found guilty only of manslaughter and given a light sentence, the city rioted in what became known as "White Night."

THE PLAGUE YEARS: 1980s

After all the hard-won political gains of the previous decades, the community was decimated by a new adversary. In 1981, the first incidence of a rare form of cancer was reported and within months, word spread of a disease dubbed "the gay cancer." The disease was later named AIDS (Auto-Immune Deficiency Syndrome), which is caused by the HIV virus (Human Immunodeficiency Virus). The city's gay community became one of the hardest hit, with as many as half of the city's gay men infected with HIV. It also became a model in developing a response. People rapidly mobilized to establish education and prevention efforts and community-based services to care for people with AIDS. San Francisco also leapt to the forefront of research, establishing the San Francisco AIDS Foundation and the Center for AIDS Prevention Studies at the UCSF Medical School.

The San Francisco AIDS Fund, now AIDS Emergency Fund (AEF), established in 1982

The right to a same-sex wedding is an on-going political battle

RECOVERY: 1990–PRESENT

The 1990s were perhaps most marked by the increase in political clout for gay people, with the passage of domestic partnership laws, more gay politicians being elected, military policies on gays being challenged, and much more.

The AIDS epidemic bred new forms of participation in San Francisco's gay community and to some degree made it more cohesive. But the sheer numbers of members lost means that the community is once again redefining itself, this time with an influx of diverse young people whose sexual identities have been formed in a much more open society. In these days of same-sex on-screen kissing and prom dating, gender roles are more fluid, and there's less of a sense of urgency to sorting out the "rules" of sexuality.

That said, the politics of being gay are very much in the forefront, and were put famously on view by Mayor Gavin Newsom's attempt at legalizing same-sex marriage. Some 3,000 couples were wed at City Hall in February of 2004, a historic event broadcast around the world. The marriages were later invalidated by the courts, but it was clearly the opening salvo of an ongoing battle.

FAIRS, FESTIVALS, AND EVENTS

AIDS Candlelight Vigil
May, usually 3rd Sunday.
Tel 415-331-1500 ext 2437.
AIDS Walk San Francisco
July, date varies.
Tel 415-615-9255.
Castro Street Fair
October, usually first Sunday.
Tel 415-841-1824.
Dyke March
June, Saturday evening before Pride March.
Tel 415-777-3247.
Folsom Street Fair
September, usually last Sunday.
Tel 415-648-3247.
Last and main event for popular Leather Week. Not only for the leather and fetish community.
Gay Pride Month
June, various events.
Gay Pride Parade
June, last Sunday of the month.
Tel 415-864-3733.
Halloween
October 31. Party along Market and Castro Streets. **Map** 10 D2.
Home for the Holidays
December 24, SF Gay Men's Chorus Christmas concert at the Castro Theatre (*see p136*).
Pink Saturday
June, Saturday evening before Pride March (men and women). Women's alternate Pride parade and party in the Castro.
SF International Lesbian and Gay Film Festival
June, usually ten days before Gay Pride Day.
Tel 415-703-8650.
Up Your Alley Fair
August, usually first Sunday.
Tel 415-777-3247.
SoMa's Dore Street fair. **Map** 11 A2.

CONTACT INFORMATION

Betty's List
Tel 415-861-1637.
www.bettyslist.com
Online community directory.
GLBT Historical Society
657 Mission Street. **Map** 6 D4.
Tel 415-777-5455.
HIV/AIDS Hotline
Tel 415-863-2437.
James C. Hormel Gay and Lesbian Center
100 Larkin St. **Map** 11 A1.
Tel 415-557-4400.
SF City Clinic
356 7th Street. **Map** 11 B2.
Tel 415-487-5500.
STD testing/counseling.
SF LGBT Community Center
1800 Market Street. **Map** 10 E1.
Tel 415-865-5555.
Sex Information Hotline
Tel 415-989-7374.
Suicide Prevention Hotline
Tel 415-781-0500.

San Francisco's Best: Architecture

Architectural highlights in San Francisco are mostly small-scale; the overall fabric, rather than specific buildings, lends the city its unique character. One memorable aspect is the wide variety of house styles, ranging from Arts and Crafts rustic chalets to grand Victorian mansions. Commercial buildings reflect a gamut of styles from Beaux Arts to Postmodern. This map gives some highlights, with a detailed overview on pages 46–7.

Octagon House
Octagonal houses were popular in the mid-1800s because they allowed in more sunlight than traditional Victorian designs.

Haas-Lilienthal House
This large Queen Anne style house is a typical upper-middle-class dwelling of the late 1880s.

Presidio

Pacific Heights and the Marina

Civic Center

Golden Gate Park and Land's End

Haight Ashbury and the Mission

0 kilometers 2

0 miles 1

City Hall
Many of the city's civic buildings are examples of Classical Beaux Arts style.

Goslinsky House
The charming Arts and Crafts style was popular at the turn of the century in San Francisco.

Hotaling Building (1866)
This Jackson Square edifice was the largest of many neighboring Gold Rush buildings to survive the 1906 earthquake. It was a whisky distillery and warehouse.

Coit Tower (1934)
The fluted column of Coit Tower on Telegraph Hill is one of the city's best known landmarks.

Old St. Mary's Church
Standing among the pagodas of Chinatown, the brick walls of this Gothic church date back to the Gold Rush.

Financial District and Union Square

Hallidie Building
Built in 1917 by prolific local architect Willis Polk, this was the world's first glass-curtain-walled building. It is topped with an elaborate cast-iron cornice.

Union Square
Before he built New York's famous Guggenheim Museum in 1959, architect Frank Lloyd Wright experimented with the use of ramps in this small Union Square shop.

MOMA
Built in 1995 at a cost of $60 million, the San Francisco Museum of Modern Art is one of the largest modern art museums in the United States.

Exploring San Francisco's Architecture

Few structures survive from the Mission or Gold Rush eras, and the 1906 earthquake and fire destroyed many major Victorian buildings. As the city was rebuilt, architecture became a focus of civic pride, and grand Neo-Classical edifices in the Beaux Arts style embodied the city's resurgence. By the 1930s, the Financial District's office towers proclaimed its importance as the commercial center of the west. Engineering advances and soaring property values in the late 1960s gave rise to San Francisco's towering skyscrapers.

Mission Dolores

two are open to the public: **Haas-Lilienthal House** and **Octagon House**. Also worth a visit are the houses along the east side of **Alamo Square**, the group of well-preserved working-class cottages in **Cottage Row**, and **Clarke's Folly**, an elaborate 1892 Queen Anne-style "country house" now stranded in the cityscape.

MISSION

Between 1776 and 1823, Spanish missionaries employed American Indian laborers to construct seven missions and three fortresses, or "presidios," in the Bay Area. Known as the mission style, this architecture is characterized by thick walls of rough adobe bricks, red tile roofs and arcaded galleries surrounding courtyards. Fine examples of the style are **Mission Dolores**, San Francisco's oldest building, and the mission at **Carmel**.

GOLD RUSH

At the height of the Gold Rush, most buildings were only temporary, but as the population stabilized, fireproof brick was used. The best survivors from the time are preserved as part of **Jackson Square Historical District**. Particularly noteworthy examples include Hotaling's Warehouse and Distillery, which dates from the 1860s,

with cast-iron pilasters and fireproof shutters, and three 1850s buildings on the 700 block of Montgomery Street.

VICTORIAN

The most distinctive aspect of the city's architecture is its array of Victorian houses with their elaborate ornamentation *(see pp76–7)*. Examples of these timber-frame houses can be found throughout the city, but only

ARTS AND CRAFTS

A more rustic, down-to-earth style was adopted after the turn of the century, inspired by the English Arts and Crafts movement. Architects used redwood and uncut stone, borrowing decorative Japanese motifs, to achieve a natural look. An entire block of Arts and Crafts houses surrounds Bernard Maybeck's **Goslinsky House** in Pacific Heights, and across the bay in Berkeley, his **Church of Christ, Scientist** is a particularly fine example.

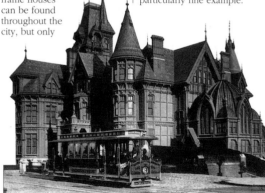

Victorian mansion built for Mark Hopkins on Nob Hill, destroyed in the fire that followed the 1906 earthquake

RELIGIOUS ARCHITECTURE

The architectural diversity of the city is most apparent in its churches. Since the first simple, white-walled and red-tile-roofed missions, the city's churches have been built in an array of styles from Gothic to Baroque with numerous hybrids in between. Many prominent churches were built during the eclectic Victorian era of the late 19th century, and their architectural styles reflect the traditions of the countries from which their congregations came.

St. Stephen's Lutheran German Renaissance

First Unitarian Church Gothic Revival

Beaux Arts style Palace of Fine Arts

BEAUX ARTS

The rigorously Neo-Classical style of the Parisian *Ecole des Beaux Arts* was favored by designers in San Francisco for major buildings following the 1906 earthquake. Opulent colonnades, sculptures and pediments are typical of this lavish style, which was readily adopted in a city eager to signal to the world its recovery from devastation.

The most perfect illustration of Beaux Arts style in the city is Bernard Maybeck's **Palace of Fine Arts**, built as the focus of the 1915 Panama–Pacific Exposition, and acclaimed as the city's most vibrant celebration of the art of architecture.

Other impressive examples surround Civic Center Plaza: the **City Hall** (Arthur Brown, 1915); the old **Main Library**, now the **Asian Art Museum** (George Kelham, 1915); the **War Memorial Opera House** and the **Veteran's Building**

(both by Arthur Brown, 1932); and the oldest building in the Civic Center, the **Bill Graham Civic Auditorium** (John Galen Howard, 1915).

COMMERCIAL

Two early office buildings that are of architectural significance are Willis Polk's **Hallidie Building** (1917), the world's first glass-curtain-walled structure, and his stately **Merchant's Exchange** (1906).

Timothy Pflueger's building at **450 Sutter Street** (1929) is a shining example of Art Deco design. Its lobby is beautifully detailed with red marble and embossed aluminum.

The **Union Square Frank Lloyd Wright Building** (Xanadu Gallery) was designed in 1949 by Wright. The interior spirals up to a mezzanine, while the façade is broken by an arched, tunnel-like entrance. The 853-ft (256-m) **Transamerica Pyramid** (William Pereira, 1972) is also a notable piece of commercial architecture.

Highly ornate Art Deco lobby of 450 Sutter Street

CONTEMPORARY

A legacy of the 1980s real estate boom, the **Marriott Hotel** (Anthony Lumsden, 1989) is the city's most disliked recent building. The imaginative projects of the 1990s were more welcome, especially the **Yerba Buena Center for the Arts** designed by Fumihiko Maki (1993), and the **Museum of Modern Art** by Mario Botta in 1994.

The imaginative façade of the Museum of Modern Art

WHERE TO FIND THE BUILDINGS

St. Paulus
Gothic

St. Boniface
Romanesque

Notre Dame des Victoires
Roman and Byzantine

SAN FRANCISCO
THROUGH THE YEAR

Springtime in San Francisco sees a city awakening from winter slumbers, with leaves returning to the trees, and the last gray whales migrating north along the coast. By May and June the air is often warm, and windsurfers can be seen on the bay. In August, morning fog rolls in from the sea, but summer weather returns in September. Cool clear nights set in at the end of the year, with occasional snowfalls on Mount Diablo. The main annual events are listed below. For up-to-date information, the San Francisco Convention and Visitors Bureau *(see p278)*, provides a free calendar of year-round city events.

SPRING

Springtime is the season for long walks around San Francisco, wandering through the parks or along city center streets washed by overnight rains. In April, bulbs come into bloom in the parks and gardens, and wildflowers cover the headlands on either side of the Golden Gate. In May, thousands of runners join the Bay to Breakers race.

MARCH

St. Patrick's Day Parade *(Sun nearest Mar 17)*. The day is marked by a parade down Market St, and the bars are filled with merrymakers.
Bay Area Music Awards *(early–mid-Mar)*. Local musicians win special "Bammie" awards from their fans.

EASTER

Easter Sunrise Services. Thousands of worshipers gather at dawn in front of the huge cross on Mount Davidson, the highest hill in the city.

APRIL

Cherry Blossom Festival *(mid- to late Apr)*. This celebration of traditional Japanese arts and crafts attracts dancers, drummers, artists and craftspeople from all around the Bay Area. It takes place at the Japan Center *(see p128)*, where there are lively performances and a colorful parade.
San Francisco International Film Festival *(late Apr–early May)*. For two weeks there are screenings every day at the Kabuki *(see p262)*, and other theaters. American and international films are shown, many of them for the first time in the US.
Wildflower Walks. Guided walks are offered at various San Francisco natural areas by volunteers. Commercial guided tours are offered in the Marin Headlands *(see pp174–5)*.
Opening Day of Baseball Season *(late Apr–early May)*. Sports fans turn out to see their baseball heroes perform at AT&T Park and Oakland Coliseum.

Glittering Carnaval celebrations in the Mission District of San Francisco

MAY

Bay to Breakers *(late May)*. Partly a serious race, partly a mad dash in funny costumes, contenders run 7.5 miles (12.5 km) from the Ferry Building to Ocean Beach *(see p153)*.

The Bay to Breakers run

Cinco de Mayo *(early May)*. Mexican cultural celebration, with a carnival in the Civic Center and special events in the Mission District.
Carnaval SF *(last weekend)*. Latin American and Caribbean festival in the Mission District, with salsa and reggae bands.

Colorful traditional costumes at the Japanese Cherry Blossom Festival

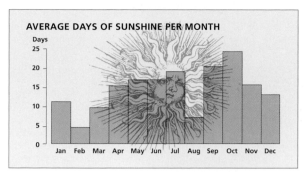

AVERAGE DAYS OF SUNSHINE PER MONTH

Days

25

20

15

10

5

0

Jan Feb Mar Apr May Jun Jul Aug Sep Oct Nov Dec

Sunshine Chart
The sunniest months in San Francisco are September and October. In mid-summer almost everywhere else in the Bay Area is both warmer and sunnier. The Napa Valley (see pp190–93) and other inland valleys are baking hot and dry.

SUMMER

Mark Twain is said to have commented that the coldest winter he ever spent was a summer in San Francisco. June and July see the city besieged by tourists from all over the world, who often complain about the "cold" that can ruin their otherwise perfect days.

Golden Gate Bridge in fog

FOGGY DAYS

Afternoon and evening fogs are common in San Francisco during the summer months. They form far out over the sea and roll in through the Golden Gate, shrouding parts of the city with a cold, damp cloud. These fogs are some-times so dense that they can cause the temperature to fall by as much as 20° F (10° C) in a matter of hours.

JUNE

Lesbian and Gay Pride Day *(Sun in late Jun)*. The biggest show in San Francisco and the largest of its kind in the US – more than 300,000 people every year attend the Market St parade and Civic Center celebrations.
Haight Street Fair *(Sat or Sun in late Jun)*. Bands play, and there are food stalls along Haight St *(see p134)*.
North Beach Festival *(mid Jun)*. Arts and crafts, bands and food stalls in the Italian district on Grant Ave, Green St and Washington Sq.

Juneteenth *(late Jun)*. African-American cultural celebration, with jazz and blues bands along Oakland's Lake Merritt *(see p164)*.

JULY

4th of July Fireworks *(Jul 4)*. Held along the waterfront at Crissy Field National Recreation Area *(see p59)*, American Independence Day is celebrated with a spectacular pyrotechnic dis-play at Golden Gate Bridge.
San Francisco Marathon *(late Jul)*. 3,500 athletes race around the city, starting at the Golden Gate Bridge.

AT&T Park is home to the San Francisco Giants baseball team

AUGUST

Baseball *(season Apr–Sep)*. San Francisco Giants and Oakland Athletics (A's) play games throughout the summer *(see p272)*. Tickets are usually available on the day of play, although the best seats sell out in advance. AT&T Park opened to the public in 2000.
San Francisco Playwright's Festival *(last week Jul–first week Aug)*. Fort Mason Center *(see pp74–5)*. Readings, workshops and performances of new works. Audiences can discuss the performances with the artists at special sessions.

Lesbian and Gay Pride Parade to the Civic Center

AVERAGE MONTHLY TEMPERATURE

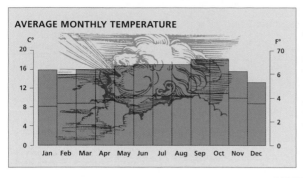

Temperature Chart
The chart shows the average minimum and maximum temperatures for each month. San Francisco and the Bay area enjoy mild weather all year round, with temperatures seldom rising above 70° F (21° C) or falling below 40° F (4° C).

AUTUMN

San Franciscans reclaim their city from the visitors in September, just as the Bay Area summer begins. Many outdoor festivities and cultural events take place in the parks and on the streets, while the football, opera and symphony seasons all open in the autumn.

SEPTEMBER

49ers and Raiders Football (*season begins Sep*). Various arenas. To December, or January if teams are in the playoffs (*see p272*).
San Francisco's Opera Opening Night. This glamorous gala event launches the San Francisco opera season which runs from September through December. It is a formal black-tie ball held at War Memorial Opera House, Van Ness Ave (*see p264*).
Valley of the Moon Vintage Festival (*late Sep*). California's oldest wine festival takes place at Sonoma Plaza, Sonoma.
San Francisco's Blues Festival (*last weekend*). This two-day outdoor event draws some of the world's best blues stars to the Great Meadow at Fort Mason (*see p267*).
Folsom Street Fair (*last Sun*). Predominantly gay and lesbian event between 11th and 17th Streets. Music, comedy, dancing, crafts, and beer garden. All proceeds from the fair are donated to charity.

49ers game season starts September

OCTOBER

Castro Street Fair (*first Sun*). One of the city's largest and longest-running street celebrations (*see p136*).
Columbus Day Parade (*Sun nearest Oct 12*). Pageant and procession down Columbus Ave in North Beach, finishing at Fisherman's Wharf.
Halloween (*Oct 31*). The autumn night is celebrated by thousands of revelers dressed in costume all converging on Market St. and Castro St. Though no longer sanctioned by the city, many die-hards still take part.
Shakespeare in the Park (*Sats and Suns from Labor Day*). Free performances in Golden Gate Park (*see p259*). A temporary outdoor theater is erected in Liberty Meadow especially for the event.

Day of the Dead procession

Columbus Day Parade

Fleet Week (*early Oct*). A celebration of the US Navy. Aerial displays by the Blue Angels; naval vessels gather near Golden Gate Bridge.
Harvest Festival and Christmas Crafts Market (*late Oct to mid-Nov*). Popular crafts fair on two weekends.

NOVEMBER

Dia de los Muertos/Day of the Dead (*Nov 2*). Mexican Halloween, marked by a nighttime procession through the Mission District. Costumes, dances, Halloween food.
San Francisco Jazz Festival (*late Oct–early Nov*). All-star jazz festival (*p266*).
The Big Game (*third Sat*). Major university football event when California Golden Bears play Stanford Cardinal, alternately at Stanford and UC Berkeley (*see p272*).
International Auto Show (*late Nov*) is now held at the Moscone Center (*see pp114–15*).

AVERAGE MONTHLY RAINFALL

Rainfall Chart
The average annual rainfall for San Francisco is about 19 in (122 cm). Most rain falls from November to March, sometimes for days at a time, and there are often torrential storms. The driest months are May to September.

WINTER

The Christmas shopping season starts the day after Thanksgiving with the lighting of the Union Square tree, while appealing pets appear in the windows of Gump's store *(see p120)*. Families of gray whales pass on their annual migration between Alaska and Mexico.

DECEMBER

Christmas Displays in Union Square store windows *(see p116)* compete to be the best.
The Nutcracker *(3rd week)* is performed by the San Francisco Ballet at the War Memorial Opera House *(see p264)*.
Sing-It-Yourself Messiah *(early Dec)* at Louise M. Davies Symphony Hall *(see p126)*. Audience performs under the direction of various conductors.
Sing for your Life *(Dec 30–31)*. 24 hours of singing in Grace Cathedral *(see p103)*.

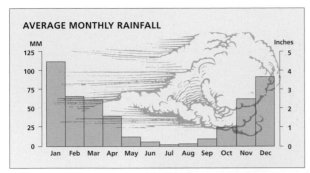

Chinese New Year celebrations in Chinatown

JANUARY

New Year's Day Swim *(Jan 1)*. Sponsored swim at Aquatic Park *(see pp172–3)*.
Russian Orthodox Christmas *(Jan 7–8)*. Ceremony in Holy Virgin Cathedral *(see p63)*.
Gray Whale Migration *(Jan– Apr)*. Watch from the coast, or take a boat *(see p272)*.

FEBRUARY

Black History Month. African-American events take place throughout the city.
Chinese New Year Parade *(date varies, usually early Feb)*. Parade through Financial District and Chinatown featuring a colorful dragon *(see pp94–100 and 107–121)*.

Christmas tree and decorations in Nieman Marcus department store

PUBLIC HOLIDAYS

New Year's Day (Jan 1)
Martin Luther King Day (3rd Mon in Jan)
President's Day (3rd Mon in Feb)
Memorial Day (last Mon in May)
Independence Day (Jul 4)
Labor Day (1st Mon in Sep)
Columbus Day (2nd Mon in Oct)
Election Day (1st Tue in Nov)
Veterans Day (Nov 11)
Thanksgiving Day (4th Thu in Nov)
Christmas Day (Dec 25)

SAN FRANCISCO AREA BY AREA

The 49-Mile Scenic Drive

Official sign

Linking the city's most intriguing neighborhoods, fascinating sights and spectacular views, the 49-Mile Scenic Drive (79 km) provides a splendid overview of San Francisco for the determined motorist. Keeping to the well-marked route is simple enough – just follow the blue-and-white seagull signs. Some of these are hidden by overhanging vegetation or buildings, so you need to be alert. You should set aside a whole day for this trip; there are plenty of places to stop to take photographs or admire the views.

Marina Green ㉗
This is an excellent vantage point from which to view or photograph Golden Gate Bridge.

The Palace of Fine Arts and the **Exploratorium** ㉘ stand near the entrance to the wooded Presidio.

Stow Lake ⑨
There is a waterfall and a Chinese pavilion on the island in this picturesque lake. Boats are for rent.

San Francisco Zoological Gardens ⑧ is one of the six best zoos in the US. Among its attractions are Gorilla World and the Primate Discovery Center.

Twin Peaks ⑬
From both summits, the views over the city and bay are magnificent and well worth the climb.

◁ A view of the Transamerica Pyramid Building

TIPS FOR MOTORISTS

Starting point: *Anywhere. The circuit is designed to be followed in a counterclockwise direction starting and ending at any point.*
When to go: *Avoid driving during rush hours: 7–10am, 4–7pm. Most of the views are as spectacular by night as by day.*
Parking: *Use parking garages in Financial District, Civic Center, Nob Hill, Chinatown, North Beach and Fisherman's Wharf. Elsewhere, street parking is usually available.*
Stopping-off points: *There are numerous cafés, bars and restaurants (see pp222–43).*

Civic Center ⑰ is the stately official and administrative heart of San Francisco, where imposing Beaux Arts buildings surround a central plaza.

Maritime National Historic Park Visitor Center ㉕ has a fine collection of ship models, photographs and relics, with many historic ships moored nearby at Hyde Street Pier.

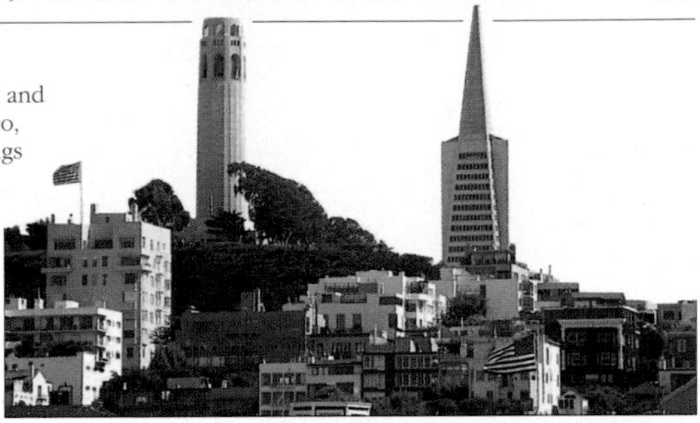

Coit Tower ㉔
Overlooking North Beach, Telegraph Hill is topped by this tower, which has stunning murals and a viewing terrace.

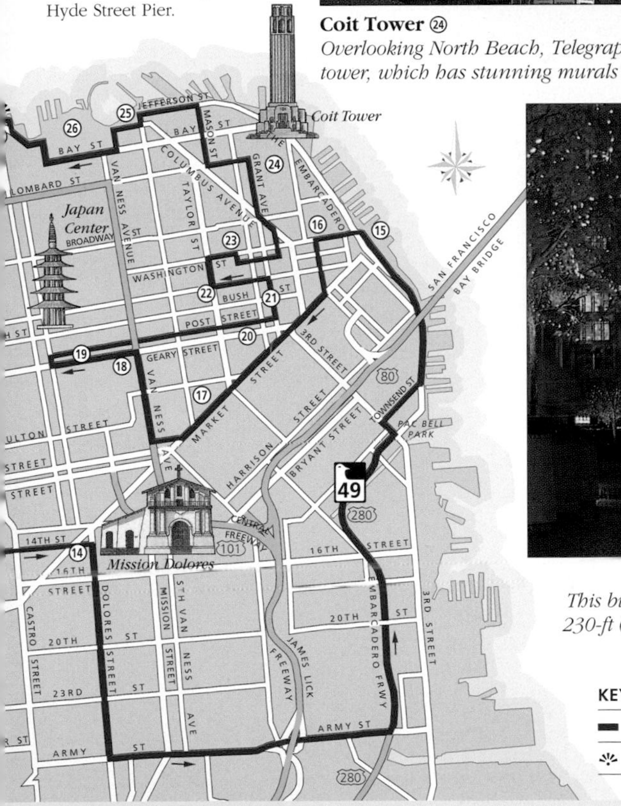

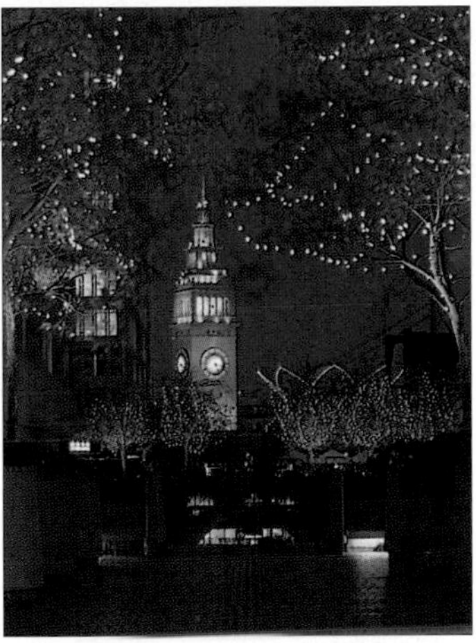

Ferry Building ⑮
This building with its distinctive 230-ft (70-m) tower survived the 1906 earthquake intact.

KEY

▬ 49-Mile Scenic Drive

Viewing point

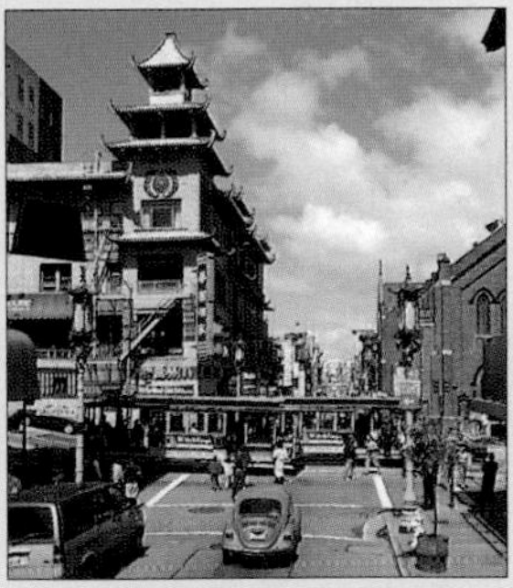

Grant Avenue in San Francisco's Chinatown *(see p99)*

FINDING THE SIGHTS

① Presidio *p62*
② Fort Point *p62*
③ Land's End *p157*
④ Legion of Honor *p156*
⑤ Sutro Heights Park *p157*
⑥ Cliff House *p157*
⑦ Queen Wilhelmina Tulip Garden *p153*
⑧ San Francisco Zoological Gardens *p160*
⑨ Stow Lake *p152*
⑩ Conservatory of Flowers *p152*
⑪ Haight Street *p134*
⑫ Sutro Tower *p139*
⑬ Twin Peaks *p139*
⑭ Mission Dolores *p137*
⑮ Ferry Building *p112*
⑯ Embarcadero Center *p110*
⑰ Civic Center *pp126–7*
⑱ St Mary's Cathedral *p128*
⑲ Japan Center *p128*
⑳ Union Square *p116*
㉑ Chinatown Gateway *p98*
㉒ Grace Cathedral *p103*
㉓ Cable Car Barn *p103*
㉔ Coit Tower *p93*
㉕ Maritime National Historic Park Visitor Center *p83*
㉖ Fort Mason *pp74–5*
㉗ Marina Green *p75*
㉘ Palace of Fine Arts and the Exploratorium *pp60–61*

PRESIDIO

This beautiful wooded corner of the city has stunning views over both Golden Gate Bridge and the mouth of San Francisco Bay. First established as an outpost of Spain's New World empire in 1776, the Presidio was, for many years, the site of an army base. But in 1994 its ownership passed to the National Park Service and it is now an area of

Cannon at Fort Point

contrasting attractions: visitors may take in Civil War gun sites, and parade grounds and barracks from the 19th century, or enjoy an invigorating stroll through miles of forest land. The area is planted with pine and eucalyptus trees, and is a wildlife haven. You can reach Baker Beach via the park, and a notable landmark, the Palace of Fine Arts, lies to the east.

SIGHTS AT A GLANCE

Historic Streets and Buildings
Clement Street ⑧
Golden Gate Bridge pp64–7 ⑤
Palace of Fine Arts and the Exploratorium pp60–61 ①
Presidio Officers' Club ③

Museums and Galleries
Fort Point and Crissy Field ④
The Walt Disney Family Museum ②

Churches and Temples
Holy Virgin Cathedral ⑦
Temple Emanu-El ⑨

Parks and Gardens
Baker Beach ⑥

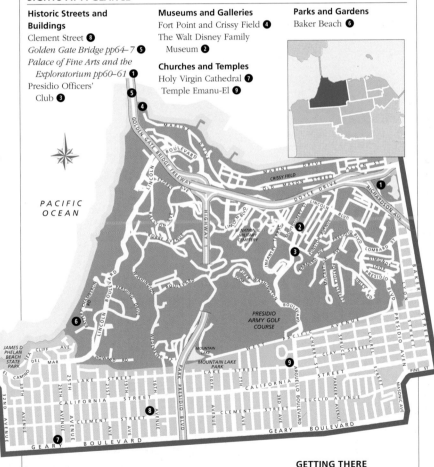

GETTING THERE
The area is best seen by car or bicycle, though Muni bus 29 stops at the main sights. Bus 43 from Haight Ashbury serves the eastern end, and the 28 runs along the northern boundary.

KEY

Street-by-Street map
See pp58–9

0 meters 750
0 yards 750

◁ **Golden Gate Bridge from Baker Beach**

A Tour of the Presidio

Presidio Park sign

The winding roads and lush landscaping of the Presidio belie its long military history. This prominent site has played a key role in San Francisco's growth, and has been occupied longer than any other part of the city. Remnants of its military past, including well-preserved barracks and artillery emplacements, can be seen everywhere, and there are many hiking trails, bicycling paths and beaches. Golden Gate Bridge crosses the bay from the northwest corner of the Presidio.

Fort Point
This impressive brick fortress, now a national historic site, guarded the Golden Gate during the Civil War of 1861–5 **4**

Golden Gate Bridge Visitor Gift Center

The Gorbachev Foundation aims to foster international cooperation.

★ **Golden Gate Bridge**
Opened in 1937, the bridge has a single span of 4,200 ft (1,280 m) **5**

Marine Drive is a waterfront road, lined with palm trees.

Coastal Trail start

Lobos Creek is a small stream that flows from Mountain Lake and provides the Presidio with drinking water.

Baker Beach
Separated from the rest of the Presidio, and extending along the foot of steep bluffs, this is the best of the city's beaches **6**

The Pet Cemetery was once used to bury army guard dogs. Since 1945 it has been the final resting place for family pets.

LOCATOR MAP
See Street Finder, map 1

Crissy Field, reclaimed from marshland for the 1915 Pan–Pacific Exposition, was used as an airfield from 1919–36. It is now a National Recreation Area.

The Military Cemetery holds the remains of almost 15,000 American soldiers killed during several wars.

★ **Palace of Fine Arts and the Exploratorium**
Conceived as a Roman ruin, the palace now houses the Exploratorium science museum ❶

The Ecology Trail starts at Boulevard Gate.

Golf course

The parade ground was first laid out in 1776. The buildings around it include barracks from the 1880s and Civil War officers' quarters.

Mountain Lake is a large spring-fed lake. The original Presidio was established nearby in 1776.

0 meters 500
0 yards 500

Presidio Officers' Club
The club is built over the remains of the old Spanish Presidio, still preserved inside the building ❸

Captured Cannon
This 19th-century cannon from the Spanish–American War is still on the grounds.

STAR SIGHTS

★ Palace of Fine Arts

★ Golden Gate Bridge

Palace of Fine Arts and the Exploratorium ●

Sole survivor of the many grandiose monuments built as part of the 1915 Panama–Pacific Exposition *(see pp30–31)*, the Neo-Classical Palace of Fine Arts was an Expo centerpiece. Inside the Palace is the Exploratorium, one of the most engaging science museums in the US. Established in 1969 by Frank Oppenheimer, whose brother Robert helped develop the atom bomb, it has hundreds of interactive exhibits, a webcast studio, and a multimedia Learning Center.

Detail from the base of the Rotunda

★ **The Rotunda**
The dome of the Rotunda is supported by a Classical frieze and an octagonal arcade.

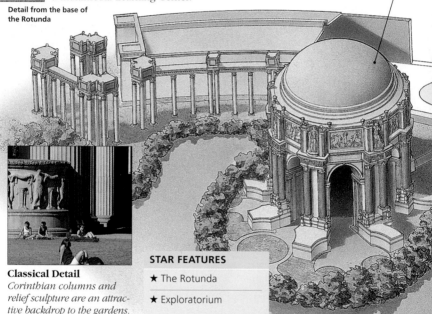

Classical Detail
Corinthian columns and relief sculpture are an attractive backdrop to the gardens.

STAR FEATURES

★ The Rotunda

★ Exploratorium

BUILDING THE PALACE OF FINE ARTS

The beautiful Palace of Fine Arts is one of San Francisco's most prominent pieces of architecture. Designed by the noted Bay Area architect Bernard R. Maybeck, this landmark structure is composed of a central rotunda on the edge of a landscaped lagoon, flanked by an open-air peristyle of intricately detailed Corinthian columns. Intended as a melancholic evocation of vanquished grandeur, it was inspired by Piranesi's Baroque etchings and by *L'Isle des Morts*, a painting by the well-known Swiss artist Arnold Böcklin.

Since it was not supposed to last beyond the end of the 1915 Exposition, the Palace of Fine Arts was originally constructed of inexpensive wood and plaster, at a total cost of $700,000. After being

Bernard Maybeck

The Palace of Fine Arts in a state of severe decay

spared demolition, the fabric of the structure was left to crumble gracefully until 1962, when it was rebuilt using reinforced concrete.

Seeing
Learn about optical illusions and investigate how eyes work.

Motion
In this area visitors can choose a winning wheel in Downhill Race or try the thrilling Momentum Machine.

★ **Inside the Exploratorium**
Hundreds of exhibits encourage visitors to explore the world of science and to make discoveries.

Tactile Dome

Electricity and Magnetism

Heat and Temperature, Patterns

Sound and Hearing

Complexity

Life Sciences

Pendulums

MUSEUM GUIDE TO THE EXPLORATORIUM
Exhibits are divided into five broad thematic areas located on the main floor and the mezzanine level. The Tactile Dome is pitch-black inside; visitors must crawl, climb, and slide through it.

McBean Theater — **Entrance**

Colored Shadows
Whenever your shadow blocks one color, the two other primary colors combine in a new color.

KEY TO FLOOR PLAN

☐	Seeing
☐	Motion
☐	Electricity and Magnetism
☐	Heat and Temperature, Patterns
☐	Life Sciences
☐	Sound and Hearing
☐	Complexity
☐	Pendulums

Palace of Fine Arts and the Exploratorium ❶

See pp60–61.

Historic barracks on the Presidio

The Walt Disney Family Museum ❷

104 Montgomery Street. **Map** 3 A2.
Tel 345-6800 ☐ 10am–6pm
Wed–Mon ☐ Jan 1, July 4,
Thanksgiving, Dec 25. ☒
www.waltdisney.org

Opened in 2009, this museum documents the life and achievements of Walt Disney. A series of ten interactive galleries incorporate film clips, storyboards and scripts to tell the story of the man and his amazing career. Visitors will find Hollywood's first feature length animated film and early drawings of Mickey Mouse alongside exhibits dedicated to Disney's home life including photographs and home movies.

Presidio Officers' Club ❸

50 Moraga Ave. **Map** 3 A2.
🚌 29. ☐ 9am–5pm daily.
☐ some public hols.

Situated in the south-west corner of the Plaza de Armas, over-looking the parade grounds of the Presidio and the 19th-century

barracks, the Officers' Club is built in the Spanish Mission style *(see p46)*. It dates from the 1930s, but incorporates the adobe (sun-dried brick) remains of the original 18th-century Spanish fort.

Fort Point and Crissy Field ❹

Marine Drive. **Map** 2 E1. 📞 556-1693. ☐ 10am–5pm Fri–Sun.
📷 ♿ partial.

Completed by the US Army in 1861, this fort was built partly to protect San Francisco Bay from any attack, and partly to defend ships carrying gold from California mines. It is the most prominent of the many fortifications constructed along the coast, and is a classic example of a pre-Civil War brick fortress. The building soon became obsolete, because its 10-ft-thick (3-m) brick walls would not have stood up to powerful modern weaponry. It was closed in 1900, never having come under attack.

The brickwork vaulting is extremely unusual for San Francisco, where the ready availability of good timber was an incentive to build wood-frame constructions. This may have saved the fort from collapse in the 1906 earthquake *(see pp28–9)*. It was nearly demolished in the 1930s to make way for the Golden Gate Bridge, but it survived and is now a good place from which to view the bridge. National Park Service rangers

in Civil War costume conduct guided tours. A tidal marsh once covered the area called Crissy Field. After two centuries of military use, the Field has been transformed into a waterfront park for recreation and education. The Crissy Field Center offers a rich array of programs including many geared towards kids, from wildlife treks to kite-flying.

Golden Gate Bridge ❺

See pp64–7.

Golden Gate Bridge seen from Baker Beach

Baker Beach ❻

Map 2 D4. ☐ dawn–dusk daily.

Baker Beach is the largest and most popular stretch of sand in the city and is often crowded with sunbathers. The chilly water and strong currents make it a dangerous place to swim, but it is a fine place to go for a walk. Fishing is also good here. There are forests of pine and cypress on the bluffs above the beach, where visitors can explore Battery Chamberlin, a gun emplacement from 1904. On the first weekend of each month rangers show the "disappearing gun," a heavy rifle that can be lowered behind a thick wall to protect it from enemy fire, and then raised again in order to be fired.

Cannon in the courtyard of Fort Point

Holy Virgin Cathedral ⑦

6210 Geary Blvd. **Map** 8 D1.
221-3255. 2, 29, 38. 8am and 6pm daily.

Shining gold onion-shaped domes crown the Russian Orthodox Holy Virgin Cathedral of the Russian Church in Exile, a startling landmark in the suburban Richmond District. Built in the early 1960s, it is generally open only during services. In contrast to those of many other Christian denominations, the services here are conducted with the congregation standing, so there are no pews or seats.

The cathedral and the many Russian-owned businesses nearby, such as the lively Russian Renaissance restaurant, are situated at the heart of San Francisco's extensive Russian community *(see p41)*. This has flourished since the 1820s, but expanded greatly when new immigrants arrived after the Russian Revolution of 1917, and especially in the late 1950s and late 1980s.

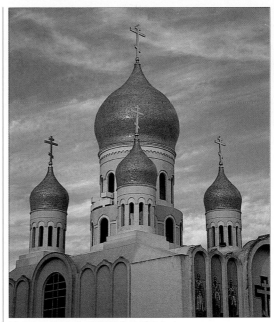

The Russian Orthodox Holy Virgin Cathedral

Clement Street ⑧

Map 1 C5. 2, 28, 29, 44.

This is the bustling main thoroughfare of the otherwise sleepy Richmond District. Bookshops and small boutiques flourish here, and the inhabitants of the neighborhood meet together in a lively mix of bars, fast-food cafés and ethnic restaurants. Most of these are patronized more by locals than by tourists. Clement Street is surrounded by an area known as New Chinatown, home to more than one-third of the Chinese population of San Francisco. As a result, some of the city's best Chinese restaurants can be found here,

and the emphasis in general is on East Asian cuisine. However, the area is known for the diversity of its restaurants, and Peruvian, Russian and French establishments, among many others, also flourish here. The street stretches from Arguello Boulevard to the north-south cross-streets which are known as "The Avenues." It ends near the Legion of Honor *(see pp156–7)*.

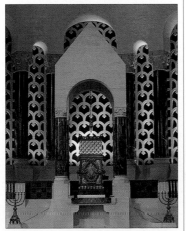

Interior of Temple Emanu-El, showing Holy Ark

Temple Emanu-El ⑨

Lake St and Arguello Blvd. **Map** 3 A4. **Tel** 751-2535. guided tours only; available 1–3pm daily. www.emanuelsf.org

After World War I hundreds of Jews from Russia and Eastern Europe moved into the Richmond District and built religious centers that are still major landmarks. Among these is the Temple Emanu-El, its dome inspired by that of the 6th-century Santa Sophia in Istanbul. The temple is a majestic piece of architecture. It was built in 1925 for the city's longest-established Jewish congregation (which was founded in 1850). The architect was Arthur Brown, who also designed San Francisco's City Hall *(see p125)*. With its red-tiled dome, Emanu-El is a Californian architectural hybrid, combining the local Mission style *(see p46)* with Byzantine ornament and Romanesque arcades. Its interior, which holds nearly 2,000 worshipers, is especially fine when bright sunlight shines through the earth-toned stained-glass windows.

Golden Gate Bridge ❺

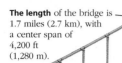

Named after that part of San Francisco Bay called "Golden Gate" by John Fremont in 1844, the bridge opened in 1937, connecting the city with Marin County. Breathtaking views are offered from this spectacular, world-famous landmark, which has six lanes for vehicles plus a free pedestrian walkway. It is the world's third-largest single-span bridge and, when it was built, was the longest and tallest suspension structure.

Bridge builder wearing protective mask

The length of the bridge is 1.7 miles (2.7 km), with a center span of 4,200 ft (1,280 m).

The Foundations
The foundations of the twin towers are a remarkable feat of engineering. The south pier, 1,125 ft (345 m) offshore, was sunk 100 ft (30 m) below the surface in open water.

Pier base 65-ft (20-m) thick

Fender 155-ft (47-m) high

Reinforcing iron frame

The roadway is 220 ft (67 m) above water 318-ft (97-m) deep.

Divers
To reach bedrock, divers were employed to dynamite 20-ft (6-m) deep holes in the ocean floor.

The Concrete Fender
During construction, the south pier base was protected from the force of the tides by a fender of concrete. Water was pumped out to create a vast watertight locker.

THE GOLDEN GATE BRIDGE

The Roadway
The original steel-supported concrete roadway was constructed from the towers in both directions, so weight on the suspension cables was evenly distributed.

Construction of the Towers
The twin steel towers rise to a height of 746 ft (227 m) above the water. The towers are hollow.

Catching the Hot Rivets
Working in gangs of four, one man heated the rivets and threw them to another, who caught them in a bucket. The other two fastened sections of steel with the hot rivets.

Joseph Strauss
Joseph Strauss is officially credited as the bridge's designer, though his assistant Charles Ellis has been given major credit for the span's design. Irving F. Morrow acted as consulting architect.

TIMELINE OF THE BRIDGE'S CONSTRUCTION

	1933		1934		1935		1936		1937

January Anchorages and San Francisco pier and trestle are started

October Work begins on towers

December San Francisco pier is finished

June Towers are complete

July Cable laying begins

June Work ends on cables and starts on roadway

April Roadway is finished

June Part of trestle is destroyed by a ship

February Official groundbreaking

May Marin Tower is topped off

Marin Tower topping-off ceremony

July First cable across Golden Gate

June Earthquake shakes towers violently

September Last suspender rope in place

May Opening Day

February Last rivet is driven

The Opening of the Bridge

The bridge that most people said could never be built was completed on time and under budget in the midst of the Great Depression. Joseph Strauss finally won widespread support for the bridge, and a major bond issue financed its $35 million, four-year construction. When it opened, every siren and church bell in San Francisco and Marin sounded simultaneously as part of a huge celebration.

First Vehicles Cross
At 9:30am on May 28, 1937, the toll gates lifted and an official convoy of black limousines became the first vehicles to cross the bridge.

Opening Day Crowd
On May 27, 1937 the bridge opened only for pedestrians. Nearly 18,000 people waited at the barriers, held back by large numbers of police.

THE BRIDGE IN FIGURES

- Every year more than 40 million vehicles cross the bridge; every day about 120,000 vehicles use it.
- The original coat of paint lasted for 27 years, needing only touch-ups. But since 1965, a crew has been stripping off the old paint and applying a more durable coating.
- The two great 7,650-ft (2,332-m) cables are more than 3 ft (1 m) thick, and contain 80,000 miles (128,744 km) of steel wire, enough to encircle the earth at the equator three times.
- The volume of concrete poured into the piers and anchorages during the bridge's construction would be enough to lay a 5-ft-wide (1.5 m) sidewalk stretching from New York to San Francisco, a distance of more than 2,500 miles (4,000 km).
- The bridge was designed to withstand 100 mph (160 km/h) winds.
- Each pier has to withstand a tidal flow of more than 60 mph (97 km/h), while supporting a 21,500-ton steel tower above.

Original painting of the bridge

View from Vista Point
The best view of both the bridge and San Francisco is from the Marin side.

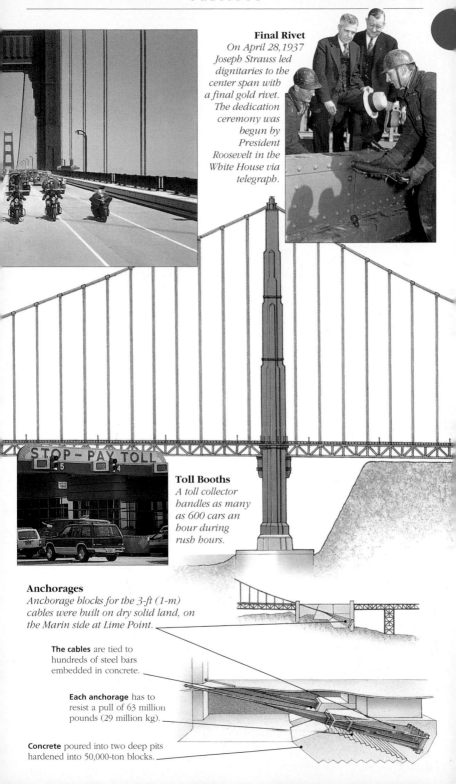

Final Rivet
On April 28, 1937 Joseph Strauss led dignitaries to the center span with a final gold rivet. The dedication ceremony was begun by President Roosevelt in the White House via telegraph.

Toll Booths
A toll collector handles as many as 600 cars an hour during rush hours.

Anchorages
Anchorage blocks for the 3-ft (1-m) cables were built on dry solid land, on the Marin side at Lime Point.

The cables are tied to hundreds of steel bars embedded in concrete.

Each anchorage has to resist a pull of 63 million pounds (29 million kg).

Concrete poured into two deep pits hardened into 50,000-ton blocks.

PACIFIC HEIGHTS
AND THE MARINA

Pacific Heights is an exclusive neighborhood that clings to a hillside rising 300 ft (100 m) above the city. The area was developed in the 1880s, after cable cars linking it with the city center were introduced. With its magnificent views, it quickly became a desirable place to live, and elegant Victorian houses still line its tree-shaded streets. Most of these are privately owned, but the Queen Anne-style Haas-Lilienthal House is open to the public. To the north of Broadway, the streets drop steeply to the Marina District, ending at San Francisco Bay. The houses here are built on a once-marshy site that was cleared and drained for the Panama–Pacific Exposition (see p72), and the ambience is that of a seaside resort for the wealthy, with boutiques, lively cafés and two prestigious yacht clubs.

Fort Mason logo

SIGHTS AT A GLANCE

Historic Streets and Buildings
Convent of the Sacred Heart **6**
Cow Hollow **8**
Fort Mason **15**
Haas-Lilienthal House **1**
Octagon House **11**
Spreckels Mansion **2**
Trinity Episcopal Church **7**
Wave Organ **14**

Parks and Gardens
Alta Plaza **4**
Lafayette Park **3**
Marina Green **13**

Churches and Temples
Church of St. Mary the Virgin **9**
Vedanta Temple **10**

Shopping Streets
Chestnut Street **12**
Fillmore Street **5**

KEY
Street-by-Street map
See pp70–71

Cable car terminus

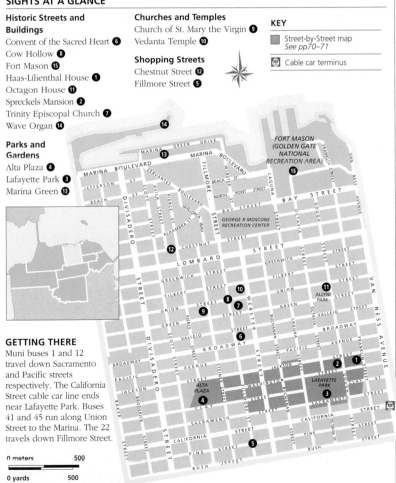

GETTING THERE
Muni buses 1 and 12 travel down Sacramento and Pacific streets respectively. The California Street cable car line ends near Lafayette Park. Buses 41 and 45 run along Union Street to the Marina. The 22 travels down Fillmore Street.

0 meters   500
0 yards   500

◁ Detail of the southern façade of Spreckels Mansion, overlooking Washington Street

Street-by-Street: Pacific Heights

The blocks between Alta Plaza and Lafayette Park are at the heart of Pacific Heights. The streets here are quiet and tidy, lined with smart apartment blocks and palatial houses. Some date from the late 19th century, while others were built after the fire of 1906 *(see pp28–9)*. To the north of the area, the streets drop steeply toward the Marina District, affording outstanding views of the bay. Wander through the two large parks and past the luxuriant gardens of the mansions in between, then visit one of the numerous good bars, cafés and restaurants on lively Fillmore Street.

Toy rabbit in Haas-Lilienthal house

The view from Alta Plaza down hilly Pierce Street to the north encompasses the Marina District and offers a splendid panorama of the bay beyond.

★ Alta Plaza
Set aside as a public park in the 1850s, this hilltop green space has a playground, tennis courts and good views ④

Washington Street lies to the east of Alta Plaza. Here Victorian houses, in various architectural styles, fill an entire block.

BUCHANAN

WEBSTER STREET

FILLMORE STREET

STEINER STREET

To bus no. 12

0 meters   100

0 yards   100

STAR SIGHTS

★ Spreckels Mansion

★ Alta Plaza

KEY

– – – Suggested route

Webster Street Row houses (terraced houses) have been declared an historic landmark. They were built for a middle-class clientèle in 1878 and have since been restored.

LOCATOR MAP
See Street Finder, maps 3 & 4

★ **Spreckels Mansion**
This impressive limestone building, constructed on the lines of a French Baroque palace, has been home to the family of best-selling novelist Danielle Steele since 1990 ❷

No. 2004 Gough Street, one of the more elaborate Victorian houses in Pacific Heights, was built in 1889.

To bus nos. 47, 76

Lafayette Park
This quiet park gives good views of the Victorian houses that surround it ❸

No. 2151 Sacramento Street is an ornate French-style mansion. A plaque commemorates a visit by the author Sir Arthur Conan Doyle in 1923.

Haas Lilienthal House
Furnished in Victorian style, this mansion is the headquarters of the Architectural Heritage Foundation ❶

Haas-Lilienthal House ❶

2007 Franklin St. **Map** 4 E3. **Tel** 441-3004. 🚌 1, 19, 27, 47, 49, 83. 📷 noon–3pm Wed & Sat, 11am–4pm Sun (times may vary; call ahead). 📷 📷 www.sfheritage.org/house

This exuberant Queen Anne-style mansion *(see pp76–7)* was built in 1886 for the rich merchant William Haas. Alice Lilienthal, his daughter, lived there until 1972, when it was given to the Foundation for San Francisco's

The Haas-Lilienthal House, a Queen Anne mansion from 1886

Architectural Heritage. It is the only intact private home of the period open as a museum, and is complete with authentic furniture. A fine example of an upper-middle-class Victorian dwelling, the house has elaborate wooden gables, a circular corner tower and luxuriant ornamentation.

A display of photographs in the basement describes the history of the building and reveals that this grandiose house was modest in comparison with some of the dozens of mansions destroyed in the fire of 1906 *(see pp28–9)*.

Spreckels Mansion ❷

2080 Washington St. **Map** 4 E3 🚌 1, 47, 49. ⚫ to the public.

Dominating the north side of Lafayette Park, this imposing Beaux Arts mansion *(see pp46–7)* is sometimes known as the "Parthenon of the West." It was built in 1912 for the flamboyant Alma de Bretteville Spreckels and her husband Adolph, who was heir to the sugar fortune of Claus Spreckels *(see p134)*. Today the house is privately owned and occupies a block on Octavia Street, which is paved and landscaped in the style of curvy Lombard Street *(see p88)*.

Imposing façade of Spreckels Mansion at Lafayette Park

The architect of the mansion was George Applegarth, who in 1916 designed the Legion of Honor *(see p156)*. The Palace was donated to the city by the Spreckels in 1924.

Lafayette Park ❸

Map 4 E3. 🚌 1, 12.

One of San Francisco's prettiest hilltop gardens, Lafayette Park is a leafy green haven of pine and eucalyptus trees, although its present tranquillity belies its turbulent history. Along with Alta Plaza and Alamo Square, the land was set aside in 1855 as city-owned open space, but squatters and others, including a former City Attorney, laid claim to the land and built houses on it. The largest of the houses stood at the center of the hilltop

---

PANAMA-PACIFIC EXPOSITION (1915)

San Francisco celebrated its recovery from the 1906 earthquake and fire with a monumental fair *(see pp30–31)*. Officially it was planned to celebrate the opening of the Panama Canal, and it was designed to be the most extravagant world's fair ever held. It was described by one highly enthusiastic visitor as "a miniature Constantinople."

The fair was held on land reclaimed from San Francisco Bay, on the site of today's Marina District. Its impressive pavilions were donated by all the states and by 25 foreign countries and lined a concourse 1 mile (1.6 km) long. Many of the buildings were based on such architectural gems as a Turkish mosque and a Buddhist temple in Kyoto. The lavish Tower of Jewels, at the center of the concourse, was encrusted with glass beads and lit by spotlights. To the west stood the Palace of Fine Arts *(see pp60–61)*, today the sole surviving structure from the fair, which visitors reached by gondola across a lagoon.

Ferry Building during Pan-Pacific Exposition

Panorama across the site of the Panama-Pacific Exposition

park until 1936, because the squatter who had built it refused to move. It was finally torn down after the city authorities agreed to swap it for land on Gough Street. Steep stairways now lead to the summit of the park and its delightful views. In the surrounding streets there are scores of palatial buildings, with particularly ornate examples along Broadway, Jackson Street and Pacific Avenue going east–west, and on Gough, Octavia and Laguna streets going north–south.

Alta Plaza 4

Map 4 D3. 1, 3, 12, 22, 24.

Situated in the center of Pacific Heights, Alta Plaza is a beautifully landscaped urban park, where San Francisco's elite come to relax. There are angular stone steps (offering great city views) rising up from Clay Street on the south side of the park. These steps may be familiar to you from films – Barbra Streisand drove down them in *What's Up Doc?* The park has tennis courts and a playground, and from the north side of the park you can see splendid mansions, including the Gibbs House at 2622 Jackson Street, built by Willis Polk in 1894.

Fillmore Street 5

Map 4 D4. 1, 2, 3, 4, 22, 24.

Fillmore Street survived the devastating 1906 earthquake *(see pp28–9)* virtually intact, and for several years afterward served as the civic heart of the city. Government departments, as well as private businesses, were housed in the district's shops, homes and even churches. Today the main commercial district of Pacific Heights is located here, from Jackson Street to Japantown *(see p128)* around Bush Street. This area boasts an abundance of bookstores, restaurants and boutiques.

Relaxing in Alta Plaza

Convent of the Sacred Heart 6

2222 Broadway. **Map** 4 D3.
563-2900. 22, 24.
to the public.

This Neo-Classical villa was formerly known as the Flood Mansion. It was designed by the architects Bliss and Faville for James Leary Flood, son of the Comstock Mine magnate *(see p102)*, and was completed in 1915. With its harmonious proportions, impeccable detailing, and Tennessee marble façade, the house is the most refined of the Pacific Heights mansions. In 1939 the building became home to one of the oldest private schools in California.

Trinity Episcopal Church 7

1668 Bush Street. **Map** 4 D4. *Tel* 775-1117. 2, 3, 4, 19, 22, 49.

The dramatic edifice of Trinity Episcopal Church is based on Durham Cathedral in northern England, which is arguably one of the finest examples of Norman architecture. The oldest Episcopal church on the Pacific Coast, Trinity celebrated its 150th anniversary in 1999. Its colorful stained-glass windows were designed by a pupil of John LaFarge, a leading figure in the New York art scene during the late 19th century. The high altar displays the 100-year old jewel-encrusted Trinity Cross, which was presented as a gift on Trinity Sunday by the women of the parish. The church is also home to the San Francisco Bach Choir.

Cow Hollow 8

Map 4 D2. 22, 41, 45.

Cow Hollow, a shopping district along Union Street, is so called because it was used as grazing land for the city's dairy cows up until the 1860s. It was then taken over for development as a residential neighborhood. In the 1950s the area became fashionable, and chic boutiques, antique shops and art galleries took over the old neighborhood shops. Many of these are in restored 19th-century buildings, lending an old-fashioned air to the district, in stark contrast to the sophistication of the merchandise on display.

The view from Fillmore Street, overlooking Cow Hollow

Church of St. Mary the Virgin ❾

2325 Union St. **Map** 4 D3. **Tel** 921-3665. 🚌 22, 41, 45. ☐ 9am–5pm Mon–Fri. ✝ 8, 9, 11am and 5:30pm Sun. 📷 during services.

Evoking the more rural early 19th-century years of Cow Hollow (see p73), this rustic, wooden-shingled Episcopal church stands at the west end of what is now the busy Union Street shopping area.

One of the natural springs that provided water for the Cow Hollow dairy herds still bubbles up in the grounds, now largely hidden from the view of passersby on the street by the church's original lych-gate and hedge.

The small, plainly ornamented building is an early example of the Arts and Crafts style (see p46) later used in more prominent Bay Area churches. Below the steeply sloping roof, the walls are faced with "shingles," strips of redwood nailed in overlapping rows

onto the building's wooden frame. Part of the church was remodeled in the 1950s, when the entrance was moved from Steiner Street to the opposite end of the building, but the fabric has been well preserved.

Ornate decoration on the Vedanta Temple

Vedanta Temple ❿

2963 Webster St. **Map** 4 D2. **Tel** 922-2323. 🚌 22, 41, 45. ☐ to the public except for services. ✝ 8pm Fri only. 📷 during services.

One of the bay area's most unusual structures, the Vedanta Temple is an eclectic combination of a host of divergent decorative traditions. The roof is crowned by a rusty red onion-shaped dome similar to those seen on Russian Orthodox churches. It also has a tower resembling a crenellated European castle, and an octagonal Hindu temple cupola. Other archi-

tectural features include highly decorated Moorish arches, medieval parapets and elements of Queen Anne (see p77) and Colonial styles. It was built in 1905 by the architect Joseph A. Leonard, working closely with the Northern California Vedanta Society minister, Swami Trigunatitananda.

Vedanta is the highest of the six schools of Hinduism, and the building symbolizes the Vedanta concept that every religion is just a different way of reaching one god. The Temple is now a monastery, but it is worth a visit just to marvel at this bizarre building from the outside.

Fort Mason ⓯

Map 4 E1. 🛂 441-3400. 🚌 22, 28, 30, 43. 📷 ♿ partial. **Events Line Tel** 345-7544. **www**.fortmason.org. See **Five Guided Walks** pp172–3.

Fort Mason reflects the military history of San Francisco. The original buildings were private houses, erected in the late 1850s, which were confiscated by the US Government when the site was taken over by the US army during the Civil War (1861–65).

The Fort remained an army command post until the 1890s, and also housed refugees left homeless by 1906 earthquake (see pp28–9). In World War II, Fort Mason Army Base was the point of embarkation for around 1.6 million soldiers.

Fort Mason was converted to peaceful use in 1972, although some of the white-painted, mid-19th-century buildings still house military personnel. Other buildings, however, are

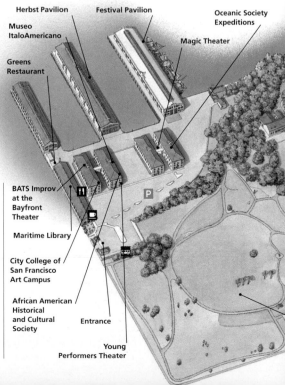

Herbst Pavilion

Festival Pavilion

Oceanic Society Expeditions

Museo ItaloAmericano

Magic Theater

Greens Restaurant

BATS Improv at the Bayfront Theater

Maritime Library

City College of San Francisco Art Campus

African American Historical and Cultural Society

Entrance

Young Performers Theater

Octagon House ⓫

2645 Gough St. **Map** 4 E2.
***Tel** 441-7512.* 🚌 *41, 45, 47, 49.*
⏰ *noon–3pm on second Sun and
second and fourth Thu of the month,
except Jan.* ***Donation suggested.***
📷 ♿ *limited.* **www**.nscda.com

Built in 1861, the Octagon
House is named for its eight-
sided cupola. It houses a
small, but engaging,
collection of decorative arts
and historic documents of the
Colonial and Federal periods.
Included are furniture, paintings, Revolutionary playing
cards and signatures of 54
of the 56 signers of the
Declaration of Independence.

Chestnut Street ⓬

Map 3 C2. 🚌 *22, 28, 30, 43.*

The main shopping and nightlife center of the Marina
District, Chestnut Street has a
varied mix of movie theaters,
markets, cafés and restaurants.
The commercial strip stretches
just a few blocks from
Fillmore Street west to Divisadero Street, after which the
neighborhood becomes
predominantly residential
in character.

Marina Green ⓭

Map 4 D1. 🚌 *22, 28, 30.*

A long thin strip of lawn
running the length of the
Marina District, Marina Green
is popular with kite-flyers and
for picnics, especially on July 4,
when the city's largest firework
show can be seen from here
(see p49). Paths along the
waterfront are the
city's prime spots
for bicyclists,
joggers and roller
skaters. Golden
Gate Promenade
leads from the
west end of the
green to Fort
Point, or you can
turn east to the
Wave Organ at
the harbor jetty.

Wave Organ ⓮

Map 4 D1. 🚌 *30.*

Sitting at the tip of the
breakwater that protects the
Marina is the world's most
peculiar musical instrument.
Built by scientists from the
Exploratorium *(see pp60–61),*
the Wave Organ consists of a
number of underwater pipes
that echo and hum with the
changing tides. Listening
tubes are imbedded in a mini-
amphitheater that has views
of Pacific Heights and the
Presidio. The sounds you
hear are more like gurgling
plumbing than organ music.

Wave Organ at the end of the West Harbor jetty

**International Youth
Hostel**

**Fort Mason
Officer's Club**

Chapel

**Golden Gate
National
Recreation Area
headquarters**

Great Meadow

Meta III (1905) by Italo
Scanga at Museo
ItaloAmericano chapel

open to the public. These
include the original barracks,
and the old hospital, which
serves as a Visitor Center and
headquarters of the Golden
Gate National Recreation
Area (GGNRA).
    Fort Mason has some of the
city's finest views, looking
across the bay toward Golden
Gate Bridge and Alcatraz.

Fort Mason Center
    Part of the Fort is now
    occupied by one of San
    Francisco's prime art
    complexes. Fort Mason
    Center is home to over
    25 cultural organizations,
    art galleries, museums,
    and theaters, including
    the Cowell Theater, the
    BATS Improv at the Bay-
    front Theater, the Magic
    Theater, and the Young
    Performers Theater. The
    SFMOMA Rental Gallery
    offers artworks from
    Northern Californian
    artists for sale or
    rent. Italian and
    Italian-American
    artists display

their works at the Museo
ItaloAmericano. The Maritime
Library holds a wonderful
collection of maritime history
books, oral histories, and
ships' plans. The Maritime
Museum (partly closed for
renovation until 2012) itself
(see p83) is located near
Fisherman's Wharf. Among
the places to eat at the Fort
Mason Center is Greens *(see
p229),* one of the city's best
vegetarian restaurants.
    The Conference Center
produces a monthly calendar
of events.

**The SS *Balclutha*, at Hyde Street
Pier, part of the Maritime Museum**

Victorian Houses in San Francisco

Despite earthquakes, fires, and the inroads of modern life, thousands of ornate, late 19th-century houses still line the streets of San Francisco. In fact, in many neighborhoods they are by far the most common type of housing. Victorian houses are broadly similar, in that they all have wooden frames, elaborately decorated with mass-produced ornament. Most were constructed on narrow plots to a similar floor plan, but they differ in the features of the façade. Four main styles prevail in the city, although in practice many houses, especially those built in the 1880s and 1890s, combine aspects of two or more styles.

Italianate window

Detail of Queen Anne-style gateway at Chateau Tivoli

GOTHIC REVIVAL (1850–80)

Gothic Revival houses are the easiest to identify, since they always have pointed arches over the windows and sometimes over the doors. Other features are pitched gabled roofs, decorated vergeboards (again, with pointed arch motifs) and porches that run the width of the building. The smaller, simpler houses of this type are usually painted white, rather than the vibrant colors often associated with later styles.

No. 1111 Oak Street *is one of the city's oldest Gothic Revival buildings. Its front garden is unusually large.*

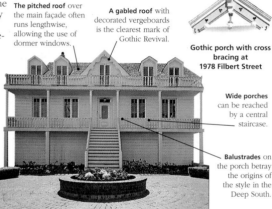

The pitched roof over the main façade often runs lengthwise, allowing the use of dormer windows.

A gabled roof with decorated vergeboards is the clearest mark of Gothic Revival.

Gothic porch with cross bracing at 1978 Filbert Street

Wide porches can be reached by a central staircase.

Balustrades on the porch betray the origins of the style in the Deep South.

ITALIANATE (1850–85)

Italianate houses were more popular in San Francisco than elsewhere in the US, perhaps because their compact form was suited to the city's high building density. The most distinctive feature of the Italianate style is the tall cornice, usually with a decorative bracket, which adds a palatial air even to modest homes. Elaborate decoration around doors and windows is another feature typical of the style.

No. 1913 Sacramento Street *displays a typical formal Italianate façade, modeled on a Renaissance palazzo. The wooden exterior is made to look like stone.*

Tall cornices, often with decorative brackets, conceal a pitched roof.

Imposing entrance with Italianate porch

Symmetrical windows are capped by decorative arches.

Neo-Classical doorways, sometimes with ornate pedimented porches, are a typical Italianate touch.

STICK (1860–90)

This architectural style, with its ungainly name, is perhaps the most prevalent among Victorian houses in the city. Sometimes also called "Stick-Eastlake" after London furniture designer Charles Eastlake, this style was intended to be architecturally "honest." Vertical lines are emphasized, both in the wood-frame structure and in ornamentation. Bay windows, false gabled cornices and square corners are key identifying features.

No. 1715–1717 Capp Street *is a fine example of the Stick-Eastlake style, with a plain façade enlivened by decorative flourishes.*

Gabled roof with Eastlake windows at 2931 Pierce Street

Wide bands of trim often form a decorative truss, emphasizing the underlying structure of Stick houses.

Decorative gables filled with "sunburst" motifs are used on porches and window frames.

Adjoining front doors can be protected by a single projecting porch.

QUEEN ANNE (1875–1905)

The name "Queen Anne" does not refer to a historical period; it was coined by the English architect Richard Shaw. Queen Anne houses freely combine elements from many decorative traditions, but are marked by their turrets and towers and large, often decorative, panels on wall surfaces. Most houses also display intricate spindle-work on balustrades, porches and roof trusses.

Palladian windows were used in gables to give the appearance of an extra floor.

Queen Anne gable filled with ornamental panels at 818 Steiner Street

Queen Anne turret topped by a finial at 1015 Steiner Street

Round, square and polygonal turrets and towers are typical of Queen Anne-style houses.

Gable pediments hold ornamental windows and decorative panels.

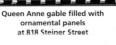

The curved window frame is not itself characteristic of Queen Anne style, but many houses include features borrowed from other styles.

The asymmetrical façade *of 850 Steiner Street, with its eclectic ornament, is typical of a Queen Anne house. Such features are often painted in various bright colors.*

WHERE TO FIND VICTORIAN HOUSES

1715–1717 Capp St. **Map** 10 F4
Chateau Tivoli, 1057 Steiner St. **Map** 4 D4
1978 Filbert St. **Map** 4 D2
1111 Oak St. **Map** 9 C1
2931 Pierce St. **Map** 4 D3
1913 Sacramento St. **Map** 4 E3
818 Steiner St. **Map** 4 D5
850 Steiner St. **Map** 4 D5
1015 Steiner St. **Map** 4 D5
2527–2531 Washington St. **Map** 4 D3
Alamo Square *p129*
Clarke's Folly *p139*
Haas-Lilienthal House *p72*
Liberty Street. **Map** 10 E3
Masonic Avenue. **Map** 3 C4
Octagon House *p75*
Sherman House *p73*
Spreckels Mansion *p72*

FISHERMAN'S WHARF AND NORTH BEACH

ishermen from Genoa and Sicily first arrived in the Fisherman's Wharf area in the late 19th century, and here they founded the San Francisco fishing industry. The district has slowly given way to tourism since the 1950s, but brightly painted boats still set out from the harbor on fishing trips early each morning. To the south of

Fisherman's Wharf entrance sign

Fisherman's Wharf lies North Beach, sometimes known as "Little Italy." This lively part of the city has an abundance of aromatic delis, bakeries and cafés, from which you can watch the crowds. It is home to Italian and Chinese families, with a sprinkling of writers and bohemians; Jack Kerouac *(see p32)*, among others, found inspiration here.

SIGHTS AT A GLANCE

Historic Streets and Buildings
Alcatraz Island pp84–7 ❶
Pier 39 ❷
Lombard Street ❾
Vallejo Street Stairway ⓫
Filbert Steps ⓲
Greenwich Steps ⓳
Upper Montgomery Street ⓴

Monuments
Coit Tower ⓱

Churches
Saints Peter and Paul Church ⓯

Shopping Centers
The Cannery ❻
Ghirardelli Square ❼

Restaurants and Bars
Club Fugazi ⓬

Parks and Gardens
Washington Square ⓭
Bocce Ball Courts ⓰
Levi's Plaza ㉑

Museums and Galleries
USS *Pampanito* ❸
Wax Museum ❹
Ripley's Believe It Or Not! Museum ❺
San Francisco Maritime National Historical Park Visitors' Center ❽
San Francisco Art Institute ❿
North Beach Museum ⓭

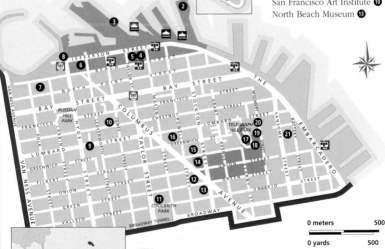

KEY

	Street-by-Street map *See pp80–81*
	Street-by-Street map *See pp90–91*
	Cable car turntable
	Ferry terminal
	Historical trolley line

| | 0 meters | 500 |
| | 0 yards | 500 |

GETTING THERE
The Powell–Hyde cable car line goes to Ghirardelli Square and Russian Hill. The Powell–Mason line goes through North Beach, to Fisherman's Wharf and Pier 39. Many buses run through the district.

 Detail of Coit Tower mural showing Fisherman's Wharf in the 1930s

Street-by-Street: Fisherman's Wharf

Italian seafood restaurants have
replaced fishing as the primary focus
of the Fisherman's Wharf local
economy. Restaurants and outdoor
crab stands serve San Francisco's
celebrated Dungeness crab from
November to June. Besides sampling
the seafood, visitors also take in the
shops, museums and attractions for
which Fisherman's Wharf is noted.

**Fisherman's and
Seaman's Chapel**
was built on the pier
so that the devout
could pray before
they sailed and after
they returned.

Pier 45

★ **USS *Pampanito***
*An audio tour gives an idea of the
hardships endured by sailors in
this World War II submarine* ❸

Fisherman's Wharf is
now a street lined with
seafood restaurants
and crab stands.

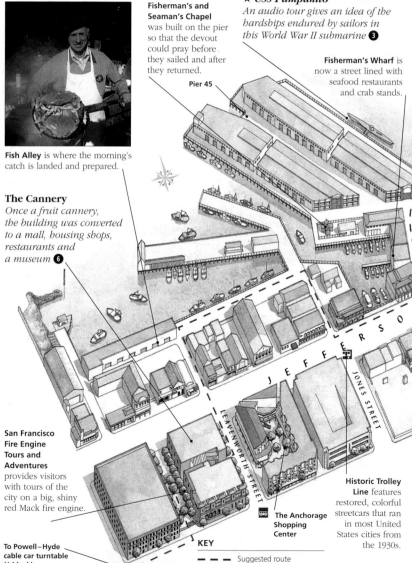

Fish Alley is where the morning's
catch is landed and prepared.

The Cannery
*Once a fruit cannery,
the building was converted
to a mall, housing shops,
restaurants and
a museum* ❻

**San Francisco
Fire Engine
Tours and
Adventures**
provides visitors
with tours of the
city on a big, shiny
red Mack fire engine.

**Historic Trolley
Line** features
restored, colorful
streetcars that ran
in most United
States cities from
the 1930s.

**The Anchorage
Shopping
Center**

**To Powell–Hyde
cable car turntable
(1 block)**

KEY

- - - Suggested route

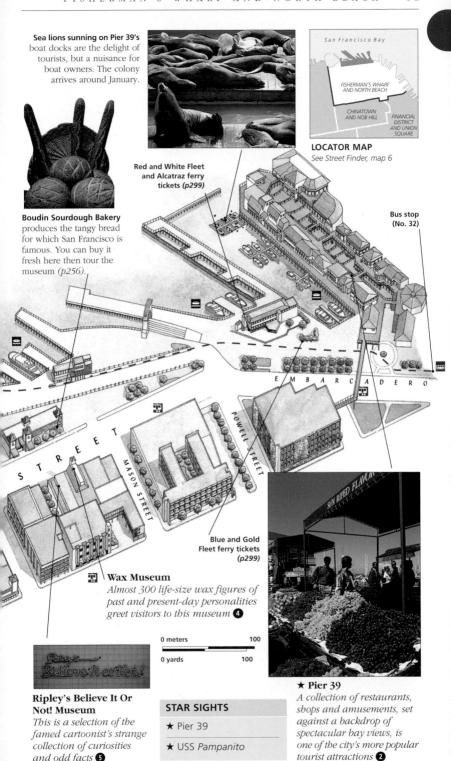

Sea lions sunning on Pier 39's boat docks are the delight of tourists, but a nuisance for boat owners. The colony arrives around January.

LOCATOR MAP
See Street Finder, map 6

San Francisco Bay

FISHERMAN'S WHARF AND NORTH BEACH

CHINATOWN AND NOB HILL

FINANCIAL DISTRICT AND UNION SQUARE

Boudin Sourdough Bakery produces the tangy bread for which San Francisco is famous. You can buy it fresh here then tour the museum *(p256)*.

Red and White Fleet and Alcatraz ferry tickets *(p299)*

Bus stop (No. 32)

EMBARCADERO

POWELL STREET

MASON STREET

STREET

Blue and Gold Fleet ferry tickets *(p299)*

Wax Museum
Almost 300 life-size wax figures of past and present-day personalities greet visitors to this museum ❹

0 meters   100
0 yards   100

Ripley's Believe It Or Not! Museum
This is a selection of the famed cartoonist's strange collection of curiosities and odd facts ❺

STAR SIGHTS

★ Pier 39

★ USS *Pampanito*

★ **Pier 39**
A collection of restaurants, shops and amusements, set against a backdrop of spectacular bay views, is one of the city's more popular tourist attractions ❷

Alcatraz Island **❶**

See pp84–87.

Pier 39 **❷**

Map 5 B1. 🚃 F. *See Shopping in San Francisco p245.*

Refurbished in 1978 to resemble a quaint wooden fishing village, this 1905 cargo pier now houses many tourist shops and specialty stores spread through two levels.

The pier's street performers and amusements are popular with families. You can try the two-story carousel, play games at the Riptide arcade, or brave the Turbo Ride, a roller-coaster simulator where a film gives the illusion of speed and danger. An aquarium is also planned.

A sensational multimedia show, the San Francisco Experience, whisks visitors through an historical tour of the city, complete with Chinese New Year celebrations, fog and an earthquake.

The two-story Venetian Carousel on Pier 39

USS *Pampanito* **❸**

Pier 45. **Map** 4 F1. **Tel** *(415) 775-1943.* 🚌 *47.* ⬜ *9am–6pm daily (sometimes stays open later; call ahead for details).* 🎟 📷 🔓 **www.**maritime.org

This World War II submarine-fought in, and survived, several bloody battles in the Pacific, sinking six enemy ships and severely damaging others. Tragically for the allies, two of its fatal targets were carrying British and Australian POWs. The *Pampanito* managed to rescue 73 men and carry them to safety in the US. A tour of the ship takes visitors from

USS *Pampanito*'s torpedo room

stern to bow to see the torpedo room, the claustrophobic kitchen and officers' quarters. When the *Pampanito* was in service, it had a full crew of 10 officers and 70 seamen.

Wax Museum **❹**

145 Jefferson St. **Map** 5 B1. 📠 *(800) 439-4305.* 🚃 F. ⬜ *10am–9pm Mon–Fri, 9am–11pm Sat & Sun.* 🎟 📷 🔓 **www.**waxmuseum.com

One of the world's largest and most absorbing collections of life-size wax figures is displayed here. The ancient tomb of Egyptian King Tutankhamun is re-created in one special exhibit, while a tableau of the Last Supper dominates the Hall of Religions. In the Hall of Living Art, portraits such as the *Mona Lisa* are rendered in wax. A host of fictional characters rubs shoulders with historical luminaries, including 14 US presidents, members of the British Royal family, Sir Winston Churchill, William Shakespeare, Mozart, Mark Twain, Elvis Presley, Marilyn Monroe and Al Capone. While a gruesome assortment can be found in the compelling Chamber of Horrors.

Ripley's Believe It Or Not! Museum **❺**

175 Jefferson St. **Map** 4 F1. **Tel** *771-6188.* 🚃 F. ⬜ *10am–10pm Sun–Thu, 10am–12am Fri–Sat; mid-Jun–Labor Day: 9am–11pm Sun–Thu, 10am–midnight Fri–Sat.* 🎟 📷 🔓 **www.**ripleysf.com

California native Robert L. Ripley, was an illustrator with a penchant for collecting peculiar facts and artifacts. He earned his fame and fortune by syndicating his celebrated US newspaper cartoon strip, which was called "Ripley's Believe It Or Not!"

Among the 350 oddities on display are a cable car built of 275,000 matchsticks, a two-headed calf, a shrunken torso, and a life-size image of a man who had two pupils in each eyeball. There are also samples of Ripley's famous cartoon strips.

The Cannery **6**

2801 Leavenworth St. **Map** 4 F1.
🚌 19, 30. 🚋 Powell–Hyde. See
Shopping in San Francisco p245.

The interior of this 1909 fruit-canning plant was refurbished in the 1960s. It now incorporates footbridges, rambling passages and sunny court-yards, with restaurants and specialty shops selling clothing, collector dolls and American Indian arts and crafts.

The Cannery also used to house the Museum of the City of San Francisco, but a fire forced the premises to close. However, the collection has moved to the City Hall

(see p127), where all the exhibits are now on display. Among these is the massive head of the statue that capped City Hall before the 1906 earthquake *(see pp28–9)*. The illuminated crown on the head is an example of early electric illumination. You can also visit www.sfmuseum.org.

Ghirardelli Square **7**

900 North Point St. **Map** 4 F1. 🚌
19, 30, 47, 49. 🚋 Powell–Hyde. See
Shopping in San Francisco p244.

Once a chocolate factory and woollen mill, this is the most attractive of San Francisco's many refurbished factories. It is a blend of old, red-brick buildings with new, elegant shops and restaurants. The shopping center retains the famous Ghirardelli trade-mark clock tower and the original bright electric roof sign. Ghirardelli Chocolate

Ghirardelli Square

Manufacturing on the plaza beneath the tower still houses vintage chocolate-making machinery and sells the confection, although the famous chocolate bars are now made in San Leandro, across the bay.

Fountain Plaza is a colorful outdoor attraction for shoppers day and evening.

San Francisco Maritime National Historical Park Visitors' Center **8**

900 Beach St. **Map** 4 F1. 🚌 10, 19,
30. 🚋 Powell–Hyde. **Museum Tel**
561-7100. 🔵 partly closed for renovation until 2012. **Hyde Street Pier**
Tel 447-5000. 🔵 11am–4pm daily
(during renovations). 🔵 Jan 1,
Thanksgiving, Dec 25 🎫 Pier only.
📷 ♿ Pier and museum only. 🚻
See **Five Guided Walks** pp172–3.
www.maritime.org

Built in 1939, this building first housed the Maritime Museum in 1951. Though partly closed for renovation,

Hyde Street Pier

visitors can still take time to admire the Streamline Modern style building with its clean lines of an ocean liner. Moored at nearby Hyde Street Pier is one of the world's largest collections of old ships.

Among the most spectacular is the *CA Thayer*, a three-masted schooner built in 1895 and retired in 1950. The *Thayer* carried lumber along the North California coast, and later was used in Alaskan fishing. Also at the pier is the 2,560-ton side-wheel ferry-boat, *Eureka*, built in 1890 to ferry trains between the Hyde Street Pier and the counties north of San Francisco Bay. It carried 2,300 passengers and 120 cars, and was the largest passenger ferry of its day.

BALCLUTHA
This ship is the star of Hyde Street Pier. Launched in 1886, she sailed twice a year between Britain and California, trading wheat for coal.

Mainmast

Mizzenmast

Quarterdeck

Foremast

Bowsprit

Alcatraz Island ❶

Alcatraz means "pelican" in Spanish, a reference to the first inhabitants of this rocky, steepsided island. Lying 3 miles (5 km) east of the Golden Gate, its location is both strategic and exposed to harsh ocean winds. In 1859, the US military established a fort here that guarded San Francisco Bay until 1907, when it became a military prison. From 1934–63, it served as a maximum-security Federal Penitentiary. Unoccupied until 1969, the island was seized by members of the American Indian Movement (see p32) laying claim to the island as their land. The group was expelled in 1971, and Alcatraz is now a part of the Golden Gate National Recreation Area.

Badge on entrance to cell house

★ Cell Block

The cell house contains four free-standing cell blocks. No cell has an outside wall or ceiling. The dungeon-like foundation of the "Big House," as inmates called the main prison block, shares the original foundation of the old military fortress.

Lighthouse

The original Alcatraz lighthouse, the first on the Pacific coast of the United States, was built in 1854 and replaced in 1909 by the present structure.

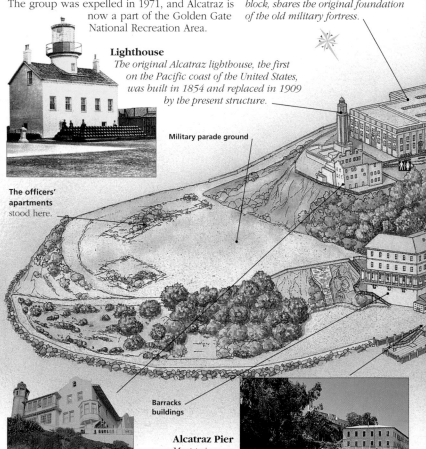

Military parade ground

The officers' apartments stood here.

Barracks buildings

Warden's House

This house suffered extensive fire damage during the American Indian occupation of 1969–1971.

Alcatraz Pier

Most prisoners took their first steps ashore here. Now visitors alight at this pier.

Alcatraz Island from the Ferry
*"The Rock" has no natural soil. Earth was
shipped from Angel Island to make
garden plots.*

Metal detectors checked
prisoners when they passed to
and from the dining hall and
exercise yards. The "machine"
on display is a prop from the
filming of *Escape from Alcatraz*.

The Military Morgue is tiny and
cramped and not open to
the public.

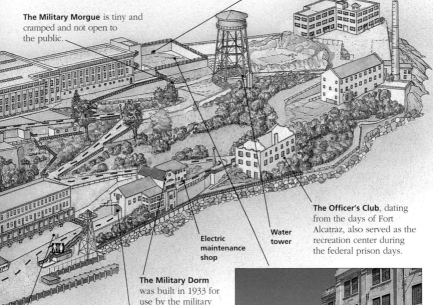

The Officer's Club, dating
from the days of Fort
Alcatraz, also served as the
recreation center during
the federal prison days.

**Water
tower**

**Electric
maintenance
shop**

The Military Dorm
was built in 1933 for
use by the military
prison guards.

The Visitor Center is in
the old barracks building
behind the ferry jetty.
It houses a bookstore,
exhibits and multimedia
show providing an
historical overview
of Alcatraz, and an
information counter.

Sally Port dates from
1857. Equipped with
drawbridge and dry
moat, this guardhouse
defended the approach
to Fort Alcatraz.

★ **Exercise Yard**
*Meals and walks around
the exercise yard were the
highlights of a prisoner's
day. The walled yard
featured in films made
at the prison.*

KEY

- – – Suggested route

0 meters   75

0 yards   75

STAR FEATURES

★ Cell Block

★ Exercise Yard

Inside Alcatraz

The maximum-security prison on Alcatraz, dubbed "The Rock" by prisoners, housed an average of 264 of the country's most incorrigible criminals, who were transferred here for disobedience while serving time in prisons elsewhere in the US. The strict discipline at Alcatraz was enforced by the threat of a stint in the isolation cells and by loss of privileges, including the chance at special jobs, time for recreation, use of the prison library and visitation rights.

Typical cell key

D Block
In the silent, solitary confinement cells of D Block, prisoners had to endure hours of unrelieved boredom.

Library from which prisoners could order "approved" books

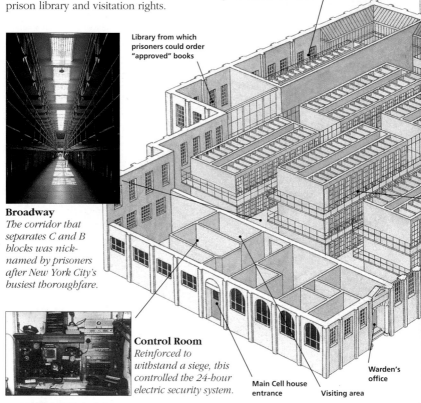

Broadway
The corridor that separates C and B blocks was nick-named by prisoners after New York City's busiest thoroughfare.

Control Room
Reinforced to withstand a siege, this controlled the 24-hour electric security system.

Main Cell house entrance

Visiting area

Warden's office

TIMELINE

1775 Spanish explorer Juan Manuel de Ayala names Alcatraz after the pelicans that inhabit it

1859 Fort Alcatraz completed; equipped with 100 cannon and 300 troops

1909–12 Army prisoners build the cell house

1972 Alcatraz becomes a national park

1962 Frank Morris and the Anglin brothers escape

1750	1800	1850	1900	1950

John Fremont

1848 John Fremont buys Alcatraz for US government

1857 Sally Port built

1854 First Pacific Coast lighthouse built on Alcatraz

Sally Port

1963 Prison closed

1934 Federal Bureau of Prisons turns Alcatraz into a civilian prison

1969–71 Island occupied by American Indians

Gun Gallery
Guards armed with pistols and rifles patrolled along the caged walkways at the ends of the cell blocks.

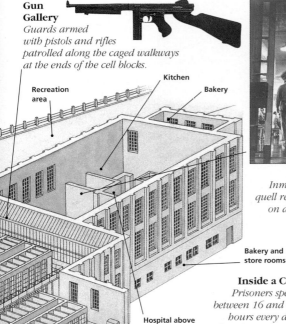

Kitchen

Recreation area

Bakery

Dining Room
Inmates were well fed, the better to quell rebellion. Note the sample menu on display at the kitchen entrance.

Bakery and store rooms

Inside a Cell
Prisoners spent between 16 and 23 hours every day alone in stark cells, equipped with only a toilet and bunk. Many cells measured 5 ft by 9 ft (1.5 m by 2.7 m).

Hospital above dining room

Barber shop

FAMOUS INMATES

Al Capone
The notorious Prohibition-era gangster, "Scarface" Capone was actually convicted, in 1934, for income tax evasion! He spent much of his five-year sentence on Alcatraz in a hospital isolation cell, and finally left the prison mentally unbalanced.

Robert Stroud
During his 17 years on The Rock, Stroud spent most of his time in solitary confinement. Despite assertions to the contrary in the film *The Birdman of Alcatraz* (1962), Stroud was in fact prohibited from keeping birds in his prison cell.

Carnes, Thompson and Shockley
In May 1946, prisoners led by Clarence Carnes, Marion Thompson and Sam Shockley overpowered guards and captured their guns. The prisoners failed to break out of the cell house, but three inmates and two officers were killed in the "Battle of Alcatraz." Carnes received an additional life sentence, and Shockley and Thompson were executed at San Quentin prison, for their part as ringleaders of the insurrection.

Anglin Brothers
John and Clarence Anglin, along with Frank Morris, chipped through the back walls of their cells, hiding the holes with cardboard grates. They left dummy heads in their beds and made a raft to enable their escape. They were never caught. Their story was dramatized in the film, *Escape from Alcatraz* (1979).

George Kelly
"Machine Gun" Kelly was The Rock's most dangerous inmate. He served 17 years for kidnapping and extortion.

Cars negotiating the steep and crooked section of Lombard Street

Lombard Street ❾

Map 5 A2. 🚌 45. 🚋 Powell–Hyde.

Banked at a natural incline of 27°, this hill proved too steep for vehicles to climb. In the 1920s the section of Lombard Street close to the summit of Russian Hill was revamped, and the severity of its gradient lessened by the addition of eight curves.

Today it is known as "the crookedest street in the world." Cars can travel downhill only, while people take the steps or use the cable car.

San Francisco Art Institute ❿

800 Chestnut St. **Map** 4 F2. **Tel** 771-7020. 🚌 30. **Diego Rivera Gallery** ⬜ 8am–9pm daily. 🔵 public hols. **Walter and McBean Galleries** ⬜ 11am–6pm Tue–Sat. ♿ partial. 📷 💻

San Francisco's Art Institute dates from 1871 and once occupied the immense wooden mansion built for the family of Mark Hopkins on Nob Hill

A 30-Minute Walk through North Beach

Settlers from Chile, and later those from Italy, created the North Beach nightlife that earned this quarter its exuberant reputation. Its café-oriented atmosphere has long appealed to bohemians, particularly the 1950s Beat Generation (see p32).

Neighborhood of the Beats
Start from the southwest corner of Broadway and Columbus Avenue at City Lights Book-store ①. Owned by Beat poet Lawrence Ferlinghetti, City Lights was the first book-shop in the US to sell only paperbacks. It was author Jack Kerouac, a friend of Ferlinghetti, who coined the word "Beat," later made popular as "Beatnik."

One of the most popular Beat haunts was Vesuvio ②, south of City Lights, across Jack Kerouac Alley. Welsh poet Dylan Thomas was a patron of this watering hole, which is still a favorite of poets and artists.

Jack Kerouac

From Vesuvio continue south to Pacific Avenue and cross to the opposite side of Columbus Avenue. Walk back toward Broadway, stopping first at Tosca ③. The walls of this old-world bar and café display evocative murals of rural Tuscany, and a jukebox plays selections from Italian opera. A few steps north bring you to Adler Alley. Specs ④, an exuberant, cozy bar filled with memora-bilia of the Beat era, is at No. 12. Retrace the route to Columbus Avenue, then turn right into Broadway and walk as far as Kearny Street, taking in the hustle and bustle of Broadway.

Columbus Café ❿

The Strip
This stretch of Broadway is known as The Strip ⑤, and is noted for its "adult entertainment." At the junction of Broadway and Grant Avenue is the former Condor Club ⑥, where the world's first topless stage show was performed in June 1964 by Carol Doda, a waitress at the club.

(see p102), which burned down in the fire of 1906 *(see pp28–9)*. Today it is housed in a Spanish colonial-style building, constructed in 1926, complete with cloisters, courtyard fountain and bell tower. The Diego Rivera Gallery, named after the Mexican muralist, sits to the left of the main entrance. The Walter and McBean Galleries are the primary exhibition venues and feature changing shows from contemporary photography and film screenings to design and technology.

Vallejo Street Stairway ⓫

Mason St and Jones St. **Map** 5 B3.
🚌 30, 45. 🚋 *Powell–Mason.*

The steep climb from Little Italy to the southernmost summit of Russian Hill reveals some of the city's best views of Telegraph Hill, North Beach and the encompassing bay. The street gives way to

A gallery at the North Beach Museum

steps at Mason Street, which climb up through quiet and pretty Ina Coolbrith Park. Higher still, above Taylor Street, there is a warren of lanes, with several Victorian-style wooden houses *(see pp76–7)*. At the crest of the hill is one of the rare pockets of the city that was not destroyed in the earthquake and fire of 1906 *(see pp28–9)*.

Club Fugazi ⓬

678 Green St. **Map** 5 B3. **Tel** 421-4222. 🚌 30, 41, 45. ○ *Wed–Sun.* See **Entertainment** p263.

Built in 1912 as a North Beach community hall, the

Club Fugazi is the home of the musical cabaret *Beach Blanket Babylon (see p263).* This lively show, famous for its topical and outrageous songs, has been running for over two decades and has become a favorite San Francisco institution.

North Beach Museum ⓭

1435 Stockton St. **Map** 5 B3.
Tel 391-6210. 🚌 30, 41, 45.
○ *9am–4pm Mon–Thu, 9am–6pm Fri.* ● *public hols.* 📷

This small museum, on the second floor of the Eureka Bank, documents the history of North Beach and Chinatown through exhibitions of old photographs. These celebrate the heritage of the Chileans, Irish, Italians and Chinese who have arrived here since the 19th century. Other photographs illustrate the bohemian community of North Beach.

Upper Grant Avenue
Turn right into Grant Avenue where you will find The Saloon ⑦ with its original 1861 bar. On the corner of Vallejo Street is Caffè Trieste ⑧, the oldest coffeehouse in San Francisco and a

genuine writers' and artists' rendezvous since 1956. Very much a part of Italian-American culture, it offers live opera on Saturday afternoons. Follow Grant Avenue north past the Lost and Found Saloon ⑨, now a blues club but formerly the Coffee Gallery, haunt of the Beats. Turn left at Green Street and look for

Vesuvio, a popular Beat bar ②

Columbus Café ⑩ and its exterior murals. Go left at Columbus Avenue, and follow this main North Beach street south past many more Italian coffeehouses, to return to your starting point.

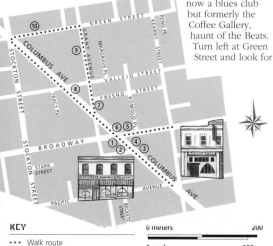

KEY

••• Walk route

0 meters 200
0 yards 200

TIPS FOR WALKERS

Starting point: *Corner of Broadway and Columbus Avenue.*
Length: *1 mile (1.5 km).*
Getting there: *Muni bus No. 41 runs along Columbus Avenue.*
Stopping-off points: *All the bars and cafés mentioned are worth visiting for a drink and the atmosphere. Children are not usually allowed in bars.*

Street-by-Street: Telegraph Hill

Telegraph Hill was named after the semaphore installed on its crest in 1850 to alert merchants of the arrival of ships. Today's hill falls away abruptly on its eastern side, where it was dynamited to provide rocks for landfill and paving. There are steep paths on this side of the hill, bordered by gardens. The western side slopes more gradually into "Little Italy," the area around Washington Square. In the past the hill has been home to immigrants and to artists who appreciated the panoramic views. These days the quaint pastel clapboard homes are much sought after and this is one of the city's prime residential areas.

The Fire Department Memorial

Telegraph Hill is dominated by Coit Tower. At night the tower is bathed in yellow light and is visible from many parts of the city.

The Christopher Columbus Statue was erected in 1957.

The Statue of Benjamin Franklin stands above a time capsule planted in 1979, containing Levis, a poem and a recording of the Hoodoo Rhythm Devils.

Bus stop (No. 39)

Washington Square
This small park at the heart of Little Italy is dominated by Saints Peter and Paul Catholic Church, known as the "Italian Cathedral" **14**

KEY

– – – Suggested route

★ **Saints Peter and Paul Church**
The Neo-Gothic church, consecrated in 1924, has an ornate interior with this fine image of Christ in the apse **15**

★ **Coit Tower**
The frescoes inside were painted by local artists in 1933, as part of the Federal Art Project set up by President Roosevelt ⑰

Bus stop (No. 39)

Greenwich Steps
These formally landscaped steps contrast with the charmingly rustic Filbert Steps ⑲

LOCATOR MAP
See Street Finder, map 5

Napier Lane is a small lane lined with 19th-century cottages. It is the last of San Francisco's wooden plank streets and a tranquil retreat from the city.

No. 1360 Montgomery Street is decorated with an Art Deco figure of a modern Atlas.

| 0 meters | 100 |
| 0 yards | 100 |

★ **Filbert Steps**
The descent through flower gardens down these steps gives fine views over the harbor to the East Bay ⑱

STAR SIGHTS

★ Saints Peter and Paul Church

★ Coit Tower

★ Filbert Steps

The façade of Saints Peter and Paul Church

Washington Square ⓮

Map 5 B2. 🚌 *30, 39, 41, 45.*

The square consists of a simple expanse of lawn, surrounded by benches and trees, set against the twin towers of Saints Peter and Paul Church. It has an almost Mediterranean atmosphere, appropriate for the "town square" of Little Italy, although the Italian community is less evident in this neighborhood now than it was when the park was first laid out in 1955. Near the center of the square stands a statue of Benjamin Franklin. A time capsule was buried under this in 1979 and is scheduled to be reopened in 2079. It is said to contain some Levi jeans, a bottle of wine and a poem by Lawrence Ferlinghetti, San Francisco's famous Beat poet (*see p88*).

Saints Peter and Paul Church ⓯

666 Filbert St. **Map** 5 B2.
Tel *421-0809.* 🚌 *30, 39, 41, 45.*
✝ *Italian mass and choir 11:45am Sun; phone for other masses.* ♿

Still known by many as the Italian Cathedral, this large church is situated at the heart of North Beach, and many Italians find it a welcome haven when they first arrive in San Francisco. It was here that the local baseball hero, Joe Di Maggio, was photographed after his marriage to the actress Marilyn Monroe in 1957, although the actual wedding ceremony was held elsewhere. The building, designed by Charles Fantoni, has an Italianesque façade, with a complex interior notable for its many columns and ornate altar. There are also statues and mosaics illuminated by stained-glass windows. The concrete and steel structure of the church, with its twin spires rising over the surrounding rooftops, was completed in 1924.

Cecil B. DeMille filmed the workers working on the foundations of Saints Peter and Paul, and used the scene to show the building of the Temple of Jerusalem in his film *The Ten Commandments*, made in 1923.

The church is sometimes known as the Fishermen's Church (many Italians once earned their living by fishing), and there is a mass to celebrate the Blessing of the Fleet in October. Masses here can be heard in Italian and Chinese, as well as English.

Bocce Ball Courts ⓰

Lombard St and Mason St, North Beach Playground. **Map** 5 B2.
Tel *274-0201.* 🚌 *30, 39, 41.*
🚋 *Day–Taylor.* ⭘ *dawn till dusk Mon–Sat.* ♿

Italians have been influential in North Beach since the main wave of immigration from Italy in the late 19th and early 20th centuries. Along with their food, customs and religion, they also brought games to their new home. Among these was *bocce*, an Italian version of lawn bowling, played on a narrower and shorter court than the English version. In North Beach it is played most afternoons on the public court in a corner of the North Beach Playground. There are four participants (or four teams), who roll a wooden ball at a smaller, target ball, at the opposite end of an earth court. The aim is for the balls to lightly "kiss" (*bocce*), and the highest score goes to the player whose ball gets closest to this target.

Playing *bocce* at North Beach Playground

View of Coit Tower at the top of Telegraph Hill

Coit Tower ⑰

1 Telegraph Hill Blvd. **Map** 5 C2. **Tel** 362-0808. 🚌 39. ⭕ 10am–6:30pm daily. 🎫 to tower. ♿ murals only. 📷

Coit Tower was built in 1933 at the top of 284-ft-high (87-m) Telegraph Hill, with funds left to the city by Lillie Hitchcock Coit, an eccentric San Franciscan pioneer and philanthropist. The 210-ft (63-m) reinforced concrete tower was designed as a fluted column by the architect Arthur Brown. When floodlit at night it is an eerie white and can be seen from most parts of the eastern half of the city. The encircling view around the North Bay Area

from the observation platform (reached by elevator) is spectacular.

In the lobby of the tower are murals that are even more absorbing *(see p140)*. These were sponsored in 1934 by a government-funded program designed to keep artists employed during the Great Depression *(see pp30–31)*. Twenty-five artists joined efforts to paint a vivid portrait of life in modern California. Scenes range from the teeming streets of the city's Financial District (with a robbery in progress) to factories, dockyards and Central Valley wheat fields. There are many fascinating details, and viewers can find a real light switch cleverly incorporated into a painting, a poor family of migrants encamped by a river, plus newspaper headlines, magazine covers and book titles. The murals are effective social commentary and yet also whimsical in spirit. Various political themes depicting labor problems and social injustice run through them. Many of the faces in the paintings are those of the artists and their friends, along with local figures such as Colonel William Brady, caretaker of Coit Tower. The work's political content initially caused some public controversy.

Filbert Steps ⑱

Map 5 C2. 🚌 39.

Telegraph Hill falls away sharply on its eastern side, and the streets here become steep steps. Descending from Telegraph Hill Boulevard, Filbert Street is a rambling stairway, made of wood, brick and concrete, where fuchsia, rhododendron, bougainvillea, fennel and blackberries thrive.

Greenwich Steps ⑲

Map 5 C2. 🚌 39.

Descending roughly parallel to Filbert Steps, the steps of Greenwich Street have splendid views, with luxuriant foliage from adjoining gardens overflowing onto them. Going up one set of steps and down the other makes a delightful walk around the eastern side of Telegraph Hill.

Upper Montgomery Street ⑳

Map 5 C2. 🚌 39.

Until it was paved in 1931, the Telegraph Hill end of Montgomery Street was mostly inhabited by working-class families. There was also a sprinkling of artists and writers, attracted by the seclusion, the cheap rents and the views. It is now, however, a distinctly fashionable place to live, with some lovely walks nearby.

Julius Castle restaurant on Montgomery Street

Levi's Plaza ㉑

Map 5 C2.

This square is where the headquarters of Levi Strauss, the manufacturers of blue jeans *(see p135)*, can be found. It was landscaped by Lawrence Halprin in 1982, with the aim of recalling the company's history in California. The plaza is studded with granite rocks and cut by flowing water, thus evoking the Sierra Nevada canyon scenery in which the miners who first wore the jeans worked. Telegraph Hill in the background adds another mountainous element.

Steps at the bottom of Filbert Street leading up to Telegraph Hill

CHINATOWN AND NOB HILL

The Chinese settled in the plaza on Stockton Street in the 1850s, and today the shops and markets recall the atmosphere of a typical southern Chinese town, although the architecture, customs and public events are distinctly American hybrids on a Cantonese theme. This densely populated neighborhood with its colorful façades, teeming markets, temples, theaters and unique restaurants and stores, is "a city"

Chinese symbol outside the Bank of America

within the city and a place most visitors want to see.

Nob Hill is San Francisco's most celebrated hilltop, famous for its cable cars, plush hotels and views. In the late 19th century, the "Big Four," who built the first transcontinental railway, were among its richest tenants, in their large mansions on the hill. The earthquake and fire of 1906 *(see pp28–9)* leveled all but one of these, but today's hotels still recall the opulence of Victorian times.

SIGHTS AT A GLANCE

Historic Streets and Buildings
Bank of Canton **8**
Chinatown Alleys **6**
Chinatown Gateway **1**
Golden Gate Fortune Cookies **5**
Grant Avenue **7**
The Pacific-Union Club **14**

Historic Hotels
Fairmont Hotel **13**
Mark Hopkins Inter-Continental Hotel **12**

Galleries and Museums
Cable Car Museum **15**
Chinese Historical Society **11**
Pacific Heritage Museum **10**

Churches and Temples
Grace Cathedral **16**
Kong Chow Temple **3**
Old St. Mary's Cathedral **2**
Tin How Temple **4**

Parks and Squares
Portsmouth Square **9**

GETTING THERE
Visit on foot, if possible. Car drivers can sometimes park in one of the Nob Hill hotel garages, or under Portsmouth Plaza or at St. Mary's Square in Chinatown. All cable car lines go to Nob Hill and Chinatown.

KEY

▮	Street-by-Street map *See pp96–7*
▮	Street-by-Street map *See p101*
🚋	Cable car turntable

0 meters 500
0 yards 500

◁ Chinatown's bustling main street, Grant Avenue

Street-by-Street: Chinatown

Grant Avenue is the tourist Chinatown of dragon lampposts, up-turned roof-lines and neighborhood hardware stores packed to the rafters with everything from kites to cooking utensils. Locals shop up the hill on Stockton Street, where the freshest vegetables, produce and fish spill over in boxes on to crowded pavements. In the alleys in between, look for traditional temples, shops, laundries and family-run restaurants.

A street lamp in Chinatown

★ **Chinatown Alleys**
Authentic sights and sounds of the Far East echo in these busy alleys **6**

Ross Alley

JACKSON STREET

To bus no. 83

WASHINGTON STREET

Golden Gate Fortune Cookies
Visitors can see San Francisco cookies being made **5**

Chinese Historical Society **11**

Kong Chow Temple
Fine Cantonese wood carvings are a feature of this temple **3**

POWELL STREET

SACRAMENTO STREET

GRANT AVE

Tin How Temple
This was founded in 1852 by Chinese people grateful for their safe arrival in San Francisco **4**

CALIFORNIA STREET

STOCKTON STREET

Bank of Canton
Between 1909 and 1946 this was home to Chinatown's telephone exchange **8**

STAR SIGHTS

★ Chinatown Gateway

★ Chinatown alleys

★ Grant Avenue

Cable Cars run down two sides of Chinatown and are an essential part of the area's bustling atmosphere. Any of the three lines will take you there.

BUSH STREET

| 0 meters | 100 |
| 0 yards | 100 |

Portsmouth Plaza
Laid out in 1839, this was the social center for the village of Yerba Buena. Today it is a gathering place for players of cards and mahjong **9**

★ **Grant Avenue**
In the 1830s and early 1840s this was the main thoroughfare of Yerba Buena. It is now the busy commercial center of Chinatown **7**

LOCATOR MAP
See Street Finder, map 5

FISHERMAN'S WHARF AND NORTH BEACH

CHINATOWN AND NOB HILL

CIVIC CENTER

FINANCIAL DISTRICT AND UNION SQUARE

KEY

– – – Suggested route

The Chinese Cultural Center
contains an art gallery and a small crafts shop. It sponsors a lively series of lectures and seminars.

Pacific Heritage Museum
Housed in an elegant building below the Bank of Canton, this small museum has fine exhibitions of Asian art that are regularly changed **10**

KEARNY STREET

CLAY STREET

Old St. Mary's Cathedral
The clock tower of this church, built while the city was still in its infancy, bears an arresting inscription **2**

SON, OBSERVE THE TIME AND FLY FROM EVIL. ECC.IV.23.

PINE STREET

St. Mary's Square is a quiet haven in which to rest.

To bus nos. **31, 38**

★ **Chinatown Gateway**
Also known as the "Dragons' Gate," this marks Chinatown's southern entrance **1**

Chinatown Gateway ❶

Grant Ave at Bush St. **Map** 5 C4.
🚌 *2, 3, 4, 30, 45.*

This ornate portal, opened in 1970 and designed by Clayton Lee, spans the entrance to Chinatown's main tourist street, Grant Avenue. Inspired by the ceremonial entrances of traditional Chinese villages, the three-arched gateway is capped with green roof tiles and a host of propitiatory animals – including two dragons and two carp chasing a large, round pearl – all of glazed ceramic. Village gateways are often commissioned by wealthy clans to enhance their status, and the names of these benefactors are inscribed on the gates. This structure was erected by a peculiarly American institution, the Chinatown Cultural Development Committee, with materials that were donated by the Republic of China (Taiwan).

It is guarded by two stone lions suckling their cubs through their claws, in accordance with ancient lore. Once through the gate, you find yourself among some of the most elegant shops in Chinatown. Here you can buy antiques, silks and gems, but sometimes at high prices, aimed at tourists.

Chinatown Gateway dragon

Old St. Mary's Cathedral ❷

660 California St. **Map** 5 C4. **Tel** 288-3800. 🚌 *1, 30, 45.* 🚋 *California St.* **Mass** *7:30 am, 12:05pm daily, also 5pm Sat, 8:30, 11am Sun.* 📷

San Francisco's first Catholic cathedral, Old St. Mary's served a largely Irish congregation from 1854 to 1891, when a new St. Mary's Church was

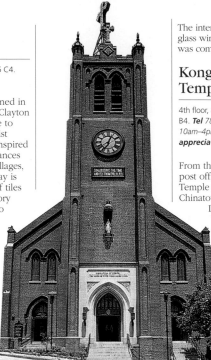

Entrance to Old St. Mary's Church below the clock tower

built on Van Ness Avenue. Because of the unavailability of suitable building materials in California, the bricks for the old church were imported from the East Coast, while the granite foundation stones came from China. The clock tower bears a large inscription, "Son, observe the time and fly from evil," said to have been directed at the brothels that stood across the street at the time it was built. Though twice damaged by fire, the church today retains its original foundations and walls.

The interior, with its stained-glass windows and balcony, was completed in 1909.

Kong Chow Temple ❸

4th floor, 855 Stockton St. **Map** 5 B4. **Tel** 788-1339. 🚌 *30, 45.* ⭕ *10am–4pm daily.* **Donations appreciated.** 🚫 ♿

From the top floor above the post office, the Kong Chow Temple looks out over Chinatown and the Financial District. Although the building dates only from 1977, the temple altar and statuary are possibly the oldest Chinese religious shrine in North America. One altar is known to have been carved in Guangzhou (Canton), and shipped to San Francisco in the 19th century. The main shrine is presided over by a carved wooden statue of Kuan Di, also dating from the 19th century. He is the deity most often found in shrines in Cantonese cities.

Kuan Di is also frequently seen in Chinatown: his distinctive face looks down from Taoist shrines in many Chinatown restaurants. He is typically depicted with a large sword in one hand and a book in the other – symbols of his unswerving dedication to both the martial and the literary arts.

Carved statue of Kuan Di inside the Kong Chow Temple

Three-floor climb to the Tin How Temple, founded in 1852

Tin How Temple ❹

Top floor, 125 Waverly Pl. **Map** 5 C3. 🚎 1, 30, 45. ⏲ 9am–4pm daily. **Donation requested.** 📷

This unusual temple is dedicated to Tin How (Tien Hau), Queen of Heaven and protector of seafarers and visitors, and is the longest-operating Chinese temple in the United States. Originally founded in 1852, it is now situated at the top of three steep, wooden flights of stairs. The narrow space is smoky with incense and burnt paper offerings, and hung with hundreds of gold and red lanterns. It is lit by red electric bulbs and burning wicks floating in oil. Gifts of fruit lie on the carved altar in front of the wooden statue of the temple's namesake deity.

Golden Gate Fortune Cookies ❺

56 Ross Alley. **Map** 5 C3. **Tel** 781-3956. 🚎 30, 45. ⏲ 10am–8:30pm daily. 7

Although there are a number of other fortune cookie bakeries in the San Francisco Bay area, Golden Gate Fortune Cookies has been in business longer than most, since 1962. The cookie-making machine nearly fills the small bakery, where dough is poured onto small griddles and then baked on a

conveyor belt. An attendant inserts the "fortunes" (slips of paper bearing predictions of a generally positive nature), before the cookies are folded.

Ironically, the fortune cookie, despite its close association with Chinese food and culture, is a phenomenon entirely unknown in China. It was actually invented in 1909 in San Francisco's Japanese Tea Garden (see p147), by the chief gardener of the time, Makota Hagiwara.

Chinatown Alleys ❻

Map 5 B3. 🚎 1, 30, 45.

Contained within a busy neighborhood, the Chinatown Alleys are situated between Grant Avenue and Stockton Street. These four narrow lanes intersect Washington Street within half a block of each other. Of these, the largest is Waverly Place, known as the "Street of Painted Balconies," for reasons that are apparent to every passerby. The alleys contain many old buildings, as well as traditional shops and restaurants. There are

Final touches in the cookie factory

also atmospheric, old-fashioned herbalist shops, displaying elk antlers, sea horses, snake wine and other exotic wares in their windows. Small restaurants, both above and below street level, serve cheap, delicious, home-cooked food.

Grant Avenue ❼

Map 5 C4. 🚎 1, 30, 45. 🚋 California St.

The main tourist street in Chinatown, Grant Avenue is also distinguished for being the first street of Yerba Buena, the village that preceded San Francisco. A plaque at No. 823 Grant Avenue marks the block where William A. Richardson and his Mexican wife erected Yerba Buena's first edifice, a canvas tent, on June 25, 1835. By October, they had replaced this with a wooden house, and the following year with a yet more permanent adobe (sun-dried brick) home, called Casa Grande. The street in which the Richardsons' house stood was named Calle de la Fundacion, the "Street of the Founding." It was finally renamed Grant Avenue in 1885 in memory of Ulysses S. Grant, the US president and Civil War general who died that year.

Effigy of the god of longevity on Grant Avenue

Bank of Canton ❽

743 Washington St. **Map** 5 C3.
Tel 421-5215. ▦ 1, 30, 45.
⬜ 9am–5pm Mon–Thu, 9am–6pm
Fri, 9am–4pm Sat.

Before being acquired by
the Bank of Canton in the
1950s, this building was the
Chinese Telephone Exchange.
It was built in 1909 on the site
where Sam Brannan printed
California's first newspaper.
The three-tiered tower is like
a pagoda, with upward-curving
eaves and a ceramic tiled roof,
and is the most distinctive work
of architectural chinoiserie in
the neighborhood.
 The telephone operators
worked on the main floor and
lived on the second floor. They
were multilingual, speaking
Cantonese and four other
Chinese dialects. One of their
original telephone books can
be seen on display in the
Chinese Historical Society on
Clay Street.

Bank of Canton entrance

Portsmouth Square ❾

Map 5 C3. ▦ 1, 41.

San Francisco's original town
square, now on the land-
scaped top of an underground
garage, was laid out in 1839.
It was once the social center
for the small village of Yerba
Buena. On July 9, 1846, less
than a month after American
rebels in Sonoma declared

Portsmouth Square

California's independence from
Mexico, a party of marines
rowed ashore. They raised the
American flag above the plaza,
officially seizing the port as
part of the United States *(see
pp24–5)*. Two years later, on
May 12, 1848, it was here that
Sam Brannan announced the
discovery of gold in the Sierra
Nevada *(see pp24–5)*. Over
the next two decades, the plaza
became the hub of an increasingly dynamic city. In the 1860s
the business district shifted
southeast to flatlands reclaimed
from the bay, and the plaza
declined in civic importance.
 Portsmouth Plaza today is
the social center of Chinatown.
In the morning, people
practice *t'ai chi*, and from midday to evening others gather
to play checkers and cards.

Pacific Heritage Museum ❿

608 Commercial St. **Map** 5 C3. **Tel**
399-1124. ▦ 1, 41. ⬜ 10am–4pm
Tue–Sat, except public hols. 📷 ♿

The building itself is as
elegant as the frequently
changing collections of
Asian arts displayed within
the museum. It is actually a
synthesis of two distinct
buildings. The US Sub-
Treasury was built here
in 1875–77 by William
Appleton Potter, on the
site of San Francisco's
original mint. You can
look into the old coin
vaults through a cutaway
section on the ground floor,
or descend in the elevator
for closer inspection.
 In 1984 architects
Skidmore, Owings and
Merrill designed and built

the impressive 17-story headquarters of the Bank of Canton
above the existing building, incorporating the original street-
level façade and basement.

Chinese Historical Society ⓫

965 Clay St. **Map** 5 B3. **Tel** 391-1188.
▦ Powell–Clay. ▦ 1, 30, 45. ⬜
12pm–5pm Tue–Fri, 11–4pm Sat. ⬤
Sun, Mon, public hols. 📷 except first
Thu of month. 🚪 🚫 www.chsa.org

Founded in 1963, the Chinese
Historical Society of America
is the oldest and largest
organization dedicated to the
study, documentation, and
dissemination of Chinese
American history. Exhibits
include the Daniel Ching
collection, the original hand-
written Chinatown telephone
book, a ceremonial dragon
costume, and a "tiger fork."
This triton was wielded in
one of the battles during the
reign of terror known as the
Tong Wars. Many objects,
documents, and photographs
illuminate the daily life of
Chinese immigrants in San
Francisco in the late 19th and
early 20th centuries.
 The Chinese contribution to
California's development was
extensive. Chinese helped
build the western half of the
first transcontinental railroad
and constructed dikes throughout the Sacramento River delta.
The CHSA sponsors oral history projects, an "In Search of
Roots" program,
and a monthly
speakers forum.

**Dragon's head in the
Chinese Historical Society**

Street-by-Street: Nob Hill

Nob Hill is the highest summit of the city center, rising 338 ft (103 m) above the bay. Its steep slopes were treacherous for carriages and kept prominent citizens away until the opening of the California Street cable car line in 1878. After that, the wealthy "nobs" soon built new homes on the peak of the hill. Though the grandiose mansions were burned down in the great fire of 1906 *(see pp28–9)*, Nob Hill still attracts the affluent to its splendid hotels.

LOCATOR MAP
See Street Finder, map 5

Fairmont Hotel
This renovated hotel is known for its marble lobby and elegant dining in one of the city's best restaurants **13**

The Pacific-Union Club
Now an exclusive men's club, this was once the mansion of Comstock millionaire James Flood **14**

Stouffer Renaissance Stanford Court Hotel occupies the site of Stanford's mansion; the original boundary walls remain.

★ **Grace Cathedral**
The cathedral is a replica of Notre Dame in Paris **16**

Huntington Park is on the site of Collis P. Huntington's great mansion.

The Masonic Auditorium honors Freemasons who died in American wars.

STAR SIGHTS

★ Mark Hopkins Inter-Continental Hotel

★ Grace Cathedral

Huntington Hotel with its Big Four Bar and Restaurant exudes the opulent urbane atmosphere of the Victorian era on Nob Hill.

0 meters   150

0 yards   150

★ **Mark Hopkins Inter-Continental Hotel**
The hotel's Top of the Mark penthouse bar is celebrated for its spectacular views **12**

Mark Hopkins Inter-Continental Hotel ⑫

999 California St. **Map** 5 B4. *Tel 392-3434.* 📷 *1.* 🚋 *California St, Powell–Mason, Powell–Hyde.* **www**.markhopkins.net

At the behest of his wife Mary, Mark Hopkins *(see below)* arranged for a fantastic wooden mansion, surpassing every other for ostentatious ornamentation, to be built on Nob Hill *(see below)*. When Mrs. Hopkins died, the house became home to the fledgling San Francisco Art Institute. It burned in the fire of 1906 *(see pp28–9)*, and only the granite retaining walls remain. The present 25-story tower, capped by a flag visible from all over the city, was built in 1925 by architects Weeks and Day. Top of the Mark *(see p271)*, the glass-walled bar on the 19th floor, is one of the most celebrated of the city's drinking establishments. World War II servicemen customarily drank a farewell toast to the city here before leaving for overseas.

Forecourt of the Mark Hopkins Inter-Continental Hotel

Fairmont Hotel ⑬

950 Mason St. **Map** 5 B4. **Tel** 772-5000. 📷 *1.* 🚋 *California St, Powell–Mason, Powell–Hyde. See **Where to Stay** p213.* **www**.fairmont.com

Built by Tessie Fair Oelrichs *(see below)*, this Beaux Arts building was completed on the eve of the 1906 earthquake *(see pp28–9)*, and stood for only two days before it was burned down. It was rebuilt by Julia Morgan within the original white terracotta façade, and opened for business one year later. After World War II it was the scene of meetings that led to the founding of the United Nations. For stunning views, ride the glass-walled elevator to the city's highest observation point, the Fairmont Crown; or, enjoy a cocktail at the hotel's famed Tonga Room and Hurricane Bar.

The Pacific-Union Club ⑭

1000 California St. **Map** 5 B4. **Tel** 775-1234. 📷 *1.* 🚋 *California St, Powell–Mason, Powell–Hyde.* 🔵 *to the public.*

Augustus Laver built this townhouse for the "Bonanza King" James Flood *(see below)* in 1885. Its Italianate, brown sandstone façade survived the 1906 fire *(see pp28–9)*, though the other mansions, built of wood, were destroyed. The gutted building was bought by the Pacific-Union Club, an exclusive gentlemen's club that had its origins in Gold Rush San Francisco *(see pp24–5)*.

THE NOBS OF NOB HILL

"Nob" was one of the kinder names reserved for the unscrupulous entrepreneurs who amassed vast fortunes during the development of the American West. Many of the nobs who lived on Nob Hill acquired other nicknames that hint at the wild stories behind their vast wealth. "Bonanza King" James Flood joined in a partnership with Irish immigrants

Mark Hopkins 1814–78

James Fair, John Mackay, and William O'Brien. In 1872, the four men bought controlling interests in some dwindling Comstock mines, sinking new shafts and striking a "bonanza" – a rich pocket of high-grade silver ore. Flood returned to San Francisco as a millionaire and bought a parcel of land on the summit of Nob Hill, across the street from a plot owned by James Fair. The Flood Mansion (now the Pacific-Union Club) still stands. The monument on Fair's property, the Fairmont Hotel, was built by his daughter, Tessie, after his death *(see above)*.

Bonanza Jim

The Big Four
Other distinguished residents of Nob Hill were the "Big Four," Leland Stanford, Mark Hopkins, Charles Crocker and Collis P. Huntington. This shrewd quartet made up the principal investors behind the first transcontinental railway. Their biggest enterprise, the Central Pacific Railroad (it was later renamed Southern Pacific) was an influential corporation in the burgeoning West. It acquired great wealth and influence as a result of the generous land grants bestowed by the US Congress to encourage railroad construction. Bribery and corruption made the Big Four among the most hated men of 19th-century America. In this capacity, they were characterized by yet another popular nickname: the "Robber Barons." All four built big mansions on Nob Hill, but these did not survive the devastation of the 1906 earthquake and fire.

Cable Car Museum ⑮

1201 Mason St. **Map** 5 B3.
Tel 474-1887. 🚌 1, 12, 30, 45, 83.
🚋 Powell–Mason, Powell–Hyde.
⏰ Apr 1–Sep 30: 10am–6pm daily;
Oct 1–Mar 31: 10am–5pm daily. ⏰
Jan 1, Easter Sunday, Thanksgiving,
Dec 25. 📷 ♿ mezzanine only. 🚻

This is both a museum and the powerhouse of the cable car system *(see pp104–5)*.

Anchored to the ground floor are the engines and wheels that wind the cables through the system of channels and pulleys beneath the streets. Observe them from the mezzanine, then walk downstairs to see under the street. The museum houses an early cable car and specimens of the mechanisms that control the individual cars. The system is the last of its kind in the world.

Entrance to the Cable Car Barn Museum

Grace Cathedral ⑯

1100 California St. **Map** 5 B4.
Tel 749-6300. 🚌 1. 🚋 California
St. 🎵 Choral evensong 5:15pm Thu,
3pm Sun; Choral Eucharist 7:30am,
8:15am, 11am, 6pm Sun. ♿
📷 12:30–2pm Sun, 1–3pm Mon–
Fri, 11:30am–1:30pm Sat. 🚻
www.gracecathedral.org

Grace Cathedral is the main Episcopal church in San Francisco. Designed by Lewis P. Hobart, it stands on the site of Charles Crocker's mansion *(see p102)*. Preparatory work began in February 1927, and building started in September

1928, but the cathedral was not finally completed until 1964. Despite its modern construction, the building was inspired by Notre Dame in Paris, incorporating traditional elements.

The interior is replete with marble and stained glass. Its leaded-glass windows were designed by Charles Connick, inspired by the blue glass of Chartres. The rose window is

Stained glass detail

made using 1-inch (2.5-cm) thick faceted glass, which is illuminated from inside at night. Other windows are by Henry Willet and Gabriel Loire. These include depictions of modern heroes such as Albert Einstein.

Objects in the cathedral include a 13th-century Catalonian crucifix and a 16th-century silk and gold Brussels tapestry. The doors of the main entrance are cast from molds of Lorenzo Ghiberti's "Doors of Paradise," made for the Baptistry in Florence.

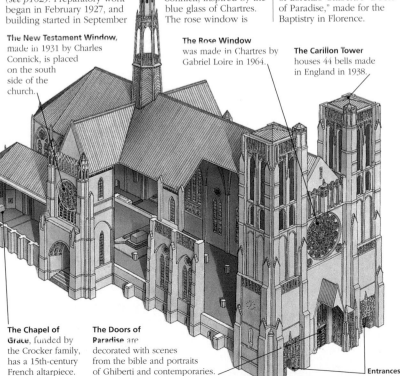

The New Testament Window, made in 1931 by Charles Connick, is placed on the south side of the church.

The Rose Window was made in Chartres by Gabriel Loire in 1964.

The Carillon Tower houses 44 bells made in England in 1938.

The Chapel of Grace, funded by the Crocker family, has a 15th-century French altarpiece.

The Doors of Paradise are decorated with scenes from the bible and portraits of Ghiberti and contemporaries.

Entrances

San Francisco's Cable Cars

The cable car system was launched in 1873, with its inventor Andrew Hallidie riding in the first car. He was inspired to tackle the problem of transporting people up the city's steep slopes after seeing a horrible accident: a horse-drawn tram slipped down a hill, dragging the horses with it. His system was a success, and by 1889 cars were running on eight lines. Before the 1906 earthquake *(see pp28–9)*, more than 600 cars were in use. With the advent of the internal combustion engine, cable cars became obsolete, and in 1947 attempts were made to replace them with buses. After a public outcry the present three lines, using 17 miles (25 km) of track, were retained.

Cable car traffic lights

The Cable Car Barn *garages the cars at night and is a repair shop, museum and powerhouse for the entire cable car system* (see p103).

Bell

POWEL

The gripman *has to be strong, with good reflexes. Only a third of candidates pass the training course.*

Sandbox

Grip handle

Center plate and jaws grip the cable

Emergency brake

Wheel brake

Cable

HOW CABLE CARS WORK

Engines in the central powerhouse wind a looped cable under the city streets, guided by a system of grooved pulleys. When the gripman in the cable car applies the grip handle, the grip reaches through a slot in the street and grabs the cable. This pulls the car along at a steady speed of 9.5 mph (15.5 km/h). To stop, the gripman releases the grip and applies the brake. Great skill is needed at corners where the cable passes over a pulley. The gripman must release the grip to allow the car to coast over the pulley.

Cable car grip mechanism

Grip handle

Destination board

Wooden beams

Grip crotch

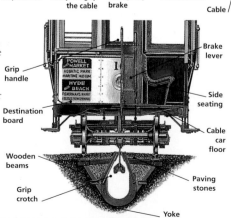

POWELL AND MARKET
AQUATIC PARK
MARITIME MUSEUM
HYDE BEACH
FISHERMAN'S WHARF

Brake lever

Side seating

Cable car floor

Paving stones

Yoke

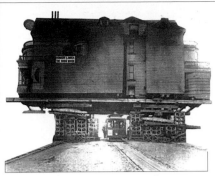

Hatch House *is the name given to a four-story house that needed moving in its entirety in 1913. Herbert Hatch used a system of jacks and hoists to maneuver the house across the cable car line without causing any cessation of the service.*

A cable car celebration *was held in 1984 after a two-year renovation of the system. Each car was restored, and all lines were replaced with reinforced tracks. The system should now work safely for 100 years.*

Brake block   Brake shoe

The original *San Francisco cable car, tested by Hallidie on Clay Street on August 2, 1873, is on display in the Cable Car Barn (see p103). The cable car system has remained essentially unchanged since its invention.*

A cable car bell-ringing contest *is held in Union Square every July, when conductors ring out their most spirited rhythms. On the street, the bell signals a warning to other traffic.*

Rebuilding the cable cars *is done with attention to historical detail because they are designated historic monuments.*

ANDREW SMITH HALLIDIE

Andrew Smith was born in London in 1836 and later adopted his uncle's surname. He trained as a mechanic, moving to San Francisco in 1852, where he formed a company that made wire rope. In 1873 he tested the first cable car, which soon became profitable and opened the hills of the city to development.

FINANCIAL DISTRICT AND UNION SQUARE

Montgomery Street, now in the heart of the Financial District, was once a street of small shops, where miners came to weigh their gold dust. It roughly marks the old shoreline of the shallow Yerba Buena Cove, which was filled in during the Gold Rush years *(see pp24–5)*

Motif on Union Bank

to create more land. Today, old-style banking halls from the early 20th century stand in the shadow of glass and steel skyscrapers, and crowds of office workers throng the streets. Union Square is at the center of the city's main shopping district, and has a wealth of fine department stores.

SIGHTS AT A GLANCE

Historic Streets and Buildings
California Historical Society ⓫
Ferry Building ❿
Jackson Square Historical District ❷
Merchant's Exchange ❼
Old United States Mint ㉕
Pacific Coast Stock Exchange ❽
Powell Street Cable Car Turntable ㉓
Union Bank of California ❻

Museums and Galleries
Contemporary Jewish Museum ⓮
Museum of African Diaspora ⓬
Museum of Modern Art pp118–21 ⓰
Wells Fargo History Museum ❸

Modern Architecture
Bank of America ❹
Embarcadero Center ❶
Rincon Center ⓭
Transamerica Pyramid ❺
Yerba Buena Gardens pp114–15 ⓯

Hotels
Sheraton Palace Hotel ⓱

Visitors Information
San Francisco Visitor Information Center ㉖

Shops
Crocker Galleria ⓲
Gump's ⓳
Union Square Shops ㉒
Westfield Shopping Centre ㉔

Theaters
Theater District ㉑

Parks and Squares
Justin Herman Plaza ❾
Union Square ⓴

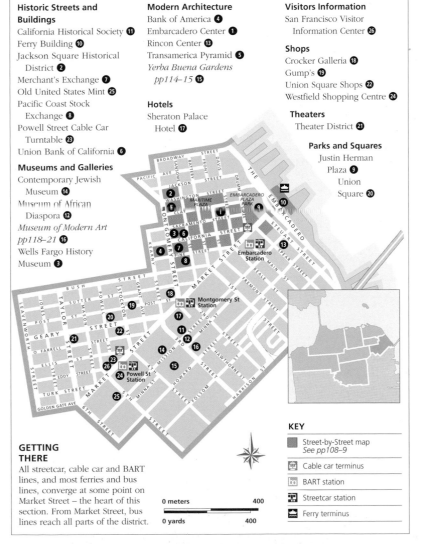

KEY

🟪	Street-by-Street map See pp108–9
🚋	Cable car terminus
Ⓑ	BART station
🚈	Streetcar station
⛴	Ferry terminus

0 meters   400
0 yards   400

GETTING THERE

All streetcar, cable car and BART lines, and most ferries and bus lines, converge at some point on Market Street – the heart of this section. From Market Street, bus lines reach all parts of the district.

◁ Interior of the Hyatt Regency Hotel, showing *Eclipse*, a sculpture by Charles Perry

Street-by-Street: Financial District

San Francisco's economic engine is fueled predominantly by the Financial District, one of the chief commercial centers in the US. It reaches from the imposing modern towers and plazas of the Embarcadero Center to staid Montgomery Street, sometimes known as the "Wall Street of the West." All the principal banks, brokers, exchanges and law offices are situated within this compact area. The Jackson Square Historical District, north of Washington Street, was once the heart of the business community.

**La Chiffonière (1978)
by Jean Dubuffet,
Justin Herman Plaza**

★ **Embarcadero Center**
The center houses both commercial outlets and offices. A shopping arcade occupies the first three tiers of the towers ❶

Hotaling Place, a narrow alley leading to the Jackson Square Historical District, has several good antiques shops.

Jackson Square Historical District
This district recalls the Gold Rush era more than any other ❷

The Golden Era Building, was built during the Gold Rush. It was the home of the paper *Golden Era*, for which Mark Twain wrote.

Bus stop (No. 41)

★ **Transamerica Pyramid**
Since 1972, this 853-ft (256-m) skyscraper has been the tallest on the city's skyline ❺

Union Bank of California
The grand banking hall is guarded by fierce stone lions carved by sculptor Arthur Putnam ❻

Merchant's Exchange
Epic paintings of local shipping scenes line the walls ❼

Wells Fargo History Museum
An original stagecoach, evoking the wilder days of the old West, is one of the many exhibits in this transportation and banking museum ❸

Bank of America
There are fine views from the 52nd floor of this important banking institution ❹

| 0 meters | 100 |
| 0 yards | 100 |

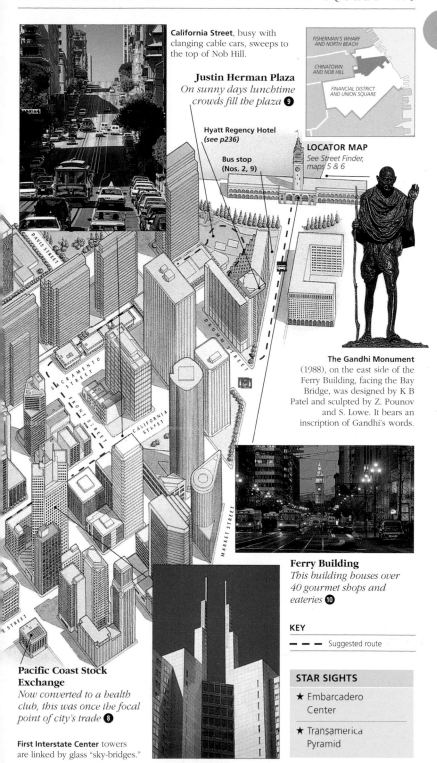

California Street, busy with clanging cable cars, sweeps to the top of Nob Hill.

Justin Herman Plaza
On sunny days lunchtime crowds fill the plaza 9

Hyatt Regency Hotel
(see p236)

Bus stop
(Nos. 2, 9)

LOCATOR MAP
See Street Finder,
maps 5 & 6

FISHERMAN'S WHARF
AND NORTH BEACH

CHINATOWN
AND NOB HILL

FINANCIAL DISTRICT
AND UNION SQUARE

The Gandhi Monument
(1988), on the east side of the Ferry Building, facing the Bay Bridge, was designed by K B Patel and sculpted by Z. Pounov and S. Lowe. It bears an inscription of Gandhi's words.

DAVIS STREET

SACRAMENTO STREET

FRONT STREET

CALIFORNIA STREET

DRUMM STREET

MARKET STREET

Ferry Building
This building houses over 40 gourmet shops and eateries 10

KEY

— — — Suggested route

Pacific Coast Stock Exchange
Now converted to a health club, this was once the focal point of city's trade 8

First Interstate Center towers are linked by glass "sky-bridges."

STAR SIGHTS

★ Embarcadero Center

★ Transamerica Pyramid

Embarcadero Center ➊

Map 6 D3. 🚌 *1, 32.* 🚋 *J, K, L, M, N.* 🚎 *California St. See **Shopping in San Francisco** p245 and **Where to Stay** p215.*

Completed in 1981 after a decade of construction, San Francisco's largest redevelopment project reaches from Justin Herman Plaza to Battery Street. Four separate high-rise towers reach upward 35 to 40 stories above the landscaped plazas and elevated walkways.

Embarcadero Center's most spectacular interior is the lobby of the Hyatt Regency Hotel. Its 17-story atrium contains an immense sculptured globe by Charles Perry, entitled *Eclipse*. Glass elevators glide up and down one wall, carrying visitors to and from the Equinox, a revolving rooftop restaurant that completes a full circle every 40 minutes. Also housed in the center is a cinema screening an impressive array of independent and foreign films.

Lobby of the Hyatt Regency Hotel at the Embarcadero Center

Hotaling Place in Jackson Square

Jackson Square Historical District ➋

Map 5 C3. 🚌 *12, 41, 83.*

Renovated in the early 1950s, this low-rise neighbor-hood contains many historic brick, cast-iron and granite façades dating from the Gold Rush era. From 1850–1910, it was notorious for its squalor and the crudeness of its inhabitants and was known as the Barbary Coast *(see pp26–7)*. The Hippodrome at 555 Pacific Street used to be a theater; the bawdy relief sculptures in the recessed front recall the risqué shows that were performed there. Today the buildings are used as showrooms, law offices and antique shops; the best can be seen on Jackson Street, Gold Street, Hotaling Place and Montgomery Street.

Wells Fargo History Museum ➌

420 Montgomery St. **Map** 5 C4. **Tel** 396-2619. 🚌 *1, 12, 41.* 🚎 *California St.* 🚇 *Montgomery* ⏰ *9am–5pm Mon–Fri.* ⬤ *public hols.* ♿
🖥 www.wellsfargohistory.com

Founded in 1852, Wells Fargo & Co. became the greatest banking and transport company in the West and was influential in the development of the American frontier. The company moved people and goods from the East to the West Coast, and between California mining camps and towns. It also transported gold from the West Coast to the East and delivered

Black Bart, the poet bandit

mail. Wells Fargo put mail boxes in convenient locations and messengers sorted the letters en route. The Pony Express was another mail venture in which Wells Fargo played a major role.

The splendid stage coaches *(see p108)*, like the one on display in the museum, are famous for the legendary stories of their heroic drivers and the bandits who robbed them. The best-known bandit was Black Bart, who left poems at the scene of his crimes. He stalked the lonely roads from Calaveras County to the Oregon border between 1875 and 1883, holding up stage coaches. In one hold-up he mistakenly left a handkerchief with a distinctive laundry mark, revealing him to be a mining engineer named Charles Boles.

Museum visitors can experience how it felt to sit for days in a jostling stage coach, and listen to the recorded diary of Francis Brocklehurst, an immigrant. Exhibits include Pony Express mail, photographs, early checks, weaponry, gold nuggets, and Emperor Norton's imperial currency *(see p26)*.

Bank of America ❹

555 California St. **Map** 5 C4.
Tel 433-7500 (Carnelian Room).
🚌 1, 41. 🚋 California St. See
San Francisco's Bars pp270–71.

The red granite-clad building housing the world head-quarters of the Bank of America opened in 1972. Its 52 stories make it the largest skyscraper in San Francisco, and there are incredible views of the city from the Carnelian Room Restaurant on the 52nd floor.

The Bank of America was originally the Bank of Italy, founded by A. P. Giannini in San Jose, California. It built up a huge clientèle early in the 20th century by catering to immigrants and by investing in the booming farmlands and small towns. In the great fire of 1906 (see pp28–9) Giannini personally rescued his bank's deposits, carting them to safety hidden in fruit crates, so there were sufficient funds for the bank to invest in the rebuilding of the city.

Transcendence by Masayuki Nagari outside the Bank of America

Transamerica Pyramid ❺

600 Montgomery St. **Map** 5 C3.
Tel 983-4100. 🚌 1, 41. ⬤ to the public. ♿ www.tapyramid.com

Capped with a pointed spire on top of its 48 stories, the pyramid reaches 853 ft (256 m) above sea level. It is the tallest and most widely recognized building in the city, and although San Franciscans disliked it when it opened in 1972, they have since accepted it as part of their city's skyline. Since September 11, 2001, the pyramid has been closed to the public.

Designed by William Pereira & Associates, the pyramid houses 1,500 office workers on a site that is historically one of the richest in the city. The Montgomery Block, which contained many important offices and was the largest building west of the Mississippi, was built here in 1853. In the basement was the Exchange Saloon, which was frequented by Mark Twain. In the 1860s artists and writers took up residence in the Montgomery Block. The Pony Express terminus, marked by a plaque, was at Merchant Street opposite the pyramid.

The spire is hollow, rising 212 ft (64 m) above the top floor. Lit from inside, it casts a warm yellow glow at night. Its purpose is purely decorative.

Vertical Wings
The wings of the building rise vertically from the middle of the ground floor and extend beyond the frame, which tapers inward. The east wing houses 18 elevator shafts; the west wing houses a smoke tower and stairs.

Earthquake Protection
The exterior is covered with white precast quartz aggregate, interlaced with reinforcing rods on each floor. Clearance between the panels allows lateral movement in case of an earthquake.

The 3,678 windows take cleaners one month to wash.

City Views
Workers in the upper-floor offices have stupendous 360° views of the entire city, and right across San Francisco Bay.

The Shape
The building tapers so that it casts a smaller shadow than a conventional design.

The foundation rests on a steel-and-concrete block, sunk 52 ft (15.5 m) into the ground, and designed to move with earth tremors.

Classical façade of the Union Bank of California

Union Bank of California **6**

400 California St. **Map** 5 C4.
Tel 765-0400. 🚌 1, 41.
🚋 California St. & ✪

William Ralston and Darius Mills founded this bank in 1864. Ralston, known as "the man who built San Francisco," invested profitably in Comstock mines *(see p27)*. He, in turn, used the bank and his personal fortune to finance many civic projects in San Francisco. These included the city's water company, a theater and the Palace Hotel *(see p113)*. However, when economic depression struck in the 1870s, Ralston's empire also collapsed.

The present colonnaded building was completed in 1908. In the basement there is a pleasant arcade of shops, restaurants and small art and photography exhibits.

Merchant's Exchange **7**

465 California St. **Map** 5 C4.
Tel 421-7730. 🚌 1, 3, 4, 10, 15.
🚋 Montgomery. ◯ 8:30am–6pm
Mon–Fri, 9am–6pm Sat & Sun by
appt only. ◯ public hols. & ✪
www.merchantsexchange.com

The exchange, designed by Willis Polk in 1903, survived the great fire of 1906 with little damage. Inside, fine seascapes by the Irish painter William Coulter line the walls. These depict epic maritime scenes from the age of steam and sail. The building was the focal point of San Francisco's commodities exchange in the early 20th century, when lookouts in the tower relayed news of ships arriving from abroad.

Pacific Coast Stock Exchange **8**

301 Pine St. **Map** 5 C4. **Tel** 393-
4000. 🚌 3, 4, 41. **Not open** to the
public. **www**.pacificex.com

This was once America's largest stock exchange outside New York. Founded in 1882, it occupied these buildings, which were remodeled by Miller and Pflueger in 1930 from the existing US Treasury. The monumental granite statues that flank the Pine Street entrance to the building were made by Ralph Stackpole, also in 1930. Due to changing trading methods, the building is no longer a stock exchange and has been converted into a fitness club.

Justin Herman Plaza **9**

Map 6 D3. 🚌 many buses. 🚃 J, K,
L, M, N. 🚋 California St.

Popular with lunchtime crowds from the nearby Embarcadero Center and other offices, this plaza is mostly known for its avant-garde Vaillancourt Fountain, made in 1971 by the Canadian artist Armand Vaillancourt. The fountain is modeled from huge concrete blocks, and some people find it ugly, especially when it is allowed to run dry in times of drought. However, you can climb on and through it, and its pools and columns of falling water make it an intriguing public work of art when it is functioning as intended.

The Vaillancourt Fountain in Justin Herman Plaza

The clock tower on the Ferry Building

Ferry Building **10**

Embarcadero at Market St. **Map** 6
E3. 🚌 many buses. 🚃 J, K, L, M, N.
🚋 California St.

Constructed between 1896 and 1903, the Ferry Building survived the great fire of 1906 *(see pp28–9)* through the inter-cession of fireboats pumping water from the bay. The clock tower is 235 ft (71 m) high, and was inspired by the Moorish bell tower of Seville Cathedral. In the early 1930s more than 50 million passengers a year passed through the building. Redeveloped in 2003, the Ferry building houses many gourmet shops selling a huge variety of fresh produce, as well as several restaurants and eateries. On Tuesdays and Saturdays, a Farmers' Market is held around the outside of the building.

With the opening of the Bay Bridge in 1936, the Ferry Building ceased to be the city's main point of entry. Today, only a few ferries cross the bay to Larkspur and Sausalito in Marin County *(see p161)*, and Alameda and Oakland in the East Bay *(see pp164–7)*.

California Historical Society ⓫

678 Mission St. **Map** 6 D5. *Tel 357-1848.* 🚌 *5, 9, 38.* 🚃 *J, K, L, M, N, T.* 🚇 *Montgomery.* ◯ *noon–4:30pm Wed–Sat (library closed Sat).* **www**.californiahistoricalsociety.org

The society provides research libraries, museum galleries, and a bookstore. There is an impressive photographic collection, more than 900 paintings and watercolors by American artists, a decorative arts exhibit, and a unique costume collection.

Fishing in the harbor

Museum of the African Diaspora ⓬

685 Mission St. **Map** 5 C5. 📞 *358-7200.* 🚌 *7, 9, 21, 38, 71.* 🚃 *J, K, L, M, N, T.* ◯ *11am–6pm Wed–Sat, noon–5pm Sun.* **www**.moadsf.org

The central idea of this museum is that we all share

Rincon Annex mural depicting the Spanish discovery of San Francisco

a common African past. Permanent exhibits cover African music, culinary traditions, and explain the slave trade. There are also interactive exhibits, lectures, and workshops.

Rincon Center ⓭

Map 6 B4. 🚌 *14. See* **Shopping in San Francisco** *p245.*

This shopping center, with its soaring atrium, was added onto the old Rincon Annex Post Office Building in 1989. The Rincon Annex is known for its murals by Anton Refregier showing aspects of the city's history.

Contemporary Jewish Museum ⓮

736 Mission St. **Map** 5 C5. *Tel 655-7800.* 🚌 *7, 9, 21, 38, 71.* 🚃 *J, K, L, M, N, T.* ◯ *11am–5:30pm Mon, Tue, Fri–Sun, 1–8:30pm Thu.* 🅰 🏠 🅲 🖥 **www**.thecjm.org

This museum partners with national and international cultural institutions to present a variety of art, photography, and installations celebrating and exploring Judaism.

Yerba Buena Gardens ⓯

See pp114–115.

Museum of Modern Art ⓰

See pp118–121.

Sheraton Palace Hotel ⓱

2 New Montgomery St. **Map** 5 C4. *Tel 512-1111.* 🚌 *7, 9, 21, 31, 66, 71.* 🚃 *J, K, L, M, N, T. See* **Where to Stay** *p215.*

The original Palace Hotel was opened by William Ralston, one of San Francisco's best-known financiers, in 1875. It was the most luxurious of San Francisco's early hotels and was regularly frequented by the rich and famous. Among its patrons were Sarah Bernhardt, Oscar Wilde, and Rudyard Kipling. The celebrated tenor Enrico Caruso was a guest at the time of the earthquake of 1906 *(see pp28–9),* when the hotel caught fire. It was rebuilt by the architect George Kelham, and reopened in 1909.

The Garden Court at the Sheraton Palace Hotel

Yerba Buena Gardens ⑮

The construction of the Moscone Center, San Francisco's largest venue for conventions was the start of ambitious plans for Yerba Buena Gardens. New housing, hotels, museums, shops, galleries, restaurants and gardens have followed or are planned, rejuvenating a once depressed area. Development is almost complete, with the exception of the Moscone Convention facility at Fourth and Howard Streets.

★ Yerba Buena Center for the Arts
Galleries, Forum and a screening room featuring contemporary films and videos are the highlights.

Esplanade Gardens
Visitors can wander along the paths or relax on benches.

The Martin Luther King Jr. Memorial has words of peace in several languages.

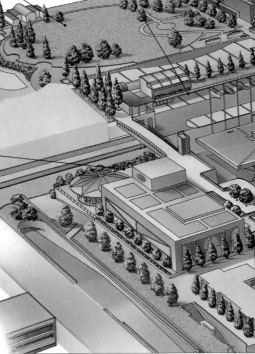

Zeum

Zeum is located at the Yerba Buena Rooftop. It has an ongoing program of events and provides opportunities for youngsters and artists to collaborate in the design and creation of anything from airplanes, robots, and futuristic buildings to mosaics and sculptures.

STAR SIGHTS

★ Yerba Buena Center for the Arts

★ SF Museum of the Modern Art

MOSCONE CENTER

Engineer TY Lin found an ingenious way to support the children's center above this huge underground hall without a single interior column. The bases of the eight steel arches are linked, like an archer's bowstrings, by cables under the floor. By tightening the cables, the arches exert enormous upward thrust.

Yerba Buena Center for the Arts Theater
Performing arts reflecting the cultural diversity of San Francisco are presented in the 755-seat indoor theater. There is also an outdoor theater.

VISITORS' CHECKLIST

Mission, 3rd, Folsom and 4th Sts.
Map 5 C5. ☎ 978-2787. 🚌 9, 14, 15, 30, 45, 76. 🚃 J, K, L, M, N, T. **Zeum** ☎ 820-3320. ☐ 11am–5pm Tue–Sun (summer), 1–5pm Wed–Fri & 11am–5pm Sat–Sun (school year). ● Dec 25. 📷 ♿ 🛍 **Yerba Buena Center for the Arts** ☐ noon–5pm Tue, Wed, Sun, noon–8pm Thu–Sat. ● Mon, public hols. 📷 (free first Tue of month). ✗ ♿ 🛍 SF **Museum of Modern Art** (see pp 118–21). www.yerbabuena.org

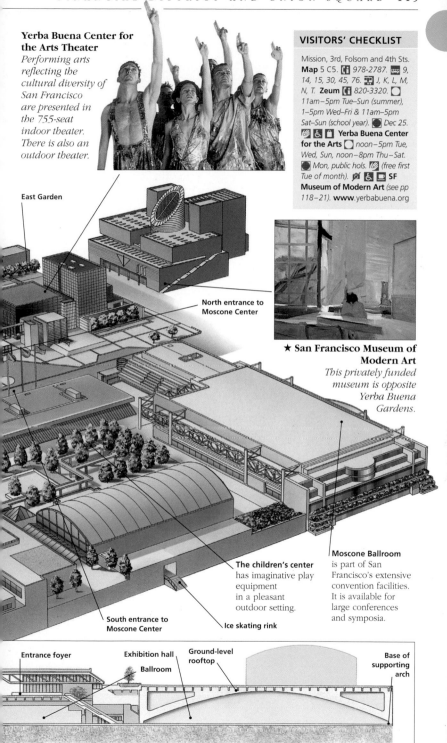

East Garden

North entrance to Moscone Center

★ San Francisco Museum of Modern Art
This privately funded museum is opposite Yerba Buena Gardens.

The children's center has imaginative play equipment in a pleasant outdoor setting.

Moscone Ballroom is part of San Francisco's extensive convention facilities. It is available for large conferences and symposia.

South entrance to Moscone Center

Ice skating rink

Entrance foyer

Exhibition hall

Ballroom

Ground-level rooftop

Base of supporting arch

Central plaza of the Crocker Galleria

Crocker Galleria ⑱

Between Post, Kearny, Sutter and Montgomery Sts. **Map** 5 C4. 🚌 *2, 3, 4.* 🚃 *J, K, L, M, N, T. See* **Shopping in San Francisco** *p245.*

The Crocker Galleria was built in 1982, by architects Skidmore, Owings and Merrill. Inspired by the Galleria Vittorio Emmanuelle in Milan, this building features a central plaza under a vaulting skylight roof. More than 50 shops and restaurants are housed here on three floors, with displays promoting the best of American and European designers.

Gump's ⑲

135 Post St. **Map** 5 C4. **Tel** *982-1616.* 🚌 *2, 3, 4, 30, 38, 45.* 🚃 *J, K, L, M, N, T.* 🚃 *Powell–Mason, Powell–Hyde.* 🕙 *10am–6pm Mon–Sat, 12pm–5pm Sun.* ♿ *See* **Shopping in San Francisco** *p249.*

Founded in 1861 by German immigrants who were former mirror and frame merchants, this homegrown San Francisco department store is an institution. Many local couples register their wedding present list with the store. Gump's has the largest collection in the US of fine china and crystal, which includes famous names such as Baccarat, Steuben and Lalique.

The store is also celebrated for its oriental treasures, furniture, and the rare works of art in the art department. The Asian art is particularly fine, especially the remarkable jade collection, which enjoys a world-wide reputation. In 1949 Gump's imported the great bronze Buddha and presented it to the Japanese Tea Garden *(see p147).* Gump's has an exclusive, refined atmosphere and is frequented by the rich and famous. It is renowned for its colorful and extravagant window displays.

Union Square ⑳

Map 5 C5. 🚌 *2, 3, 4, 30, 38, 45.* 🚃 *J, K, L, M, N, T.* 🚃 *Powell–Mason, Powell–Hyde.*

Union Square was named for the big, pro-Union rallies held there during the Civil War of 1861–65. The rallies galvanized popular support in San Francisco for the Northern cause, and this was instrumental in bringing California into the war on the side of the Union. The square is at the heart of the city's shopping district and marks the edge of the Theater District. It is bordered on the west side by the famous Westin St. Francis Hotel *(see p216),* and at the center there is a statue of *Victory* at the top of a 90-ft (27-m) column. This monument commemorates Admiral Dewey's victory at Manila Bay during the Spanish–American War of 1898.

Victory monument in Union Square

Theater District ㉑

Map 5 B5. 🚌 *2, 3, 4, 38.* 🚃 *Powell–Mason, Powell–Hyde.* 🚃 *J, K, L, M, N, T.* *See* **Entertainment** *p263.*

Several theaters are located near Union Square, all within a six-block area. The two biggest are on Geary Boulevard, two blocks west of the square. These are the Curran Theater, built in 1922, and the Geary Theater, built in 1909 and now home to the American Conservatory Theater (ACT). Drama has flourished in San Francisco since the days of the Gold Rush *(see pp24–5),* and great actors and opera stars have been attracted to the city. Isadora Duncan, the famous, innovative 1920s dancer, was born in the Theater District at 501 Taylor Street.

San Francisco's famous stores overlooking Union Square

Union Square Shops ㉒

Map 5 C5. 🚌 *2, 3, 4, 30, 38, 45.* 🚃 *Powell–Mason, Powell–Hyde.* 🚃 *J, K, L, M, N, T. See* **Shopping** *p245.*

Many of San Francisco's largest department stores can be found here, including Macy's, Sak's Fifth Avenue, Neiman Marcus, and Gumps *(see pp244–5),* as well as grand hotels, antiquarian bookshops and boutiques. The Union Square Frank Lloyd Wright Building, at 140 Maiden Lane, is the precursor to New York's Guggenheim Museum.

Powell Street Cable Car Turntable **㉓**

Hallidie Plaza, Powell St at Market St. **Map** 5 C5. 🚌 *many buses.* 🚊 *J, K, L, M, N, T.* 🚋 *Powell–Mason, Powell–Hyde.*

The Powell-Hyde and the Powell-Mason cable car lines are the most spectacular routes in San Francisco. They start and end their journeys to Nob Hill, Chinatown and Fisherman's Wharf at the corner of Powell Street and Market Street. Unlike the double-ended cable cars on the California Street line, the Powell Street cable cars were built to move in one direction only – hence the need for a turntable at every terminus.

After the car's passengers have disembarked, it is pushed onto the turntable and rotated manually by the conductor and gripman. Prospective customers for the return journey wait amid an ever-moving procession of street musicians, shoppers, tourists and office workers.

Rotating a cable car on the Powell Street turntable

Westfield Shopping Centre **㉔**

Market St and Powell St. **Map** 5 C5. **Tel** 512-6776. 🚌 *5, 7, 9, 14, 21, 71.* 🚊 *J, K, L, M, N.* 🚋 *Powell–Mason, Powell–Hyde.* ⏰ *9:30am–9pm Mon–Sat, 10am–7pm Sun.* **www. westfield.com** See **Shopping in San Francisco** p245.

Shoppers are carried upward on semi-spiral escalators through this vertical mall, which consists of a soaring, central atrium with nine floors of elegant shops. It is topped by a dome, 150 ft (45 m) above the ground floor. The basement levels provide access to the Powell Street Station. Nordstrom's department store is located on the top five levels and is the mall's main tenant. Entrances to Bloomingdale's, famed for its Classical rotunda, are on the lower floors.

Old United States Mint **㉕**

Fifth St and Mission St. **Map** 5 C5. 🚌 *14, 14L, 26, 27.* 🚊 *J, K, L, M, N, T.* ● *closed indefinitely.*

One of San Francisco's three mints, the Old Mint operated as a museum from 1973–1994; its last coins were produced in 1937. Designed in a Classical style, the building is constructed of sturdy granite, hence its nickname, "Granite Lady." It was built by AB Mullet between 1869 and 1874, its windows fortified by iron shutters and its basement vaults impregnable. The building was one of the few to survive the 1906 earthquake and fire (*see pp28–9*). It is currently closed to the public.

San Francisco Visitor Information Center **㉖**

Powell St at Market St under Hallidie Plaza. **Map** 5 B5. **Tel** 391-2000. 📠 391-2001. 🚌 *many buses. J, K, L, M, N, T.* 🚋 *Powell–Mason, Powell–Hyde.* ⏰ *9am–5pm Mon–Fri, 9am–3pm Sat & Sun.* ● *Sun (Nov–Apr).* ♿ *limited.* **www**.sfvisitor.org

Inquire here for information on tours of the city and surrounding areas, festivals, special events, restaurants, accommodations, nightlife, sightseeing and shopping. Maps and a wide range of brochures are available in English and other languages, while a multilingual staff is on hand to answer any questions. You can make inquiries by telephone, or use their 24-hour information recording.

The impregnable "Granite Lady" Old Mint

San Francisco Museum of Modern Art 🔟

This dramatic museum forms the nucleus of San Francisco's reputation as a leading center of modern art. Created in 1935 with the aim of displaying works from 20th-century artists, it moved into its new quarters in 1995. The focus of Swiss architect Mario Botta's modernist building is the 125-ft (38-m) cylindrical skylight, which channels light down to the first-floor atrium court. It has more than 23,000 works of art housed in its 50,000 sq ft (4,600 sq m) of gallery space on four floors. The museum offers a dynamic schedule of changing exhibits from around the world.

Zip Light (1990) by Sigmar Willnauer

Personal Values
Belgian Surrealist René Magritte created this late masterpiece in 1952. It features his use of everyday objects in strange and often unsettling surroundings, all painted in a realistic style.

MUSEUM GUIDE

The museum shop, Phyllis Wattis Theater, café and special events space are on the first floor. The Koret Visitor Education Center and works from the permanent collection of paintings, sculptures, architecture and design are on the second floor. Photography and special exhibitions are displayed on the third floor, with media arts, special exhibitions and a sculpture terrace on the fourth floor. The fifth floor galleries feature contemporary works of painting and sculpture from the museum's collection.

★ No. 14, 1960
This oil on canvas was painted by Mark Rothko, a leading Abstract Expressionist. It is one of the artist's most beautiful and hypnotic works.

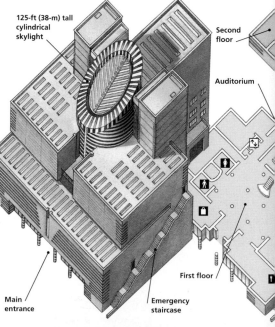

The Nest
Louise Bourgeois created this spidery sculpture in 1994, at the age of 83. The elongated forms are typical of her work.

125-ft (38-m) tall cylindrical skylight

Second floor

Auditorium

First floor

Main entrance

Emergency staircase

KEY TO FLOOR PLAN

- Painting and sculpture
- Architecture and design
- Photography and works on paper
- Media arts
- Koret Visitor Education Center
- Special exhibitions
- Non-exhibition space

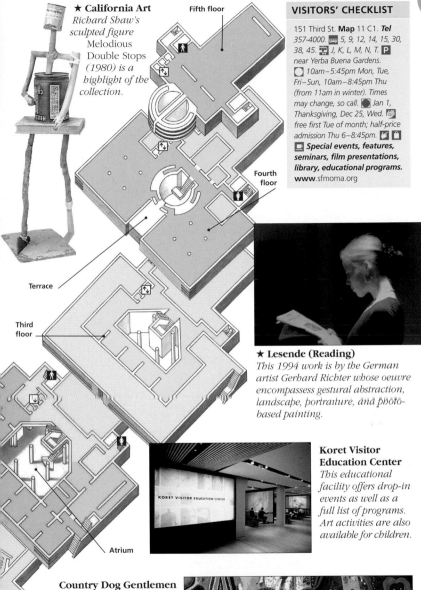

★ **California Art**
Richard Shaw's sculpted figure Melodious Double Stops *(1980) is a highlight of the collection.*

Fifth floor

Fourth floor

Terrace

Third floor

Atrium

VISITORS' CHECKLIST

151 Third St. **Map** 11 C1. **Tel** 357-4000. 5, 9, 12, 14, 15, 30, 38, 45. J, K, L, M, N, T. near Yerba Buena Gardens. 10am–5:45pm Mon, Tue, Fri–Sun, 10am–8:45pm Thu (from 11am in winter). Times may change, so call. Jan 1, Thanksgiving, Dec 25, Wed. free first Tue of month; half-price admission Thu 6–8:45pm. *Special events, features, seminars, film presentations, library, educational programs.* www.sfmoma.org

★ **Lesende (Reading)**
This 1994 work is by the German artist Gerhard Richter whose oeuvre encompasses gestural abstraction, landscape, portraiture, and photo-based painting.

Koret Visitor Education Center
This educational facility offers drop-in events as well as a full list of programs. Art activities are also available for children.

Country Dog Gentlemen
Bay Area artist Roy De Forest painted this fantasy of a universe guarded by animals in 1972.

STAR EXHIBITS

★ No14, 1960

★ California Art

★ Lesende (Reading)

Exploring the San Francisco Museum of Modern Art

The Museum of Modern Art is both an outstanding repository of modern and contemporary art and a powerhouse of inspiration and encouragement to the local art scene. With thousands of works by American artists, its strengths lie in the American Abstract Expressionist school, the art of California, and artists of the San Francisco Bay Area. However, it is also renowned for its international collection, particularly in the areas of Mexican painting, Fauvism and German Expressionism.

Stuart Davis, Marsden Hartley, Frida Kahlo, Wilfredo Lam, Georgia O'Keeffe, Rufino Tamayo and Joaquin Torres-Garcia. One of the museum's most powerful images is *The Flower Carrier*, a 1935 oil painting by Mexican artist Diego Rivera, who is celebrated for his murals *(see p140)*. Another exhibition area permanently shows works by Jasper Johns, Robert Rauschenberg and Andy Warhol, among others, from the Anderson Collection of American Pop Art.

There is a good collection of the European Modernists, including notable paintings by Jean Arp, Max Beckmann, Constantin Brancusi, Georges Braque, Andre Derain, Franz Marc and Pablo Picasso.

Large collections of works by Swiss-born Paul Klee, and the famous French painter of the Fauvist school, Henri Matisse, are accommodated in individual galleries. Henri Matisse's *Femme au Chapeau (Woman with a Hat)* is perhaps the museum's best known painting.

The survey of 20th-century art examines Surrealism, with works by Salvador Dali, Max Ernst and Yves Tanguy.

Women of Algiers (1955) by Pablo Picasso

PAINTINGS AND SCULPTURE

Included in the museum's permanent holdings are over 6,000 paintings, sculptures and works on paper. Major artists and schools of European, North American and Latin American art from the 20th century are represented. Paintings and sculpture from 1900 through to 1960 are in the second-floor galleries, while post-1960 contemporary painting, sculpture and works on paper are displayed on the fifth floor.

American Abstract Expressionism is well represented at the museum by Philip Guston, Willem de Kooning, Franz Kline, Joan Mitchell and Jackson Pollock, whose *Guardians of the Secret* is a masterpiece of the genre.

Separate galleries have been allocated for paintings by Clyfford Still, who in the mid-20th century served on the faculty of the California

School of Fine Arts, now the San Francisco Art Institute *(see p88)*. Clyfford Still donated 28 of his paintings to the museum in 1975.

Other prominent North and Latin American artists whose works are displayed in the museum collections include

92 Chaise (1992) by Holt Hinshaw Pfau Jones

ARCHITECTURE AND DESIGN

The Department of Architecture and Design was founded in 1983. Its function is to procure and maintain a collection of historical and contemporary architectural drawings, models and design objects, and to examine and illuminate their influences on modern art. Its current holding of over 4,000 items focuses on architecture, furniture, product design and graphic design.

Among items on display in the second-floor galleries are models, drawings, prints and prototypes by well-known and emerging designers. These include the famous architect Bernard Maybeck, who was responsible for some of the most beautiful buildings in the Bay Area, including the Palace of Fine Arts *(see pp60–61)*. Other noted San Francisco Bay Area architects represented are Timothy Pflueger, William Wurster, William Turnbull and Willis Polk, known for his design of the glass and steel Halladie Building *(see p45)*, as well as the California design team of Charles and Ray Eames.

Fumihiko Maki, Frank Lloyd Wright and Frank Gehry have all exhibited in the permanent collections. There are also regular, museum-sponsored programs in the Design Lecture Series and the Architectural Lecture Series.

Michael Jackson and Bubbles
(1988) by Jeff Koons

PHOTOGRAPHY

Drawing on its permanent collection of over 12,000 photographs, the museum presents a historical survey of the photographic arts. A rotating display of photographs is housed in the third-floor galleries. The collection of Modernist American masters includes Berenice Abbott, Walker Evans, Edward Steichen and Alfred Stieglitz, with special attention paid to California photographers Edward Weston, John Gutmann, Imogen Cunningham and Ansel Adams. There are also collections from Japan, Latin America and Europe, including German avant-garde photographers of the 1920s, and European Surrealists of the 1930s.

Graphite to Taste **(1989) by Gail Fredell**

MEDIA ARTS

The Department of Media Arts on the fourth floor was established in 1987. It collects, conserves, documents and exhibits art of the moving image, including works in video, film, projected image, electronic arts and time-based media. The galleries have state-of-the-art equipment to present photographic, multi-image and multimedia works, film, video and selected programs of interactive media artwork.

The museum's growing permanent collection includes pieces by accomplished artists such as Nam June Paik, Don Graham, Peter Campus, Joan Jonas, Bill Viola, Doug Hall and Mary Lucier.

CALIFORNIA ARTS

On the second and fifth floors there are works by California artists. These painters and sculptors have drawn their inspiration from local materials and scenes to create an influential body of art that is unique to the West Coast. Important Bay Area Figurative painters include Elmer Bishoff, Joan Brown and David Park, and there is a significant collection by Richard Diebenkorn.

Collage and assemblage artists exhibited from the museum's collection include Bruce Connor, William T. Wiley and Mission District resident Jess. The use of everyday materials such as felt-tip pen, junkyard scrap and old paintings, has produced art with a distinctive West Coast flavor.

CONTEMPORARY ART AND SPECIAL EXHIBITIONS

Gallery space on the third and fourth floors is reserved for special exhibitions. Included among these are displays of newly acquired gifts and purchases for the permanent collection, and around ten traveling exhibitions per year. An actively changing schedule of contemporary art exhibits supplements the museum's historical collection and does much to encourage today's art scene.

Cave, Tsankawee, Mexico **(1988) photographed by Linda Connor**

CIVIC CENTER

The administrative center of San Francisco has as its focal point the Civic Center Plaza. This includes some of the best architecture in the city. Its grand government buildings and palatial performing arts complex are the source of a great deal of local pride. The former City Hall was destroyed in the earthquake of 1906 (see pp28–9), creating an opportunity to build a civic center more in keeping with San Francisco's fast-emerging role as a major port. The challenge was taken up by "Sunny Jim" Rolph (see p29)

Reclining Nudes by Henry Moore outside the Louise M. Davies Symphony Hall

after he became mayor in 1911. He made the building of a new Civic Center a top priority, and the funding for the project was found in 1912. The buildings provide an outstanding example of the Beaux-Arts style (see p47), and in 1987 the whole area was declared an historic site. It is perhaps the most ambitious and elaborate city center complex in the US and well worth an extended visit. Fulton Street climbs gently to nearby Alamo Square where there are several fine late Victorian houses.

SIGHTS AT A GLANCE

Historic Streets and Buildings
Alamo Square ⑬
Bill Graham Civic Auditorium ②
City Hall ⑦
Cottage Row ⑪
University of San Francisco ⑭
Veterans Building ⑥

Shopping Area
Hayes Valley ⑫

Modern Architecture
Japan Center ⑩

Theaters and Concert Halls
Great American Music Hall ⑧
Louise M. Davies Symphony Hall ④
War Memorial Opera House ⑤

Museums and Galleries
Asian Art Museum ①
San Francisco Arts Commission Gallery ③

Churches
St. Mary's Cathedral ⑨

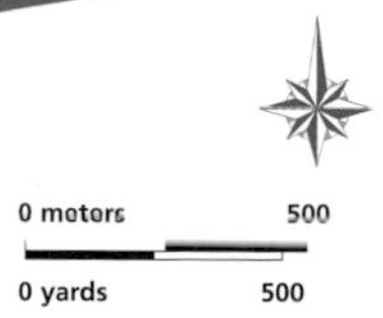

KEY

▪ Street-by-Street map
See pp124–5

🚇 BART station

🚃 Streetcar station

0 meters   500
0 yards   500

GETTING THERE

The Civic Center BART/Muni station on Market Street is two blocks east of City Hall. Buses 5, 19, 47 and 49 travel into the area. The immediate Civic Center district is best seen on foot, but take a car to visit outlying sights.

◁ View from Alamo Square across the Civic Center toward the city center

Street-by-Street: Civic Center

Simon Bolivar sculpture in UN Plaza

San Francisco's main public space is a triumph of planning and design. Its well-balanced Beaux Arts architecture *(see p47),* with the impressive dome of City Hall, is a tribute to San Francisco's energy in the years after the 1906 earthquake *(see pp28–9).* Construction started with the Civic Auditorium, completed in 1915 for the Pan–Pacific Exposition *(see p72).* This was followed by the City Hall, Library and War Memorial Arts complex.

The State Building, completed in 1986, was designed by Skidmore, Owings and Merrill. The building mirrors the curves of the Davies Symphony Hall, one block away.

Veterans Building
Home to the Herbst Theater and various veterans' associations. **6**

San Francisco Art Commission Gallery *is also here.* **3**

★ War Memorial Opera House
The distinguished San Francisco Opera and Ballet companies both perform in this elegant spot **5**

Louise M. Davies Symphony Hall
The San Francisco Symphony Orchestra, founded in 1911, is based here. Completed in 1981, to a design by Skidmore, Owings and Merrill, the hall has a grand lush interior **4**

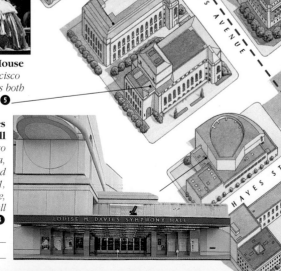

LOUISE M. DAVIES SYMPHONY HALL

MCALLISTER STREET

VAN NESS AVENUE

HAYES STR

KEY

- - - Suggested route

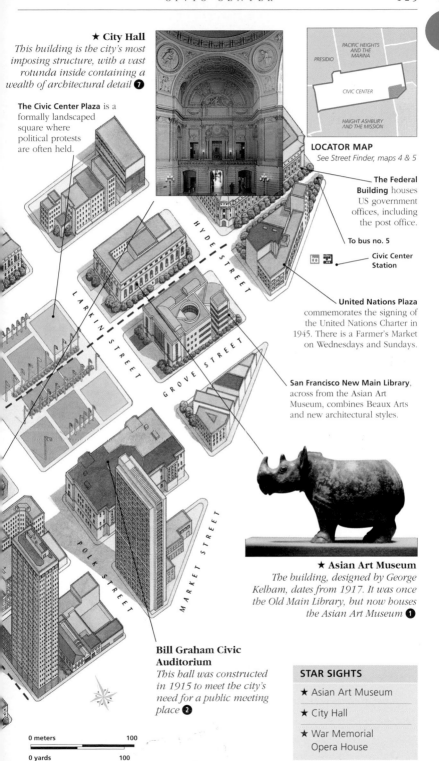

★ City Hall
This building is the city's most imposing structure, with a vast rotunda inside containing a wealth of architectural detail ❼

The Civic Center Plaza is a formally landscaped square where political protests are often held.

LOCATOR MAP
See Street Finder, maps 4 & 5

PACIFIC HEIGHTS AND THE MARINA

PRESIDIO

CIVIC CENTER

HAIGHT ASHBURY AND THE MISSION

The Federal Building houses US government offices, including the post office.

To bus no. 5

Civic Center Station

United Nations Plaza commemorates the signing of the United Nations Charter in 1945. There is a Farmer's Market on Wednesdays and Sundays.

San Francisco New Main Library, across from the Asian Art Museum, combines Beaux Arts and new architectural styles.

★ Asian Art Museum
The building, designed by George Kelham, dates from 1917. It was once the Old Main Library, but now houses the Asian Art Museum ❶

Bill Graham Civic Auditorium
This hall was constructed in 1915 to meet the city's need for a public meeting place ❷

0 meters 100
0 yards 100

STAR SIGHTS

★ Asian Art Museum

★ City Hall

★ War Memorial Opera House

Asian Art Museum ❶

200 Larkin St. **Map** 4 F5. **Tel** 581-3500. 🚌 5, 19, 21, 26, 47, 49. 🚋 F, J, K, L, M, N, T. ⏰ 10am–5pm Tue, Wed, Fri–Sun, 10am–9pm Thu. ⬤ Mon, public hols. 🎟 except first Tue of month. ♿ 🛍 ⬛ ▣
www.asianart.org

The Asian Art Museum is located on Civic Center Plaza across from City Hall in a building that was the crown jewel of the Beaux Arts movement in San Francisco. The former Main Library, built in 1917, underwent major renovation in 2001 to create the largest museum outside Asia devoted exclusively to Asian art.

The museum's holdings include more than 17,000 art objects spanning 6,000 years of history and representing cultures and countries throughout Asia. Among the exhibits is a gilt bronze Buddha, one of the oldest Chinese Buddhas in the world. There are also venues for performances and festivals, a library, a hands-on discovery center where families can explore Asian art and culture, and classrooms for educational programs.

The café's beautiful outdoor terrace overlooks the Civic Center and Fulton Street mall.

Grand staircase in the Asian Art Museum

Interior of San Francisco Art Commission Gallery

Bill Graham Civic Auditorium ❷

99 Grove St. **Map** 4 F5. **Tel** 974-4060. 🚌 5, 7, 19, 21, 26, 47, 49, 71. 🚋 J, K, L, M, N, T. ⬤ for performances.

Designed in Beaux Arts style (see pp46–7) by architect John Galen Howard to form a major part of the Panama-Pacific Exposition (see pp30–31), San Francisco's Civic Auditorium was opened in 1915, and since then has been one of the city's most prominent performance venues. It was inaugurated by the French pianist and composer Camille Saint Saens. The building was completed along with City Hall, in the course of the massive architectural renaissance that followed the disasters of 1906 (see pp28–9). It was built, together with the adjoining Brooks Exhibit Hall, beneath the Civic Center Plaza. The Civic Auditorium now serves as the city's main conference center, and has the capacity to seat 7,000 people. In 1992 its name was changed in honor of the legendary Bill Graham (see p129), the local rock music impresario who was a pivitol figure in both the development and promotion of the city's trademark psychedelic sound.

San Francisco Art Commission Gallery ❸

401 Van Ness Ave. **Map** 4 F5. 🎫 554-6080. 🚌 5, 19, 21, 26, 47, 49. 🚋 J, K, L, M, N, T. ⏰ noon–5pm Wed–Sat. (call for late opening hours). ♿
www.sfacgallery.org

Located in the Veterans Building (see p127), this dynamic art gallery shows paintings, sculptures, and multimedia works produced by local artists. The gallery's previous location is now View 155, an annex gallery south-east of the main gallery at 155 Grove Street between Polk and Van Ness.

Louise M. Davies Symphony Hall

Louise M. Davies Symphony Hall ❹

201 Van Ness Ave. **Map** 4 F5. **Tel** 552-8000. 🚌 21, 26, 47, 49. 🚋 J, K, L, M, N, T. ♿ 🎫 552-8338. **www**.sfsymphony.org
See **Entertainment** p264.

Loved and loathed in equal measure by the citizens of San Francisco, this curving, glass-fronted concert hall was constructed in 1980 – the creation of architects Skidmore, Owings and Merrill. The ultramodern hall is named for the prominent philanthropist who donated $5 million of the $35 million construction cost. It is home to the San Francisco Symphony Orchestra and also welcomes many visiting artists.

The acoustics of the building were disappointing when it was first opened, but after ten years of negotiations a new sound system has been installed. The interior was also redesigned, and the walls were resculpted to reflect sound better. These measures improved the acoustics.

Front entrance of War Memorial Opera House, built in 1932

War Memorial Opera House ➎

301 Van Ness Ave. **Map** 4 F5. **Tel** 621-6600. 🚌 5, 21, 47, 49. 🚈 J, K, L, M, N, T. 🅾️ except during performances. 🚻 🎫 call 552-8338. **www**.sfwmpac.org

Opened in 1932, the War Memorial Opera House, designed by Arthur Brown, was dedicated to the memory of World War I soldiers. In 1951 it was used for the signing of the peace treaty between the US and Japan, marking the formal end of World War II. The building is now home to the San Francisco Opera (see p264).

Veterans Building ➏

401 Van Ness Ave. **Map** 4 F5. **Tel** 621-6600; **Herbst Theater** 392-4400. 🚌 5, 19, 21, 47, 49. 🚈 J, K, L, M, N, T. 🅾️ 8am–5pm Mon–Fri. 🅾️ except during performances. 🚻 limited. 🎫 call 552-8338. **www**.sfwmpac.org

Like its almost identical twin, the War Memorial Opera House, the multipurpose Veteran's Building was designed by Arthur Brown and built in 1932 to honor World War I soldiers. In addition to displays of historic weapons, there are showcases of military memorabilia. The building is also home to the Herbst Theater, a 928-seat concert hall and theater. Because of its good acoustics, many classical music recitals are held here regularly. The theater was the site of the signing of the United Nations Charter in 1945.

City Hall ➐

400 Van Ness Ave. **Map** 4 F5. **Tel** 554-4000. 🚌 5, 8, 19, 21, 26, 47, 49. 🚈 J, K, L, M, N, T. 🅾️ 8am–8pm Mon–Fri. 🅾️ 🚻 🎫 call 554-6023. **www**.sfgov.org

City Hall, completed in 1915, just in time for the Panama–Pacific Exposition (see pp30–31), was designed by Arthur Brown when he was at the height of his career. The original building was completely destroyed in the 1906 Earthquake. Its Grand Baroque dome was modeled on St. Peter's Church in Rome and is higher than the US Capitol in Washington, DC. The upper levels of the dome are accessible to the public.

The restored building is at the center of the Civic Center complex and is a magnificent example of the Beaux Arts style (see p47).

There are allegorical figures evoking the city's Gold Rush past in the pediment above the main Polk Street entrance. This entrance leads into the marble floored Rotunda.

Great American Music Hall ➑

859 O'Farrell St. **Map** 4 F4. **Tel** 885-0750. 🚌 19, 38, 47, 49. **www**.musichallsf.com

Built in 1907 as a place for bawdy comedy shows, the Great American Music Hall was soon in use as a brothel. Since then, it has become an excellent performance space, with a rich interior containing tall marble columns and elaborate balconies, adorned with ornate gilt plasterwork.

Sign over Great American Music Hall

The venue is intimate, stylish and known throughout the US, and famous artists such as Carmen McCrae, BB King, Duke Ellington, the Grateful Dead, Van Morrison and Tom Paxton have played every kind of music here, from blues, jazz, and folk to rock 'n' roll. The views here are good from almost every table.

The imposing façade of the Beax Arts style City Hall in the heart of the Civic Center of San Francisco

The altar in St. Mary's Cathedral

St. Mary's Cathedral ❾

1111 Gough St. **Map** 4 E4. **Tel** 567-2020. 🚌 38. ⬭ 8:30am–4:30pm Mon–Fri, 9am–6:30pm Sat, Sun. ✝ 5:30am (Sat only), 6:45am, 8am, 12:10pm Mon–Sat; 7:30am, 9am, 11am, 1pm, Sun. 🚫 during services. 📷 ♿ www.stmarycathedralsf.org

Situated at the top of Cathedral Hill, the ultra-modern St. Mary's is one of the city's most prominent architectural landmarks. Designed by architect Pietro Belluschi and engineer Pier Luigi Nervi, it was completed in 1971.

The four-part arching para-boloid roof stands out like a white-sailed ship on the horizon, though critics say it resembles a giant food mixer. The 200-ft-high (60-m) concrete structure, which supports a cross-shaped stained-glass ceiling representing the four elements, seems to hover effortlessly over the 2,500-seat nave. A sunburst canopy made of aluminum rods sparkles above the plain stone altar.

Japan Center ❿

Post St and Buchanan St. **Map** 4 E4. **Tel** 922-6776. 🚌 2, 3, 4, 38. ⬭ 10am–6pm daily.

The Japan Center was built as part of an ambitious 1960s scheme to revitalize the Fillmore District. Blocks of aging Victorian houses were demolished and replaced by the Geary Expressway and the large shopping complex of the Japan Center. At the heart of the complex, and centered upon a five-tiered, 75-ft (22-m) concrete pagoda,

is the remodeled Peace Pagoda Garden. Taiko drummers and others perform here at the annual Cherry Blossom festival each April (see p48). Both sides of the Garden are lined with Japanese shops, restaurants, and the eight-screen AMC Kabuki (see p262). This neighborhood has been the heart of the Japanese community for over 75 years. More authentic Japanese shops are on Post Street, where there are twin steel sculptures by Ruth Asawa.

Cottage Row ⓫

Map 4 D4. 🚌 2, 3, 4, 22, 38.

One of the few surviving remnants of working-class Victorian San Francisco, this short stretch of flat-fronted cottages was built in 1882, at the end of the Pacific Heights building boom. Unusual for San Francisco, the cottages share dividing walls, like terraced houses in Europe or on the East Coast of America. Their utter lack of ornament, and their siting on what was a dark and crowded back alley,

Japan Center by night

emphasize their lower-class status. The Cottage Row houses were saved from destruction during the process of slum clearance in the 1960s. A pro-gram organized by Justin Herman awarded grants to help people restore their existing houses, rather than replace them. All but one of the houses have now been restored, and they face a small attractive city park.

Cottage Row

Hayes Valley ⓬

Map 4 E5. 🚌 21, 22.

Just west of City Hall, these few blocks of Hayes Street became one of San Francisco's trendier shopping districts after US 101 highway was damaged in the 1989 earthquake (see p18). The road was then torn down, having previously cut Hayes Valley off from the wealthy power brokers and theatergoers of the Civic Center. A few of the local cafés and restaurants, like Hayes Street Grill and Mad Magda's Russian Tea Room, had already mixed in with the Hayes Street secondhand furniture and thrift shops. The influx of expensive art galler-ies, interior design shops and clothing boutiques has made the area noticeably more upscale.

Alamo Square ⑬

Map 4 D5. 🚌 21, 22.

San Francisco's most photo-graphed row of colorful Victorian houses lines the eastern side of this sloping green square, which is some 225 ft (68 m) above the Civic Center, giving grand views of City Hall backed by the Financial District skyscrapers. The square was laid out at the same time as the pair of Pacific Heights squares *(see pp72–3)*, but it developed later and much more quickly, with speculators building large numbers of nearly identical houses.

The "Six Sisters" Queen Anne-style houses *(see p77)* built in 1895 at 710–20 Steiner Street are good examples. They appear on many San Francisco postcards. So many grand old Victorian houses line the streets around Alamo Square that the area has been declared an historic district.

St. Ignatius Church on the University of San Francisco campus

University of San Francisco ⑭

2130 Fulton St. **Map** 3 B5. *Tel* 422-5555. 🚌 5, 31, 33, 38, 43. www.usfca.edu

Founded in 1855 as St. Ignatius College, the University of San Francisco (USF) is still a Jesuit-run institution, though classes are now coeducational and non-denominational. The landmark of the campus is St. Ignatius Church, completed in 1914. Its buff-colored twin towers are visible from all over the western half of San Francisco, especially when lit up at night. The university campus and residential neighborhood that surrounds it occupy land that historically formed San Francisco's main cemetery district, on and around Lone Mountain.

THE SOUNDS OF 1960S SAN FRANCISCO

During the Flower Power years of the late 1960s, and most notably during the 1967 Summer of Love *(see p32)*, young people from all over the US flocked to San Francisco. They came not just to "turn on, tune in and drop out," but also to listen to music. Bands such as Janis Joplin's Big Brother and the Holding Company, Jefferson Airplane and the Grateful Dead emerged out

Hippies lounging on a psychedelic bus

of a thriving music scene. They were nurtured at clubs like the Avalon Ballroom and the Fillmore Auditorium.

Premier music venues

The Avalon Ballroom, now the Regency II theater on Van Ness Avenue, was the first and most significant rock venue. Run by Chet Helms and the Family Dog collective, the Avalon pioneered the use of colorful psychedelic posters by designers such as Stanley Mouse and Alton Kelly.

Fillmore Auditorium, facing the Japan Center *(see p128)*, used to be a church hall. In

1965 it was taken over by rock impresario Bill Graham, after whom the Civic Auditorium *(see p126)* is named. Graham put such unlikely pairs as Miles Davis and the Grateful Dead on the same bill, and brought in big-name performers from Jimi Hendrix to The Who. The Fillmore was damaged in the 1989 earthquake but reopened in 1994.

Bill Graham also opened the Winterland and the Fillmore East, and by the time he died in 1992 had become the most successful rock music promoter in the US.

Janis Joplin (1943–70), hard-edged blues singer

HAIGHT ASHBURY AND THE MISSION

To the north of Twin Peaks – two windswept hills rising 900 ft (274 m) above the city – lies Haight Ashbury. With its rows of beautiful late Victorian houses *(see pp76–7)*, it is mostly inhabited by the wealthy middle classes, although this is where thousands of hippies lived in the 1960s *(see p129)*. The Castro

Figure from Mission Dolores

District, to the east, is the center of San Francisco's gay community. Well known for its wild hedonism in the 1970s, the area has become quieter in recent years, although its cafés and shops are still lively. The Mission District, farther east still, was originally settled by Spanish monks *(see p22)* and is home to many Hispanics.

SIGHTS AT A GLANCE

Historic Streets and Buildings
Castro Street ❽
Clarke's Folly ❿
Dolores Street ❿
Haight Ashbury ❷
Lower Haight
　Neighborhood ❺
Noe Valley ⓮
(Richard) Spreckels
　Mansion ❸

Churches
Mission
　Dolores ❾

Landmarks
Sutro Tower ⓲

Parks and Gardens
Buena Vista Park ❹
Corona Heights Park ❻
Dolores Park ⓫
Golden Gate Park
　Panhandle ❶
Twin Peaks ⓰
Vulcan Street Steps ⓱

Museums and Galleries
Carnaval Mural ⓭
Mission Cultural Center for
　the Latino Arts ⓬

Theaters
Castro Theatre ❼

KEY

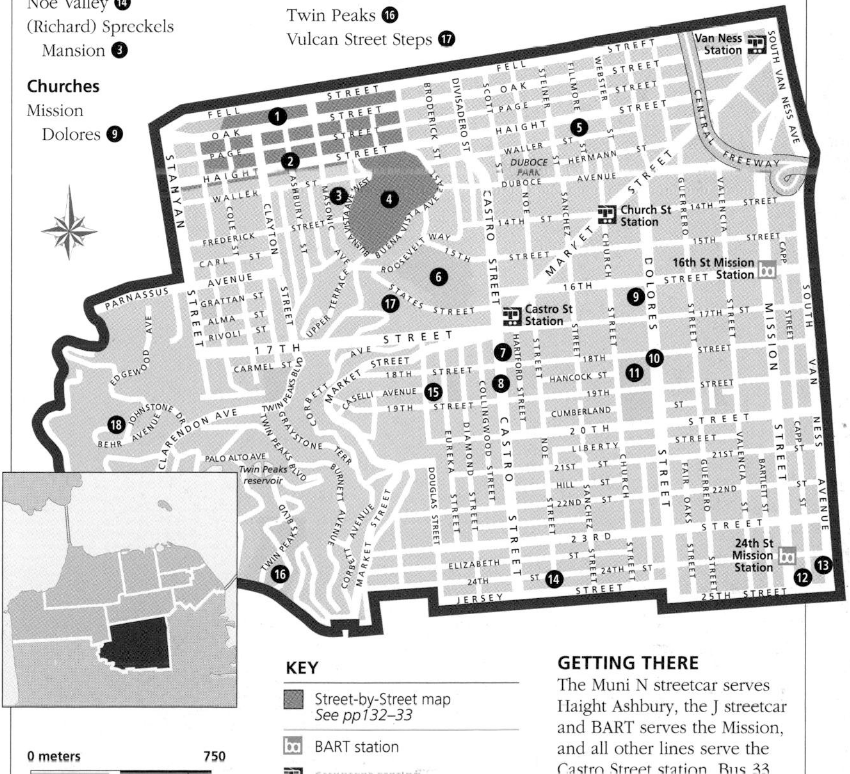

▨ Street-by-Street map
　See pp132–33

🅱 BART station

🚉 Streetcar station

0 meters　　　750
0 yards　　　750

GETTING THERE

The Muni N streetcar serves Haight Ashbury, the J streetcar and BART serves the Mission, and all other lines serve the Castro Street station. Bus 33 links all three neighborhoods.

◁ **Street scene in Haight Ashbury**

Street-by-Street: Haight Ashbury

HAIGHT ASHBURY FREE MEDICAL CLINIC

Plaque outside the Free Clinic

Stretching from Buena Vista Park to the flat expanses of Golden Gate Park, in the 1880s Haight Ashbury was a place to escape to from the city center. It developed into a residential area, but between the 1930s and '60s changed dramatically from middle-class suburb to center of the "Flower Power" world, with a free clinic to treat hippies. It is now one of the liveliest and most unconventional places in San Francisco, with an eclectic mix of people, excellent book and record stores, and good cafés.

Haight Ashbury
In the 1960s hippies congregated at this major intersection, from which the area takes its name ❷

Wasteland, at 1660 Haight Street, is an anarchic used clothing, curio and furniture emporium housed in a colorful painted Art Nouveau building. Bargain hunters will find plenty to delight them in this unconventional store.

Golden Gate Panhandle
This thin green strip runs west into the heart of Golden Gate Park ❶

To bus nos. 7, 33

0 meters   100

0 yards   100

Cha Cha Cha is one of the liveliest places to eat in San Francisco, serving Latin American food in a variety of small dishes *(see p236)*.

The Red Victorian Bed and Breakfast, a relic of the hippie 1960s, caters to a New Age clientèle with health food and rooms with transcendental themes *(see p218)*.

No. 1220 Masonic Avenue is one of many ornate Victorian mansions built on a steep hill to the south of Haight Street.

LOCATOR MAP
See Street Finder, map 9

★ **(Richard) Spreckels Mansion**
This grand home at No.737 Buena Vista Avenue was built in 1897 ❸

STAR SIGHTS

★ (Richard) Spreckels Mansion

★ Buena Vista Park

★ **Buena Vista Park**
Through its mass of twisting trees growing closely together, this dramatic park offers magnificent views over the city ❹

KEY

– – – Suggested route

To bus no. 37

Golden Gate Park Panhandle ❶

Map 9 C1. 6, 7, 21, 43, 66, 71. N.

This one-block-wide, eight-block-long stretch of parkland forms the narrow "Panhandle" to the giant rectangular pan that is Golden Gate Park (see pp142–55). It was the first part of the park to be reclaimed from the sand dunes that rolled across west San Francisco, and its stately eucalyptus trees are among the oldest and largest in the city. The Panhandle's winding carriage roads and bridle paths were first laid out in the 1870s, and the upper classes came here to walk and ride. They built large mansions on the outskirts of the park; many can still be seen today. In 1906 the Panhandle was a refuge for families made homeless by the earthquake

Guitar hero Jimi Hendrix in concert

(see pp28–9). Today the old roads and paths are used regularly by large crowds of joggers and bicyclists.

The Panhandle is still remembered for its "Flower Power" heyday of the 1960s (see p129), when bands gave impromptu concerts here.

Haight Ashbury ❷

Map 9 C1. 6, 7, 33, 37, 43, 66, 71. N.

Taking its name from the junction of two main streets, Haight and Ashbury, this district contains independent bookstores, large Victorian houses, cafés, and hip clothing boutiques. Following the reclamation of Golden Gate Park (see p146) and the opening of a large amusement park called The Chutes, the area was rapidly built up in the 1890s as a middle-class suburb – hence the dozens of elaborate Queen Anne-style houses

(see p77) lining its streets. The Haight survived the 1906 earthquake and fire (see pp28–9), and experienced a brief boom, followed by a long period of decline.

After the streetcar tunnel under Buena Vista Park was completed in 1928, the middle classes began their exodus to the suburbs in the Sunset. The area reached its lowest ebb in the years after World War II. The big Victorian houses were divided into apartments and the low rents attracted a mixed population. By the 1960s the Haight had become host to a bohemian community that was a hotbed of anarchy. A component of this "hippie scene" was the music of rock bands such as the Grateful Dead, but the area stayed quiet until 1967. Then the media-fueled "Summer of Love" (see p129) brought some 75,000 young people in search of free love, music and drugs, and the area became the focus of a worldwide youth culture.

Today, the Haight retains its anti-establishment atmosphere, but there are problems of crime, drug abuse and homelessness. However, from the congenial cafés to the second-hand clothing shops, you will still find the aura of the past here.

Mansion built for Richard Spreckels

(Richard) Spreckels Mansion ❸

737 Buena Vista West. **Map** 9 C2. 6, 7, 37, 43, 66, 71. ● to the public.

This house should not be confused with the larger and grander Spreckels Mansion on Washington Street (see p72). It was, however, also built by the millionaire "Sugar King" Claus Spreckels, for his nephew Richard. The elaborate Queen Anne-style house (see p77), built in 1897, is a typical late-Victorian Haight Ashbury home. It was once a recording studio, and later a guest house, but is now in private hands. Guests have included the acerbic journalist and ghost-story writer Ambrose Bierce, and the adventure writer Jack London, who wrote White Fang here in 1906.

The mansion is situated on a hill near Buena Vista Park. Rows of Victorian houses, many of them well preserved and some palatial, are nearby. One of these, a block away at 1450 Masonic Street, is an onion-domed house, one of the most unusual of the many eccentric mansions built in the Haight since the 1890s.

The Cha Cha Cha restaurant on Haight Street

Buena Vista Park ❹

Map 9 C1. 🚌 6, 7, 37, 43, 66, 71.

Buena Vista Park rises steeply, 569 ft (18 m) above the geographical center of San Francisco. First landscaped in 1894, it is a pocket of land left to nature. A network of paths winds up from Haight Street to the crest, where densely planted trees frame views of the Bay Area. Many of the trails are overgrown and eroded, but there is a paved route up to the summit from Buena Vista Avenue. It is best to avoid the park at night.

Lower Haight Neighborhood ❺

Map 10 D1. 🚌 6, 7, 22, 66, 71. 🚋 K, L, M, N, T.

Halfway between City Hall and Haight Ashbury, and marking the southern border of the Fillmore District, the Lower Haight is an area in transition. Unusual art galleries and boutiques, including the Used Rubber USA shop, which sells clothes and accessories made entirely of recycled rubber, began to open here in the mid-1980s. These were in addition to the inexpensive cafés, bars and restaurants serving a bohemian clientèle that were already in business in the area. This combination has created one of the most lively districts in San Francisco.

As in nearby Alamo Square (see p129), the Lower Haight holds dozens of houses known

LEVI STRAUSS AND HIS JEANS

First manufactured in San Francisco in the days of the Gold Rush *(see pp24–5)*, denim jeans have had a great impact on popular culture. One of the leading producers of jeans is Levi Strauss & Co., founded in the city in the 1860s. The company's story started in

1853, when Levi Strauss left New York to set up a branch of his family's cloth firm in San Francisco.

Levi Strauss

In the 1860s, though still primarily a seller of cloth, he pioneered the use of durable blue canvas to make workpants, sold directly to miners. In the 1870s his company began to use metal rivets to strengthen stress points in the garments, and demand increased. The company expanded, and early in the 20th century moved to 250 Valencia Street in the Mission District, where it remained until 2002. Levi's jeans are now produced and worn all over the world, and the company that was founded by Levi Strauss is still owned by his descendants.

Two miners wearing Levis at the Last Chance Mine in 1882

as "Victorians" *(see pp76–7)*, built from the 1850s to the early 1900s. These include many picturesque cottages such as the Nightingale House at 201 Buchanan Street, built in the 1880s.

But public housing projects from the 1950s have discouraged wholesale gentrification. The area is safe during the day, but like Alamo Square, it can seem quite threatening after dark.

Corona Heights and Randall Museum ❻

Map 9 D2. *Tel* 554-9600. 🚌 24, 37. **Randall Museum Animal Room** 199 Museum Way. 🕐 10am–5pm Tue–Sat. 🌑 public hols. 👶 limited. **www**.randallmuseum.org

Corona Heights Park is a dusty and undeveloped rocky peak. Clinging to its side is an unusual museum for children. The Randall Museum Animal Room has an extensive menagerie of raccoons, owls, snakes and other animals. The emphasis of the museum is on participation, and there are many hands-on exhibits and workshops.

Children can also enjoy climbing on the craggy outcrops in the park. Corona Heights was gouged out by brick-making operations in the 19th century. It was never planted with trees, so its bare red-rock peak offers an unimpeded panorama over the city and East Bay, including the winding streets of Twin Peaks.

View from Corona Heights across the Mission

Castro Theatre ❼

429 Castro St. **Map** 10 D2. *Tel 621-6120.* ▥ *24, 33, 35, 37.* ▦ *F, K, L, M, T. See* **Entertainment** *p240.* **www**.*thecastrotheatre.com*

Completed in 1922, this brightly lit neon marquee is a Castro Street land-mark. It is the most sumptuous and best preserved of San Francisco's neighborhood film palaces, and one of the first commissions of the architect Timothy Pflueger. With its lavish, Arabian Nights interior, complete with a glorious Wurlitzer organ that rises from the floor between screenings, it is well worth the price of admission. The ceiling of the auditorium is particularly noteworthy; it is cast in plaster and resembles the interior of a large tent, with imitation swathes of material, rope and tassels. The theater seats 1,500 and shows mainly revival classics. It also hosts the Gay and Lesbian Film Festival, held each June *(see p49).*

The historic Castro Theatre

Castro Street ❽

Map 10 D2. ▥ *24, 33, 35, 37.* ▦ *F, K, L, M, T.*

The hilly neighborhood around Castro Street between Twin Peaks and the Mission District is the heart of San Francisco's high-profile gay and lesbian community. Focused on the intersection of Castro Street and 18th Street,

the self-proclaimed "Gayest Four Corners of the World" emerged as a homosexual nexus during the 1970s. Gays of the Flower Power generation moved into this predominantly working-class district and began restoring Victorian houses and setting up such businesses as the bookstore A Different Light, at 489 Castro Street. They also opened such gay bars as the Twin Peaks on the corner of Castro Street and 17th Street. Unlike earlier bars, where lesbians and gays hid in dark corners out of public view, the Twin Peaks installed large windows. Though the many shops and restaurants attract all kinds of people, the Castro's openly

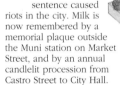

View down Castro Street

homosexual identity has made it a place of pilgrimage for gays and lesbians. It symbol-izes for this minority group a freedom not generally found in cities elsewhere.

The city's first prominent and openly gay politician, Harvey Milk, was known as the Mayor of Castro Street before he was assassinated on November 28, 1978. He and Mayor George Moscone were killed by an ex-policeman, whose lenient sentence caused riots in the city. Milk is now remembered by a memorial plaque outside the Muni station on Market Street, and by an annual candlelit procession from Castro Street to City Hall.

The AIDS Memorial Quilt on display in Washington in 1992

THE NAMES PROJECT

The NAMES Project's AIDS Memorial Quilt was conceived by San Francisco gay rights activist Cleve Jones, who organized the first candlelit procession on Castro Street for Harvey Milk in 1985. Jones and his fellow marchers wrote the names of all their friends who had died of AIDS on placards, which they then taped to the San Francisco Federal Building. The resulting "patchwork quilt" of names inspired Jones to create the first panel for the AIDS Memorial Quilt in 1987. Public response to the quilt was immediate – both in the US and across the world. It is now made up of over 60,000 panels, some sewn by individuals and others by "quilting bees" – friends and relatives who have come together to commemorate a person lost to AIDS. All panels are the same size – 3 by 6 ft (90 by 180 cm) – but each is different: the design, colors, and material reflect the life and personality of the person commemorated. In 2002 the Memorial Quilt moved from its base in San Francisco to permanent headquarters in Atlanta, Georgia.

Mission Dolores ❾

16th St and Dolores St. **Map** 10 E2.
📞 621-8203. 🚌 22. 🚃 J. ☐ 8am–
noon daily, 1–4pm Mon–Fri. 🌀
Thanksgiving, Dec 25.
📷 📵 ♿ 🚻 **www**.
missiondolores.org

Preserved intact since
it was built in 1791,
Mission Dolores is the
oldest building in the
city and an embodiment
of San Francisco's
religious Spanish colonial
roots *(see pp22–3)*. The
mission was founded by a
Franciscan monk, Father
Junipero Serra, and is
formally known as the
Mission of San Francisco
de Asis. The name
Dolores reflects its
proximity to Laguna de

**Figure of saint
in the Mission
Dolores**

los Dolores (Lake of Our
Lady of Sorrows). The building is modest by mission
standards, but its 4-ft-thick
(1.2-m) walls have
survived the years
without serious decay.
Paintings by American
Indians adorn the
ceiling, which has
been restored.
There is a fine
Baroque altar and
reredos, as well
as a display of
historical docu-
ments in the
small museum
(see p39). Most
services are held in
the basilica, which
was built next to
the original
mission in 1918.
The white-walled

cemetery contains graves of
prominent San Franciscans
from pioneering days. A
statue marking the mass
grave of 5,000 Indians, most
of whom died in the great
measles epidemics of 1804
and 1826, was stolen; all that
remains is a pedestal reading
"In Prayerful Memory of our
Faithful Indians." The famous
graveyard scene in Hitchcock's
Vertigo was filmed here.

**The Statue of Father Junipero
Serra**, founder of the mission, is
a copy of the work of local
sculptor Arthur Putnam.

The ceramic mural was created
by Guillermo Granizo, a
native San Francisco artist.

Museum and
display

**The painted and gilded
altarpiece** was imported from
Mexico in 1780.

The ceiling paintings
are based on original
Ohlone designs using
vegetable dyes.

Entrance for
the disabled

The mission cemetery
originally extended
across many streets.
The earliest wooden
grave markers have
disintegrated, but the
Lourdes Grotto
commemorates the
forgotten dead.

**Statue of Our Lady of
Mount Carmel**

**The front of
the mission**
has four columns
that support niches
for three bells. The
bells are inscribed
with their names
and dates.

Entrance and
gift shop

Sculpture commemorating soldiers in the Spanish–American War

Dolores Street ⑩

Map 10 E2. 🚌 22, 33, 48. 🚊 J.

Lined by lovingly maintained late-Victorian houses *(see pp76–7)* and divided by an island of palm trees, Dolores Street is one of San Francisco's most attractive public spaces. The broad straight boulevard runs for 24 blocks, parallel to Mission Street, forming the western border of the Mission District. It starts at Market Street, where a statue in honor of Spanish–American War soldiers is overwhelmed by the hulking US Mint.

The Mission High School, with the characteristic white walls and red tile roof of Mission-style architecture, is on Dolores Street, as is the historic Mission Dolores *(see p137)*. The street ends near prosperous Noe Valley.

Dolores Park ⑪

Map 10 E3. 🚌 22, 33. 🚊 J.

Originally the site of the city's main Jewish cemetery, Dolores Park transformed in 1905 into one of the Mission District's few large open spaces.

Bounded by Dolores, Church, 18th and 20th streets, it is situated high on a hill with a good view of the city center.

Dolores Park is popular during the day with tennis players, sunbathers and dog walkers, but after dark can draw drug dealers. Above the park to the south and west, the streets rise so steeply that many turn into pedestrian-only stairways. Here are some of the city's finest Victorian houses, especially on Liberty Street.

Mission Cultural Center for the Latino Arts ⑫

2868 Mission St. **Map** 10 F4. **Tel** 821-1155 (Events Hotline: 643-5001). 🚌 14, 26, 48, 49. 🚊 J. **Gallery** ⬚ 10am–4pm Tue–Sat. ♿ **www**.mission culturalcenter.org

This dynamic arts center caters for the Latino population of the Mission District. It offers classes and workshops to people of all ages, and stages theatrical events and exhibitions. Chief among these is the parade held in November to celebrate the Day of the Dead *(see p50)*.

Carnaval Mural ⑬

24th St and South Van Ness Ave. **Map** 10 F4. 🚌 12, 14, 48, 49, 67. 🚊 J.

One of the many brightly painted murals to be seen on walls in the Mission District, the *Carnaval Mural* celebrates the diverse people who come together for the Carnaval

festival *(see p48)*. This event, held annually in late spring, is the high spot of the year.

Guided tours of other murals, some with political themes, are given by civic organizations *(see p257)*. There is also an outdoor gallery with murals in Balmy Alley *(see pp140–41)*, near Treat and Harrison streets.

Noe Valley Ministry

Noe Valley ⑭

🚌 24, 35, 48. 🚊 J.

Noe valley is known as "Noewhere Valley" by its residents, who are intent on keeping it off the tourist map. It is a comfortable neighborhood mainly inhabited by young professionals. Named after its original land-grant owner, José Noe, the last *alcalde* (mayor) of Mexican Yerba Buena, the area was first developed in the 1880s following the completion of a cable car line over the steep Castro Street hill. Like many other areas of San Francisco, this once working-class district underwent wholesale gentrification in the 1970s, resulting in today's engaging mix of boutiques, bars and restaurants. The Noe Valley Ministry, at 1021 Sanchez Street, is a late 1880s Presbyterian church in the "Stick Style" *(see p77)*, with emphasis on vertical lines. It was converted into a community center in the 1970s.

Detail from the *Carnaval Mural*

Clarke's Folly **⑮**

250 Douglass St. **Map** 10 D3. 🚌 33, 35, 37, 48. ⬤ to the public.

This resplendent white manor house was originally surrounded by extensive grounds. It was built in 1892 by Alfred Clarke, known as Nobby, who worked in the San Francisco Police Department at the time of the Committee of Vigilance (see pp26–7). The house is said to have cost $100,000, a huge sum in the 1890s. Now divided into private apartments, its turrets and other features make it an evocative example of Victorian-era domestic architecture.

Twin Peaks **⑯**

Map 9 C4. 🚌 33, 36, 37.

These two hills were first known in Spanish as El Pecho de la Chola, the "Bosom of the Indian Girl." At the top there is an area of parkland with steep and grassy slopes, from which you can enjoy incomparable views of the whole of San Francisco.

Twin Peaks Boulevard circles both hills near their summits, and there is a parking and viewing point from which to look out over the city. Those who are prepared to climb up the steep footpath to the very top can leave the crowds behind and get a 360° view. The residential districts on the slopes lower

View of the city and of Twin Peaks Boulevard from top of Twin Peaks

down have curving streets that wind around the contours of the slopes, rather than the formal grid that is more common in San Francisco.

Vulcan Street Steps **⑰**

Vulcan St. **Map** 9 C2. 🚌 37.

Apart from a tiny figure of Spock standing on a mailbox, there is no connection between the popular television program Star Trek and this block of almost rural houses climbing between Ord Street and Levant Street. Like the Filbert Steps on Telegraph Hill (see p93), however, Vulcan Steps does feel light years away from the busy streets of the Castro District below. The small vegetable and flower gardens of the houses spill out and soften the edges of the steps, and a canopy of pines muffles the city sounds. There are grand views of the Mission District and beyond.

Sutro Tower **⑱**

Map 9 B3. 🚌 36, 37. ⬤ to the public.

Marking the skyline like an invading robot, Sutro Tower is 970 ft (290 m) high. It was named after the local philanthropist and landowner Adolph Sutro, and it carries antennae for the signals of most of San Francisco's TV and radio stations. Built in 1973, it is still much used, despite the rise of cable networks. The tower is visible from all over the Bay Area, and sometimes seems to float above the summer fogs that roll in from the sea. On the north side of the tower there are dense eucalyptus groves, first planted in the 1880s by Adolph

Sutro Tower

Sutro. They drop down to the medical center campus of the University of California at San Francisco, one of the most highly rated teaching hospitals in the United States.

Nobby Clarke's Folly

San Francisco's Murals

San Francisco is proud of its reputation as a culturally rich and cosmopolitan city, qualities evident in the vivid elaborate murals that decorate walls and fences in several areas of the city. Many were painted in the 1930s, and many more in the 1970s, with some appearing spontaneously while others were commissioned. One of the best is the *Carnaval Mural* on 24th Street in the Mission District *(see p138)*; further examples are shown here.

Mural at Balmy Alley

503 Law Office at Dolores and 18th streets

PAST AND PRESENT

Some of the best examples of San Francisco's historical mural art can be found inside Coit Tower, where a series of panels, funded during the Great Depression of the 1930s by President Roosevelt's New Deal program, is typical of the period. Many local artists participated in creating the work, and themes include the struggles of the working class and the rich resources of California. The city has since been decorated with a number of modern murals, most notably by the Precita Eyes Mural Arts Studio.

Detail from Coit Tower mural focuses on California's rich resources

Coit Tower mural showing life during the Depression years

Precita Eyes Mural Arts Association *is a community-based organization that seeks to promote the mural arts through collaborative projects. They also sponsor new murals by established artists and run lively mural tours around San Francisco.*

Mosaic mural (2007) by Precita Eyes, Hillcrest school

Balloon Journey, Precita Eyes

This mural *was designed and painted by AYPAL (Asian Pacific Islander Youth Promoting Advocacy and Leadership) students in 2007, in association with Precita Eyes. The organization runs a number of community and youth workshops, which produce between 15 and 30 new murals every year. Visitors can see examples of these throughout the Bay Area.*

Stop the Violence at 1212 Broadway #400, Oakland

LIFE TODAY

Life in the modern metropolis is one of the major themes of mural art in San Francisco, as much now as it was in the 1930s. In the Mission District particularly, every aspect of daily life is illustrated on the walls of banks, schools and restaurants, with lively scenes of the family, community, political activity and people at work and play. The Mission District contains around 200 murals, many painted in the 1970s, as part of a city program that paid young people to create works of art in public places. The San Francisco Arts Commission continues to foster this art form.

Golden Gate Bridge

Palace of Fine Arts

Cable car

BART

Tourists

This Balmy Alley mural *is a view of the city as tourists see it. The alley, in the Mission District, is decorated with numerous vivid murals, first painted by local children, artists and community workers in the 1970s. The works are now a major attraction.*

The Learning Wall, Franklin St., depicts education and art

Positively Fourth Street, a weathered mural at Fort Mason

THE MULTICULTURAL CITY

San Francisco's heritage of diversity and tolerance comes alive in the murals that enliven its ethnic neighborhoods. In Chinatown, Chinese-American artists evoke memories of the "old country." The Mission District is filled with art, some of it politically inspired, celebrating the struggles and achievements of its Mexican and Latin American population.

Mexican American dancer

American Indian drummer

Caucasian bass player

African American maracas player

Mural in Washington Street encapsulating life in China

Multicultural San Francisco *is celebrated at Park Branch Library in Haight Ashbury.*

WHERE TO FIND THE MURALS

Balmy Alley. **Map** 11 A5
Clarion Alley. **Map** 10 F2
Coit Tower *p93*
Dolores and 18th St. **Map** 10 E3
Fort Mason *pp74–5*
Franklin Street. **Map** 4 E1
Oakland. *p164*
Park Branch Library
    1833 Page St. **Map** 9 B1
Precita Eyes Mural Arts Studio
    348 Precita Ave. **Map** 10 F5
Washington Street. **Map** 11 A2

GOLDEN GATE PARK AND LAND'S END

Lying to the south of the Richmond District is the spectacular Golden Gate Park, a masterpiece of landscape gardening, created in the 1890s out of a sandy wasteland. Little grows here by chance, and trees have been planted where they will best deflect the prevailing winds. All shrubs and bushes are carefully chosen to ensure there is color at every season.

Auguste Rodin's The Shades, the Legion of Honor

Among the many attractions of the park are meandering paths, sports facilities ranging from archery to golf, and three major museums. More parklands lie to the north and west of the Richmond District, linked by the Coastal Trail. This is where rugged Land's End, the scene of so many shipwrecks, meets the sea. Nearby Lincoln Park, with its manicured golf course, makes a dramatic contrast.

SIGHTS AT A GLANCE

Museums and Galleries
California Academy of Sciences pp150–1 **2**
de Young Museum **4**
Legion of Honor **16**

Parks and Gardens
Buffalo Paddock **12**
Children's Playground **6**
Conservatory of Flowers **8**
Japanese Tea Garden **3**
Polo Fields **11**
Queen Wilhelmina Tulip Garden **13**
Shakespeare Garden **1**
Stow Lake **10**
Strybing Arboretum **9**
Ocean Beach **14**
Seal Rocks **15**
Lincoln Park **17**
Land's End **18**

Historic Buildings
Cliff House **19**
Columbarium **7**
McLaren Lodge **5**

KEY

Street-by-Street map
See pp144–5

GETTING THERE
Muni streetcars and buses serve the neighborhood. Bus 44 goes to the area of Golden Gate Park near the Music Concourse. Take buses 5, 7, 21 or 71, or the N streetcar, for the east end of the park, or the 73 for the southern edge. Bus 18 goes to Lincoln Park, Land's End and Cliff House. Bus 38 goes as far as Point Lobos.

0 meters   1000

0 yards   1000

Distinctive architecture of the de Young Museum in Golden Gate Park

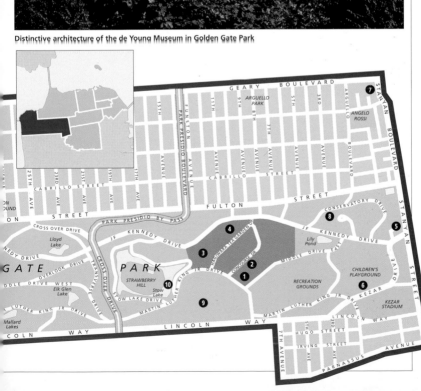

Street-by-Street: Golden Gate Park

Golden Gate Park is one of the largest urban parks in the world. It stretches from the Pacific Ocean to the center of San Francisco, forming an oasis of greenery and calm in which to escape from the bustle of city life. Within the park an amazing number of activities are possible, both sporting and cultural. The landscaped area around the Music Concourse, with its fountains, plane trees and benches, is the most popular and developed section. Here you can enjoy free Sunday concerts at the Spreckels Temple of Music. Two museums stand on either side of the Concourse, and the Japanese and Shakespeare gardens are in walking distance.

Lamp in the Japanese Tea Garden

★ de Young Museum
This state-of-the-art, landmark museum showcases collections from around the world. Exhibits include this mahogany chest, made in Philadelphia in 1780.

The Great Buddha, nearly 11 ft (3 m) high, is probably the largest statue of its kind outside Asia.

Japanese Tea Garden
This exquisite garden, with its well-tended plants, is one of the most attractive parts of the park ❸

The bridge in the Japanese Tea Garden is known as the Moon Bridge. It arches steeply, and its reflection in the water below forms a perfect circle.

The bust of Verdi reflects the city's passion for opera.

The Spreckels Temple of Music is an ornate band shell, the site for free Sunday concerts since 1899.

HAGIAWARA TE

MARTIN LUTHER KING DRIVE

STAR SIGHTS

★ California Academy of Sciences

★ de Young Museum

0 meters		80
0 yards		80

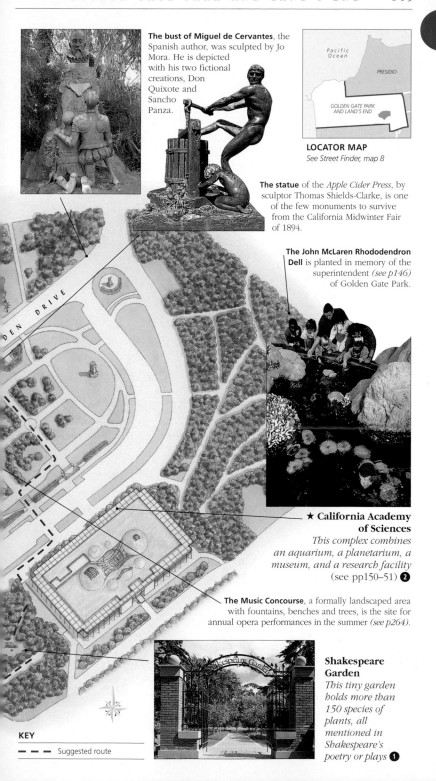

The bust of Miguel de Cervantes, the Spanish author, was sculpted by Jo Mora. He is depicted with his two fictional creations, Don Quixote and Sancho Panza.

LOCATOR MAP
See Street Finder, map 8

The statue of the *Apple Cider Press*, by sculptor Thomas Shields-Clarke, is one of the few monuments to survive from the California Midwinter Fair of 1894.

The John McLaren Rhododendron Dell is planted in memory of the superintendent *(see p146)* of Golden Gate Park.

★ California Academy of Sciences
This complex combines an aquarium, a planetarium, a museum, and a research facility (see pp150–51) **2**

The Music Concourse, a formally landscaped area with fountains, benches and trees, is the site for annual opera performances in the summer *(see p264).*

Shakespeare Garden
This tiny garden holds more than 150 species of plants, all mentioned in Shakespeare's poetry or plays **1**

KEY

– – – Suggested route

The Creation of Golden Gate Park

As San Francisco prospered and matured in the 1860s, its citizens demanded the same amenities as other great cities. Prominent among these was a large city park, for which they petitioned in 1865. New York had recently finished building its trendsetting Central Park, created largely by landscape designer Frederick Law Olmsted. San Francisco's mayor, HP Coon, sought Olmsted's advice on a piece of land that the city had recently secured for a park. This vast, undeveloped wasteland to the west of the city by the Pacific Ocean was known as the "Outside Lands."

William H. Hall

John McLaren

Reclaiming the Land

The city planners turned to a surveyor and engineer named William Hammond Hall. He had already achieved some success in dune reclamation in the Outside Lands, and in 1870 he applied his methods to Golden Gate Park. Hall was appointed the park's first superintendent in 1871. He started work at the east end, laying out meandering roads and trying to create a seemingly natural landscape. The developing park soon proved popular. Families came to picnic and young dandies raced their carriages.

Cyclists in Golden Gate Park

The Plan Falters

Despite the popularity of the park, it was nearly prevented from reaching maturity by public corruption. Throughout the 1870s city officials siphoned off funds and the budget was repeatedly cut. In 1876 Hall was falsely accused of corruption and resigned in protest. The park fell into a period of decline, but after a decade of decay, Hall was asked to resume the task of managing it. The remarkable man he chose as superintendent in 1890 was a Scotsman named John McLaren, who agreed with Hall that a park should be a natural environment. He planted thousands of trees, bulbs, flowers and shrubs, chosen so

blooms would appear each month. He also imported exotic plants from around the world. These thrived in his care, despite the poor soil and foggy climate of San Francisco. McLaren devoted his whole life to the park, personally fighting the developers who threatened encroachment. He died at the age of 93, after 53 years in office.

The Changing Park

The park still reflects the vision of McLaren and Hall, but contrary to their plans, the park today is scattered with buildings, and McLaren's most prominent defeat became a popular attraction. In what is now the Music Concourse, the California Midwinter Fair opened in 1894, despite his protests. Urban encroachment continued to press upon the park in the 20th century, but for most San Franciscans the park remains what it was intended to be – a place in which to escape from city life.

1894 California Midwinter Fair

Plaques in the Shakespeare Garden

Shakespeare Garden **❶**

Music Concourse, Golden Gate Park. **Map** 8 F2. 44.

Gardeners here have tried to cultivate all the plants mentioned in William Shakespeare's works. The relevant quotes are written on plaques set in a wall at the back of the garden.

California Academy of Sciences **❷**

See pp150–51.

Japanese Tea Garden **❸**

Music Concourse, Golden Gate Park. **Map** 8 F2. **Tel** 752-4227. 🚌 44. ⏰ Mar–Oct: 9am–6pm daily; Nov–Feb: 9am–4:45pm daily. 🎫 📷 🖥 🚻

Established by the art dealer George Turner Marsh for the California Midwinter Fair of 1894 *(see p146)*, this garden is a very popular attraction. The best time to visit is when the cherry trees bloom in April. Paths wind through the carefully manicured Japanese trees, shrubs and flowers. The steeply arched Moon Bridge forms a dramatic circular reflection in the pond below. The largest bronze Buddha to be found outside Asia, which was cast in Japan in 1790, is seated at the top of the garden stairs.

de Young Museum **❹**

50 Tea Garden Drive, Golden Gate Park. **Map** 8 F2. **Tel** 863-3330. 🚌 5, 21, 44. 🚇 N. ⏰ 9:30am–5:15pm daily (to 8:45pm Fri). 🎫 (free first Tue of month). ♿ **www**.thinker.org

Founded in 1895, the de Young Museum houses one of the city's finest art collections. In 1989 the building was too damaged by an earthquake to be saved. However, an exciting state-of-the-art facility opened in 2005. The museum contains a broad range of American art, as well as extensive pre-Columbian-American, African, and Oceanic works. The American art collection comprises more than 1000 paintings.

McLaren Lodge **❺**

Nr junction of Stanyan St and Fell St on the park's east side. **Map** 9 B1. **Tel** 831-2700. ⏰ 8am–5pm Mon–Fri. 🚌 7, 21.

This sandstone villa, designed by Edward Swain, was built in 1896. As superintendent of the park, John McLaren lived here with his family until his death in 1943. His portrait hangs on the wall, and every December the cypress tree outside is lit with colored lights in his memory. The lodge is now a park office that also dispenses maps and information.

Gateway in the Japanese Tea Garden

Children's Playground **❻**

Kezar Drive, near First Ave. **Map** 9 A1. 🚌 5, 7, 71. 🚇 N. *No adults allowed unless accompanied by children.*

This is the oldest public children's playground in the United States, and it set the style for many later ones. In 1978 it was redesigned with sandboxes, swings, sprawling slides and a climbing "fortress." On the Herschell-Spillman merry-go-round, housed in a Greek-inspired structure that dates from 1892, children ride on brightly painted beasts.

Inside the Columbarium

Columbarium **❼**

1 Loraine Court. **Map** 3 B5. **Tel** 752-7891. 🚌 33, 38. ⏰ 9am–5pm Mon–Fri, 10am–3pm Sat–Sun. ⛔ Jan 1, Thanksgiving and Dec 25. 📷 ♿ ground floor only.

The San Francisco Columbarium is the sole survivor of the old Lone Mountain Cemetery, which once covered sizable tracts of the Richmond District. Most of the remains were disinterred and moved to Colma in 1914. This Neo-Classical rotunda houses the remains of 6,000 people in elaborate decorated urns. Unused for several decades, it was rescued and restored by the Neptune Society in 1979. The ornate, bright interior under the dome has lovely stained-glass windows. The narrow passages encircling the dome are remarkable for their acoustics.

Carousel ride at the Children's Playground in Golden Gate Park ▷

California Academy of Sciences ❷

The California Academy of Sciences moved back to its permanent home in Golden Gate Park in late 2008. The building, housing Steinhart Aquarium, Morrison Planetarium, and the Kimball Natural History Museum, combines innovative green architecture with flexible exhibition spaces.

A penguin in the African Hall

Guide and child meeting a resident alligator

A lovely piazza is at the heart of the building, with excellent views overlooking Golden Gate Park.

MUSEUM GUIDE

Steinhart Aquarium displays are spread throughout the museum, but most of the tanks can be found in the basement beneath the Piazza. An auditorium above the café hosts traveling exhibits as well as special performances and programs. The back of the building holds the museum's collection of over 20 million scientific specimens along with staff offices and research laboratories.

The Swamp

Coral Reef Tank

Sharks

Morrison Planetarium
State-of-the-art exhibits and digital technology transform the ceiling here into a night sky.

KEY TO FLOOR PLAN

- African Hall
- Kimball Natural History Museum
- Morrison Planetarium
- Rainforests of the World
- Steinhart Aquarium
- Aquarium Tanks
- Non-exhibition space

African Hall
Realistic models of animals from Africa's jungles and savannas are displayed here, in lifelike dioramas.

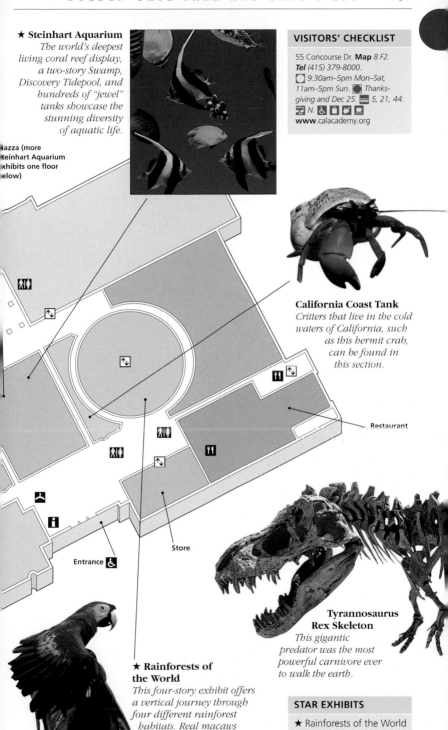

★ **Steinhart Aquarium**
The world's deepest living coral reef display, a two-story Swamp, Discovery Tidepool, and hundreds of "jewel" tanks showcase the stunning diversity of aquatic life.

VISITORS' CHECKLIST

55 Concourse Dr. **Map** *8 F2.*
***Tel** (415) 379-8000.*
◯ *9:30am–5pm Mon–Sat, 11am–5pm Sun.* ◯ *Thanksgiving and Dec 25.* 🚌 *5, 21, 44.*
🚉 *N.* ♿ 🅿 📷 💷
www.calacademy.org

Piazza (more Steinhart Aquarium exhibits one floor below)

California Coast Tank
Critters that live in the cold waters of California, such as this hermit crab, can be found in this section.

Restaurant

Store

i

Entrance ♿

Tyrannosaurus Rex Skeleton
This gigantic predator was the most powerful carnivore ever to walk the earth.

★ **Rainforests of the World**
This four-story exhibit offers a vertical journey through four different rainforest habitats. Real macaws and other exotic birds live in the canopy of this exhibit.

STAR EXHIBITS

★ Rainforests of the World

★ Steinhart Aquarium

Conservatory of Flowers, prior to hurricane damage

Conservatory of Flowers ❽

John F. Kennedy Drive, Golden Gate Park. **Map** 9 A1. *Tel* 666-7001. 🚌 33, 44. ◯ 9am–4:30pm Tue–Sun. 📷 (free 1st Tue of the month.) ♿ **www**.conservatoryofflowers.org

This ornate glass-house was the oldest building in Golden Gate Park. A jungle of ferns, palms and orchids thrived here but a hurricane battered the city in December 1995, and the conservatory was largely destroyed. A campaign for its repair was launched and it reopened in 2003.

Strybing Arboretum ❾

9th Ave at Lincoln Way, Golden Gate Park. **Map** 8 F2. 🚌 44, 71. 🚈 N. ◯ 8am–4:30pm Mon–Fri, 10am–5pm weekends and public hols. 📷 ♿ 📷 1:30pm daily. 🏛 www.strybing.org

On display are 7,500 species of plants, trees and shrubs from many different countries. There are Mexican, African, South American and Australian gardens, and one devoted to native California plants.

Well worth a visit is the enchanting Moon-Viewing Garden. It exhibits East Asian plants in a setting that, unlike that of the Japanese Tea Garden *(see p147)*, is naturalistic rather than formal. Both medicinal and culinary plants grow in the Garden of Fragrance, which is designed for blind plant-lovers. Here the emphasis is on the senses of taste, touch and smell, and the plants are identified in braille. Another area is planted with indigenous California redwood trees, with a small stream winding through. This re-creates the flora and atmosphere of a northern California coastal forest. There is also a New World Cloud Forest, with flora from the mountains of Central

America. Surprisingly, all these gardens thrive in the California fogs. The Arboretum has a shop, selling seeds and books, and it also houses the Helen Crocker Russell Library of Horticulture, which is open to the public. A flower show is held in the summer *(see p49)*.

Stow Lake ❿

Stow Lake Drive, Golden Gate Park. **Map** 8 E2. 🚌 28, 29, 44. 📷 *Boat rental* 752-0347.

In 1895 this artificial lake was created encircling Strawberry Hill, so that the summit of the hill now forms an island in the lake, linked to the mainland by two stone-clad bridges. Stow Lake's circular stream makes an ideal course for rowing laps from the boathouse, though leisurely drifting seems more appropriate. There is a Chinese moon-watching pavilion on the island's shore, which was the gift of San Francisco's sister city in Taiwan, Taipei. The red and green pavilion was shipped to San Francisco in 6,000 pieces and then assembled on the island.

The millionaire Collis P. Huntington *(see p102)* donated the money to create the reservoir and the waterfall that cascades into Stow Lake. This is known as Huntington Falls and is one of the park's most attractive features.

Moon-watching pavilion on Stow Lake

Queen Wilhelmina Tulip Garden and the Dutch Windmill

Polo Fields ⓫

John F. Kennedy Drive, Golden Gate Park. **Map** 7 C2. 🚌 *5, 29.*

You are increasingly likely to see joggers rather than polo ponies using the Polo Fields stadium in the more open western half of Golden Gate Park. Horses, on which to explore the park's equestrian trails and the Bercut Equitation Field, are available by the hour at the adjacent riding stables. For anglers, there is a fly-casting pool nearby.

To the east of the stadium, in the green expanse of Old Speedway Meadows, many celebrations were held during the late 1960s, including some notable rock concerts. The Grateful Dead and Jefferson Airplane, among others, played here. Here in the spring of 1967, thousands attended a huge "Be-in," one of many events that led to the "Summer of Love" *(see pp32–3)*.

Buffalo Paddock ⓬

John F. Kennedy Drive, Golden Gate Park. **Map** 7 C2. 🚌 *5, 29.*

The shaggy buffalo that graze in this paddock are the largest of North American land animals. With its short horns and humped back, the buffalo is the symbol of the American plains and is more properly known as the American bison. This paddock was opened in 1892, at a time when the buffalo was on the

verge of extinction. In 1902 William Cody, alias "Buffalo Bill," traded one of his bulls for one from the Golden Gate Park herd. Both parties thought that they had rid themselves of an aggressive beast, but Cody's newly purchased bull jumped a high fence once back at his encampment and escaped. According to one newspaper of the day, the *San Francisco Call*, it took a total of 80 men to recapture it.

Queen Wilhelmina Tulip Garden ⓭

Map 7 A2. 🚌 *5, 18.* **Windmill** ♿

The Dutch windmill was built near the northwest corner of Golden Gate Park in 1903. Its original purpose was to pump water from an underground source for irrigating the park, but now it is no longer in use. Its companion, the Murphy Windmill, was erected in the

park's south-west corner in 1905. The garden was named after the Dutch Queen Wilhelmina, and tulip bulbs are donated each year by the Dutch Bulb Growers' Association.

Ocean Beach ⓮

Map 7 A1–5. 🚌 *5, 18, 31, 38, 71.* 🚋 *L, N.*

Most of San Francisco's western boundary is defined by this broad sweep of sand. Though sublime when viewed from Cliff House or Sutro Heights, the beach is dangerous for swimming because of its icy waters and a strong undertow. Surfers in wetsuits are a common sight, but there is often a stiff wind, or fog. On rare hot days, it is also a popular spot for sun-bathers and picnickers.

Seal Rocks ⓯

Map 7 A1. *Not accessible* to visitors. View from Ocean Beach, Cliff House or Sutro Heights Park. 🚌 *18, 38.*

Bring binoculars to watch the sea lions and birds in their natural setting. At night, from the beach or Cliff House promenade, the barking of the sea lions is both reassuring and eerie, especially when it is foggy. On a clear day you can see the Farallon Islands 32 miles (51 km) off the coast. These are also inhabited by sea lions and contain a rookery that has been protected by the state since 1907.

Looking out toward Seal Rocks from Ocean Beach

Golden Gate Bridge from Lincoln Park golf course ▷

Legion of Honor ⑯

Inspired by the Palais de la Légion d'Honneur in Paris, Alma de Bretteville Spreckels built this museum in the 1920s to promote French art in California and to commemorate the state's casualties in World War I. Designed by the architect George Applegarth, it contains European art from the last eight centuries, with paintings by Monet, Rubens, and Rembrandt, as well as over 70 sculptures by Rodin. The Achenback Foundation, a famous collection of graphic works, is also part of the gallery.

Bust of Camille Claudel by Rodin

★ The Thinker
This original bronze casting of Rodin's Le Penseur *(1904) is in the colonnaded Court of Honor.*

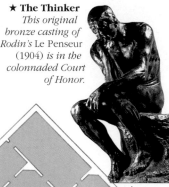

★ Waterlilies
Claude Monet's famous work (c.1914–17) is one of a series depicting his lily pond.

Florence Gould Theater

Entrance

St. Wenceslaus
Figurine, made c.1732, after a model by Johann Gottlieb Kirchner.

Stairs down from first floor

GALLERY GUIDE
The museum's permanent collection is displayed in 19 galleries on the first floor. Beginning at the left of the entrance, works are arranged chronologically from the medieval period to the 20th century. Current exhibitions are on the lower level.

KEY TO FLOOR PLAN

- Permanent displays
- Achenbach Foundation Library
- Porcelain gallery
- Theater storage
- Temporary displays
- Non-exhibition space

Old Woman
Georges de la Tour painted this study in about 1618.

The Impresario
In this portrait (c.1877), artist Edgar Degas emphasizes the subject's size by making him appear too large for the frame.

STAR EXHIBITS

★ The Thinker

★ Waterlilies

Golden Gate Bridge from Lincoln Park Golf Course

Lincoln Park ⑰

Map 1 B5. 18.

This splendid park, located above the Golden Gate Park is the setting for the Legion of Honor. The land was originally allocated to Golden Gate Cemetery, where graves were segregated according to the nationality of their occupants. When these graves were cleared in the first decade of the 20th century, the park was established and landscaped by John McLaren *(see p146)*.

The park now boasts an 18-hole golf course and scenic walks. City views from the hilltop course are superb.

Land's End ⑱

Map 1 B5. 18, 38.

A rugged seascape of rock, cliff and matted cypress woods, Land's End is the wildest part of San Francisco. It is reached by foot along the Coastal Trail, which can be accessed by stairs from the Legion of Honor, or from the Point Lobos parking area near Sutro Heights Park. The Coastal Trail is safe, ending in a spectacular viewing point overlooking the Golden Gate. Do not leave the trail. Those who do risk being stranded by incoming tides or swept away by high waves. Call the National Parks Service Visitors Center (tel: 556-8642) for

tide information. Mile Rock Lighthouse can be seen offshore from here.

Cliff House ⑲

1090 Point Lobos. **Map** 7 A1. **Tel** 386-3330 (Visitor Center). 18, 38. daily. Camera Obscura only (9am–11pm daily). www.cliffhouse.com

Built in 1909, the present building, which was renovated in 2004, is the third on this site. Its predecessor, an elaborate eight-story Gothic structure that burned down in 1907, was built by the flamboyant entrepreneur Adolph Sutro. His estate on the hill overlooking Cliff House is now Sutro Heights Park. There are several restaurants on the upper levels, occasional live music, and three observation decks with panoramic views. Camera Obscura is located on the lower level.

View across to Mile Rock Lighthouse from Land's End

FARTHER AFIELD

San Francisco is the smallest in size of the nine counties that encircle the bay. The settlements that were once summer retreats are today sprawling suburbs or cities in their own right. To the north of Golden Gate Bridge, Marin County has a wild, wind-swept coastline, forests of redwoods, and Mount Tamalpais, which offers magnificent views of the Bay Area.

Detail from Sather Gate at UC Berkeley

Marin's settlements have retained their village atmosphere, and the county is the perfect escape for visitors who want an after-noon away from the metropolis. In the East Bay, the most popular destinations are Oakland's museum and harbor, and Berkeley's gardens and famous university. To the south, San Francisco Zoo has plenty to entertain younger sightseers.

SIGHTS AT A GLANCE

Museums and Galleries
Judah L. Magnes Museum ⑯
Lawrence Hall of Science ⑬
Oakland Museum of California pp166–7 ㉓

Parks and Gardens
Angel Island ⑧
Mount Tamalpais ⑤
Muir Woods ④
San Francisco Zoological Gardens ①
Tilden Park ⑨
University Botanical Gardens ⑭

Churches and Temples
Mormon Temple ⑲

15 km = 10 miles

Shops, Markets and Restaurants
Fourth Street ⑩
Gourmet Ghetto ⑪
Jack London Square ㉒
Oakland Chinatown ㉕
Rockridge ⑱
Telegraph Avenue ⑮

Historic Streets and Buildings
Bay Bridge ⑳
Claremont Resort and Spa ⑰
Old Oakland ㉔
University of California at Berkeley ⑫

Historic Towns
Sausalito ⑥
Tiburon ⑦

Lakes
Lake Merritt ㉑

Beaches
Point Reyes National Seashore ②
Stinson Beach ③

KEY

▨	Main sightseeing areas
▢	Urban areas
✈	Airport
🚉	Amtrak station
═	Freeway
━	Major road
═	Minor road

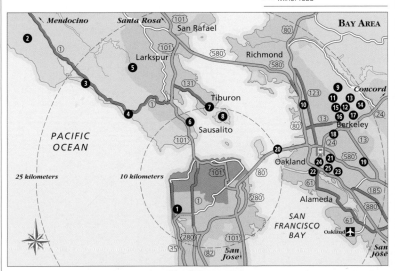

Orangutan in the San Francisco Zoological Gardens

San Francisco Zoo ❶

Sloat Blvd and 45th Ave. *Tel 753-7080.* 18, 23. L. 10am–5pm daily. free first Wed of every month. **www**.sfzoo.com

San Francisco Zoo is at the far southwestern corner of the city, between the Pacific Ocean and Lake Merced. The complex houses more than 1,000 species of birds and mammals. Among which 30 are considered to be endangered, including snow leopards, a Bengal tiger and a jaguar. At the innovative Primate Discovery Center there are 15 different species of primates, including monkeys, langurs, and macaques.

One of San Francisco Zoo's highlights is the Koala Crossing, which is designed like an Australian outback station. Otter River features cascading waterfalls and a live fish feeder for North American river otters. Gorilla World is one of the world's largest naturalistic exhibits.

Dairy farm at picturesque Point Reyes

At 2pm every day except Monday, the big cats are fed at the Lion House. Nearby is the Children's Zoo, where animals can be petted.

Point Reyes National Seashore ❷

US Highway 1 to Olema; once past town follow signs for Point Reyes National Seashore. *Golden Gate Transit bus 50 or 80 to San Rafael Center, then bus 65 (Sat, Sun & hols).*

Point Reyes peninsula is wild and windswept, and a haven for wildlife, including a herd of tule elk. There are cattle and dairy ranches, and three small towns: Olema, Point Reyes Station and Inverness.

The peninsula is due west of the San Andreas Fault, which caused the 1906 earthquake *(see pp18–19).* A displaced fence on the Earthquake Trail near Bear Valley Visitor Center is evidence of how the Fault caused the peninsula to move a full 20 ft (6 m) north of the mainland.

In 1579 the British explorer Sir Francis Drake is said to have anchored in Drake's Bay *(see pp24–5),* named the land Nova Albion, and claimed it for England.

The Visitor Center has tide tables and trail maps. From December to mid March, whales can be seen offshore.

Stinson Beach ❸

US 101 N to Highway 1, continue to Stinson Beach. *Tel Stinson Beach Park 868-9828.* Golden Gate Transit bus 20, then bus 63 (Sat, Sun & hols). 7am–one hour after sunset daily.

Since the early days of the 20th century this has been a popular vacation spot; the first visitors came on ferries from San Francisco and were met by horse-drawn carriages. Stinson remains the preferred swimming beach for the whole area. It is a stretch of soft sand, where surfers mingle with swimmers and sunbathers. The village nearby has good bookstores, a few restaurants and a grocery store.

Giant redwoods in Muir Woods

Muir Woods and Beach ❹

US 101 N, exit for Highway 1; then either turn onto Panoramic Highway and follow signs to Muir Woods, or stay on Highway 1 to Muir Beach turnoff. No public transportation. *Tel Gray Line Tours 558-9400.*

Nestling at the foot of Mount Tamalpais is Muir Woods National Monument, one of the few remaining stands of first-growth coast redwoods. These giant trees (the oldest is at least 1,000 years old) once covered the coastal area of California. The woods were named in honor of John Muir, a 19th-century naturalist

The attractive main street of Tiburon

who was one of the first to persuade Americans of the need for conservation.

Redwood Creek bubbles out of Muir Woods and makes its way down to the sea at Muir Beach, a wide expanse of sand popular with beachcombers and picnickers. The road to the beach passes the Pelican Inn. This 16th-century style English inn is extremely proud of its English menu, and its welcoming hospitality.

The beach is likely to be crowded on weekends, but visitors who are prepared to walk a mile or more are usually rewarded with solitude.

Mount Tamalpais ❺

US 101 N, exit for Highway 1, turn on to Panoramic Highway. *Tel Mount Tamalpais State Park 388-2070.* Golden Gate Transit bus 20 to Marin City, then bus 63 (Sat, Sun & hols). **Mountain Theater** *East Ridgecrest.* **Performances** *May–Jun: Sun except Memorial Day.* **Reservations Tel** *383-1100.* **www**.mountainplay.org

Mount Tamalpais State Park, a wilderness nature preserve, has extensive trails that wind through redwood groves and alongside creeks. There are picnic areas, campsites, and meadows for kite flying. Mount Tamalpais, at 2,571 ft (784 m), is the highest peak in the Bay Area; the steep, rough tracks gave rise to the invention of the mountain bike. Near the summit, the Mountain Theater is a natural amphitheater with stone seats, where musicals and plays are performed.

Sausalito ❻

US 101 N, first exit after Golden Gate Bridge, to Bridgeway. Golden Gate Transit buses 10, 50. from Ferry Building or Pier 43½. **Bay Model Visitor Center Tel** *332-3871.* Apr–Sep: 9am–4pm Tue–Fri, 10am–5pm Sat, Sun & Vacs; Oct–Mar: 9am–4pm Tue–Sat. Jul 4.

In this small town that was once a fishing community, Victorian bungalows cling to steep hills rising from the bay. Parallel to the waterfront, Bridgeway Avenue serves as a promenade for the weekend crowds that come to patronize the restaurants and boutiques and enjoy the views. Village Fair is an eclectic assembly of shops in an old warehouse. At 2100 Bridgeway, the Bay Model simulates the movement of the bay's tides and currents.

Looking over to San Francisco from Sausalito

Tiburon ❼

US 101 N, Tiburon Blvd exit. Golden Gate Transit bus 10. from Pier 43½.

The main street in this chic waterfront town is lined with shops and restaurants housed in "arks." These are turn-of-the-century houseboats that have been pulled ashore, lined up and refurbished. They now stand in what is called "Ark Row."

Less hectic than Sausalito, Tiburon is a good town for walking, with parks along the scenic waterfront that offer a place for contemplation.

View of Angel Island from the waterfront town of Tiburon

Angel Island ❽

from Pier 43½ and Tiburon. State Park 435-1915.

Angel Island is reached by ferry from Tiburon and San Francisco. The boats dock at Ayala Cove, which has a sweeping lawn with picnic tables. Hiking trails loop around the heavily wooded island, rising to 776 ft (237 m) above sea level, past an abandoned military garrison that once housed immigrants from Asia. During World War II, prisoners of war were detained here. No motor vehicles are allowed here, except for a few park service vans. Most visitors prefer to walk or bicycle on the island.

Berkeley

Carousel in Tilden Park

Tilden Park ❾

Tel (510) 843-2137. Berkeley, then AC Transit 67 bus. **Park open** 5am–10pm daily. **Steam trains** 11am–5pm Sat, Sun, and daily in summer. **Carousel open** 11am–5pm Sat, Sun, 10am–5pm daily during summer. **Pony rides open** 11am–5pm Sat, Sun, daily in summer and public hols. **Botanical Garden open** 8:30am–5pm daily. limited. www.ebparks.org

Though preserved for the most part in a natural wild condition, Tilden Park offers a variety of attractions. It is noted for the enchantingly landscaped Botanical Garden, specializing in California plants. Visitors can stroll from alpine meadows to desert cactus gardens by way of a lovely redwood glen, and there are also guided nature walks. If you have children, don't miss the carousel, the miniature farmyard and the model steam train.

Fourth Street ❿

AC Transit Z. Berkeley, then AC Transit 9, 51, 65 bus.

This gentrified enclave north of University Avenue is characteristic of Berkeley's climate of fine craftsmanship and exquisite taste. Here you can buy everything from hand-made paper, stained-glass windows and furniture, to organically grown lettuce and designer garden tools. There is also a handful of renowned restaurants *(see pp238–9)*.

Gourmet Ghetto ⓫

Upper Shattuck Ave. Berkeley, then AC Transit 7, 9, 43 bus.

This north Berkeley neighborhood acquired fame as a gourmet's ghetto when Alice Waters opened Chez Panisse *(see p239)* here in 1971. The restaurant is acclaimed for its use of fresh local ingredients in a French-inspired style that gave rise to what is known as California cuisine. In its original house on Shattuck Avenue, Chez Panisse has influenced many worthy imitators. There are also many specialty markets and coffeehouses in the surrounding neighborhood – hence its salubrious nickname.

University of California at Berkeley ⓬

Tel (510) 642-6000. Berkeley. AC Transit 9, 15, 40, 43, 51, 52, 65. **Hearst Museum of Anthropology** *Tel* (510) 643-7648. 10am–4:30pm Wed–Sat, noon–4pm Sun. public hols. **Berkeley Art Museum** *Tel* (510) 642-0808. 11am–5pm Wed–Sun. public hols. www.berkeley.edu

Some would argue that UC Berkeley's reputation for countercultural movements sometimes eclipses its reputation for academic excellence. However, Berkeley remains one of the largest and most prestigious universities in the world. Founded as a utopian

Sather Tower, built in 1914

"Athens of the Pacific" in 1868, Berkeley has more than 10 Nobel Laureates among its fellows and staff. The campus *(see pp176–7)* was laid out by Frederick Law Olmsted on the twin forks of Strawberry Creek; changes by San Francisco architect David Farquharson were later adopted. Today there are over 30,000 students and a wide range of museums, cultural amenities and buildings of note. These include the Berkeley Art Museum *(see p38)*, the Hearst Museum of Anthropology and Sather Tower, also known as the Campanile.

Lawrence Hall of Science ⓭

Centennial Drive, Berkeley. *Tel* (510) 642-5132. Berkeley, then AC Transit 8, 65 bus. from Mining Circle, UC Berkeley (except Sat, Sun). 10am–5pm daily. www.lawrencehall ofscience.org

At this fascinating science museum, workshops and classes make science fun. Hands-on exhibits encourage younger visitors to study the effects of mirrors on lasers or manipulate a hologram. They can also build a dinosaur skeleton, feed a snake, plot stars in the planetarium, or calculate odds by rolling dice. Along with a resident mechanical dinosaur, there are changing feature exhibitions, popular with families and children.
The stunning view from the outdoor plaza includes much of the northern Bay Area, as far west as the Farallon Islands. By night, the lights around the bay are an extraordinary sight.

Model of DNA at the Lawrence Hall of Science

University Botanical Garden ⓮

Centennial Drive, Berkeley. 📞 *(510) 643-2755.* 🚌 *from Mining Circle, UC Berkeley Hills (except Sat, Sun, hols).* ◯ *9am–5pm daily.* ● *public hols & first Tue of month.* 📷 ♿ *limited.* 🎞

More than 12,000 species from all over the world thrive Berkeley's Strawberry Canyon. Primarily used for research, collections are arranged in thematic gardens linked by paths. Particularly noteworthy are the Asian, African, South American, European and California gardens. The Chinese medicinal herb garden, orchid display, cactus garden and the carnivorous plants are also well worth a visit.

Telegraph Avenue ⓯

🚉 *Berkeley.* 🚌 *AC Transit U.*

Berkeley's most stimulating and fascinating street is Telegraph Avenue, which runs between Dwight Way and the University. It has one of the highest concentrations of bookstores in the country, and many coffeehouses and cheap eateries. This district was the center of student protest during the 1960s. Today it swarms with students from dawn to long after dusk, along with street vendors, musicians, protestors and eccentrics.

Judah L. Magnes Museum ⓰

2911 Russell St, Berkeley. *Tel (510) 549-6950.* 📞 *(415) 591-8800.* 🚉 *Rockridge, then AC Transit 51 bus.* 🚉 *Ashby, then AC Transit 6 bus.* ◯ *2–4pm Tue, Thu & Sun by appointment.* ● *Jewish and federal hols.* 🚫 ♿ *arrange in advance.* 🎞 *by arrangement.* **www**.magnes.org

Located in a rambling old mansion, this is California's largest collection of historical artifacts pertaining to Jewish culture, from ancient times to today. Among them are fine Jewish art treasures from

19th-century Jewish ceremonial dress, Judah L. Magnes Museum

Europe, India and Turkey, and paintings by Marc Chagall and Max Liebermann. There are also mementos of Nazi Germany, such as a burned Torah scroll rescued from a synagogue. Lectures, films, and traveling exhibits periodically enliven the halls. The Blumenthal Library has permanent resources for scholars.

Claremont Resort and Spa ⓱

41 Tunnel Road (Ashby & Domingo Aves), Oakland. *Tel (510) 843-3000.* 🚉 *Rock ridge, then AC Transit 7 bus.* ♿ 🅿 🛅 💂
www.claremontresort.com

The Berkeley Hills form a backdrop to this half-timbered fairytale castle. Construction began in 1906, and ended in 1915. In the early years the hotel failed to prosper, due partly to a law that forbade the sale of alcohol within a 1-mile (1.6-km) radius of the Berkeley university campus. An enterprising student actually measured the distance in 1937, and found that the radius line passed through the *center* of the building. This revelation led to the founding of the Terrace Bar, beyond the line, in the same corner of the hotel that it occupies today.

As well as being one of the Bay Area's plushest hotels, this is a good place to have a drink and enjoy the views.

View of the Claremont Resort and Spa at Berkeley

Gourmet shops at Rockridge Market Hall

Oakland

Rockridge ⑱

🚇 Rockridge.

A leafy residential area with large houses and flower gardens, Rockridge also attracts shoppers to College Avenue. There is a variety of shops and restaurants as well as many cafés with outdoor tables.

Mormon Temple ⑲

4770 Lincoln Ave, Oakland.
Tel (510) 531-1475 (Visitors' Center).
🚇 Fruitvale, then AC Transit 46 bus. ◯ 9am–9pm daily.
Temple ◯ Call the Visitors' Center for times. 🚫 (except Visitors' Center.) ♿ 📷 of Visitors' Center.

Designed in 1963 and built on a hilltop, this is northern California's only Mormon temple. Its full name is the

Oakland Temple of the Church of Jesus Christ of the Latter Day Saints. At night the temple is floodlit and can be seen from Oakland and San Francisco. The central ziggurat is surrounded by four shorter towers, all terraced and clad with white granite and capped by glistening golden pyramids.

From the temple there are magnificent views over the entire Bay Area. The Visitors' Center offers guided tours by missionaries, who explain the tenets of the faith with a series of multimedia presentations.

Lake Merritt ㉑

🚇 12th or 19th Street, then AC Transit 12, 13, 57, 58 bus.

Formed when a saltwater tidal estuary was dredged, embanked and partly dammed, Lake Merritt and its surrounding park form an oasis of rich blue and green in the urban heart of Oakland. Designated in 1870 as the first state game refuge in the United States, Lake Merritt still attracts migrating flocks of birds. Rowers can rent boats from two boat-houses on the west and north shores, and joggers and bicyclists can circle the lake on a 3-mile (5-km) path. The north shore at Lakeside Park has flower gardens, an aviary,

Central ziggurat of the Mormon Temple

Bay Bridge ⑳

Map 6 E4.

The compound, high-level San Francisco–Oakland Bay Bridge was designed by Charles H. Purcell. It has two distinct structures, joining at Yerba Buena Island in the middle of the Bay, and reaches 4.5 miles (7.2 km) from shore to shore. Its completion in 1936 heralded the end of the age of ferryboats on San Francisco Bay by linking the peninsular city at Rincon Hill to the Oakland

"mainland" with road and rail. The tracks were removed in the 1950s, leaving the bridge for use by more than 250,000

The East Bay Crossing

vehicles a day. Five traffic lanes wide, it has two levels: westbound traffic into San Francisco uses the top deck, eastbound to Oakland the lower.

The eastern canti-lever section is raised on more than 20 piers. It climbs up from the toll plaza causeway in Oakland to 191 ft (58 m) above the bay at Yerba Buena Island. In 1989 the bridge was

10 miles (16 km) of cable holding up the bridge

2,310 ft (704 m)

The West Bay Crossing section of Bay Bridge

and a Children's Fairyland where young visitors can enjoy pony rides, puppet shows and nursery rhyme scenes.

Jack London Square ㉒

🚢 to Oakland. 🚌 12th Street, then AC Transit 58, 72, 88 bus.

Jack London, author of *The Call of the Wild* and *White Fang*, grew up in Oakland in the 1880s, and was a frequent visitor to the Oakland Estuary waterfront. You can drive or catch the ferry to its bright, cheerful promenade of shops and restaurants, which have outdoor tables in fine weather. There are also pleasure boats offering trips along the estuary.

Little of the waterfront that London knew remains. However, the writer's footsteps can be traced to Heinold's First and Last Chance Saloon, which has now sunken with age into the street. The Yukon cabin that was purportedly occupied by London during the Gold Rush of 1898 has also been erected at the dockside.

Oakland Museum ㉓

See pp166–67.

View from Oakland across Lake Merritt

Old Oakland ㉔

🚌 12th Street.
Farmers' Market Tel (510) 745-7100. ◯ 8am–2pm Fri.

Also known as Victorian Row, these two square blocks of wood and brick commercial buildings were erected between the 1860s and 1880s, but they were thoroughly renovated in the 1980s and now contain an array of shops, restaurants, and art galleries. Fridays bring crowds of shoppers to the Farmers' Market, where stalls sell fresh produce and prepared foods. By night, the crowds move to the Pacific Coast Brewing Company on Washington Street. Don't miss 103-year-old Rattos, at 827 Washington Street an Italian delicatessen

famed for its Friday and Saturday night "Pasta Operas," when the management and visiting singers serenade the clientèle.

Oakland Chinatown ㉕

🚌 12th Street or Lake Merritt.

The bay area's second-largest Chinatown should perhaps be called "Asiatown." Its Cantonese majority is augmented by immigrants from Korea, Vietnam, and other parts of Southeast Asia. The neighborhood receives far fewer tourists than San Francisco's Chinatown. Its restaurants have a reputation for hearty, dependable, and reasonably priced home-style food.

---

closed for a month after the Loma Prieta earthquake *(see p19)*, when a 50-ft (15-m) segment disconnected where the cantilever span meets the approach ramp from Oakland. There are plans to completely rebuild the East Bay crossing from Yerba Buena Island to Oakland.

Boring through the island in a tunnel 76 ft (23 m) high and 58 ft (17 m) wide, the roadway emerges at the West Bay section of the bridge. Two

suspension spans join at the concrete central anchorage, which is deeper in the water than that of any other bridge.

The World's Fair (1939 to 1940) was held on Treasure Island, part of Yerba Buena Island, to celebrate the bridge's completion *(see p31)*. Now this small island is home to small parks and fine residences.

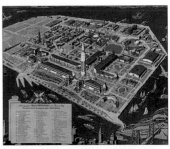

Plan of the 1939–40 World's Fair on Treasure Island

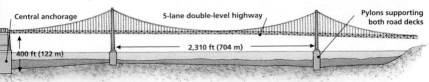

Central anchorage | 5-lane double-level highway | Pylons supporting both road decks

400 ft (122 m) | 2,310 ft (704 m)

Oakland Museum of California ㉓

California's only museum exclusively dedicated to documenting the state's art, history, and environment opened in 1969. The building, an important architectural icon for its integration of museum and landscape, is handsomely terraced with courts and gardens and was designed by architect Kevin Roche. The Natural Sciences gallery features "A walk across California" with natural history dioramas showing all of the state's ecozones and species. The Cowell Hall of California History has a large collection of Californian artifacts, while the Gallery of California Art boasts early oil paintings of Yosemite and San Francisco. Check their website for details of the latest exhibitions.

California gold miner's banjo

Welcome to California
This display celebrates past and present-day life in California.

Roof and gardens

The Great Hall is used for special changing exhibitions.

Gallery of California Art
The modern art in this collection includes the painting Ocean Park No: 107 (1978) by Richard Diebenkorn.

Level 3

Level 2

10th Street entrance

★ Dream on Wheels
A drive-in restaurant sign and jukebox in the 1951 diorama capture the atmosphere of postwar California.

KEY TO THE OAKLAND MUSEUM LEVELS

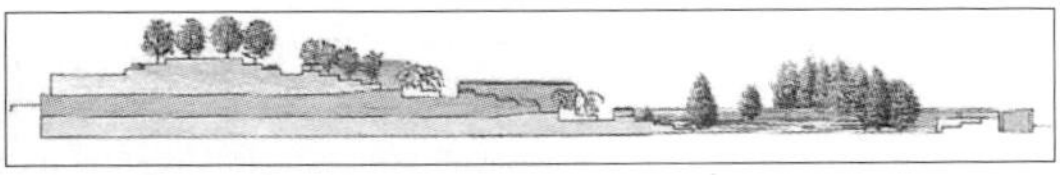

☐ Art Gallery   ☐ History   ☐ Natural Sciences

VISITORS' CHECKLIST

1000 Oak St, Oakland. 🅵 *(510) 238-2200.* 🚌 *Lake Merritt.* 🕐 *10am–5pm Wed–Sat, noon–5pm Sun (until 9pm 1st Fri of the month).* ⬤ *Jan 1, Jul 4, Thanksgiving, Dec 25, Mon–Tue.* 🅿 ♿ *free 2nd Sun* 🔲🔲🔲🔲♿
www.museumca.org

California Mud Wagon
Developed for rural life during the mid 19th century, this multipurpose vehicle could be converted easily from a field wagon to a stylish carriage.

★ **Food Chain Diorama**
This diorama features a mountain lion and its prey, to show how wildlife competes to survive.

MUSEUM GUIDE
Level 1 contains the shop and the Natural Sciences Gallery, where "A Walk Across California" covers the state's ecology from west to east. The Cowell Hall of California history and the restaurant are on level 2. Level 3 has the Art Gallery.

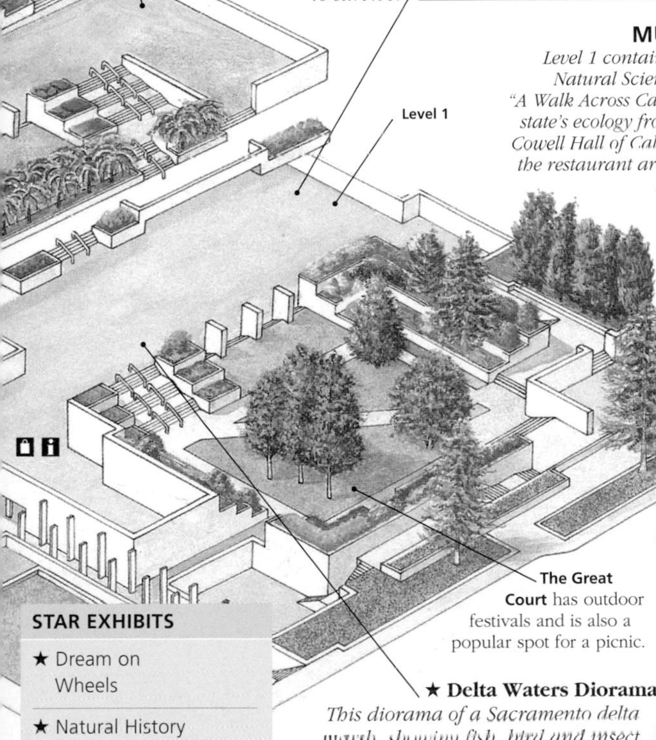

Level 1

The Great Court has outdoor festivals and is also a popular spot for a picnic.

STAR EXHIBITS

★ Dream on Wheels

★ Natural History Dioramas

★ **Delta Waters Diorama**
This diorama of a Sacramento delta marsh, showing fish, bird and insect life, typifies the high caliber of the Aquatic California Gallery.

Day Trips South of the City

South of San Francisco bay, Santa Clara County became famous in the late 1960s for its Silicon Valley. It is well worth exploring on day trips. San Jose has a variety of fascinating museums, while Filoli estate offers a mansion and garden tour. Stanford University and Pescadero are interesting for their fine architecture and history.

The Winchester Mystery House

SIGHTS AT A GLANCE

Museums

Children's Discovery Museum **4**
Rosicrucian Egyptian Museum and Planetarium **2**
History Museum of San Jose **5**
Stanford University **8**
Tech Museum of Innovation **3**
The Winchester Mystery House **1**

Historic Places

Filoli **6**   Pescadero **7**

KEY

▨	Central San Francisco
▨	Greater San Francisco
✈	Airport
▰	Freeway
▰	Major road
═	Minor road
──	Railroad line

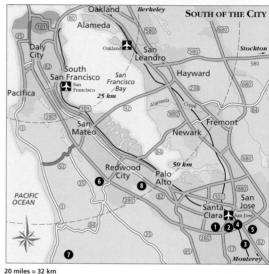

SOUTH OF THE CITY

20 miles = 32 km

The Winchester Mystery House **1**

525 S Winchester Blvd, between Stevens Creek Blvd and I-280, San Jose. **☎** *(408) 247-2101.* **☐** *Santa Clara, then Santa Clara Transportation Agency bus 32 or 34 to Franklin St and Monroe St; then bus 60.* ☐ *9am–5pm daily.* ● *Dec 25.* ✔ ✔ ☐ ☐ www.winchestermy steryhouse.com

When the heiress of the Winchester Rifle fortune, Sarah Winchester, started to build her house in 1884, a medium told her she would die if she stopped. She kept carpenters working there for 38 years, until she died at age 82. The result is a bizarre complex of 160 rooms filled with unusual treasures, set in beautiful gardens. Its features include stairways that lead nowhere and windows set into the floor. The house has a Firearms Museum with a collection of Winchester rifles.

Forecourt of the Rosicrucian Egyptian Museum

Rosicrucian Egyptian Museum and Planetarium **2**

Naglee and Park Aves, San Jose. **☎** *(408) 947-3600.* **☐** *Santa Clara, then Santa Clara Transportation Agency bus 32 or 34 to Franklin St, then bus 81.* ☐ *9am–5pm Mon–Fri, 11am–6pm Sat & Sun (Museum).* ● *Jan 1, Easter Sunday, Thanksgiving, Dec 24, 25, 31.* ✔ www.egyptianmuseum.org

Inspired by the Temple of Amon at Karnak, Egypt, this museum houses ancient Egyptian, Babylonian, Assyrian, and Sumerian artifacts. Funerary boats and models, human and animal mummies, Coptic textiles, pottery, jewelry and a full-size tomb are on display.

The Tech Museum of Innovation **3**

201 South Market St (at Park Ave), San Jose. **☎** *(408) 294-TECH.* **☐** *San Jose, then Light Rail to Convention Center.* ☐ *10am–5pm Tue–Sun.* ✔ ☐ ☐ www.thetech.org

This colorful technological museum has undergone a multi-million dollar expansion. The Tech is divided into four themed galleries, including Innovation and Exploration. Many of the exhibits have a "hands-on" element, such as making your own film, or discovering the latest tricks in animation. There is also an Imax® Dome Theater, which is open for screenings on Friday and Saturday nights.

Children's Discovery Museum ❹

180 Woz Way, San Jose.
Tel (408) 298-5437. 🚊 Arena, or to
Tamien, then Light Rail to Technology.
🕐 10am–5pm Tue–Sat, noon–5pm
Sun. 📷 🖼 ♿ **www**.cdm.org

A short walk leads from San
Jose Convention Center to this
museum, where children can
play in a real red fire-engine
or in an ambulance with
flashing lights. The more
adventurous can crawl
through a multi-level maze to
experience three-dimensional
space or step into dedicated
environments to explore the
phenomenon of rhythm. At
"Doodad Dump" creative
visitors can make their own
jewelry and gadgets using
recycled material from Silicon
Valley companies, glue and
lots of imagination.

History Museum of San Jose ❺

1650 Senter Rd, San Jose. **Tel** (408)
287-2290. 🚊 Cahill, then bus 64 to
1st and Santa Clara St, then bus 73
from 2nd St. 🕐 noon–5pm Tue–
Sun. ● Jan 1, Jul 4, Thanksgiving,
Dec 25. 🖼 **www**.historysanjose.org

This charming museum in
Kelley Park re-creates San Jose
as it was in the early 20th
century. More than 21 original
houses and businesses have
been restored and set
around a town

A popular exhibit in the Children's Discovery Museum

square. They include a fire
station, an ice cream parlor
with working soda fountain,
gas station, and a historic
trolley that travels around
the grounds.

Filoli ❻

Canada Rd, nr Edgewood Rd,
Woodside. **Tel** (650) 364-8300. 📷
Feb–Nov by appointment. 🕐 10am–
3:30pm Tue–Sat, 11am–3:30pm Sun
(last admission 2:30pm). ● federal
hols. **www**.filoli.org

The lavish 43-room Filoli
mansion was built in 1915 for
William Bourne II, owner of
the Empire Gold Mine. Gold
from the mine was used in its
decoration. The elegant house
is surrounded by a large
garden and an estate where
guided nature walks can be
arranged. "Filoli" is an acronym
for "Fight, love, live," which
refers to Bourne's love for the
Irish and their
struggle.

Pescadero ❼

 Daly City, then SamTrans routes
IC or IL to Half Moon Bay, then 96C
(weekdays only).

This quaint village with its
many two-story wooden
buildings has antique stores,
gift shops and one of the
southern peninsula's best
restaurants, Duarte's Tavern.
Families will enjoy Phipps
Ranch, a farm with a barnyard
and "pick your own" fruit.
Pigeon Point Lighthouse lies
8 miles (5 km) to the south.

Stanford University ❽

Palo Alto. **Tel** (650) 723-2053. 🚊
Palo Alto, then Santa Clara Transit
bus 35. 📷 phone (650) 723-2560
for details. **www**.stanford.edu

One of the country's most
prestigious private universities,
with 13,000 students, Stanford
was built by railroad mogul
Leland Stanford (see p102) in
memory of his son, and
opened in 1891. The heart of
the campus is the Main Quad,
built in Romanesque style
with some characteristics of
Mission architecture. Main
landmarks are the Memorial
Church, the Hoover
Tower and the Stanford
University Museum of
Art, where you can
see the Golden Spike
that completed the
transcontinental railroad
in 1869. The Museum of
Art owns a collection of
Rodins, including the
Gates of Hell and *Adam
and Eve*.

Memorial Church at Stanford University, Palo Alto

FIVE GUIDED WALKS

These five walks take in much of the Bay Area's intriguing cultural and geographical diversity and sweeping views. The Aquatic Park walk along the northern waterfront covers the area from Hyde Street Pier *(see p83)*, with its historic sailing ships and echoes of the past, to Fort Mason Center *(see pp74–5)*, a military relic transformed into a lively community with theaters, museums and arts activities. Only half an hour's drive away, the Marin Headlands walk is into another world,

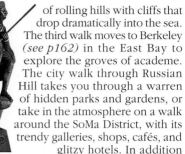

Davy Crockett figure head at the Maritime Museum
(see p83)

of rolling hills with cliffs that drop dramatically into the sea. The third walk moves to Berkeley *(see p162)* in the East Bay to explore the groves of academe. The city walk through Russian Hill takes you through a warren of hidden parks and gardens, or take in the atmosphere on a walk around the SoMa District, with its trendy galleries, shops, cafés, and glitzy hotels. In addition to these walks, each of the eight areas of San Francisco described in the *Area by Area* section of this book has a walk on its *Street-by-Street* map.

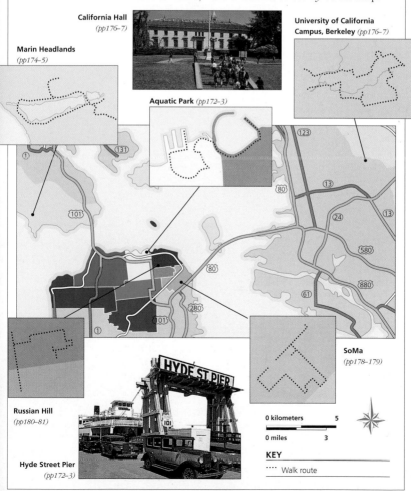

California Hall
(pp176–7)

Marin Headlands
(pp174–5)

University of California Campus, Berkeley *(pp176–7)*

Aquatic Park *(pp172–3)*

SoMa
(pp178–179)

Russian Hill
(pp180–81)

Hyde Street Pier
(pp172–3)

0 kilometers 5

0 miles 3

KEY

····· Walk route

◁ View of Point Bonita Lighthouse on the southwestern tip of the Marin Headlands

A 90-Minute Walk around Aquatic Park

Side by side on San Francisco's northern waterfront, Aquatic Park and Fort Mason offer some fascinating glimpses into the city's past, especially its colorful history as a seaport. There are no cars here, just walkers, cyclists and skaters sharing lushly overgrown paths. The route winds past historic ships moored in the bay, Depression-era swim clubs, Gold Rush cottages and military installations dating from Spanish colonial times to World War II. You can swim if you don't mind the chilly bay water, fish for crabs, paddle off a small beach or just stop to admire the view and picnic in one of the many grassy spots. For more details see pages 74–5 and 80–3.

Statue by Bufano in Fort Mason Center

Marina Green and Fort Mason

Hyde Street Pier

Begin at the seaward end of Hyde Street Pier ①. Until 1938, when the opening of the Golden Gate Bridge made it obsolete, this pier was the

Ships moored in Aquatic Park

center of activity on the city's northern waterfront. It is now part of the National Maritime Museum, used as a mooring for the museum's collection of historic ships *(see p83)*. Among these is a handsome steam-powered ferry boat, the *Eureka* ②, built in 1890 and recently restored. The ship is full of old cars and ephemera from 1941, the last year it was in service. From the landward end of the pier, where there is a bookstore ③ operated by the National Park Service, walk west along the waterfront past

the Hyde Street cable car turntable on your left. In flower-filled Victorian Park ④ street musicians perform. There is a pair of whitewashed clapboard buildings ⑤ on the sandy beach to your right, which house the South End and Dolphin swimming and rowing clubs.

Aquatic Park

Continue westward to the broad Golden Gate Promenade, popular with joggers, cyclists and skaters. This right-of-way follows the old Belt Line railroad, which once ran along the Embarcadero from the wharves and warehouses of China Basin and Potrero Hill to Fort Mason and the Presidio.

On the left is a large building known as the Casino ⑥, built in 1939 as a public bathing club. Since 1951 it has been the West Coast home of the Maritime National Historical Park Visitors' Center *(see p83)*, which is partially closed for renovation work until 2012. Visitors cannot go inside but they can still admire the unique museum building.

West of the Casino is a topiary sign spelling out "Aquatic Park." Behind this are red-and-white plastic-roofed *bocce* ball courts.

Hearst Pavilion

Bufano Statue

FORT MASON (GOLDEN GATE NATIONAL RECREATION AREA)

LAGUNA STREET

BAY STREET

Boat building in progress on Hyde St. Pier ①

The old dock and boathouse ⑦ to your right are used on weekends by sea scouts learning seamanship. Continue along the waterfront to the curving concrete pier ⑧ that marks the western end of Aquatic Park. People fish here at all hours, mostly for crabs. The Mission-style building at the foot of the pier is an emergency pumping station.

Promenade to the top of the slope, then turn left and go around to the front of the Youth Hostel ⑩. This is one of the few ornate wooden houses open to the public. Most of the buildings date from the 1850s. Today, they serve as homes for the park staff. Follow Funston Street along

The sea scouts' boathouse ⑦

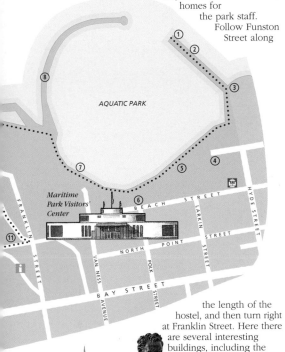

AQUATIC PARK

Maritime Park Visitors' Center

BEACH STREET
LARKIN STREET
HYDE STREET
FRANKLIN STREET
NORTH POINT STREET
POLK STREET
VAN NESS AVENUE
BAY STREET

Fort Mason

West of Aquatic Park, the Golden Gate Promenade climbs upward, rounding Black Point and giving excellent views of Alcatraz and Angel Island. Above the pathway, cypress trees cover the headland, and a series of terraces ⑨ holds the remains of artillery emplacements from the late 1800s. Follow the Golden Gate

Phillip Burton in Great Meadow ⑫

From the Great Meadow, take the narrow steps down the hill to Fort Mason Center (see pp74–5). Continue north to Pier 3, which is usually home to the SS *Jeremiah O'Brien*, the last of over 2,700 "Liberty Ships." These were built in World War II to carry troops into combat, and this vessel took part in both the 1944 D-Day invasion of Normandy and the 50th anniversary celebrations. Recently, the ship has been on temporary display at other piers in the city.

0 meters   250

0 yards   250

KEY

••• Walk route

▣ Cable car turntable

ℹ Information center

the length of the hostel, and then turn right at Franklin Street. Here there are several interesting buildings, including the exclusive Fort Mason Officers' Club on the left. Turn right by the chapel to arrive at the headquarters of the Golden Gate National Recreation Area (GGNRA) ⑪.
The grassy knolls of Great Meadow ⑫ extend westward from here. This was where refugees from the 1906 earthquake camped until they could be re-housed. A statue of Congressman Phillip Burton, the inspiration behind the formation of the GGNRA, has been erected in the middle of the field.

TIPS FOR WALKERS

Starting point: The seaward end of Hyde Street Pier.
Length: 1.5 miles (2.5 km).
Getting there: The Powell-Hyde cable car's northern terminus and turntable at Beach Street is a short walk from Hyde Street Pier. Muni bus no. 32 goes to Jefferson Street and Hyde Street.
Stopping-off points: The Buena Vista Café, opposite the cable car turntable, is always packed with customers who come for the good breakfasts and strong coffee (including a famous Irish Coffee). Greens restaurant (see p229) in Building A at Fort Mason Center, considered to be San Francisco's finest vegetarian restaurant, is run by disciples of Zen Buddhism. You can have a full meal or, if you just want a snack, buy pastries and drinks from the counter.

A 90-Minute Walk through the Marin Headlands

At its northern end, the Golden Gate Bridge is anchored in the rolling green hills of the Marin Headlands. This is an unspoiled wild area of windswept ridges, sheltered valleys and deserted beaches, once used as a military defense post and now part of the vast Golden Gate National Recreation Area. From several vantage points there are spectacular views of San Francisco and the sea and, on autumn days, you can see migrating eagles and ospreys gliding past Hawk Hill.

Schoolchildren on a trip to the Marin Headlands

Rodeo Beach ③

Visitor Center to Rodeo Beach

Before starting this walk, pause a while at the steepled Visitor Center ①, which was once the interdenominational chapel for Fort Cronkhite. It has since been refurbished and is now a museum and information center, with a natural history bookstore that specializes in books on birds. Here you can discover the history of the Marin Headlands and see a Coast Miwok Indian shelter.

The walk, which will take you around Rodeo Lagoon ②, begins at the gate on the west, ocean side, of the parking area. Take the path to the left that leads to the sea. This part of the trail is thick with trees and shrubs, including the poison oak, of which visitors should be aware. The songs of birds fill the air, and around the edges of the lagoon you will see brown pelicans, snowy egrets and mallards. A 15-minute walk will bring you to the sandy, windblown Rodeo Beach, ③, and from here you can see Bird Island ④

MARIN HEADLANDS
STATE PARK
(GOLDEN GATE NATIONAL
RECREATION AREA)

⑥ MITCHELL ROAD

Cooper's Hawk

Rodeo

②

White Egret

③ Rodeo Beach

Herring Gull

PACIFIC OCEAN

Turkey Vulture

④

Battery Smith-Guthrie

COAST

Bird Island

MENDELL RO

Batter Mende

KEY

••• Walk route

❊ View point

P Parking

Rodeo Lagoon ②

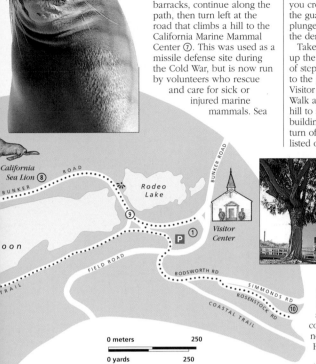

Seal at the Marine Mammal Center ⑦

barracks, continue along the path, then turn left at the road that climbs a hill to the California Marine Mammal Center ⑦. This was used as a missile defense site during the Cold War, but is now run by volunteers who rescue and care for sick or injured marine mammals. Sea

brackish lagoon with its tall grasses. Stay on the path as you cross the bridge. Before the guard rail ends, a path ⑨ plunges down to the right into the dense shrubbery.

Take this, and then continue up the hill again, via a series of steps that will return you to the path at the end of the Visitor Center parking area. Walk across the lot and up the hill to a three-story wooden building, constructed at the turn of the century. This is listed on the National Historic

Visitor Center ①

Registry and has been officers' headquarters, a hospital and a missile command center. It is now the Golden Gate Hostel ⑩ for travelers. The Marin Headlands also offer a wide range of longer, more challenging wilderness walks. Wolf Ridge and Bobcat Trail are two popular routes to try.

lying off-shore to the south. Fishing boats may be seen bobbing out at sea, but the beach is mostly empty of people, although sometimes you might see groups of children studying the coastal ecology: educational programs are run by the Headlands Institute, based in the nearby former army barracks.

Barracks to the California Marine Mammal Center

From the beach, turn inland again as you approach the tip of the lagoon, crossing a wooden footbridge ⑤. Here there are restrooms and barracks ⑥ housing various offices, among them the Headlands District Office, the Raptor Observatory and an energy and resources center. Walking past the

lions and seals, including elephant seals, are examined and treated here, in specially designed pens, then put back in the sea when they have recovered. You can watch the vets at work and get a close view of the mammals, many of which are orphaned pups. There are also displays on the marine ecosystem.

Lagoon to the Golden Gate Hostel

Make your way back down the hill and return to the paved road that runs past the lagoon ⑧. There is a separate roadside pathway for hikers, but you have to climb over a guard rail to get on to it. Just before the road crosses a bridge, there is a large bench where you can watch the water birds. There are plenty of these to be seen in this

Horse Trail

Bike Trail

Sign marking a trail

TIPS FOR WALKERS

Starting point: The Visitor Center at Fort Cronkhite.
Length: 2 miles (3 km).
Getting there: San Francisco Muni bus 76 leaves from the intersection of Fourth Street and Townsend Street on Sundays only. **Tel** (415) 673-6864 (Muni). By car, drive across the Golden Gate Bridge, taking the Alexander Avenue exit. Turn under the freeway, following signs for the Headlands, Fort Cronkhite and Fort Barry.
Stoping-off points: Water is available, but there are no refreshment facilities in the Marin Headlands. You will need to bring your own picnic lunch, which can be enjoyed at any number of tables dotted along the trails and on the beaches.

A 90-Minute Walk around the University of California Campus in Berkeley

This walk concentrates on a distinct area of Berkeley, the campus of the University of California, allowing a stimulating glimpse into the intellectual, cultural and social life of this vibrant university town *(see pp162–63)*.

West Entrance to Sather Tower

From University Avenue ①, cross Oxford Street and follow University Drive past the Valley Life Sciences Building ②. Wellman Hall can be seen on the north fork of Strawberry Creek as you follow the road to the right, keeping California Hall ③ on your right. Turn left on the Cross Campus Road ④. Wheeler Hall lies to the right and ahead is the main campus landmark, the 307-ft (94-m)

Inside are ore samples and pictures of old mining operations. Return to University Drive, turn left and out of the East Gate to the Hearst Greek Theater ⑩.

Faculty Club to the Eucalyptus Grove

Follow Gayley Road, which straddles a major earthquake fault, and turn right down the first path past Lewis Hall and

Students outside Wheeler Hall

Esplanade near Sather Tower ⑤

tall Sather Tower ⑤. Built by John Galen Howard in 1914, it was based on the campanile in the Piazza San Marco in Venice. Before going there, visit the Doe Library ⑥ and the AF Morrison Memorial Library ⑦ in the north wing. The adjacent Bancroft Library houses the plate supposedly left by Sir Francis Drake, claiming California for Queen Elizabeth I *(see p22)*. Return to Sather Tower, which is open 10am–3:30pm Monday to Saturday and offers fine views from the top. Across the way lies South Hall ⑧, the oldest building on campus.

Hearst Mining Building to the Greek Theatre

Continuing north, pass LeConte Hall then cross University Drive to the Mining Circle. Here is the Hearst Mining Building ⑨, built by Howard in 1907.

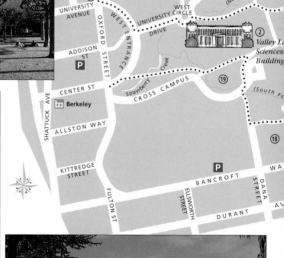

Wellman Hall on the University of California Campus

Musicians on lower Sproul Plaza ⑰

proceed to the wildly modern Berkeley Art Museum ⑮. Continue along Bancroft Way to Telegraph Avenue ⑯, famous for the student activism of the 1960s and '70s. The entrance to the university opposite Telegraph Avenue opens onto Sproul Plaza ⑰. Step into the lower courtyard with its modern Zellerbach Hall ⑱, then pass Alumni House, noting the state-of-the-art Harmon Gym, and turn right. Cross over the south fork of Strawberry Creek at Bay Tree Bridge, and bear left for the

Sather Tower ⑤

nature area, with its eucalyptus trees, some of the tallest in the world ⑲. The path ends near the start of the walk.

0 meters — 250

0 yards — 250

KEY

• • • Walk route

🚇 Bart station

🅿 Parking

Map labels

HEARST AVENUE

CYCLOTRON ROAD

Hearst Mining Building

GAYLEY RD

⑨

MINING CIRCLE

UNIVERSITY DRIVE

⑩ *Hearst Greek Theater*

STADIUM RINGWAY

⑤

⑧ ⑫ ⑪

⑬

Sather Gate

PIEDMONT AVENUE

BARROW LANE

Sproul Hall 🅿

BANCROFT WAY

⑭ COLLEGE AVENUE

⑮

BOWDITCH STREET

AVENUE

⑰

TELEGRAPH AVENUE

⑯ DURANT AVENUE

Hildebrand Hall, then left over a footbridge. The path winds between a log house and the Faculty Club ⑪. This rambling, rustic building, partly designed by Bernard Maybeck, dates from 1903. Faculty Glade ⑫ in front of the club is a favorite picnic spot.

The path now swings to the right, then sharply left. Take a look at Hertz Hall ⑬, then go down the diagonal walk that passes Wurster Hall to Kroeber Hall. Here you can visit the PA Hearst Museum of Anthropology. Cross Bancroft Way to the Caffè Strada ⑭, and then

Within (1969) by A. Lieberman at UCB Art Museum ⑮

A 90-Minute Walk around South of Market

Once a grubby warehouse district, SoMa is a model of urban revitalization. The acronym, SoMa, comes from an old nickname referring to the "wrong side" of the Market Street cable car track when Gold Rush-era immigrants worked in the factories here. Today, a four-block square area surrounding the Moscone Convention Center is chock-a-block with major art and history museums, high-rise hotels, trendy galleries, and shops. On this walk you will encounter vestiges of the city's rip-roaring past among its dazzling 21st-century architecture, as well as trendy cafés and bars.

and children's games and plan to return for a full tour of the displays of contemporary art. On either side of SFMOMA are skyscraper hotels, the St. Regis Museum Tower, and W San Francisco. At the base of the St. Regis, a turn-of-the-century building houses the new Museum of the African Diaspora (MOAD), where multimedia displays

The SoMa skyline with its mix of old and new architecture

Mission Street
Begin at St. Patrick's Church ① , a soaring brick landmark built in 1851. Notice the green open space of Yerba Buena Gardens across the street, and the variety of vintage and contemporary buildings that characterize this diverse district. Walk north-east a block to the California Historical Society ② *(see p113)*, where the colorful story of the Golden State is told through art and photography. You might like to return here another time to delve into manuscripts in the library, or to sign up for narrated history walks. Step into the Cartoon Art Museum ③ to see exhibitions of comic book super-heroes, great women cartoonists or the work of Charles Schultz, the Peanuts creator – it depends on what is on display at the time. In the same building, Foto-Graphix Books offers books on photography and graphic art including a stunning collection by famed California photographer, Ansel Adams. You can pick up collectible posters of San Francisco here, too. Stroll up to Second Street and turn left to find the Alexander Book Company ④ , an old favorite, that is unassuming

on the outside with three floors of treasures inside.

SFMOMA
Retrace your steps to Mission Street and walk south two blocks to Third Street. Across from Yerba Buena Gardens, admire the cylinder of the San Francisco Museum of Modern Art ⑤ *(see pp118–21)*, one of the architectural wonders of the city. The architect, Mario Botta, described the tilting skylight as "the eye for the city." Browse in the museum store for art books, jewelry

SF Museum of Modern Art ⑤ , a stunning work of architecture

present such subjects as celebrations, slavery, art and origins. At the sleek W hotel, take a look into the "Living Room," the octagonal, three-story lobby that's walled with glass and flowing drapes. Here, you can rest with a drink or a coffee.

Yerba Buena Gardens to the Old United States Mint
Cross Third Street to enter Yerba Buena Gardens ⑥ *(see p114–15)*. Take a stroll beneath the sycamores and around the flower gardens, and walk behind the Martin

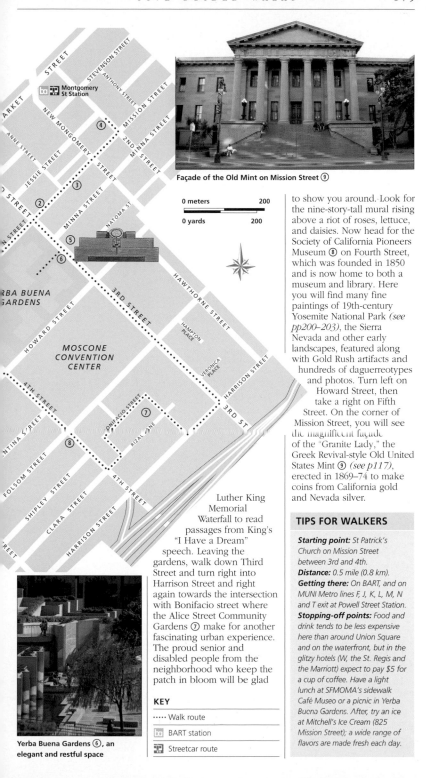

Façade of the Old Mint on Mission Street ⑨

0 meters 200
0 yards 200

STEVENSON STREET
ANTHONY STREET
MISSION STREET
STREET
Montgomery
St Station
NEW MONTGOMERY
STREET
2ND STREET
MINNA STREET
ANNE STREET
JESSIE STREET
STREET
④
③
②
MARKET
STREET
MINNA STREET
NATOMA ST
⑤
⑥
HAWTHORNE STREET
RBA BUENA
GARDENS
3RD STREET
HOWARD STREET
HAMPTON PLACE
MOSCONE
CONVENTION
CENTER
VERONICA PLACE
HARRISON STREET
4TH STREET
HARRISON STREET
3RD ST
BONIFACIO STREET
RIZAL LANE
⑦
NTINA STREET
⑧
4TH STREET
FOLSOM STREET
4TH STREET
SHIPLEY STREET
CLARA STREET
HARRISON STREET

to show you around. Look for the nine-story-tall mural rising above a riot of roses, lettuce, and daisies. Now head for the Society of California Pioneers Museum ⑧ on Fourth Street, which was founded in 1850 and is now home to both a museum and library. Here you will find many fine paintings of 19th-century Yosemite National Park *(see pp200–203)*, the Sierra Nevada and other early landscapes, featured along with Gold Rush artifacts and hundreds of daguerreotypes and photos. Turn left on Howard Street, then take a right on Fifth Street. On the corner of Mission Street, you will see the magnificent façade of the "Granite Lady," the Greek Revival-style Old United States Mint ⑨ *(see p117)*, erected in 1869–74 to make coins from California gold and Nevada silver.

TIPS FOR WALKERS

Starting point: *St Patrick's Church on Mission Street between 3rd and 4th.*
Distance: *0.5 mile (0.8 km).*
Getting there: *On BART, and on MUNI Metro lines F, J, K, L, M, N and T exit at Powell Street Station.*
Stopping-off points: *Food and drink tends to be less expensive here than around Union Square and on the waterfront, but in the glitzy hotels (W, the St. Regis and the Marriott) expect to pay $5 for a cup of coffee. Have a light lunch at SFMOMA's sidewalk Café Museo or a picnic in Yerba Buena Gardens. After, try an ice at Mitchell's Ice Cream (825 Mission Street); a wide range of flavors are made fresh each day.*

Luther King Memorial Waterfall to read passages from King's "I Have a Dream" speech. Leaving the gardens, walk down Third Street and turn right into Harrison Street and right again towards the intersection with Bonifacio street where the Alice Street Community Gardens ⑦ make for another fascinating urban experience. The proud senior and disabled people from the neighborhood who keep the patch in bloom will be glad

KEY

····· Walk route

🚇 BART station

🚋 Streetcar route

Yerba Buena Gardens ⑥, an elegant and restful space

A 90-Minute Walk around Russian Hill

A hilltop warren of parks and rare pre-earthquake architecture are the rewards for this scramble up the steep stairways and leafy alleyways of Russian Hill. Here, you will encounter few cars and fewer people as you wander among carefully preserved buildings from the city's lively and notorious past, and enjoy the dazzling views, the birdsong and the luxuriant hillside gardens that are the pride of the neighborhood. At the end of your walk, descend to indulge in the European-style cafés and boutiques at the foot of the hill.

Russian Hill, fabulous views and pre-quake houses

his own house (at 1013), which is a shingle-sided, six-story arrangement reminiscent of the English Arts and Crafts movement. After the quake, Polk was appointed supervising architect of the 1915 Panama Pacific International Exposition, a world fair that celebrated the building of the Panama Canal and the rebuilding of San Francisco (see p72). Below his house, he created the zigzagging, Beaux Arts-style Vallejo

Russian Hill Place

Start the walk from the corner of Jones and Vallejo Streets on the whimsical, Beaux-Arts balustrade ①, designed in 1915 by Willis Polk, one of the architects of the post-1906 earthquake reconstruction (see pp28–9). Before climbing the stone stairway, notice the Spanish-tile-roofed, Mission Revival-style houses, with their fanciful balconies and arched windows on either side. Then take the stairs and walk into the short alleyway of Russian Hill Place ② to see the backs of those homes and their gardens. No. 6 is a turn-of-the-century Bay Area Tradition-style house. Vallejo Street has a variety of homes and apartments built between 1888 and the 1940s.

Florence Street to Coolbrith Park

Turn right into short Florence Street ③ and, at the end, look across the rooftops to Nob Hill. Once called Snob Hill, it is sprinkled with 19th-century mansions and grand hotels – look for the towers of Grace Cathedral (see p103). No. 40, one of the oldest houses on the hill, built in 1850, is hidden within additions from later decades. Peek through

the fence to see an 8-ft-tall rabbit, and a contemporary mobile sculpture. Note the Pueblo-Mission Revival-style homes along this street. Back on Vallejo Street, the gems of Russian Hill are two steep-roofed, gabled houses in the Bay Area Tradition-style at Nos. 1013–19 ④. Here, leading a move away from the gingerbread-house design of the Victorian era, Polk designed a home (at 1019) in 1892 for a wealthy client (who hosted, among others, Robert Louis Stevenson and Laura Ingalls Wilder) and next door,

Part of the rambling Vallejo Street steps ④ or "the ramps"

---

0 meters 100

0 yards 100

KEY

····· Walk route

Street steps, known as "the ramps." All along the extensive, three-part stairway are gardens overflowing with blue hydrangeas, azaleas, palms, magnolias, and over-arching pines and cypress trees. There is also a bench where tired walkers can rest. At the bottom of the steps at Taylor and Vallejo, stroll across the street to enjoy the sun at tiny Coolbrith Park ⑤. From here you can see islands in the bay, North Beach,

earthquake survivor. Turn left on Leavenworth Street, then right onto Green Street. The block between Hyde and Leavenworth Streets is also called "the Paris Block" ⑦, a reference to the house at No. 1050, which is reminiscent of those in Paris. A number of buildings on the block are on the National Register of Historic Places, including the last firehouse

A local relaxing in Macondray Lane, scene of TV's "Tales of the City" ⑥

cafés and shops cluster between Jackson and Union Streets ⑧. Lovers of all things French will like the Hyde Street Bistro (at No. 1521), the boutiques, and charming antiques shops. After browsing here, catch a bus directly from Hyde Street to various points across the city.

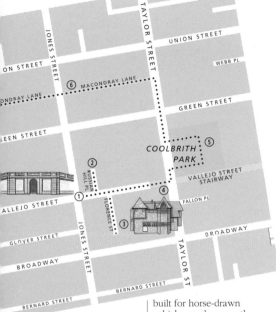

the Bay Bridge and the lower Financial District. On 4th of July, locals gather here to watch the fireworks display.

Macondray Lane to Green Street

Proceed north on Taylor Street to Macondray Lane ⑥ on the left, which is accessed by a creaky wooden stairway winding through dense vegetation. Along the two-block walkway are shingled "Edwardian" cottages, ballast stones from sailing ships, and rustic country houses set in flower gardens. The lane was the location for Barbary Lane in the "Tales of the City" television series. At Nos. 5–17, extravagant plaster garlands drape over the doorways of this rare

built for horse-drawn vehicles, and, across the street, the flamboyant 1857 Freusier Octagon House, with its mansard roof and cupola.

Hyde Street

Continue west on Green Street to Hyde Street where

TIPS FOR WALKERS

Starting point: The stone stairway at Jones and Vallejo Streets.
Distance: 0.75 miles (1.2 km).
Getting there: Take the Hyde-Powell cable car or the 45 MUNI line to Vallejo Street and walk east two blocks.
Stopping-off points: On Hyde Street, Frascati (at 1901) caters to neighborhood regulars with a pan-European menu of paella, and coq au vin in a cozy setting. The young and the hip hang out on leather love seats in the window of Bacchus Wine & Sake Bar (at 1954).

Hyde Street, with its French-style boutiques, cafés, and antique shops

Tunnel View, Yosemite Valley ▷

NORTHERN CALIFORNIA

Exploring Northern California

San Francisco sits at the apex of a beautiful,
varied and historical region of California.
The sheltered valleys of the coastal
ranges, perfect for vineyards, have
given the state a rich array of wineries
to explore, and the extensive coastline
is ideal for relaxing on pristine
beaches or birdwatching. There
are scores of old and fascinating
towns, and visitors can ski or
hike among the lofty summits of
the Sierra Nevada, all within a
few hours of the city. The
excursions described on
pages 186–203 have been
selected to give visitors a
sample of what beyond San
Francisco has to offer.

View north over Lake Tahoe in winter

SIGHTS AT A GLANCE

Carmel **1**
Lake Tahoe **8**
Lassen Volcanic National
    Park **5**
Mendocino **2**
The Napa Wine Country **3**

Redwood National Park **4**
Sacramento **7**
Sonoma Valley **6**
Yosemite National Park **9**

Oak trees in Yosemite Valley in the fall

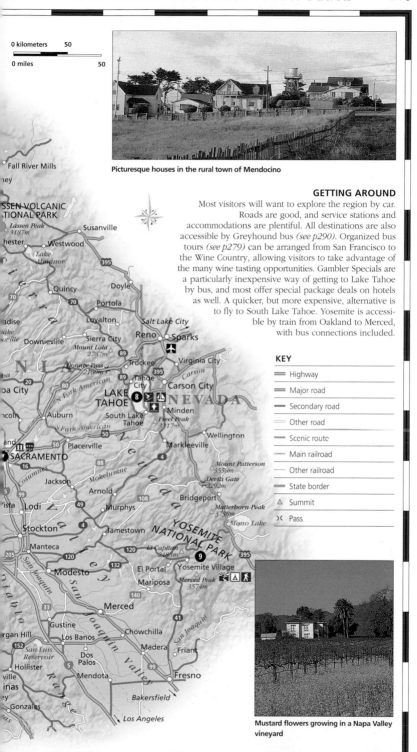

0 kilometers 50

0 miles 50

Fall River Mills

hey

SSEN VOLCANIC
TIONAL PARK
*Lassen Peak
3187m*
hester
Westwood
Susanville

Quincy

Doyle

Portola

Loyalton

Downieville
*Mount Lola
2787m*

Sierra City

Truckee

Tahoe
City

LAKE
TAHOE

South Lake
Tahoe

Auburn

Placerville

SACRAMENTO

Jackson

Lodi

Stockton

Manteca

Modesto

Merced

Gustine
Los Banos

Hollister

Mendota

Gonzales

Reno
Sparks

Virginia City

Carson City

NEVADA

Minden
*Freel Peak
3317m*

Markleeville

Wellington

*Mount Patterson
3558m*
*Devils Gate
2292m*

Bridgeport

*Matterhorn Peak
3738m*
Mono Lake

YOSEMITE
NATIONAL PARK
*El Capitan
2495m*
El Portal   Yosemite Village
Mariposa   *Merced Peak
3574m*

Chowchilla

Madera   Friant

Fresno

Bakersfield

Los Angeles

Donner Pass

Salt Lake City

Picturesque houses in the rural town of Mendocino

GETTING AROUND

Most visitors will want to explore the region by car.
Roads are good, and service stations and
accommodations are plentiful. All destinations are also
accessible by Greyhound bus *(see p290)*. Organized bus
tours *(see p279)* can be arranged from San Francisco to
the Wine Country, allowing visitors to take advantage of
the many wine tasting opportunities. Gambler Specials are
a particularly inexpensive way of getting to Lake Tahoe
by bus, and most offer special package deals on hotels
as well. A quicker, but more expensive, alternative is
to fly to South Lake Tahoe. Yosemite is accessible by train from Oakland to Merced,
with bus connections included.

KEY

▬▬	Highway
▬▬	Major road
▬▬	Secondary road
▬▬	Other road
▬▬	Scenic route
▬▬	Main railroad
▬▬	Other railroad
▬▬	State border
△	Summit
✕	Pass

Mustard flowers growing in a Napa Valley
vineyard

A Two-Day Tour to Carmel ❶

Skirting cliffs and coves, pocket beaches, lighthouses, parks and old historic towns, coastal Hwy 1 is a highly scenic route from San Francisco to Carmel. The region has a colorful history, particularly in old Monterey, the original capital of Spanish California. Carmel itself, a pretty seaside town, has been a haven for artists and writers since the early 20th century. Here you can visit the Carmel Mission, burial place of Father Junípero Serra *(see p137)*.

Santa Cruz roller coaster

San Francisco to Santa Cruz

Leaving the city at Pacifica, Hwy 1 narrows to a two-lane road. At Sharp Park, you can hike to Sweeny Ridge ①, a distance of 1.5 miles (2 km). From here, in 1769, Gaspar de Portolá's party of Spanish explorers became the first Europeans to see the Bay of San Francisco *(see pp24–5)*.

The strong currents and cold waters of the Pacific discourage most swimmers at the state-owned beaches at Gray Whale Cove ② and Montara. At low tide, the exposed rock pools reach from Fitzgerald Marine Preserve south to Pillar Point, the most extensive along the San Mateo County coast.

The fishing fleet still docks at nearby Princeton ③, while the big event of the year at Half Moon Bay ④ is the Pumpkin Festival in October. Princeton's main street retains the flavor of an old coastal town, and many Portuguese and Italian immigrants have settled here. To the south, the countryside quickly becomes much less populated. At Pigeon Point ⑤, just south of

Pescadero *(see p169)*, is a lighthouse built in 1872, which is closed for renovation, though the grounds remain open. From here, side roads

Child at the Pumpkin Festival in Half Moon Bay ④

climb into the Santa Cruz Mountains. The spectacular Ano Nuevo State Park ⑥ lies 20 miles (32 km) north of Santa Cruz, along Hwy 1. You can make a reservation with a ranger to hike a 3-mile (5-km) round-trip to the beach to see the colony of elephant seals.

Santa Cruz to Monterey

At Monterey Bay's northern end, Santa Cruz offers some excellent swimming beaches. Though the sandstone bridge of the Natural Bridges State

Beach ⑦ disappeared long ago into the waves, the beach here is protected and provides a safe harbor for swimmers.

Santa Cruz is famous for the Boardwalk ⑧, an amusement park that stretches for 0.5 mile (1 km) along the beach. The Big Dipper roller coaster has thrilled riders since 1923.

From Santa Cruz the highway curves around the bay to Monterey, 28 miles (45 km) away. Midway between them is the University of California's marine science station at Moss Landing ⑨, where visitors can watch birds and learn about the area's flora and fauna.

Monterey to Pacific Grove

The first capital of California, Monterey ⑩ was established by the Spanish in 1770. Many Spanish, Mexican and early

SAN FRANCISCO

San Francisco Bay

Pescadero

0 kilometers   20

0 miles   10

View of Pigeon Point lighthouse ⑤

Fisherman's Wharf, Monterey ⑩

American buildings still stand in the central part of the city. A free walking map, produced by the Chamber of Commerce, is readily available. This map indicates sights such as Robert Louis Stevenson's home and Colton Hall, where California's first constitution was written.

In the 1940s John Steinbeck, author of *Cannery Row* and *Tortilla Flat*, wrote about Monterey, describing it as a collection of sardine canneries and whorehouses. The spectacular Monterey Bay aquarium stands on the 3.3-acre site of the largest of the old canneries. The galleries and exhibits at the Aquarium utilize the unique marine habitats of the Bay itself. On the edge of the Monterey Peninsula is Pacific Grove ⑪, where in the autumn thousands of butterflies cluster in the trees. The 17-Mile Drive ⑫ starts here, following a scenic route past the world-famous golf courses of Pebble Beach and Spyglass Hill.

The drive ends at Carmel ⑬, with its

TIPS FOR TRAVELERS

Distance from San Francisco: *137 miles (220 km).*
Duration of journey: *About four hours, excluding stops.*
Getting back to San Francisco: *Monterey Peninsula is linked to US 101. It takes two and a half hours to reach San Francisco via San Jose.*
When to go: *The peak tourist season is summer when the sea air is fresh. Winter is often wet, sometimes with torrential rain.*
Where to stay and eat: *Santa Cruz, Monterey, Carmel, Pacific Grove and Pebble Beach have a wide selection of hotels, motels and bed-and-breakfast inns. Municipal Wharf in Santa Cruz has numerous snack bars for a light meal en route. Restaurants and eateries abound in Monterey on Cannery Row and Fisherman's Wharf. Carmel has a variety of restaurants, from French bistros to seafood restaurants.*
Visitor information: *Monterey Peninsula Chamber of Commerce and Visitors Bureau, 380 Alvarado Street, Monterey.* **Tel** *(831) 648-5360. Carmel Tourist Information Center, Mission Patio, Carmel.* **Tel** *(831) 624-1711.* **www**.montereyinfo.org

quaint streets and eccentric houses. This hillside town was founded as an artists' colony in the early 20th century, and there are several art galleries where visitors can browse. Many of the houses were designed by artists, inspired perhaps by romanticized impressions of old France. The quaint streets, quiet courtyards and shops encourage strollers. Father Junipero Serra, founder of the missions, is buried in Mission Carmel, which is one of the most beautiful churches in California.

⑬ *Carmel*

KEY

- Tour route
- Main road
- River
- Viewing point

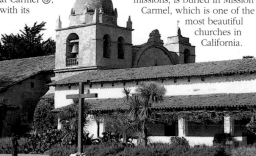

The Mission at Carmel, dating from 1793 ⑬

A Two-Day Tour to Mendocino ❷

A trip to Mendocino will take you along the rugged coastline of northern California, through wild and unspoiled country, to a small picturesque town that was once a logging village. It became a haven for artists in the 1950s, and was so well restored that it was declared an historic monument. Inland there are valleys with forests of redwood trees, best seen from the "Skunk Train" out of Fort Bragg, 10 miles (16 km) north of Mendocino.

Russian Orthodox chapel in Fort Ross

Western Marin to Bodega Bay

Start the trip north by crossing Golden Gate Bridge and then continue on US 101 through southern Marin County *(see pp160–61)*. At Mill Valley take a turn west on to Hwy 1, which climbs up the 1,500-ft-high (450-m) coastal hills then hugs the coast through Stinson Beach. At the town of Point Reyes Station ①, you can detour left and follow the road leading to Point Reyes National Seashore *(see p160)*, which takes about two hours. Hwy 1 continues along the edge of Tomales Bay ②, one of California's prime oyster growing estuaries. Beyond the bay the road winds inland for 30 miles (48 km) through the dairy farms of west Marin County, returning to the coast at Bodega Bay ③, where Alfred Hitchcock filmed *The Birds* in 1962.

Russian River and Fort Ross

North of Bodega Bay, Hwy 1 continues along the Pacific coastline, reaching the wide

mouth of the Russian River at Jenner ④, where there is a broad beach. Guerneville,

Coastal redwoods

the area's main town, lies up the river. The road climbs up the steep switchback of the Jenner Grade high above the Pacific, where you can stop to admire the views. On a windswept headland 12 miles (19 km) north of Jenner you

Johnson's Beach at Guerneville, on the Russian River

0 kilometers   20

0 miles   10

KEY

— Tour route

= Other road

— River

☆ Viewing point

A "Skunk Train" on its way through the redwood forest

will find the Fort Ross State Historic Park ⑤, a restored Russian fur trading outpost that stood from 1812 until it was closed in 1841. The original house of the fort's last manager, Alexander Rotchev, is still intact, and other buildings have been carefully reconstructed within a wooden palisade. The highlight is the Russian Orthodox chapel, built from local redwood in 1824. The park, which has a visitor center, is open from 10am to 4:30pm. Beyond Fort Ross, Hwy 1 snakes along the coast, passing through several coastal state parks, including the Kruse

Rhododendron Reserve ⑥. The best time to visit is during April and May, when the flowers are in bloom. This stretch of coast is ruggedly beautiful, with windswept headlands and hidden coves.

Point Arena and Manchester State Beach

The drive continues through open meadows and cypress groves to Point Arena ⑦. Here visitors can climb up the 147 steps in the old lighthouse for a spectacular view of the coast.

Manchester State Beach ⑧ hugs the coastline for the next 5 miles (8 km), and from here you can take a detour of about three hours to visit northern California's breweries, who have earned a name for themselves in recent years. Among the best brews are Red Tail Ale from Mendocino Brewing in Hopland ⑨ on US 101, and Boont Amber, made in Boonville ⑩ in the heart of the Anderson Valley. Both have pubs on the premises. Three miles (5 km) south of Mendocino on Hwy 1 is

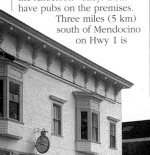

19th-century buildings in Mendocino ⑬

Van Damme State Park ⑪, a redwood forest with several good hiking trails. Mendocino Headlands State Park ⑫ is a bit farther along the highway – a greenbelt area where no development is allowed.

Mendocino ⑬ itself is tucked away west of the highway, on a rocky promontory above the Pacific. The town has retained the picturesque charm of its logging days, and although tourism is now its main industry, it remains unspoiled by commercialism, and is a thriving center for the arts, ideal for a stroll around.

The Napa Wine Country ❸

The narrow Napa Valley, with its rolling hillsides and fertile valley floor, is the heart and soul of the California wine industry. It supports over 250 wineries, some dating from the 19th century, with one or two down every country lane. Many welcome visitors for tours and tastings, and each part of the valley has its own distinctive wines *(see pp226–7)*. The rural beauty of the valley is striking at every season, and can be viewed from a balloon, a bike or a train. Other attractions include museums, galleries and the hot springs in Calistoga.

Ballooning in Napa Valley

Napa Valley Sign
Located at the entrance to the valley, this sign cheerfully welcomes visitors to its lush vineyards.

Old Faithful, a geyser, discharges hot water and steam every 40 minutes or so.

CALISTOGA

Schramsberg Vineyards

Beringer Vineyards has operated continuously since 1876.

ST HEL

Clos Pegase Winery
With its free tours and private art collection, this winery actively encourages visitors. It is housed in an award-winning Postmodern building.

RUTHERFO

KEY

═══	Road
〜〜	River
▦▦	Vineyard
▬▬▬	Railroad
• • •	Silverado Trail

Nelbaum-Coppola dates back to 1879. Tours start from the original winery, now the tasting room.

Robert Mondavi Winery uses the latest technology in its Mission-style building.

Domain Chandon produces 500,000 cases of sparkling wines annually.

Hess Collection Winery has both distinctive wines and fine works of art.

NAPA

Napa Valley Wine Train
Gourmet meals and excellent wines are served on this luxury train as it makes its three-hour trip along the valley, but some passengers come just for the ride.

Trefethen Vineyards

Silverado Hill Cellars

Sterling Vineyard
Perched on a rocky knoll overlooking the vineyards below, this unusual Greek-style winery is reached via an overhead gondola. The tour is marked by signs, allowing visitors to set their own pace.

Frog's Leap Winery

Duckhorn Vineyards

V Sattui Vineyard
French oak barrels are used for ageing the wine in some wineries.

Beaulieu Vineyard surrounds a château-style building. Tours are free.

Lake Hennesey

ILLE

OUNTVILLE

Joseph Phelps Vineyard
Grape-pickers harvest the year's crop in one of California's most prestigious wineries. Tours are by appointment.

Mumm Napa Valley is known for its classic sparkling wines.

Clos du Val, despite its small size, has a reputation for high-quality wines.

The Silverado Trail is a quiet road that offers fine views overlooking the vineyards.

TIPS FOR TRAVELERS

Distance from San Francisco: 55 miles (120 km).
Duration of journey: About one hour to Napa.
Getting there: Take US 101 north, then Hwy 37 to Vallejo, then Hwy 29 to Napa. Hwy 29 runs along the valley to Calistoga. Several bus companies offer tours, often including lunch.
When to go: In early spring the fields are carpeted with bright yellow mustard. Grapes begin to ripen in the summer heat. In September and October grapes are harvested and pressed, and vine leaves turn gold and red. Winter is the rainy season, when vines are pruned in preparation and new wine is bottled.
Where to stay and eat: For information contact the Visitors Bureau.
Visitor information: Napa Valley Visitors Bureau, 1310 Napa Town Center. Tel (707) 226-7459. www.napavalley.com

THE FIGHT AGAINST PHYLLOXERA

The phylloxera louse destroyed crops in the Napa Valley late in the 19th century, almost putting an end to the wine industry. Research found that new vines could thrive if grafted onto resistant rootstock, and disaster was averted. In 1980 the louse reappeared, and again infected plants had to be uprooted.

Infected vines being cleared for new resistant rootstock

Exploring the Napa Wine Country

A hedonist's dream, the long Napa Valley specializes in rich, distinctive wines, designer winery buildings, modern art collections, spas and artisan crafts. Indulging in a few wine tastings with a picnic and some shopping can easily consume one day. A dawn balloon ride, mud bath treatment and visits to art galleries will fill another. Before 1976, the *phylloxera* louse, Prohibition, and dull flavors haunted Napa winemakers. In that year, Chateau Montelena Chardonnay and Stag's Leap Cabernet Sauvignon won a blind tasting competition in Paris, and with a fresh marketing approach from Robert Mondavi the Napa Valley morphed into a competitive wine region with wineries in every field and hillock.

Wine tasting at one of Napa Valley's many wineries

WINE TASTING

www.napavalley.com/wineries

Many wineries have tasting rooms for sampling of the latest bottling, or will do so by appointment. Employees know products, prices, the characteristics of a vineyard's soil and the climate that gives each wine its flavor. Some wineries offer tours with a tasting at the end. Visitor volume and tasting room popularity have inspired some wineries to charge for tastings and tours. Robert Mondavi Winery bustles with tastings, presentations, tours and cooking demonstrations. Grgich Hills Cellars, Chateau Montelena Winery, Heitz Wine Cellars, Duckhorn Vineyards, Rutherford Hills, Franciscan Oakville Estates, V. Sattui Winery, Beaulieu Vineyard, and Stag's Leap all have wines with distinctive styles to taste. Sparkling wine fans should head to Mumm Cuvée Napa, Domaine Chandon and Domaine Carneros.

ART MUSEUMS AND GALLERIES

Wineries are a superb venue for art exhibits, adding cultural cachet to the experience.

Film Director Francis Ford Coppola transformed the 1879 Inglenook Winery into the Niebaum-Coppola Estate Winery, which includes his movie memorabilia museum.

The Hess Collection gallery has the contemporary European and US painting and sculpture collection of owner Donald Hess and includes artists Robert Motherwell and Frank Stella.

Artesa Winery's visitor center features artist-in-residence Gordon Huether's glass, metal and canvas art. Clos Pegase has a famed modern-era sculpture garden and Peju Province's contemporary art collection is on display in its Liana Gallery. Mumm Cuvée Napa's Fine Art photography galleries offer changing exhibitions while

the Private Collection Gallery includes images by famed photographers such as Ansel Adams. Evolved beyond a winery to a nature and art setting, di Rosa Preserve features a lake, a glass chapel, the Gatehouse Gallery and gardens to showcase recent exhibits from artists from the California Bay area.

ARCHITECTURE

There are several buildings of architectural note in the valley. The hospitality center at St. Helena's Beringer Vineyards, the oldest continuously-operating winery in the area, is the Rhine House, dating from 1883, with wooden panelling, a long bar and stained glass windows.

Whitewashed, Mykonos-style Sterling Vineyards perches prettily on a Calistoga hill, while Robert Mondavi Winery adopted a California Mission style, with statues of animals and St. Francis by renowned sculptor Beniamino Bufano.

Architect Michael Graves was commissioned to design the Clos Pegase Winery, with its spare, Post-modern lines. Some wineries, like Domaine Carneros by Taittinger, acknowledge French wine-making roots with grand chateau structures. In 2004, in deference to his origins, Darioush Khaledi gave the Silverado Trail a row of columns leading to his golden Darioush winery building built to look like Persepolis, Persia's ancient capitol city.

The Rhine House at Beringer Vineyards

Hot-air balloon rides over Napa Wine Country vineyards

BALLOON, BICYCLE AND TRAIN TRAVEL

Napa Valley Wine Train 1275 McKinstry Street, Napa, CA 94559. **Reservations Tel** *(707) 253-2111.* www.winetrain.com

Pre-dawn Napa Valley skies reveal a parade of colorful hot-air balloons ascending above vineyards or descending to almost touch the tops of vines. Prevailing winds coming north from San Francisco Bay dictate the early launch. Morning fog makes the journey surreal and chilly, warmed by the balloon burner's flame. Floating above the orderly rows of vineyards and springtime fields of yellow mustard is rewarded upon landing with a traditional toast of sparkling wine, often accompanied by a gourmet breakfast.

Cyclists find the long, generally flat valley a delight, and take to the Silverado Trail on the valley's east side to visit some of the more than 30 wineries between Napa and Calistoga. Summer heat is most intense in the afternoon. Savvy cyclists start early to avoid vehicular traffic that is extremely congested on weekends and holidays.

The Napa Valley Wine Train trip from Napa to St. Helena and back lasts three hours. Tours include brunch, lunch or dinner prepared on board, and served in restored 1915-17 Pullman Dining and Lounge Cars. Special itineraries stop for tours of Domaine Chandon, Raymond Vineyards or Grgich Hills Winery. Informal wine tasting seminars are conducted in the Napa Valley Wine Train's McKinstry station before passengers board the sleek silver and maroon train.

Themed events are organized in the glass-topped dining car including a five-course Moonlight Escapade Dinner held each full moon, and 1915 is recreated on Murder Mystery Theatre Gourmet Dinner trips.

SPAS

See www.napavalley.com for information on the best local spas

Calistoga mud treatment

Calistoga, at the north end of Napa Valley, is literally a hotbed of geothermal activity. Hot springs and local volcanic mud from an ancient eruption of Mount St. Helena created an industry here today that was started thousands of years ago. Most of the spas are located on Calistoga's main streets, Lincoln Avenue and Washington Street.

Mud bath treatments are a return to a natural form of relaxation, and for some, detoxification and rejuvenation, too. Guests immerse their bodies from the neck down in a deep tub filled with brown mud consisting of peat, clay and mineral water from the local hot springs. Spa visits also include a swim in a hot springs pool. In the last few decades, many of the original no-nonsense mud spas have added the type of amenities and treatments offered in European-style spas. Most spas also offer simple on-site accommodation.

SHOPPING

A winery tasting room may be the only place to taste and buy a delightful wine that is in limited production, and veteran wine country shoppers advise visitors to taste and buy on the spot. Wineries will check legal restrictions on shipping to other states or internationally. Winery gift shops stock everything from cookbooks to corkscrews, embellished with the establishment's name. Comestibles, convenient for picnics, are also often on sale.

The Oakville Grocery on Highway 29 is a landmark where shoppers can buy local wines, condiments and olive oils, or order a sandwich piled with local cheese and meats.

Artists of the Valley, a gallery of the Napa Valley Art Association, is one of many places to browse and shop in St. Helena. New York's artisan-producer temple, Dean & DeLuca, also has an outpost in St. Helena featuring fresh local Napa area produce and 1,400 California wines. Vintage 1870, in an historic red brick Groezinger Winery complex in Yountville, has clothing shops, a wine shop and wine-tasting room, and several art galleries.

The luxurious Napa Valley Wine Train

Redwood National Park ❹

Visitor Center *1111 Second St, Crescent City.* **Tel** *(707) 464-6101.* Arcata to Crescent City is 78 miles (125 km). Best route is US Hwy 101. **www**.redwood.national-park.com

Some of the largest original redwood forests in the world are preserved in this national park. Stretching along the coastline, the 58,000-acre (23,500-ha) park includes many smaller state parks and can be explored along a day-long drive. A two-day trip, however, allows time to walk away from the roads and experience the tranquility of the stately groves, or spot one of the world's last remaining herds of Roosevelt elk.

The park's headquarters are in **Crescent City**, a few miles north of which lies the 9,200-acre (3,720-ha) Jedediah Smith Redwoods State Park, with the most awe-inspiring coastal redwoods. Named after the fur trapper Jedediah Smith, the first white man who walked across the US, it has excellent campground facilities. South from Crescent City, the **Trees of Mystery** grove features unusual looking giant fiberglass statues.

The park's main attraction is the world's tallest tree, a 368-ft (112-m) giant, standing in the **Tall Trees Grove**. Farther south is Big Lagoon, a fresh-water lake stretching for 3 miles (5 km) and two other estuaries. Together, they form **Humboldt Lagoons State Park**. The headlands at Patrick's Point State Park, at the southern end, are great for spotting

Lassen Volcanic National park

migrating gray whales in winter. Rock pools abound with smaller marine life.

Lassen Volcanic National Park ❺

🚌 Chester, Red Bluff. **Visitor Center Tel** *(530) 595-4444.* ◯ *daily.* **www**.nps.gov/lavo

Before the eruption of Mount St. Helens in Washington in 1980, the 10,457-ft (3,187-m) high Lassen Peak was the last volcano to erupt on mainland US. In nearly 300 eruptions between 1914 and 1917, it laid 100,000 acres (40,500 ha) of the surrounding land to waste.

Lassen Peak is considered to be still active. Numerous areas on its flanks show clear signs of the geological processes. The boardwalk trail of Bumpass Hell (named for an early guide, who lost his leg in a boiling mudpot in 1865) leads past a series of steaming sulfurous pools of boiling water, heated by molten rock deep underground. In summer, visitors can take the winding road through the park, climbing more than 8,500 ft (2,590 m) high to Summit Lake. The road continues winding its way through the so-called Devastated Area, a bleak gray landscape of rough volcanic mudflows, which terminates at the Manzanita Lake, and the **Loomis Museum**.

🏛 **Loomis Museum**
Lassen Park Rd, N Entrance.
Tel *(530) 595-4444.* ◯ *late May–late-Sep only. Call for times.*

Sonoma Valley ❻

🏠 8,600. ✈ 🚌 90 Broadway & W Napa Sts, Sonoma Plaza. 🛈 *453 1st St E, (707) 996-1090.* 🍷 *Valley of the Moon Vintage Festival (late Sep).*

Nestling picturesquely in the crescent-shaped Sonoma Valley are 6,000 acres (2,400 ha) of beautiful vineyards. At the foot of the valley lies the tiny town of Sonoma. This town has had a colorful past, as it was here on June 14, 1846, that about 30 armed American farmers captured Mexican General Mariano Vallejo and his men, to protest the fact that land ownership was reserved for Mexican citizens. They seized control of Sonoma, declared California an independent republic, and flew their own flag, with a crude drawing of a grizzly bear. Although the republic was annulled 25 days later when the United States annexed California, the Bear Flag design was adopted as the official state flag in 1911.

Sonoma's main attractions are its world-famous wineries and meticulously preserved historical sites around the Spanish-style plaza. Many of the adobe buildings house wine shops, boutiques, and restaurants serving excellent local cuisine. East of the plaza is the restored **Mission San Francisco Solano de Sonoma**, the last of California's 21 historic Franciscan missions (founded by Father José Altimira of Spain in 1823). Today, all that survives of the original building is the corridor of his quarters. The adobe chapel was built by

Coastal redwood treees

General Vallejo in 1840. A short drive northward leads to the **Jack London State Historic Park**. In the early 1900s, London, famous author of *The Call of the Wild and The Sea Wolf*, abandoned his hectic lifestyle to live in this tranquil 800-acre (325-ha) expanse of oaks, madrones, and redwoods. The park retains eerie ruins of London's dream home, the Wolf House, mysteriously destroyed by fire just before completion. After London's death, his widow, Charmian Kittredge, built a magnificent home on the ranch, called the House of Happy Walls. Today, it is a museum, worth a visit for its display of London memorabilia.

⛪ Mission San Francisco Solano de Sonoma
E Spain St. *Tel (707) 938-1519.*
◯ *10am–5pm daily.* ● *Jan 1, Thanksgiving., Dec 25.* 🏛

🌿 Jack London State Historic Park
London Ranch Rd, Glen Ellen. *Tel (707) 938-5216.* **Park & Museum** ◯ *10am–5pm daily.* ● *Jan 1, Thanksgiving, Dec 25.* 🏛 ♿ *museum only.* 🏛

Sacramento ❼

🚶 🚗 🚎 30, 31, 32. ℹ️ *(916) 442-7644.* **www**.oldsacramento.com

Founded by John Sutter in 1839, California's capital city preserves many historic buildings along the waterfront in Old Sacramento. Most of the structures date from the 1860s, when it became the supply point for miners. Both the transcontinental railroad and Pony Express had their western terminus here, with riverboats providing passage to San Francisco. The

The Capitol Rotunda was restored to its original 19th-century splendor in 1975.

Original 1860 statuary

Entrance

The Historic Offices on the first floor contain a few government offices restored to their turn-of-the-century appearance.

SONOMA VALLEY WINERIES

The arms of the Sebastiani Vineyards

The Sonoma Valley has a rare combination of soil, sun, and rain perfect for growing superior wine grapes. In 1824, Father José Altimira planted Sonoma's first grapevines to produce sacramental wine for mass at the Mission San Francisco Solano de Sonoma. In 1834, General Vallejo replanted the vines and sold the wine he made to San Francisco merchants. In 1857, Hungarian Count Agoston Haraszthy planted the nation's first European varietals at Sonoma's Buena Vista Winery, now the oldest premium winery in the state.

The Sonoma Valley includes the Sonoma Valley, Carneros, and Sonoma Mountain wine-growing regions. The climate varies slightly creating different environments suitable for particular grape varieties, including Cabernet Sauvignon and Chardonnay. Today, Sonoma has more than 35 wineries, which produce about 5.4 million cases of wine a year. Some of the most notable wineries are Sebastiani Vineyards, Glen Ellen Winery; Gundlach-Bundschu Winery; and Château St. Jean. Most wineries have picnic areas, free wine tastings, and tours.

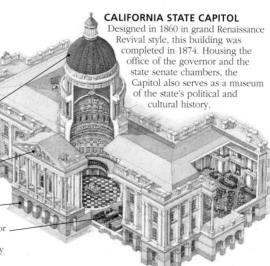
Vineyards in the Sonoma Valley

California State Railroad Museum, at the northern edge of the old town, houses some immaculately restored locomotives. A little away from the old city, the State Capitol stands in a landscaped park. To its east,

Sutter's Fort is a re-creation of the town's original settlement.

🏛 California State Railroad Museum
111 I St. *Tel (916) 445-6645.*
◯ *10am–5pm daily.* ● *Jan 1, Thanksgiving, Dec 25.*

CALIFORNIA STATE CAPITOL

Designed in 1860 in grand Renaissance Revival style, this building was completed in 1874. Housing the office of the governor and the state senate chambers, the Capitol also serves as a museum of the state's political and cultural history.

Lake Tahoe ❽

One of the most beautiful bodies of water in the world, Lake Tahoe lies in an alpine bowl on the border between Nevada and California. Surrounded by forested peaks, its shoreline measures 71 miles (114 km). The spectacular setting led Mark Twain, who spent a summer here in the 1860s, to coin it "surely the fairest picture the earth affords." Calling itself a year-round playground, Tahoe today has ski resorts, gambling, hiking trails, lakeside cabins, historic architecture, and special summer events including an Annual Celebrity Golf Tournament.

Ski lift at Home-wood ski resort

Ehrman Mansion and Visitor Center
This Queen Anne-style summer home was built in 1902. It opens for tours in summer.

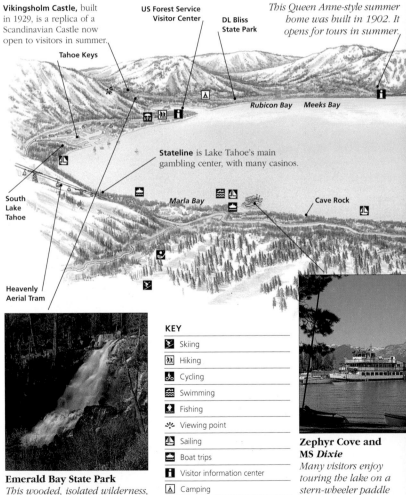

Vikingsholm Castle, built in 1929, is a replica of a Scandinavian Castle now open to visitors in summer.

Tahoe Keys

US Forest Service Visitor Center

DL Bliss State Park

Rubicon Bay   *Meeks Bay*

Stateline is Lake Tahoe's main gambling center, with many casinos.

South Lake Tahoe

Marla Bay

Cave Rock

Heavenly Aerial Tram

Emerald Bay State Park
This wooded, isolated wilderness, with its granite crags and waterfalls, is one of the natural wonders of California.

KEY

🎿	Skiing
🚶	Hiking
🚴	Cycling
🏊	Swimming
🎣	Fishing
❊	Viewing point
⛵	Sailing
🚢	Boat trips
ℹ	Visitor information center
⛺	Camping
🏞	Picnic area
⛳	Golf course

Zephyr Cove and MS *Dixie*
Many visitors enjoy touring the lake on a stern-wheeler paddle boat. The MS Dixie makes regular trips from Zephyr Cove.

SKIING AROUND LAKE TAHOE

The peaks surrounding Lake Tahoe, particularly those on the California side, are famous for their many ski resorts. These include the world-class Alpine Meadows and Squaw Valley, where the Winter Olympics were held in 1960. The area is a sunny paradise for both downhill and cross-country skiers, with miles of runs through pine forests and open

View over ski slopes near Lake Tahoe

meadows, and down ridges with splendid views of the lake. There are powder areas and challenging slopes for experts and gentle snow bowls for beginners. The runs on the Nevada side of the border are quieter.

Homewood is a popular ski resort in winter, with spectacular views all year.

Kaspian picnic area

Tahoe City is the focal point for shopping and nightlife in north Tahoe.

Incline Village is a small, sophisticated ski town.

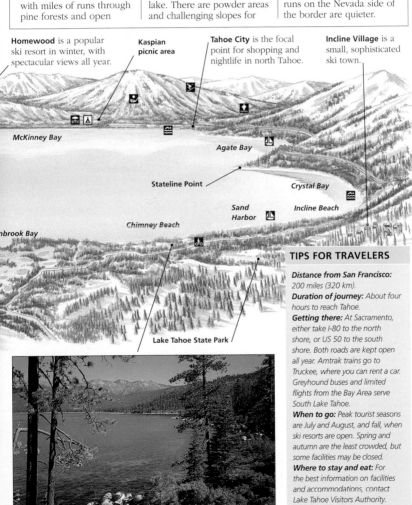

McKinney Bay

Agate Bay

Stateline Point

Crystal Bay

Sand Harbor

Incline Beach

Chimney Beach

nbrook Bay

Lake Tahoe State Park

TIPS FOR TRAVELERS

Distance from San Francisco: *200 miles (320 km).*

Duration of journey: *About four hours to reach Tahoe.*

Getting there: *At Sacramento, either take I-80 to the north shore, or US 50 to the south shore. Both roads are kept open all year. Amtrak trains go to Truckee, where you can rent a car. Greyhound buses and limited flights from the Bay Area serve South Lake Tahoe.*

When to go: *Peak tourist seasons are July and August, and fall, when ski resorts are open. Spring and autumn are the least crowded, but some facilities may be closed.*

Where to stay and eat: *For the best information on facilities and accommodations, contact Lake Tahoe Visitors Authority.*

Visitor information: *Lake Tahoe Visitors Authority, South Lake Tahoe.* **Tel** *(800) 288-2463 toll free.*

Nevada Shore during Summer
Lake Tahoe's wild, unspoiled Nevada shoreline is popular with cyclists and hikers and has some fine sandy beaches.

Exploring Lake Tahoe

Beauty, size, and a unique alpine setting distinguish Lake Tahoe from other lakes in the US. It is sometimes compared to Russia's Lake Baikal despite much more lakeshore development. Lake Tahoe offers outstanding pedestrian and bike-accessible views from a loop trail, which took some 20 years to build as well as a variety of water-based sports. There are gracious and distinctive historic mansions built as summer getaways for the rich; and a choice of California or Nevada views from casino rooms at Stateline.

Winter Olympic Games, Squaw Valley, 1960

Hiking along one of Lake Tahoe's many trails

TAHOE RIM TRAIL

Tel (775) 298-0012.
www.tahoerimtrail.org

Hikers, equestrians, and mountain bikes can travel on most stretches of the eight segments that complete the Tahoe Rim Trail's (TRT) 165-mile (266-km) loop. The TRT is open from snowmelt, usually in June, until the first major snowfall, normally in October. Some of Lake Tahoe's most scenic vistas are accessible on this trail, which features beautiful pine and aspen forests, huge grey granite boulders, alpine meadow wildflowers, and streams. Alpine elevations range from 6,300 ft (1,920 m) to 10,300 ft (3,150 m).

Moderate trails, with an average ten percent grade, are indicated with light blue triangular trailhead signs, though the TRT can be accessed almost anywhere along its well-constructed dirt path. The pedestrian-only 1.3-mile (2-km) Tahoe Meadows Interpretive Trail at the north

end is a quick introduction to TRT scenery and terrain. The most rugged segment is on the western side of the lake.

SPORTS ON THE LAKE

Fishing trips are a popular form of recreation on Lake Tahoe. Visitors may prefer a challenging search for one of the large Mackinaw trout that swim up to 400 ft (122 m) below the surface, or angling for rainbow or brown trout or Kokanee salmon.

Motorboats, some with water skiers or wake boarders in tow, speed across the lake and those in search of a further adrenaline rush can also rent waverunners. Sailors and kite surfers are challenged by winds coming down from the Sierra peaks. Hang- and para-gliders enjoy views of the blue waters from above while canoes and kayaks are a silent way to explore hidden coves and shorelines. Scuba divers seeking underwater forests or monster trout can enter the 100-ft (30-m) visibility freshwater lake from sloping beaches or kayaks.

SQUAW VALLEY

8 miles northwest of Tahoe City. *Tel* (530) 583-6985. **www**.squaw.com

Squaw Valley landed on the international ski map as host of the VIII Winter Olympic Games in 1960. This was the site of the first televised Olympics and an opening-ceremony snowfall arrived just in time to ensure a base for downhill events.

Today, the Olympic Flame and original Tower of Nations still remain at the valley's entrance. This all-season resort includes more than 30 lifts, shopping and restaurants facilities, and accommodation. Winter skiers and snow-boarders can expect an average of 450 inches of annual snowfall. High Camp, at 8,200 ft (4,500 m) above sea level, has magnificent views of Lake Tahoe. There is also a 1960 Olympic Winter Games Museum, summer ice Pavilion for skating, indoor climbing wall, swimming pool, guided hikes through slopes of wildflowers, and full moon night walks to the valley floor.

Kayaking on the clear waters of Lake Tahoe

Emerald Bay and the Eagle Falls trail

STATELINE

Situated on the border of California and the more liberal state of Nevada, Stateline is the main gambling town of the Lake Tahoe region. In the 1860s, Comstock Silver prospectors journeyed to Virginia City through Lakeside and Edgewood, and Pony Express riders made this their last stop in Nevada. In 1873, a formal state border was established along the southern end of Lake Tahoe.

There are rooms in the hotel-casinos here where your feet can straddle both states. Views of either state are fine, but the west has prized California views of the lake, shore, forests, and mountains.

EMERALD BAY

22 miles south of Tahoe City. **Tel** (530) 541-3030.

The most famous postcard view of Lake Tahoe depicts the deep blue green waters of Emerald Bay, with tiny Fannette Island in the middle. The granite rock of Fannette Island is thought to have been resistant to the glacial ice and the surviving stone ruins here were once a private teahouse.

Emerald Bay, 3-miles (4.8-km) long, is the best-known feature of the state park that adopts its name. The three-tiered Eagle Falls cascades through the park 500 ft (152 m) down to Vikingsholm, and visitors can walk the trail.

The glacier-sculpted bay became a National Natural Landmark in 1969 and draws kayakers to explore its calm waters. Emerald Bay is also a protected Underwater Park, where scuba divers can explore an ancient underwater forest, and wrecked dorries and barges.

VIKINGSHOLM CASTLE

Emerald Bay St Pk. **Tel** (530) 541-3030. ◯ mid-Jun–Labor Day.

Mrs Lora Josephine Knight's summer house, completed in 1929, is a fine example of 11th-century Scandinavian architecture, complete with turrets, sod roofs, and carved dragons. Mrs Knight visited Scandinavia with her architect in 1928 to gather ideas for the castle's design. Using local wood and granite, 200 artisans handmade, planed, carved, stained, and painted Vikingsholm's outer walls and interiors. The gaily-painted furniture and textiles are also replicated, down to hand-forged hinges and latches.

EHRMAN MANSION

Sugar Point Pine St Pk. **Tel** (530) 525-7982. ◯ Jul–Labor Day. ◻ Memorial Day–late Sep: 10am–3pm daily. ◻ $5 (adults).

Banker Isaias W. Hellman joined other wealthy landowners building summer homes around Lake Tahoe in 1903. Hellman engaged architect William Danforth Bliss to design a Queen Anne-style residence in the most sophisticated rustic style. The Ehrman Mansion is three storeys high, consisting of redwood-paneled walls and bright, large windows for maximum light. A palatial verandah with rustic chairs for rocking and lounging looks down over Lake Tahoe. A wood-burning steam generator produced electric lighting, the latest in modern technology, until the arrival of commercial energy in 1927 and there was also a modern plumbing system.

LAKE TAHOE FACTS

More than two million years ago, rain and snow formed a lake at the south end of this valley, between two parallel sections of Earth crust. Ice Age glaciers shaped the lake into a round bowl that averages a depth of 990 ft (300 m) but plunges to 1,685 ft (515 m) below the surface at one point. North America's third deepest lake, Lake Tahoe is 22 miles (35 km) long by 12 miles (19 km) wide. It lies 6,300 ft (1,920 m) above sea level and extends over 193 sq miles (99 sq km). The deep, fresh, and clear emerald green and dark sapphire blue water of this seemingly endless lake is estimated to be 99.7 per cent pure – the quality of distilled water.

A view from the surrounding peaks

Yosemite National Park ❾

A wilderness of ever-green forests, alpine meadows and sheer walls of granite, most of Yosemite National Park is accessible only to hikers or horse riders. The spectacular Yosemite Valley, however, is easily reached by vehicle along 200 miles (320 km) of paved roads. Soaring cliffs, plunging waterfalls, gigantic trees, rugged canyons, mountains and valleys give Yosemite its incomparable beauty.

Black bears

Upper Yosemite Fall
In two mighty leaps linked by a cascade, Yosemite Creek drops 2,425 ft (739 m).

Lower Yosemite Fall

Yosemite Museum

The Valley Visitor Center
features a prototype Miwok American Indian encampment.

Yosemite Village

Bicycle rental

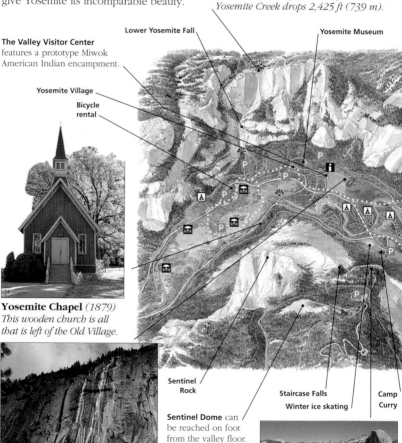

Yosemite Chapel *(1879)*
This wooden church is all that is left of the Old Village.

Sentinel Rock

Staircase Falls

Winter ice skating

Camp Curry

Sentinel Dome can be reached on foot from the valley floor. The trail continues to Glacier Point.

Ahwahnee Hotel
Rustic architecture, elegant décor and beautiful views make this hotel one of the most renowned in the country.

View from Glacier Point
The 3,200-ft (975-m) brink of Glacier Point provides a fine view down Tenaya Canyon.

BEYOND THE VALLEY

From May to October, shuttle buses carry visitors to Mariposa Grove, 35 miles (56 km) south of Yosemite Valley, where the Grizzly Giant is the largest and oldest sequoia tree in the Park. Northeast, Tuolumne Meadows is the largest Sierra alpine meadow and a good place to see deer and bears.

Giant sequoia tree

Half Dome in Autumn
A formidable trail climbs to the top of this polished cliff jutting above the wooded valley floor.

North Dome

Washington Column

Mirror Lake

Quarter Domes

Liberty Cap

Nevada Fall

```
0 meters          1500
0 yards           1500
```

Merced River

Tenaya Creek

Tenaya Canyon

KEY

═══	Road
○ ○ ○	Bicycle route
● ● ●	Suggested walk
∼∼∼	Paths and trails
∼∼∼	Rivers
🅿	Parking
🅰	Camping
⸫	Viewing point
▦	Picnic area

Vernal Fall
The Merced River pours into its canyon over the 317-ft (97-m) lip of this waterfall.

TIPS FOR TRAVELERS

Distance from San Francisco: 194 miles (312 km).
Duration of journey: About five hours to reach Yosemite.
Getting there: From Stockton, Hwy 120 is the prettiest route, but Hwy 140, the All-Weather Highway, might be preferable in winter. Bus tours operate to Yosemite Valley (see p279), but a rental car is advisable for other parts.
When to go: The waterfalls in the Valley are fullest from March to June. The peak tourist season is June to August. Crowds diminish in September and October when temperatures are mild. Snow closes many roads from November to April: tire chains are recommended.
Where to stay and eat: There is a wide variety of accommodations, from rustic tent shelters to lodges. All hotels have good restaurants.
Visitor information: Valley Visitor Center, Yosemite Village. *Tel* (209) 372-0299. www.nps.gov/yose

Exploring Yosemite National Park

Some of the world's most beautiful mountain terrain is protected within the 1,170 sq miles (3,030 sq km) of Yosemite National Park. Hundreds of thousands of visitors descend upon the park each year to admire its breathtaking views, formed by millions of years of glacial activity. Each season offers a different experience, from the swelling waterfalls in spring to the rustic colors of autumn. The summer months are the most crowded, but during the snowbound winter months several roads are inaccessible. Fall is the best time to visit, when temperatures are mild and crowds are reduced. Bus tours, cycle paths, hiking trails, and roads are all aimed at leading visitors from one awe-inspiring panoramic scene to another.

Upper Yosemite Falls, swollen with ice-melt in the spring

Half Dome
Eastern end of Yosemite Valley.
daily.
At nearly 1 mile (1.6 km) above the valley floor, the silhouette of Half Dome has become a symbol of Yosemite. Its curved back rises to a peak, before dropping vertically down to the valley. Geologists believe that Half Dome is not half, but three-quarters of its original size. It is thought that as recently as 15,000 years ago, glacial ice floes moved through the valley from the Sierra crest, scything off rock and depositing it downstream. The 8,840-ft (2,695 m) summit of Half Dome offers an amazing view of the valley. The 9-mile (14-km) trail from Happy Isles trailhead to the peak can be strenuous and long, taking around 10 to 12 hours.

Yosemite Falls
North Yosemite Valley. *daily.*
Yosemite Falls are the highest waterfalls in North America and tumble from a height of 2,425 ft (740 m) in two great drops, Upper Yosemite and Lower Yosemite Falls. One of the most recognizable features of the park, the cascades are visible all over the valley.

The top of Upper Yosemite Falls, by far the longer and more elegant of the pair, can be reached via a strenuous 7-mile (11-km) round-trip trail. The Lower Falls are easier to visit, via a short trail that starts next to Yosemite Lodge and frames an unforgettable view of both falls.

As with all the park's waterfalls, Yosemite Falls are at their peak in May and June, when the winter snows melt and fill the creek to capacity. Conversely, by September the falls often dry up and disappear altogether, their presence marked only by a dark stain on the granite wall.

Vernal and Nevada Falls
Eastern end of Yosemite Valley.
daily.
A popular half-day hike in Yosemite National Park is the Mist Trail, which visits these two waterfalls. The first fall on the 7-mile (11-km) round-trip is Vernal Fall, which plunges 320 ft (95 m) and spreads its spray across the trail (carry a poncho or rain jacket in spring.) The trail can be strenuous for the 2 miles (3 km) to the top of Nevada Fall, which drops an impressive 595 ft (180 m). Here, the Mist Trail joins the John Muir Trail, which runs around the back of Half Dome all the way south to the summit of Mount Whitney.

Sheer drop of El Capitán

Glacier Point

Glacier Point Rd. ○ *May–Oct: daily.*
The great Yosemite panorama can be experienced from Glacier Point, which rests on a rocky ledge 3,215 ft (980 m) above the valley floor. Most of the waterfalls and other features of Yosemite Valley are visible from here, but the dominant feature is Half Dome. The panorama also includes much of the surrounding landscape, a beautiful area of alpine peaks and meadows.

Glacier Point can be reached only during the summer. The road is blocked by snow during winter at Badger Pass, which was developed in 1935 as California's first commercial ski resort. Another summer route is the Four-Mile Trail, which begins at the western side of the valley. Summer bus services also allow hikers to ride up to Glacier Point then hike down to the valley.

Mariposa Grove

Visitors' Center Hwy 41, South Entrance. ○ *mid-May–Oct: daily.*
At the southern end of Yosemite, this beautiful grove was one of the main reasons the park was established. More than 500 giant sequoia trees can be seen here, some of which are more than 3,000 years old, 250 ft (75 m) tall and more than 30 ft (9 m) in diameter at their base. A series of hiking trails winds through

Tunnel View, looking across Yosemite Valley

the grove, and open-air trams make a 5-mile (8-km) circuit along roads constructed during the early years of Yosemite tourism.

Tunnel View

Hwy 41 overlooking Yosemite Valley.
○ *daily.*
One of the most photographed views of Yosemite can be seen from this lookout on Hwy 41 at the western end of the valley. Despite the name, which is taken from the highway tunnel that leads to Glacier Point Road, the view is incredible, with El Capitán on the left, Bridalveil Fall on the right and Half Dome at the center.

El Capitán

Northwestern end of Yosemite Valley.
○ *daily.*
Standing guard at the western entrance to Yosemite Valley, the granite wall of El Capitán rises more than 4,500 ft (1,370 m) above the valley floor. The world's largest exposed rock, El Capitán is a magnet to rock-climbers, who spend days on its sheer face to reach the top. The less adventurous congregate in the meadow below, watching the rock-climbers through binoculars.

Named by US soldiers, who in 1851 were the first white Americans to visit the valley, El Capitán is the Spanish phrase for "captain."

Tuolumne Meadows

Hwy 120, Tioga Rd. ○ *Jun–Sep: daily.*
In summer, when the snows have melted and the wildflowers are in full bloom, the best place to experience the striking beauty of the Yosemite landscape are these subalpine meadows along the Tuolumne River. Located 55 miles (88 km) from Yosemite valley via Tioga Pass Road, Tuolumne Meadows are also a base for hikers setting off to explore the area's many granite peaks and trails.

Black-tailed deer roaming Yosemite's meadows

Ahwahnee Hotel

Yosemite Valley. **Tel** *(209) 372-1407.* ○ *daily.*
A building that comes close to Yosemite's natural beauty is the Ahwahnee Hotel, built in 1927 at a cost of $1.5 million. It was designed by Gilbert Stanley Underwood, who used giant granite boulders and massive wood timbers to create a rustic elegance in tune with its surroundings. The interior of the Ahwahnee Hotel also emulates the natural setting, decorated in a Native American style. Examples of Native American arts and crafts are on display in the lobbies. The hotel is also noted for its high-quality restaurant, the Ahwahnee Dining Room.

Giant sequoia trees in Mariposa Grove

TRAVELERS' NEEDS

WHERE TO STAY

San Francisco offers a very-wide choice of places to stay, from spartan youth hostels to the most elegant and luxurious of hotels. There are 31,000 rooms available in the city, providing accommodations to suit every budget and taste. The top hotels are good value by international standards and have long been rated among the best in the world. For the traveler on a budget, there are many cheap and comfortable youth hostels and motels. Another option is to stay somewhere offering bed-and-breakfast facilities. There are a number of such establishments in the city, and some of them are in beautifully restored 19th-century mansions. Bed-and-breakfasts are usually smaller than hotels, and are sometimes quite opulent. We have selected a variety of places to stay that represent the best of their kind, covering all price ranges. For more details on each hotel, turn to the listings on pages 210–221.

Sign over small hotel

WHERE TO LOOK

Most of San Francisco's hotels are located in and around bustling Union Square, within easy walking distance of the Financial District and the Moscone Convention Center. Nearby Nob Hill, where many of the finer hotels are situated, is more tranquil, while the Fisherman's Wharf area has a number of hotels and motels suitable for families.

Away from the center, on the fringes of the Financial District and along Lombard Street in the Marina District, are a tremendous number of moderately priced motels. Bed-and-breakfast rooms are scattered throughout the city, often in quiet neighborhoods.

HOTEL PRICES

Considering the comfort and high level of service, hotel prices in San Francisco are generally quite reasonable, particularly in comparison with Europe or New York. Average room rates are $160–$175 a night, though this depends on when and where you stay. See *Special Rates (p208)* for details of any discounts or packages that might be available.

Single travelers receive only a small discount, if any, and most hotels charge visitors $10 to $15 a night for each additional person (in addition to the standard two) in the same room. For details on traveling with children, see page 209.

CHAIN HOTELS

You can count on good service, moderate prices, and comfortable surroundings at a chain hotel. The popular chains include the Westin, Hilton, Sheraton, Marriott, Ramada, Hyatt, and Holiday Inn. Some of these chains operate more than one hotel and designate one location as the flagship facility.

Westin St. Francis Hotel *(see p216)*

All chain hotels have Internet websites, or you can call the hotel's toll-free number to ask about rates and availability.

BED AND BREAKFAST

A notable alternative to the large city center hotels are the many fine establishments that offer bed-and-breakfast accommodations. These are often found in some of the city's extensive stock of well-preserved 19th-century houses. In San Francisco they are often referred to as bed-and-breakfast "inns"; they are unique to the city, varying from quaint, country-style cottages to converted hilltop mansions. They should not be confused with the European tradition of bed-and-breakfast accommodations, where you rent a room from a private individual in their own home and are also given breakfast. Some inns are very luxurious, and rival the city's best hotels for comfort. They vary in size,

The Room of the Dons at the Mark Hopkins Hotel *(see p213)*

◁ The Garden Court at the Sheraton Palace Hotel

from a few to no more than 30 rooms, and are generally cozier in atmosphere and decor than a normal hotel. All rates include breakfast, and sometimes a glass of wine in the afternoon.

HIDDEN EXTRAS

Room rates are generally quoted exclusive of room tax, which adds an additional 14 percent to the bill. No sales tax is levied. However, added fees are often charged for phone calls. Local calls, including access calls to toll-free services, can cost up to $1 each. Long-distance calls can cost as much as five times more than they would from a private phone, because of hefty surcharges. Wi-Fi access can also carry a fee, generally from $15 a day, so be sure to inquire before using the internet. The sending or receiving of faxes costs around $2 to $3 a page, plus any phone charges.

Parking at a city center hotel can add at least $20 a day to the bill, plus a tip for the attendant, but motels will usually have free parking. Some rooms come with stocked mini bars but you will be charged substantially for anything you eat or drink – as much as $5 for a can of beer. Prices for these will be prominently displayed.

A tip of $1 for each bag is usually paid to porters for carrying luggage to or from rooms. Room service waiters expect a tip of 15 percent of the bill, rounded up to the next full dollar and paid in cash. Visitors who stay more than a day or two may also want to leave the housekeeping staff a $5 to $10 tip next to the bed.

The luxurious lobby of the Fairmont Hotel (see p213)

FACILITIES

It is usually possible to gauge a hotel's ambience simply by setting foot in the lobby. Some of the luxury hotels, such as the Hyatt Regency with its impressive 20-story atrium or the plushly appointed Fairmont (see p213), are famous landmarks, which adds to the glamour of your stay in them. Also, most of the better establishments have excellent restaurants where hotel guests are often given preferential treatment.

Some hotels have a piano bar or nightclub on the premises, enabling visitors to enjoy a night on the town without having to set foot outside. See *Entertainment* on pages 268–9 for details.

The convention trade is an important part of the business of San Francisco's hotels, and many provide conference facilities where everything from business meetings to political jamborees are held. Some of the older establishments have large ballrooms, available for weddings and private parties. At most of the hotels in the city, guests can expect complimentary assorted toiletries and often a morning newspaper, in addition to free cable TV, a mini-bar, and tea and coffee making facilities.

JW Marriott Hotel (see p215)

HOW TO BOOK

Travelers should reserve rooms at least one month in advance during peak season which runs from July through October. Telephone bookings are accepted with a credit card, but a deposit of one night's room rate will usually be required. It is a good idea to give advance notice if you think you will be arriving later than 6pm. There is no official reservation agency but hotels may be booked via the web site (www.sfvisitor.org) of the Visitor Information Center *(see p278)*. Many hotels are listed in the center's free *Visitor Planning Guide*. Some agencies will book rooms for visitors. They do not charge for this, and can often get you discount rates.

SPECIAL RATES

It is always worthwhile to ask hotel reservation agents about any special discounts that might be available, in particular during the off-peak months between November and March. It is also useful to ask for discounts when booking

weekend visits, as many hotels that usually cater to the business traveler will cut their rates for families. Some may also provide special offers, such as a free bottle of champagne or lower-price meals, with the aim to gain the patronage of those who travel for pleasure.

Reservation services do not usually charge a fee as they receive a commission from the individual hotels, and some will offer discounted rates. A good travel agent can save its clients 10 to 20 percent of the standard nightly charge of many hotels. It is worth checking some package tours, such as those advertised in the Sunday paper, as they can offer significant savings for travelers. Many airlines also offer discounts as an incentive to those who reserve a room through them. If you are a member of a frequent-flyer program, you may be able to save as much as 50 percent off the normal rates when booking in an

The Huntington Hotel *(see p213)*

Bathroom toy at Hotel Triton

affiliated hotel, and also earn extra mileage for each night of your visit.

DISABLED TRAVELERS

All hotels in the United States are required by law to provide the disabled with accommodations, as is stated in the Americans with Disabilities Act of 1992. Older properties are exempt from this, but most of San Francisco's hotels comply with the act and provide at

---

DIRECTORY

RESERVATION AGENCIES

Hotel Locators
919 Garnet Ave, Suite 216, San Diego, CA 92109.
Tel (858) 581-1315. **www.**hotellocators.com

Hotels.Com
Suite 203, 8140 Walnut Hill Lane Dallas, TX 75231.
Tel (214) 361-7311 or *1-(800)-964-6835.* **www.**hotels.com

San Francisco Reservations
360 22nd St, Suite 300, Oakland, CA 94612.
Tel (510) 628-4450 or *1-(800)-677-1500.* **www.**hotelres.com

YOUTH AND BUDGET ACCOMMODATIONS

Hosteling International: City Center
685 Ellis St, SF, CA 94109.
Map 5 A5. *Tel 474-5721.*

Downtown
312 Mason St, SF, CA 94102. **Map** 5 B5.
Tel 788-5604.

Fisherman's Wharf
Bldg 240, Upper Fort Mason, SF, CA 94123.
Map 4 E1. *Tel 771-7277.*

European Guest House
761 Minna St, SF, CA 94103. **Map** 11 A1.
Tel 861-6634.

Hotel Herbert
161 Powell St, SF, CA 94102. **Map** 5 B5.
Tel 362-1600.

GAY AND LESBIAN ACCOMMODATIONS

Inn on Castro
321 Castro St, SF, CA 94114. **Map** 10 D2.
Tel 861-0321.
www.innoncastro.com

Chateau Tivoli
1057 Steiner St, SF, CA 94115. **Map** 10 D1.
Tel 776-5462.
www.chateautivoli.com

The Willows Inn
710 14th St, SF, CA 94114.
Map 10 E2. *Tel 431-4770.*
www.willowssf.com

FURNISHED APARTMENTS

AMSI
2800 Van Ness, SF, CA 94109. *Tel (415) 447-2000* or *1-(800)-747-7784.* **www.**amsires.com

Executive Suites
1388 Sutter St, #800, SF, CA 94109.
Tel 776-5151. **www.** executivesuites-sf.com

Grosvenor Suites
899 Pine St, SF, CA 94108. *Tel 421-1899* or *1-(800)-999-9189.* **www.** grosvenorsuites.sf.com

ROOMS IN PRIVATE HOMES

Bed and Breakfast San Francisco
PO Box 420009, SF, CA 94142. *Tel (415) 899-0060* or *1-(800)-452-8249.* **www.**bbsf.com

California Association of Bed and Breakfast Inns
2715 Porter St, Soquel, CA 95073. *Tel (831) 462-9191.* **www.**cabbi.com

least one room suitable for guests who are wheelchair-bound. You will find that staff in most establishments will do all they can to assist anyone handicapped, but if you do have special needs, it is advisable to inform the manager of the hotel when you reserve your room. All the accommodations listed in *Choosing a Hotel* on pages 210–221 allow those who are visually handicapped to bring guide dogs onto the premises. More information for disabled travelers can be found on page 280, under *Practical Information*.

GAY AND LESBIAN ACCOMMODATIONS

Though all the hotels in San Francisco welcome lesbian and gay visitors, the city also has a number of places that cater primarily, if not exclusively, to same-sex couples. Most of these are smaller properties, which are found in and around the city's predominantly gay Castro District. A few options are listed in the directory box on page 208, and gay bookstores can also provide more information.

TRAVELING WITH CHILDREN

Children are welcome at all San Francisco hotels, and few will charge extra for one or two children under 12 staying in their parents' room. It is a good idea, however, to let staff at the hotel know you are traveling with children, because not all rooms are suitable. Some hotels may provide you with a sofa that can be converted into an extra bed or alternatively may be able to set up a cot or a folding bed for an additional $10 to $15 a night. The hotel recommendations in our listings *(see pp210–221)* point out whether particular hotels offer children's facilities. Many families prefer to take rooms in an all-suite hotel, or rent a furnished apartment for extra space.

YOUTH AND BUDGET ACCOMMODATIONS

San Francisco boasts many youth hostels. These offer bunks in dormitories plus some private rooms, at affordable prices for travelers who are on a tighter budget. One of the best in the city is **Hosteling International, Fisherman's Wharf**, which is located in the old US Army barracks at Fort Mason. There are other hostels located near Union Square and at Ellis Street. The establishments are run by **Hosteling International**, a nonprofit organization, and both offer beds for around $25 a night. There are also several privately run hostels in the city. Budget hotels include the **European Guest House** and **Hotel Herbert**.

FURNISHED APARTMENTS

Renting self-contained accomodations in furnished apartments can sometimes be a good alternative to staying in a hotel, especially for family groups seeking more space and catering facilities, or visitors who plan to remain in the city for more than a few days. The drawbacks to renting apartments are that there are only a few available in the city, and they tend to be rented for full weeks only. The cost is around $500 to $800 per week. For information on renting apartments, see agencies such as **AMSI**, **Executive Suites** and **Grosvenor Suites**.

ROOMS IN PRIVATE HOMES

Some travelers may prefer European-style bed-and-breakfast accommodations in a private house. Rooms are rented out by a resident owner in his or her own home, and breakfast is always provided. Deposits may be requested and cancellation fees imposed so enquire when you book. There may also be a minimum stay period. If you do opt to stay in a private house, keep in mind that owners will expect guests to be quiet and considerate. For more details contact the special rental agencies, such as **Bed and Breakfast San Francisco** or the **California Association of Bed and Breakfast Inns**.

Guests at the Campton Place Hotel *(see p214)*

Choosing a Hotel

The choice of hotels selected in this guide is based on quality of accommodation and service as well as location. They are listed by area and within these by price, both for central San Francisco and the surrounding areas. Map references refer to the Street Finder, pages 302–312.

PRICE CATEGORIES
For a standard double room per night, including breakfast, service charges and any additional taxes:

⑤ under $100
⑤⑤ $100–$150
⑤⑤⑤ $150–$200
⑤⑤⑤⑤ over $200

PACIFIC HEIGHTS AND THE MARINA

Broadway Manor Inn   🅿 🕦 🕴   ⑤

2201 Van Ness Ave, 94109 **Tel** *(415) 776-7900* **Fax** *(415) 928-7460* **Rooms** *56*   **Map** *4 F3*

Located within walking distance of the Marina District and Fisherman's Wharf, Broadway Manor Inn is great value for tourists on a budget. The rooms are basic, but clean, and some have wireless internet access, which is also available in the lobby. Guest rooms also have microwaves and refrigerators. **www.broadwaymanor.com**

Coventry Motor Inn   🅿 🕴 ♿   ⑤

1901 Lombard Street, 94123 **Tel** *(415) 567-1200* **Fax** *(415) 921-8745* **Rooms** *69*   **Map** *4 D2*

Spacious accommodation is not easy to find in San Francisco, but the Coventry Motor Inn has it, and at a bargain price too. The rooms are clean and comfortable, parking is free, and the location in the heart of the Marina District cannot be beaten. **www.coventrymotorinn.com**

Heritage Marina Hotel   🔝 🅿 🕦 🏊 🕴 🕎   ⑤

2550 Van Ness Ave, 94109 **Tel** *(415) 776-7500* **Fax** *(415) 351-1336* **Rooms** *134*   **Map** *4 E2*

Conveniently located near the Marina and all local tourist spots. It's ideal for the budget traveler looking for no-frills accommodation and every room has a microwave. Rates include a deluxe Continental breakfast and there's an on-site Italian-style eatery. **www.heritagemarinahotel.com**

The Greenwich Inn   🅿 🕴   ⑤

3201 Steiner, 94123 **Tel** *(415) 921-5162* **Fax** *(415) 921-3602* **Rooms** *32*   **Map** *4 D2*

The Greenwich Inn is a basic and affordable option for travelers wishing to stay close to San Francisco's Marina District and Presidio Park. The rooms are comfortable and the staff is friendly. Countless restaurants and shops are within easy walking distance. **www.greenwichinn.com**

Cow Hollow Motor Inn   🅿 🕴   ⑤⑤

2190 Lombard St, 94123 **Tel** *(415) 921-5800* **Fax** *(415) 922-8515* **Rooms** *129*   **Map** *4 D2*

This hotel is situated between the fashionable Cow Hollow and Marina Districts of San Francisco, famous for world-class dining and shopping. The rooms here are simple and families traveling with children may enjoy the option to stay in one of the 12 guest suites. **www.cowhollowmotorinn.com**

Marina Inn   🔝   ⑤⑤

3110 Octavia St, 94123 **Tel** *(415) 928-1000* **Fax** *(415) 928-5909* **Rooms** *40*   **Map** *4 E2*

Well located two blocks from Fort Mason and its grassy park, this low-priced Marina District hotel has stunning views of the Bay. It is clean and the staff is friendly, though street noise from Lombard Street can be obtrusive. It is convenient for the Union Street shops and restaurants. **www.marinainn.com**

Motel Capri   🔝 🅿   ⑤⑤

2015 Greenwich St, 94123 **Tel & Fax** *(415) 346-4667* **Rooms** *46*   **Map** *4 D2*

This clean and comfortable family-owned motel is a good choice for budget-minded travelers. It is situated in a quiet residential street at the center of the Marina District. Two kitchenettes are now available. This hotel is close to public transportation, and provides free on-site parking. **www.motelcaprica.com**

Pacific Heights Inn   🅿 🕴   ⑤⑤

1555 Union St, 94123 **Tel** *(415) 776-3310* **Fax** *(415) 776-8176* **Rooms** *40*   **Map** *4 E2*

This pleasant, 1960s-era motel is on a quiet block of Union Street, just west of Van Ness Avenue. It is convenient for public transportation and has free on-site parking for guests with their own cars. The restaurants, shops, and bars of the energetic Cow Hollow neighborhood are just a few blocks away. **www.pacificheightsinn.com**

Chateau Tivoli Bed and Breakfast   🅿   ⑤⑤⑤

1057 Steiner St, 94115 **Tel** *(415) 776-5462* **Fax** *(415) 776-0505* **Rooms** *9*   **Map** *4 D4*

One of San Francisco's "painted ladies," this 100-year-old Victorian house was the center of 1970s New Age Movement, marked by rebirthing, Reichian release, and nude communal bathing. It has since been restored to its original splendor with frescoed ceilings, stained-glass windows and several antiques. **www.chateautivoli.com**

Key to Symbols *see back cover flap*

Edward II Inn and Suites P $$$

3155 Scott St, 94123 **Tel** *(415) 922-3000* **Fax** *(415) 931-5784* **Rooms** *32*   **Map** *3 C2*

Edward II Inn and Suites is a real find for those looking for a quiet place in a convenient location. The house, built in 1914, is now a three-story inn, a few blocks from San Francisco's Yacht Harbor. Some of the suites have Jacuzzis and they offer a complimentary Continental breakfast. **www.edwardii.com**

Hotel del Sol P $$$

3100 Webster St, 94123 **Tel** *(415) 921-552* **Fax** *(415) 931-4137* **Rooms** *57*   **Map** *4 D2*

Celebrating California's lively culture, this boutique hotel features a playful design with palm trees, hammocks, mosaics, and a pool. The rooms are bright and spacious with rainbow-colored bedspreads. There are also 10 themed suites. The family suite has bunk beds, board games, toys and, child-friendly furnishings. **www.hoteldelsol.com**

Laurel Inn P $$$

444 Presidio Ave, 94115 **Tel** *(415) 567-8467* **Fax** *(415) 928-1866* **Rooms** *59*   **Map** *3 C4*

This quiet, stylish boutique hotel features a hip mid-20th-century style. The comfortable, brightly-colored guest rooms come with CD players, VCRs, and writing desks and tables. Complimentary Continental breakfast and free parking are provided. The hotel's trendy G Bar is great for a pre-dinner drink. **www.laurelinn.com**

Queen Anne Hotel P $$$

1590 Sutter St, 94109 **Tel** *(415) 441-2828* **Fax** *(415) 775-5212* **Rooms** *48*   **Map** *4 E4*

The Queen Anne is a beautiful Victorian hotel, built in 1890. Each room is done up differently with antique furniture and authentic decorations. Room rates include Continental breakfast, wine in the evenings, and a weekday morning towncar airport shuttle. **www.queenanne.com**

The Hotel Majestic P $$$

1500 Sutter St, 94109 **Tel** *(415) 441-1100* **Fax** *(415) 673-7331* **Rooms** *57*   **Map** *4 E4*

One of the few top-notch San Francisco hotels to have survived the 1906 earthquake, the Majestic is an exquisite early 20th-century building in a quiet neighborhood between Pacific Heights and Civic Center. Antique furniture graces the rooms, most of which have canopied beds and open fireplaces. **www.thehotelmajestic.com**

Hotel Drisco $$$$

2901 Pacific Ave, 94115 **Tel** *(415) 346-2880* **Fax** *(415) 567-5537* **Rooms** *48*   **Map** *3 C3*

Perched at the top of the glamorous Pacific Heights neighborhood, Hotel Drisco offers stately accomodation, perfect for business travelers and tourists. Many of the guest rooms feature spectacular views of the San Francisco Bay and Golden Gate Bridge. Complimentary nightly wine service and Continental breakfast. **www.hoteldrisco.com**

Jackson Court $$$$

2198 Jackson St, 94115 **Tel** *(415) 929-7670* **Fax** *(415) 929-1405* **Rooms** *10*   **Map** *4 E3*

This beautiful, well-appointed brownstone sits in one of the loveliest neighborhoods of San Francisco. The rooms are simple and elegant, some with fireplaces, all with TV/VCR combos, hairdryers and phones. A complimentary Continental breakfast is served in the breakfast room. **www.jacksoncourt.com**

Union Street Inn $$$$

2229 Union St, 94123 **Tel** *(415) 346-0424* **Fax** *(415) 922-8046* **Rooms** *6*   **Map** *4 D3*

When you check into Union Street Inn, you'll wish you lived here. Each of the spacious guest rooms is tastefully decorated, and the idyllic back garden is the perfect setting to enjoy a complimentary glass of wine at the end of a long day of sightseeing. Two-day minimum stays are required on weekends. **www.unionstreetinn.com**

FISHERMAN'S WHARF AND NORTH BEACH

Best Inn Fisherman's Wharf P $

2850 Van Ness Ave, 94109 **Tel** *(415) 776-3220* **Fax** *(415) 921-7451* **Rooms** *42*   **Map** *4 E2*

This three-story motel, though not an architectural wonder, offers proximity to some of the major sites – Fisherman's Wharf, North Beach, and Chinatown. Clean rooms, equipped with high-speed internet access, microwaves, and refrigerators make the Best Inn a good choice for budget travelers.

San Remo Hotel $

2237 Mason St, 94133 **Tel** *(415) 776-8688* **Fax** *(415) 776-2811* **Rooms** *62*   **Map** *5 B2*

The only budget hotel in the area, San Remo is a well-maintained Italianate building, and one of the first to be constructed following the earthquake and fire of 1906. All the rooms in this non-smoking hotel share bathrooms, with the exception of the rooftop Honeymoon Suite. **www.sanremohotel.com**

Best Western Tuscan Inn P $$$

425 Northpoint St, 94133 **Tel** *(415) 561-1100* **Fax** *(415) 561-1199* **Rooms** *220*   **Map** *5 B1*

Tuscan Inn is a spacious and stylish hotel in the middle of Fisherman's Wharf. It is a popular spot for business travelers as well as for visiting film and television crews. Children under 18, accompanied by an adult, stay free of charge. Complimentary wine is served every afternoon. **www.tuscaninn.com**

Hotel Boheme
⬆⬇ Ⓦ $$$

444 Columbus Ave, 94133 **Tel** *(415) 433-9111* **Fax** *(415) 362-6292* **Rooms** *15*   **Map** *5 B3*

The stylish and hip Boheme is a homage to the Beat Generation, in the heart of where it all began. Bold color schemes and whimsical touches enhance the hotel's poetic vibe. The rooms are cozy and all are equipped with free Wi-Fi. Located amid the hustle of North Beach, it is close to many great restaurants and bars. **www.hotelboheme.com**

The Wharf Inn
Ⓟ ⛹ $$$

2601 Mason St, 94133 **Tel** *(415) 673-7411* **Fax** *(415) 776-2181* **Rooms** *51*   **Map** *5 B1*

This 1960s-style three-story motel is bright, cheerful, and clean. All the rooms are decorated in bold colors, and many feature couches and small sitting areas. The inn is located directly above the bustling Fisherman's Wharf and offers complimentary parking – a rarity in San Francisco. **www.wharfinn.com**

Argonaut Hotel
Ⓟ ⛹ 🖥 ♿ $$$$

495 Jefferson Street, 94109 **Tel** *(415) 563-0800* **Fax** *(415) 563-2800* **Rooms** *265*   **Map** *5 A1*

This historic 1907 San Francisco building is now home to a maritime-themed boutique hotel. The luxury amenities on offer include in-room spa treatments, flat screen TVs, complimentary welcome gifts for children, and an on-site fitness center. Many of the rooms have views of the Golden Gate Bridge and San Francisco Bay. **www.argonauthotel.com**

Courtyard by Marriott Fisherman's Wharf
⬆⬇ Ⓟ 🍽 ⛹ $$$$

580 Beach St, 94133 **Tel** *(415) 775-3800* **Fax** *(415) 441-7307* **Rooms** *127*   **Map** *4 F1*

Sitting just one block from Fisherman's Wharf, the Courtyard is great value for its location and amenities. Clean, modern rooms feature high-speed internet access and are perfect for both vacationing families and business travelers. On-site business meeting facilities are also available. **www.marriott.com**

Hilton Fisherman's Wharf
⬆⬇ Ⓟ ⛹ 🖥 $$$$

2620 Jones St, 94133 **Tel** *(415) 885-4700* **Fax** *(415) 771-8945* **Rooms** *234*   **Map** *4 F1*

At the Fisherman's Wharf branch of the Hilton chain, guests pay for an irresistible location in the heart of San Francisco's waterfront tourist area. The lobby is spacious and modern, while the rooms are more traditional. It's a short walk to Pier 39, the Alcatraz ferries, and Fisherman's Wharf. **www.hilton.com**

Hyatt at Fisherman's Wharf
⬆⬇ Ⓟ 🏊 🖥 $$$$

555 North Point, 94133 **Tel** *(415) 563-1234* **Fax** *(415) 749-6122* **Rooms** *313*   **Map** *5 A1*

This Hyatt is more family-oriented than the other Hyatt hotels in San Francisco, though it provides a service of the same quality. Families are offered a discount on the price of their second room, and there is a heated swimming pool. **www.fishermanswharf.hyatt.com**

Marriott Fisherman's Wharf
⬆⬇ Ⓟ 🍽 ⛹ $$$$

1250 Columbus Ave, 94133 **Tel** *(415) 775-7555* **Fax** *(415) 474-2099* **Rooms** *285*   **Map** *4 F1*

Poised precisely between Fisherman's Wharf and North Beach, the Marriott offers above-average accommodation in a central location. Many of its rooms are geared specifically toward business travelers, and a complimentary limousine service is offered daily to the Financial District. **www.marriott.com**

Suites at Fisherman's Wharf
⬆⬇ Ⓟ ⛹ $$$$

2655 Hyde St, 94109 **Tel** *(415) 771-0200* **Fax** *(415) 346-8058* **Rooms** *24*   **Map** *5 A2*

Families and groups tend to stay here, in the city's only all-suite hotel. Business people also come here regularly. Each suite, spacious enough to accommodate four people, has its own kitchen and dining facilities. The hotel is steps away from the Hyde Street cable car. **www.thesuitesatfishermanswharf.com**

Washington Square Inn
Ⓟ ⛹ $$$$

1660 Stockton St, 94133 **Tel** *(415) 981-4220* **Fax** *(415) 397-7242* **Rooms** *15*   **Map** *5 B2*

One of the few hotels in the North Beach area, this is the only one facing Washington Square Park, where you can watch people practicing Tai Chi or strolling around the park. Room rates include a complimentary breakfast, though walking to the famous Mamma's Restaurant, just across the street, is a preferred option. **www.wsisf.com**

CHINATOWN AND NOB HILL

Hotel Astoria
⬆⬇ $$

510 Bush St, 94108 **Tel** *(415) 434-8883* **Fax** *(415) 434-8919* **Rooms** *80*   **Map** *5 C4*

Travelers on their own get a good deal at the modest Hotel Astoria, where reasonably priced single rooms are available. The hotel is conveniently situated between Chinatown and Union Square, very close to the dramatic Chinatown gates. **www.hotelastoria-sf.com**

Hotel Triton
⬆⬇ 🍽 $$$

342 Grant Ave, 94108 **Tel** *(415) 394-0500* **Fax** *(415) 394-0555* **Rooms** *140*   **Map** *5 C4*

Design and media professionals frequent the small but stylish Triton, with a friendly and cheerful ambience. It is just across the street from Chinatown and in the heart of San Francisco's art gallery district. For overseas travelers, foreign newspapers are normally available at the downstairs Café de la Presse. **www.hoteltriton.com**

Key to Price Guide *see p210* **Key to Symbols** *see back cover flap*

The Hilton Financial District
P ☆ ㄲ $$$

750 Kearny Street, 94108 **Tel** *(415) 483-1498* **Fax** *(415) 765-7891* **Rooms** *551*   **Map** *5 C3*

Located in the heart of Chinatown, this Hilton hotel has undergone a $55 million renovation, and it shows. The 27-story tower boasts stunning city views and the rooms, while still a little on the small side, are exquisitely equipped for both business travelers and families. **www.hilton.com**

Fairmont Hotel
⊠ P ⅋ ☆ ㄲ $$$$

950 Mason St, 94108 **Tel** *(415) 772-5000* **Fax** *(415) 781-3929* **Rooms** *596*   **Map** *5 B4*

Famous for its gorgeous lobby and opulent public rooms, the Fairmont is the grandest of all the grand hotels at the top of Nob Hill. Reopened in 1907, a year after an earthquake and fire ravaged it, it has been much admired since. The panoramic views are unbeatable. **www.fairmont.com**

Huntington Hotel and Nob Hill Spa
⊠ P ⅋ ☰ ☆ $$$$

1075 California St, 94108 **Tel** *(415) 474-5400* **Fax** *(415) 474-6227* **Rooms** *140*   **Map** *5 B4*

Built in 1922 as a luxury apartment building, the Huntington was converted into a high-class hotel in 1945. Each of the spacious rooms is individually decorated – many have a wet bar, and some have kitchens. Indulge yourself at the world-famous Nob Hill Spa, located on the upper floors of the hotel. **www.huntingtonhotel.com**

Mark Hopkins Inter-Continental Hotel
⊠ P ⅋ ☆ ㄲ $$$$

Number One Nob Hill, 94108 **Tel** *(415) 392-3434* **Fax** *(415) 421-3302* **Rooms** *380*   **Map** *5 B4*

Located atop Nob Hill, the Mark Hopkins is a 1926 architectural landmark. Completely renovated and refurbished in 2000, it is one of the finest hotels in San Francisco, rich and lavish in style. The Top of the Mark skylounge, on the 19th floor, offers panoramic views of the city from the peak of Nob Hill. **www.markhopkins.net**

The Ritz-Carlton San Francisco
⊠ P ⅋ ☰ ☆ ㄲ $$$$

600 Stockton, 94108 **Tel** *(415) 296-7465* **Fax** *(415) 291-0288* **Rooms** *336*   **Map** *5 C4*

Since it opened in 1991, the Ritz-Carlton has been rated one of San Francisco's best hotels. It is housed in an historic Beaux Arts building in an entire block along California Street, near the top of Nob Hill. Service is excellent. There's a four-star dining room, an indoor pool, and fitness center. **www.ritzcarlton.com**

FINANCIAL DISTRICT AND UNION SQUARE

UNION SQUARE Chancellor Hotel
P ☆ & ㄲ �W $$

433 Powell Street, 94102 **Tel** *(415) 362-2004* **Fax** *(415) 362-1403* **Rooms** *137*   **Map** *5 B4*

This boutique hotel bends over backwards to offer extra amenities at a bargain price. It enjoys a great location right in the heart of Union Square and when you're not out exploring you can take advantage of the free Wi-Fi or use of the Club One fitness club. Charming hotel with friendly staff. **www.chancellorhotel.com**

Hotel Bijou
⊠ P ☆ $$

111 Mason St, 94102 **Tel** *(415) 771-1200* **Fax** *(415) 346-3196* **Rooms** *62*   **Map** *5 B5*

Movie buffs will love Hotel Bijou, with its decor themed around San Francisco's cinematic history. Even the guest room draperies are a deep and dramatic burgundy-velvet and a small theater screens double-features daily. The convenient Union Square location and complimentary breakfast round off the charm. **www.hotelbijou.com**

Hotel des Arts
⊠ ⅋ ☆ $$

447 Bush St, 94108 **Tel** *(415) 956-3232* **Fax** *(415) 956-0399* **Rooms** *51*   **Map** *5 C4*

Hotel des Arts is as much a functioning art gallery as it is a hotel. A portion of the rooms, painted and decorated by a rotating roster of local artists, makes it one of the most unusual places in the city. These rooms may be reserved by phone only. Union Square, Chinatown, and the Financial District are close by. **www.sfhoteldesarts.com**

Hotel Frank
P ☆ & ㄲ W $$

386 Geary Street, 94102 **Tel** *(415) 986-2000* **Fax** *(415) 397-2447* **Rooms** *153*   **Map** *5 B5*

This hip, boutique hotel offers a lot of pizazz at an affordable priceand has a great location near Union Square's shops and restaurants. Fashionistas will love the retro-chic decor and sophisticated feel.For extra amenities, enquire about an upgrade to "The Bold Level". **www.hotelfranksf.com**

Hotel Vertigo
P ☆ & ㄲ W $$

940 Sutter Street, 94109 **Tel** *(415) 885-6800* **Fax** *(415) 885-2115* **Rooms** *102*   **Map** *5 A4*

Playing homage to the Hitchcock movie that was partly filmed here, this hotel has undergone a wonderful renovation with plush and comfortable rooms that are elegant and whimsical yet contemporary. If you're looking for a little bit of history and fun nostalgia, the Vertigo has it. **www.hotelvertigosf.com**

San Francisco Marriott Union Square
P ☆ ㄲ & W $$

480 Sutter Street, 94108 **Tel** *(415) 398-8900* **Fax** *(415) 989-8823* **Rooms** *400*   **Map** *5 C4*

Extensively renovated, this Marriott hotel is located within walking distance of Union Square, the Theater District, and Downtown museums and shops. The hotel has all necessary amenities and is reasonably priced. Guests should note the smoke-free policy and charge for Internet use. **www.marriott.com**

Touchstone Hotel

480 Geary St, 94102 **Tel** *(415) 771-1600* **Fax** *(415) 931-5442* **Rooms** *62*

Map 5 B5

Just steps from Union Square, Touchstone Hotel is a blend of old-world charm and modern convenience. It's a small, intimate bed-and-breakfast, owned and managed by the same family for over 50 years. Rates include breakfast and there is a complementary shuttle from the airport to the hotel. **www.thetouchstone.com**

Harbor Court Hotel

165 Steuart St, 94105 **Tel** *(415) 882-1300* **Fax** *(415) 882-1313* **Rooms** *131*

Map 6 E4

Housed in what was originally a YMCA building, the Harbor Court is the only hotel in San Francisco with a location right on the waterfront. Rooms are on the small side, though some have good views of the Bay Bridge. Guests have free access to the fitness facilities of the Y gym next door. **www.harborcourthotel.com**

Hotel Diva

440 Geary St, 94102 **Tel** *(415) 885-0200* **Fax** *(415) 346-6613* **Rooms** *114*

Map 5 B5

Stepping into Hotel Diva gives one the impression of having wandered into the Museum of Modern Art. The lobby and rooms are whimsically and colorfully decorated and accented by many architectural touches. The tone is hip luxury and the rooms won't disappoint even the most style-conscious traveler. **www.hoteldiva.com**

Hotel Union Square

114 Powell St, 94102 **Tel** *(415) 397-3000* **Fax** *(415) 399-1874* **Rooms** *131*

Map 5 C5

Conveniently located two blocks from Union Square, this chic boutique hotel is ideal for those looking for good value in the heart of San Francisco's shopping hub. Rooms are small and purpose-built, but amenities include fee-based wireless internet access in the lobby and on-site currency exchange. **www.hotelunionsquare.com**

Kensington Park Hotel

450 Post St, 94109 **Tel** *(415) 788-6400* **Fax** *(415) 399-9484* **Rooms** *86*

Map 5 B5

Located in the 1920s Spanish Revivalist-style Elks Lodge building, the Kensington Park is a comfortable, medium-sized hotel close to Union Square. The lobby is gorgeous and the nicely furnished rooms are spacious. The reasonable tariff includes free Continental breakfast and afternoon wine. **www.kensingtonparkhotel.com**

Le Meridien

333 Battery Street, 94111 **Tel** *(415) 296-2900* **Fax** *(415) 296-2901* **Rooms** *360*

Map 6 D3

A luxurious experience awaits at this prime-location hotel, right next to the Embarcadero Center shops. The decor is modern and sleek, the rooms boast comfortable beds with down duvets and 300-thread-count Frette sheets and robes are provided. Room service is available 24 hours a day. **www.starwoodhotels.com/lemeridien**

Nob Hill Motor Inn

1630 Pacific Ave, 94109 **Tel** *(415) 775-8160* **Fax** *(415) 673-8842* **Rooms** *29*

Map 4 F3

This is a standard, modern motel which is clean and efficiently run. It is centrally located close to dozens of interesting shops and local eateries, and within reasonable walking distance of Fisherman's Wharf and North Beach. **www.staysf.com**

Renaissance Parc Fifty Five Hotel

55 Cyril Magnin St, 94102 **Tel** *(415) 392-8000* **Fax** *(415) 403-6002* **Rooms** *1009*

Map 5 C5

The huge Parc Fifty Five, just off Market and Powell Streets, caters to conventions and large groups. There are good views from the upper floors. Tariffs are high, but special bed-and-breakfast and weekend offers make it worth considering. **www.parc55hotel.com**

San Francisco Hilton

333 O'Farrell St, 94102 **Tel** *(415) 771-1400* **Fax** *(415) 771-6807* **Rooms** *2044*

Map 5 B5

Filling an entire block just west of Union Square, the city's largest hotel provides excellent views from its 46-story tower. The service, too, matches the establishment's grand scale. The numerous facilities include an outdoor swimming pool, five restaurants, two bars, a barber shop, and a steam room. **www.hilton.com**

Serrano Hotel

405 Taylor St, 94102 **Tel** *(415) 885-2500* **Fax** *(415) 474-4879* **Rooms** *236*

Map 5 B5

This 17-story Spanish-Revivalist-style hotel has convenient access to both Union Square and the Theatre District. Guest rooms feature high ceilings and are accented by characteristic Moroccan-influenced design. The appealing Ponzu restaurant is located on the lobby level. **www.serranohotel.com**

Campton Place Hotel

340 Stockton St, 94108 **Tel** *(415) 781-5555* **Fax** *(415) 955-5536* **Rooms** *110*

Map 5 C4

The small and elegant Campton Place is situated just off Union Square. It offers plush, well-appointed rooms, good service, and sumptuous public areas. Particular appealing is the intimate bar off the lobby. Guests can choose between dinner on the roof terrace, or in the deluxe Campton Place Restaurant. **www.camptonplace.com**

Clift Hotel

495 Geary St, 94108 **Tel** *(415) 775-4700* **Fax** *(415) 931-7417* **Rooms** *363*

Map 5 B5

The dramatic Clift is a striking example of modern design, with a lobby created by Phillippe Starck. Each room is elegantly furnished with all the amenities one would expect from a hotel of this caliber. The downstairs Redwood Room and award-winning Asia de Cuba Restaurant are enchanting. **www.clifthotel.com**

Key to Price Guide *see p210* **Key to Symbols** *see back cover flap*

Four Seasons
🛏 P 🍴 ≋ 🏃 📺 $$$$$

757 Market St, 94103 **Tel** *(415) 633-3000* **Fax** *(415) 633-3001* **Rooms** *277*   **Map** *5 C5*

Four Seasons is one of San Francisco's classiest hotels. Spacious and understatedly stylish, each room has cozy sitting areas. The ultra-chic Sports Club/LA is available for guest use. This hotel provides easy access to Union Square, the San Francisco Museum of Modern Art, and Yerba Buena Center. **www.fourseasons.com**

Grand Hyatt San Francisco
🛏 P 🍴 ≋ 🏃 📺 $$$$$

345 Stockton St, 94108 **Tel** *398-1234* **Fax** *391-178* **Rooms** *686*   **Map** *5 C4*

The 36-story Grand Hyatt towers over the north side of Union Square, offering great views from all of its rooms. The rooftop Grand View restaurant has live piano music on Friday and Saturday evenings. The location is handy for the Financial District as well as for Union Square shops and theaters. **www.grandsanfrancisco.hyatt.com**

Hotel Monaco
🛏 P 🍴 🏃 📺 $$$$

501 Geary St, 94102 **Tel** *(866) 622-5284* **Fax** *(415) 292-0111* **Rooms** *201*   **Map** *5 B5*

Funky and charming, the Monaco is a few blocks west of Union Square. The guest rooms – a study in pattern and texture – feature many luxurious extras, such as Frette robes, down pillows, and fax machines. The Grand Café is set in a spectacular turn-of-the-19th-century ballroom downstairs. **www.monaco-sf.com**

Hotel Nikko
🛏 P 🍴 ≋ 🏃 📺 $$$$

222 Mason St, 94102 **Tel** *(415) 394-1111* **Fax** *(415) 394-1106* **Rooms** *534*   **Map** *5 B5*

The ultra-modern Nikko caters primarily to business travelers, especially those from Japan. The hotel's excellent fitness center, with its glass-enclosed swimming pool and full range of exercise equipment, is among the best in the city. The lobby-level Anzu restaurant is perfect for drinking and dining. **www.hotelnikkosf.com**

Hotel Rex
🛏 P 🍴 🏃 📺 $$$$

562 Sutter St, 94102 **Tel** *(415) 433-4434* **Fax** *(415) 433-3695* **Rooms** *94*   **Map** *5 B4*

This pleasant hotel has with rooms painted in rich colors and the walls embellished with the works of local artists. A real gem – and the pride of the Rex – the downstairs lobby has a dark-hued and cozy library. The lobby bar often hosts literary events and readings. **www.jdvhospitality.com**

Hotel Vitale
🛏 P 🍴 ≋ 🏃 📺 $$$$

8 Mission St, 94105 **Tel** *(415) 278-3700* **Fax** *(415) 278-3150* **Rooms** *199*   **Map** *6 E4*

Built in early 2005, the flamboyant Hotel Vitale is the latest – and possibly, the grandest – from the JDV Hospitality Group. Situated along the Embarcadero, it has all the advantages of a destination resort, in the heart of the city. The guest rooms boast every amenity and Spa Vitale has stunning views. **www.jdvhospitality.com**

Hyatt Regency San Francisco
🛏 P 🍴 🏃 $$$$$

5 Embarcadero Center, 94111 **Tel** *(415) 788-1234* **Fax** *(415) 398-2567* **Rooms** *803*   **Map** *6 D3*

The Hyatt, built in 1973 around a 15-story atrium lobby, has had its rooms largely upgraded. Designated mainly for business travelers, the Regency Club floor has a full-time attendant, always on call. This hotel is located next to a small shopping center and theater complex. **www.sanfranciscoregency.hyatt.com**

JW Marriott
🛏 P 🍴 🏃 $$$$

500 Post St, 94102 **Tel** *(415) 771-8600* **Fax** *(415) 398-0267* **Rooms** *338*   **Map** *5 B5*

John Portman was the architect of this beautifully appointed, daringly designed modern hotel. Formerly the Pan Pacific Hotel, it has an atrium lobby 17 stories high, rising to a rooftop skylight. The public areas are glamorous, and the bed-rooms refined and elegant. Business travelers will find the staff extremely helpful. **www.jwmarriottunionsquare.com**

Mandarin Oriental
🛏 P 🍴 🏃 $$$$$

222 Sansome St, 94104 **Tel** *(415) 276-9888* **Fax** *(415) 433-0289* **Rooms** *158*   **Map** *6 D3*

Particularly convenient for business travelers, Mandarin Oriental is first class in every respect. The Mandarin Rooms have floor-to-ceiling windows, offering magnificent views of San Francisco Bay and the Golden Gate Bridge. Another attraction is the excellent restaurant, Silks, located on the second floor. **www.mandarinoriental.com**

Prescott Hotel
🛏 🍴 🏃 $$$$

545 Post St, 94102 **Tel** *(415) 563-0303* **Fax** *(415) 563-6831* **Rooms** *166*   **Map** *5 B5*

Business travelers predominate at this sumptuous hotel that resembles a gentleman's club, with dark wooden walls and a large fireplace in the entrance lobby. Complimentary drinks are served in the afternoons. Postrio Restaurant is a little past its prime, but still serves consistent food in an elegant ambience. **www.prescotthotel.com**

San Francisco Marriott
🛏 P ≋ 🍴 🏃 📺 $$$$

55 Fourth St, 94103 **Tel** *(415) 896-1600* **Fax** *(415) 486-8101* **Rooms** *1500*   **Map** *5 C5*

Someone may like the futuristic look of this 39-story tower, but no one in San Francisco has dared to say so. However, the hotel has proved a popular spot for conventions. Families always appreciate the indoor pool and the fact that children under 18, when accompanied by an adult, can stay there free. **www.sfmarriott.com**

Sheraton Palace Hotel
🛏 P 🍴 ≋ 🏃 📺 $$$$

2 New Montgomery St, 94105 **Tel** *(415) 512-1111* **Fax** *(415) 543-0671* **Rooms** *550*   **Map** *5 C4*

Early in the 20th century the Palace was one of the most famous hotels in the world, hosting royalty and heads of state, including President Harding, who died here in his sleep in 1923. Renovated in the late 1980s, it is now known for its glamorous Garden Court, where afternoon tea is served. **www.sfpalace.com**

Sir Francis Drake Hotel

🖥 🍴 🏃 📺 $$$$

450 Powell St, 94102 **Tel** *(800) 392-7755* **Fax** *(415) 392-8559* **Rooms** *417*   **Map** *5 B4*

A long-established Union Square hotel, the Sir Francis Drake glows in Art Deco splendor. It is famed for its Beefeater-uniformed doormen and Harry Denton's Starlight Room, a beautiful rooftop bar. The location, on the Powell Street cable car line, is unbeatable for access to the Financial District and North Beach. **www.sirfrancisdrake.com**

The Westin San Francisco Market Street

P 🏃 📺 ♿ $$$$

50 Third Street, 94103 **Tel** *(415) 974-6400* **Fax** *(415) 348-8207* **Rooms** *702*   **Map** *5 C5*

The hotel offers a great location from which to enjoy all Union Square has to offer. The rooms here are clean and spacious and, of course, have the signature Westin "heavenly beds" which are very comfortable. A 24-hour fitness facility is another huge plus. **www.westinsf.com**

Westin St. Francis

🖥 P 🍴 🏃 📺 $$$$

335 Powell St, 94102 **Tel** *(415) 397-7000* **Fax** *(415) 774-0124* **Rooms** *1200*   **Map** *5 B4*

Since 1904, Union Square's skyline has been defined by the triple towers of Westin St. Francis. Following earthquake and fire damage in 1906, the hotel was restored. In the 1970s, a 32-story tower was added onto the back. The best rooms have views of Union Square and the Michael Minna restaurant is one of the city's best. **www.westinstfrancis.com**

White Swan Inn

🏃 $$$$

845 Bush St, 94108 **Tel** *(415) 775-1755* **Fax** *(415) 775-5717* **Rooms** *26*   **Map** *5 B4*

A small, country-style establishment, the White Swan has rooms with bright floral prints and comfortable beds. A complimentary English breakfast is served each morning, and wine and *hors d'oeuvres* are served every evening. The inn also runs complimentary introductory tours of the city. **www.whiteswaninnsf.com**

CIVIC CENTER

Embassy Hotel

P 🏃 ♿ $

610 Polk Street, 94102 **Tel** *(415) 673-1404* **Fax** *(415) 474-4188* **Rooms** *84*   **Map** *4 F5*

Housed in a unique 1932 Art Deco building, the Embassy Hotel offers sizeable, comfortable rooms at a good price. The hotel is within easy walking distance of the Opera House, Symphony Hall, and state and federal buildings. A great place for someone on a budget. Breakfast is Continental. **www.theembassyhotelsf.com**

Albion House Inn

P 🍴 $$

135 Gough St, 94102 **Tel** *(415) 621-0896* **Fax** *(415) 621-3811* **Rooms** *9*   **Map** *10 F1*

Centrally located near the Financial District and Union Square, this inn is a favorite with businesspeople. All of the rooms include little extras such as robes, writing desks, and six pillows on each bed. A three-course American breakfast is included. **www.albionhouse.com**

Best Western Americania

🖥 P 🏊 🏃 📺 $$

121 7th St, 94105 **Tel** *(415) 626-0200* **Fax** *(415) 863-2529* **Rooms** *143*   **Map** *11 A1*

Though technically in the trendy South of Market neighborhood of San Francisco, the Americania is a short walk from Union Square. The modern, spacious, and comfortable facilities are a refreshing contrast to the buzz of the city. Free internet access is available, and the parking is free of charge. **www.theamericania.com**

Grove Inn

$$

890 Grove St, 94117 **Tel** *(415) 929-0780* **Fax** *(415) 929-1037* **Rooms** *18*   **Map** *4 E5*

Grove Inn, an Italianate-Victorian bed-and-breakfast, with a good location near Civic Center, dates to the late 1800s. The multilingual hosts have been running the place for over 20 years. The sunny rooms come with a queen-sized bed and direct dial phones. Rates include a complimentary Continental breakfast. **www.grovinn.com**

Hotel Kabuki

P 🏃 📺 ♿ $$

1625 Post Street, 94115 **Tel** *(415) 922-3200* **Fax** *(415) 614-5498* **Rooms** *218*   **Map** *4 E4*

The complimentary "welcome tea" service is a delightful treat at this Japanese-style hotel. Hotel Kabuki offers a calm and serene experience, complete with traditional, Japanese-style soaking tubs and a free pass for the Kabuki Springs and Spa. Rooms are cozy, peaceful, and clean. A great place to relax. **www.jdvhotels.com/kabuki**

Hotel Tomo

P 🏃 📺 ♿ $$

1800 Sutter Street, 94115 **Tel** *(415) 921-4000* **Fax** *(415) 563-1278* **Rooms** *125*   **Map** *4 E4*

A complete Japanese experience in the heart of Japantown. Inspired by Japanese pop culture, rooms are decorated with Japanese animation (anime) and pop art and there are gaming suites with Play-Station 3 and Wii. Cozy and clean with all-you-can-eat *shabu shabu* (meat and vegetable hot pot) in the lobby restaurant. **www.jdvhotels.com/tomo**

Monarch Hotel

P $$

1015 Geary St, 94109 **Tel** *(415) 673-5232* **Fax** *(415) 885-2802* **Rooms** *101*   **Map** *4 F4*

The Monarch is preferred by budget travelers looking for basic amenities and a central San Francisco location. All rooms have cable TV and safe-deposit boxes, some have refrigerators. Coffee is served throughout the day in the lobby and parking is available at an additional cost. **www.themonarchhotel.com**

Key to Price Guide *see p210* **Key to Symbols** *see back cover flap*

Phoenix Hotel

P ⑪ ≋ ⸙ $⑤⑤

601 Eddy St, 94109 **Tel** *(415) 776-1380* **Fax** *(415) 885-3109* **Rooms** *44*   **Map** *4 F4*

This funky two-story motel, in the heart of the Tenderloin District, conjures up images of old Route 66. Grab a drink at the house bar, Bambuddha, and head out to the courtyard pool to spot celebrities (past guests include Dave Navarro and Linda Ronstadt). The rooms are basic but great value for a central location. **www.jdvhospitality.com**

Renoir Hotel

🔲 ⑪ ⸙ 🖵 $⑤⑤

45 McAllister St, 94102 **Tel** *(415) 626-5200* **Fax** *(415) 626-0916* **Rooms** *135*   **Map** *11 A1*

The dramatically ornate Renoir is a historic landmark. With a thoroughly updated interior, the hotel provides rooms with many modern amenities, including dataports. Room service is available from Café do Brazil, the Brazilian restaurant downstairs. **www.renoirhotel.com**

Best Western Carriage Inn

🔲 P ⑪ ⸙ $⑤⑤⑤

140 7th St, 94103 **Tel** *(415) 552-8600* **Fax** *(415) 626-3973* **Rooms** *48*   **Map** *11 A1*

In the South of Market district of San Francisco, the Carriage Inn offers great value, combining fair room rates with larger-than-average rooms. An excellent choice for families, as children 17 and under stay free. There is a Jacuzzi in the common patio area, and an adjacent restaurant and bar. **www.bestwestern.com**

Cathedral Hill Hotel

🔲 P ⑪ ≋ ⸙ 🖵 $⑤⑤⑤

1101 Van Ness, 94109 **Tel** *(415) 776-8200* **Fax** *(415) 441-2841* **Rooms** *400*   **Map** *4 F4*

Sitting on a sprawling campus just off the busy Van Ness Street, the Cathedral Hill resembles a small city. Though not exactly walking distance to most of the city's sites, it's well-positioned in the middle of the city, close to public transportation. Amenities include a pool, fitness center, and a restaurant and bar. **www.cathedralhillhotel.com**

Hotel Metropolis

🔲 P ⸙ 🖵 $⑤⑤⑤

25 Mason St, 94102 **Tel** *(415) 775-4600* **Fax** *(415) 775-7606* **Rooms** *110*   **Map** *5 B5*

A funky boutique hotel, the Metropolis has a nature theme throughout, with each floor reflecting the elements. The Holistic room is perfect for escaping the hustle of nearby Union Square. All rooms offer amenities including bars, two-line phones and dataports with voicemail, and Nintendo. **www.hotelmetropolis.com**

Archbishop's Mansion Inn

🔲 ⸙ $⑤⑤⑤⑤

1000 Fulton St, 94117 **Tel** *(415) 563-7872* **Fax** *(415) 885-3193* **Rooms** *15*   **Map** *4 D5*

This imposing building, in the style of the Second French Empire, was built in 1904 but has been carefully restored. Inside there is an elaborate three-story open staircase, topped by a stained-glass skylight. All rooms are luxuriously decorated and designed around operatic themes. **www.jdvhospitality.com**

HAIGHT ASHBURY AND THE MISSION

Elements Hotel

🔲 ⑪ $

2524 Mission St, 94110 **Tel** *(415) 647-4100* **Fax** *(415) 550-9005* **Rooms** *26*   **Map** *9 F3*

This friendly, European-style hostel offers both dormitories and private rooms, right in the heart of San Francisco's Mission District. There is a restaurant and bar downstairs, but perhaps the most enticing aspect of Elements is the roofdeck – complete with sun chairs and a telescope. **www.elementshotel.com**

24 Henry

W $⑤⑤

24 Henry St, 94114 **Tel** *(415) 864-5686* **Fax** *(415) 864-0406* **Rooms** *5*   **Map** *9 D2*

In the heart of the Castro District, 24 Henry is a charming bed-and-breakfast that caters to a primarily gay clientele. It enjoys a serene ambience on a quiet, tree-lined street. Facilities include free wireless DSL, complimentary breakfast, and private phones in all rooms. Rates are reasonable. **www.24henry.com**

Beck's Motor Lodge

P $⑤⑤

2222 Market St, 94114 **Tel** *(415) 621-8212* **Fax** *(415) 241-0435* **Rooms** *57*   **Map** *10 E1*

Beck's is a standard 1960s motel, convenient for the restaurants and nightlife of the Castro, Lower Haight and Mission Districts. Free parking, cable TV, and a quiet location are its main attractions. There is also a sunny roofdeck, a perfect setting for a glass of wine before heading out for the night.

Inn on Castro

P $⑤⑤

321 Castro St, 94114 **Tel** *(415) 861-0321* **Rooms** *12*   **Map** *10 D2*

The Inn on Castro, a fully-restored Edwardian, blends old and modern, with eclectic flower bouquets and modern art adorning the traditional interiors. It's perfectly poised in the heart of the Castro District and offers guest suites and self-service apartments. A free Continental breakfast is served daily. **www.innoncastro2.com**

Inn 1890

$⑤⑤

1890 Page St, 94117 **Tel** *(415) 386-0486* **Fax** *(415) 386-3626* **Rooms** *12*   **Map** *9 B1*

One of the many imposing mansions built along the Panhandle of Golden Gate Park, this 1897 Queen Anne-style building was converted in 1984 into a comfortable and stylish bed-and-breakfast. The guest rooms, each with kitchenette, are decorated with William Morris wallpaper. A good Continental breakfast is served daily. **www.inn1890.com**

Red Victorian Bed and Breakfast $$

1665 Haight St, 94117 **Tel** *(415) 864-1978* **Fax** *(415) 863-3293* **Rooms** *18*   **Map** *9 B1*

The Red Victorian is the ubiquitous Haight Street accommodation, perfect for travelers who want to channel San Francisco in the "Summer of Love." All the rooms are individually themed, with names such as Redwood Forest and Flower Child. No radios or TVs are available, but there's a meditation room. **www.redvic.com**

The Inn San Francisco   P ⚡ W $$

943 S. Van Ness Avenue, 94110 **Tel** *(415) 641-0188* **Fax** *(415) 641-1701* **Rooms** *21*   **Map** *10 F3*

The owner of this 1872 Victorian Mansion will charm you with hospitality. The spacious rooms are individually decorated in Victorian themes. Don't miss sitting out in the English-style garden or relaxing in the redwood hot tub. The breakfast buffet is generous and it is possible to negotiate on room prices. **www.innsf.com**

Willows Bed and Breakfast   W $$

710 14th St, 94114 **Tel** *(415) 431-4770* **Fax** *(415) 431-5295* **Rooms** *12*   **Map** *10 E2*

Built in 1903, the Willows is a European-style, gay and lesbian friendly bed-and-breakfast in the Castro District. Each room comes with a sink, kimono bathrobes, and luxury soaps as well as a TV, VCR, and wireless Internet access. Eight private water closets are situated adjacent to the rooms. The staff is extremely friendly. **www.willowssf.com**

Stanyan Park Hotel   🔼 $$$

750 Stanyan St, 94117 **Tel** *(415) 751-1000* **Fax** *(415) 668-5454* **Rooms** *36*   **Map** *9 B2*

Doctors, patients, and patients' families often stay in this lovely Queen Anne-style hotel that enjoys a proximity to the San Francisco Medical Center. Opened in 1983 after extensive renovation, the hotel overlooks Golden Gate Park. The rooms are cozy, with fireplaces in many of them, while the ample suites include a full kitchen. **www.stanyanpark.com**

SOUTH OF MARKET

Marriott Courtyard San Francisco Downtown   P ▦ 🔼 📺 ♿ $$$

299 Second Street, 94105 **Tel** *(415) 947-0700* **Fax** *(415) 947-0800* **Rooms** *436*   **Map** *6 D5*

This Marriott hotel offers all the amenities of a luxury hotel without the exorbitant price. It's a great place to stay in the downtown area, especially for those traveling with children, and is conveniently located close to many of the city's museums. **www.courtyardsanfrancisco.com**

Hotel Intercontinental   P 🍴 ▦ 🔼 📺 ♿ W $$$$

888 Howard Street, 94103 **Tel** *(888) 811-4273* **Fax** *(415) 616-6501* **Rooms** *564*   **Map** *11 B1*

This architectural wonder opened to much fanfare in San Francisco. It boasts an elegant, modern interior with luxurious guest rooms. Situated south of Market Street, the hotel is near museums and the Moscone Center. Spa services are deluxe and the dining is elegant. **www.intercontinentalsanfrancisco.com**

St. Regis Hotel   P 🍴 ▦ 🔼 📺 ♿ $$$$

125 Third Street, 94103 **Tel** *(415) 284-4000* **Fax** *(415) 284-4100* **Rooms** *306*   **Map** *11 B1*

Directly adjacent to the San Francisco Museum of Modern Art, this hotel is the true epitome of luxury – their butler service brings "any request and whim to realization." Sample the handmade truffles and champagne while you wait for a spa treatment or dine in Ame, the hotel's excellent restaurant. **www.starwoodhotels.com/stregis**

BERKELEY

The French Hotel   P 🍴 🔼 $

1538 Shattuck, Berkeley, 94709 **Tel** *(510) 548-9930* **Fax** *(510) 548-9930* **Rooms** *18*

This quaint and cozy European-style hotel boasts an innately relaxed and social atmosphere. The rooms are small and comfortable – some with views and all with TVs. The downstairs French Hotel Café is a bustling venue, perfect for good coffee, food, and conversation.

Bancroft Hotel   P 🔼 $$

2680 Bancroft Way, Berkeley, 94704 **Tel** *(510) 549-1000* **Fax** *(510) 549-1000* **Rooms** *22*

The Bancroft is located directly across the street from the University of California at Berkeley and only a few blocks from the hip Telegraph Avenue. Built in 1928 in the Arts and Crafts design, this hotel offers gracious guest rooms and ample common areas. **www.bancrofthotel.com**

Rose Garden Inn   P 🔼 $$$

2740 Telegraph Ave, Berkeley, 94705 **Tel** *(510) 549-2145* **Fax** *(510) 549-1085* **Rooms** *40*

The appropriately named, turn-of-the-19th-century Rose Garden Inn is an oasis in the heart of urban Berkeley. The enchanting property takes up almost an entire street block with its four buildings and whimsically-landscaped gardens. The outdoor patio is perfect for breakfast on warm summer mornings. **www.rosegardeninn.com**

Key to Price Guide *see p210* **Key to Symbols** *see back cover flap*

Claremont Resort, Spa and Tennis Club

$$$$

41 Tunnel Road, Oakland, 94705 Tel (510) 843-3000 Fax (510) 848-6208 Rooms 279

This stunning hotel is poised at the foot of Berkeley Hills, overlooking much of East Bay and San Francisco. The sprawling grounds offer tennis courts, landscaped gardens, outdoor swimming pool and a world-class spa. Even if you don't stay here, stop by for a drink and to enjoy the views. **www.claremontresort.com**

FARTHER AFIELD

EAST PALO ALTO Four Seasons Palo Alto

$$$

2050 University Avenue, 94303 Tel (650) 566-1200 Fax (650) 566-1221 Rooms 227

Ten minutes from Stanford University, this luxury hotel offers a unique rooftop pool, relaxing spa and elegant, perfectly appointed rooms. The business elite flock here for its central location near Silicon Valley, but locals love its sophistication and outstanding restaurant. **www.fourseasons.com/siliconvalley**

HALF MOON BAY The Ritz Carlton Half Moon Bay

$$$$

1 Miramontes Point Road, 94019 Tel (650) 712-7000 Fax (650) 712-7831 Rooms 261

This romantic, luxury hotel is perched atop the cliffs of the Pacific Ocean and offers stunning views and world-class service. Enjoy hot chocolate and s'mores by the outdoor fireplaces while watching the sunset, or take a stroll down to the quaint town of Half Moon Bay where there are shops and restaurants. **www.ritzcarlton.com**

MILL VALLEY Mountain Home Inn

$$$

810 Panoramic Highway, 94941 Tel (415) 381-9000 Fax (415) 381-3615 Rooms 10

Perched atop Mount Tam, a popular hiking destination, this B&B offers incredible views of the entire San Francisco Bay from its patio deck. Each of the 10 rooms is cozy, quiet and restful. The hotel restaurant serves local fresh fare. Don't miss exploring the hiking trails or a quick drive over to Muir Woods. **www.mtnhomeinn.com**

POINT REYES Point Reyes Station Inn

$$

11591 State Route 1 N, 94956 Tel (415) 663-9372 Fax (415) 663-8842 Rooms 5

This charming B&B, in the heart of the coastal town of Point Reyes, has old-world character with modern amenities. The vaulted ceilings, whirlpool baths and in-room fireplaces make for a romantic escape. Point Reyes National Seashore boasts magnificent scenery along with boundless outdoor activities. **www.pointreyesstationinn.com**

SAUSALITO Gables Inn Sausalito

$$$

62 Princess Street, 94965 Tel (415) 289-1100 Fax (415) 339-0536 Rooms 15

Sausalito's finest historic Inn is the place to stay if you want a romantic escape. The rooms are spacious and the staff friendly and helpful. There is also a complimentary wine and cheese evening. The Ferry service to San Francisco is a three-minute walk down the hill. **www.gablesinnsausalito.com**

NORTHERN CALIFORNIA

CARMEL San Carlos Days Inn

$$

850 Abrego St, Monterey, 93940 Tel (831) 649-6332 Fax (831) 649-6353 Rooms 55

This basic, well-maintained motel is a short walk to the shops of downtown Monterey and just a mile to famous Cannery Row and Monterey Bay Aquarium. The downtown location makes San Carlos Inn a good base from which to explore the entire peninsula. Free on-site parking. **www.montereydaysinn.com**

CARMEL Carmel Wayfarer Inn

$$$

4th and Mission St, Carmel-by-the-Sea, 93921 Tel (831) 624-2711 Fax (831) 625-1210 Rooms 15

In the heart of Carmel-by-the-Sea, Carmel Wayfarer is a fair bargain option. The simple, yet tastefully appointed rooms and common areas make this a good choice for travelers who prefer to be within walking distance of the major area sites. A deluxe complimentary Continental breakfast is served daily. **www.carmelwayfarerinn.com**

CARMEL Highlands Inn

$$$$

120 Highlands Drive, Carmel, 93923 Tel (831) 620-1234 Fax (831) 626-1574 Rooms 142

High on a bluff overlooking the Pacific Ocean below, Highlands Inn represents the quintessential Monterey Peninsula drama. Over two-thirds of the rooms are suites or parlors – almost all with their own patios or balconies. Attractions include a heated outdoor pool and panoramic coastal views. **www.highlandsinn.hyatt.com**

CARMEL La Playa Hotel

$$$$

Camino Real at Eigth, Carmel, 93921 Tel (831) 624-6476 Fax (831) 624-7966 Rooms 75

The La Playa feels more like a Mediterranean estate than a standard hotel, with its extensive guest rooms and cottage complexes surrounding a central garden, lawn, and pool. It's a good option for both families with children and couples as some cottages can accommodate up to eight people. **www.laplayahotel.com**

LAKE TAHOE La Porte Cabins   P $

La Porte, CA, 95981 **Tel** *(530) 675-0850* **Rooms** *15*

Situated in the heart of La Porte, this picturesque little conglomeration of rustic cabins reminds one of the California Gold Rush era. Once a booming mine town of 900, it now only has a saloon, post office, and mini mart. Each of these original "China Alley" cabins date back to that time and have since been restored. **www.laportecabins.com**

LAKE TAHOE 3 Peaks Resort and Beach Club   P $$

931 Park Ave, Tahoe, 96150 **Tel** *(866) 500-4886* **Rooms** *54*

The 3 Peaks is one of the better choices on the California side of Lake Tahoe. It offers cabin-style guest rooms and suites – many of which have fully stocked kitchens, perfect for large groups staying together. This hotel is only two blocks away from the Heavenly Ski area. **www.3peakshotel.com**

LAKE TAHOE Christy Inn   P $$$

1650 Squaw Valley Rd, Olympic Valley, 96146 **Tel** *(530) 581-0454* **Fax** *(530) 581-5631* **Rooms** *6*

Christy Inn is located within the sprawling Squaw Valley, site of the 1960 Winter Olympics. Each of the rustic rooms has its own private bath and spectacular views of the surrounding mountains. It is a popular summer destination as well and hosts many weddings and family reunions each year.

LAKE TAHOE Harrah's Lake Tahoe   P $$$$

Highway 50 at Stateline, Nevada, 89449 **Tel** *(775) 588-6611* **Rooms** *525*

Though technically in Nevada, no trip to Lake Tahoe is complete without a quick (or not so quick) stop to pull a handle or two at the Nevada casinos. With all the conveniences of a San Francisco hotel, there is good reason to make Harrah's a home base while vacationing here. **www.harrahs.com**

LAKE TAHOE Lake Tahoe Cottages   P $$$$

7030 Highway 89, Tahoma, 96142 **Tel** *(530) 525-4411* **Fax** *(530) 525-0824*

This cluster of cabins in the North Shore area of Lake Tahoe is the perfect rustic retreat for families and couples looking for Western charm and reasonable rates. The cottages boast a year-round hot tub (perfect for après-ski) and a pool for summer use. They can accommodate large groups of up to 60 people. **www.tahoelakecottages.com**

LASSEN VOLCANIC NATIONAL PARK La Quinta Redding   P $

2180 Hilltop Drive, Redding, 96002 **Tel** *(530) 221-8200* **Fax** *(530) 223-4727* **Rooms** *144*

The La Quinta Redding is a good jumping-off point for exploring the Mount Lassen Volcanic National Park and Shasta Lake and Dam. Just off the I–5 artery, this hotel provides a pool, fitness center, airport shuttle, and a complimentary Continental breakfast. The rooms are clean, if a bit generic, but the service is consistent. **www.lq.com**

LASSEN VOLCANIC NATIONAL PARK Cornelius Daly Inn   P $$$

1125 H Street, Eureka, 95501 **Tel** *(707) 445-3638* **Rooms** *5*

This stately Victorian building is located in the atmospheric area of Eureka. Each room has been restored, but the inn-keepers have taken care to preserve the original character of the house with period-appropriate antique furniture and decor. Annie Murphy's Room has a functioning fireplace. **www.dalyinn.com**

MENDOCINO/ REDWOOD NATIONAL PARK Riverbar Farm   P $$

355 Riverbar Rd, Fortuna, 95540 **Tel** *(707) 768-9272* **Fax** *(707) 768-9273* **Rooms** *4*

It's best to book your room early at this working farm and bed-and-breakfast with only four rooms. The spartan rooms are clean and cozy, and the charm of waking up to the bustle of a functioning farm (and hearty breakfast) makes for a great vacation experience. In October there is a pumpkin patch and corn maze for children. **www.riverbarfarm.com**

MENDOCINO/ REDWOOD NATIONAL PARK Victorian Inn   P $$$

400 Ocean Ave, Ferndale, 95536 **Tel** *(707) 786-4949* **Fax** *(707) 786-4558* **Rooms** *12*

The impressive Victorian Inn anchors one of the prominent corners in downtown Ferndale. Beautifully lit at night, each of the rooms blends Victorian charm with modern conveniences. Curley's, downstairs, offers food and drink in a convivial atmosphere, perfect for unwinding after a day of sightseeing. **www.avoctorianinn.com**

MONTEREY San Carlos Inn   P $

850 Abrego Street, 93940 **Tel** *(831) 649-6332* **Fax** *(831) 649-6353* **Rooms** *55*

One of the best deals in town, the San Carlos Inn offers a great location near downtown historic Monterey and Fisherman's Wharf. The rooms are clean, large and comfortable, and the staff is eager to make your stay enjoyable. Other perks include free parking and free Internet service. **www.montereydaysinn.com**

MONTEREY Monterey Plaza Hotel and Spa   P $$$

400 Cannery Row, 93940 **Tel** *(831) 646-1700* **Fax** *(831) 646-0285* **Rooms** *300*

This luxurious get-away hotel boasts spectacular views of the Pacific from all areas of the hotel. The service here is exceptional and the restaurants serve innovative cuisine and locally sourced seafood. The nearby attractions are virtually limitless. **www.montereyplazahotel.com**

MONTEREY The Clement Monterey Hotel   P $$$

750 Cannery Row, 93940 **Tel** *(831) 375-4500* **Fax** *(831) 375-4501* **Rooms** *226*

A chic haven amidst the bustling tourist area of Cannery Row, this hotel has a wonderfully modern vibe set against the dramatic landscape of the Pacific. It offers great service, dynamic views and perfectly appointed rooms. Enjoy the spa and pool area or take a short walk to the world renowned Monterey Aquarium. **www.ichotelsgroup.com**

Key to Price Guide *see p210* **Key to Symbols** *see back cover flap*

NAPA WINE COUNTRY Hotel Sausalito   P W $$$
16 El Portal, Sausalito, 94965 **Tel** *(415) 332-0700* **Fax** *(415) 332-8788* **Rooms** *16*

Because it is not located directly on the water, Hotel Sausalito is exceptional value for its high quality of facilities and services. Each of its comfortable rooms is individually decorated. Continental breakfast is provided as are high-tech extras like wireless Internet access and in-room fax machines. **www.hotelsausalito.com**

NAPA WINE COUNTRY Hotel St. Helena   P $$$
1309 Main Street, St. Helena, 94574 **Tel** *(707) 963-4388* **Fax** *(707) 963-5402* **Rooms** *18*

This charming Victorian hotel, built in 1890, is a good base for touring the surrounding Napa Wine Country. Every room is designed differently and features four-poster beds. The elegant, flower filled lobby is the perfect place to sip a glass of wine and contemplate dinner plans. **www.hotelsthelena.net**

NAPA WINE COUNTRY River Terrace Inn   P $$$
1600 Soscol Ave, Napa, 94559 **Tel** *(707) 320-9000* **Fax** *(707) 258-1236* **Rooms** *106*

River Terrace Inn offers a more reasonably-priced option for the Wine Country visitors. Although it doesn't afford some of the spectacular views of other nearby hotels, it is good value. Amenities include high-speed Wi-Fi Internet access, a fitness center, and an outdoor pool. **www.riverterraceinn.com**

NAPA WINE COUNTRY Auberge du Soleil   P $$$$
180 Rutherford Hill Rd, Rutherford **Tel** *(707) 963-1211* **Fax** *(707) 963-8764* **Rooms** *50*

There is no finer place to stay in all of the Wine Country (or Northern California, for that matter) than the Auberge du Soleil. Guest rooms, housed in small cottages, overlook the entire Napa Valley. This resort has every imaginable amenity and all the quiet understatement of a sprawling French estate. **www.aubergedusoleil.com**

NAPA WINE COUNTRY Casa Madrona   P $$$$
801 Bridgeway, Sausalito, 94965 **Tel** *(415) 332-0502* **Fax** *(415) 332-2537* **Rooms** *63*

The gorgeous Casa Madrona, just across the bay from San Francisco, has long been an ideal weekend destination for city dwellers looking for some rest and relaxation. It is also perfect for a laid-back, yet romantic, retreat. Between the on-site restaurant and full-service spa, you may never want to leave. **www.casamadrona.com**

NAPA WINE COUNTRY Inn Above Tide   P $$$$
30 El Portal, Sausalito, 94965 **Tel** *(415) 332-9535* **Fax** *(415) 332-6714* **Rooms** *29*

Poised on pillars, directly over the San Francisco Bay, Inn Above Tide has lovely views of the ocean from all of its rooms. In-room facilities include private patios and hot tubs, making it an unparalled romantic destination. Located in the heart of downtown Sausalito, it is convenient for restaurants and shopping. **www.innabovetide.com**

SACRAMENTO Inn at Parkside   P $$$$
2116 6th St, Sacramento, 95818 **Tel** *(916) 658-1818* **Fax** *(916) 658-1809* **Rooms** *7*

A celebrated boutique, Inn at Parkside combines the holistic sensibilities of Asia, with the comfort of a California country home. The grounds feature rambling landscaping, and the full-service Spa Bloom. This unique hotel fills its rooms quickly, so book ahead. **www.Innatparkside.com**

SONOMA Best Western Dry Creek Inn   P $$
198 Dry Creek Rd, Healdsburg, 95448 **Tel** *(707) 433-0300* **Fax** *(707) 433-1129* **Rooms** *103*

One of the best value hotels in the Sonoma Valley, Dry Creek Inn offers basic rooms with a handful of amenities. A complimentary bottle of wine is presented to guests at check-in and some rooms come with free high-speed Internet access. The pool and fitness center make it a great stop for families and large groups. **www.bestwestern.com**

SONOMA The Raford Inn Bed and Breakfast Inn   P $$$
10630 Wohler Rd, Healdsburg, 95448 **Tel** *(707) 887-9573* **Fax** *(707) 887-9597* **Rooms** *6*

This cozy bed-and-breakfast was once situated on a 1,300-acre plot. These days, the Raford House sits snugly on the last four remaining acres of the original property. One of the most breathtaking features is the natural beauty of the location. Each room has a queen-sized bed and bath, and there is a wine reception in the evenings. **www.rafordhouse.com**

YOSEMITE NATIONAL PARK Curry Village   P $
Yosemite National Park **Tel** *(559) 253-5635* **Rooms** *628*

Yosemite's Curry Village offers a multitude of options for the budget traveler and a great choice for families. For the more adventurous, there is a canvas tent with a shared bath, while those preferring a less rustic option can stay in one of the standard motel rooms found on this sprawling property. **www.yosemitepark.com**

YOSEMITE NATIONAL PARK Yosemite Lodge at the Falls   P $$$
Yosemite National Park **Tel** *(209) 372-1274* **Fax** *(209) 372-1444* **Rooms** *245*

Situated at the base of Yosemite Falls, Yosemite Lodge is an excellent take-off point for exploring the park. Rooms are basic, but the hotel provides many conveniences such as wireless Internet access, a swimming pool, and bicycle rentals. The outdoor ampitheater hosts frequent naturalist programs. **www.yosemitepark.com**

YOSEMITE NATIONAL PARK Ahwahnee Hotel   P $$$$
Yosemite National Park **Tel** *(209) 372-1407* **Fax** *(209) 372-1403* **Rooms** *123*

The Ahwahnee is one of the most magnificent places to stay in all of California. Built in 1927, it is a National Historic Landmark, famous for its impeccable setting in the spectacular Yosemite National Park. Five-star dining, gorgeous common areas, and impeccable service make it a must-stop. **www.yosemitepark.com**

RESTAURANTS AND CAFÉS

Anchor beer label

There are more than 5,000 places to eat and drink in San Francisco, and because competition between restaurants is fierce, visitors can find great food at reasonable prices. Easy access to fresh produce, and particularly to seafood, has made the city a hotbed of good, innovative "California Cuisine."

San Francisco's role as an international port of entry *(see pp 40–43)* has brought a variety of ethnic cuisine to the city. The *Choosing a Restaurant* list on pages 228–41 provides a selection of representative restaurants; lighter fare and quick snacks are listed on page 243. San Francisco's cafés are on page 242.

SAN FRANCISCO'S RESTAURANTS

The city's great strength, as far as eating is concerned, is in the wide range of food from around the world that can be found here. The most fashionable restaurants are in the center of the city, with more in the South of Market area. Chestnut Street in the Marina District, and the stretch of Fillmore Street between Bush Street and Jackson Street are also worth investigating. Italian food is available in the North Beach area, while Latin American fare can be found in the Mission District. Chinatown has Cambodian, Vietnamese and Thai, as well as many Chinese, restaurants. On Geary Boulevard and Clement Street, in the Richmond District, are more Chinese restaurants.

Sign for Alioto's Restaurant *(see p231)*

A number of restaurants now follow the American Heart Association's guidelines for reducing cholesterol and dietary fat. A red heart beside a dish denotes an AHA-approved "Healthy Heart" meal, low in calories and cholesterol.

OTHER PLACES TO EAT

San Francisco offers a broad range of venues other than restaurants in which to consume food. Many hotels have excellent dining rooms open to the public. Some of these, like Campton Place or the Ritz-Carlton, are among the city's finest places to eat. Other hotels provide informal buffets at lunchtime and in

the evening. Most also have coffee shops for breakfast or for late-night eating.

Delicatessens, where you can buy a salad or a sandwich, are not very common in San Francisco, but some can be found in the Financial District. There are fast-food outlets all over the city, and many street vendors sell Mexican food. Dishes from these stalls might include fried corn tortillas, with a vegetable filling, or *burritos* (wheat-flour tortillas with meat, vegetables or beans).

MICROBREWERY BARS

In the world of beer, micro-breweries are big news. On-site brewmasters serve a selection of national and international beers as well as brewing their own specials, such as San Francisco's famous Anchor Steam beer. If a beer proves successful locally, it can go on to earn national and sometimes international

Opulent dining room decor at an upmarket restaurant

recognition. A variety of snack foods is also served at these bars to soak up the beer.

HOURS AND PRICES

Prices vary widely, and they depend partly on when you eat. Breakfast is available between 7am and 11am, and is often inexpensive, costing between $8 and $15. Brunch (a large cooked breakfast), usually served between 10am and 2pm on Saturdays and Sundays, costs about $7 to $20. At lunchtime you can buy a light meal for about $6 between 11am and 2:30pm. In the best restaurants lunchtime prices are lower than they are at dinner, but they are still by no means cheap. In the evenings, meals are generally served from 6pm, and many kitchens begin to close around 10pm. Salads and appetizers cost between $5 and $8 each and main dishes are between $10 and $25. In the very best restaurants, however, a meal can cost $75, plus $30 to $50 for a bottle of wine. A few places are open all night.

A waiter working the coffee machine in Tosca *(see p243)*

DINING ON A BUDGET

One way of stretching your budget is to eat a large, late breakfast. Eating outside can be a real treat: at midday, buy some of the fresh fruit so abundant here, and have a picnic lunch. If eating in a restaurant, you can cut expenses by sharing: portions here are often large. Or, take advantage of the free food offered by many city center bars between 4pm and 6pm: delicacies such as fried *won ton* are often included in the price of a drink. *San Francisco's Bars* on page 270 has specific recommendations. Many places offer fixed-price meals at a good price. Chez Panisse in Berkeley, for example, provides a four-course meal on Tuesdays for half the usual rate.

TAX AND TIPPING

A sales tax of 8.5 percent is added to all meal checks in San Francisco, although a service charge is rarely included unless there are six or more in your party. You are expected to leave a tip, however. About 15 percent of the total bill is average, and most locals simply double the tax, then round it up or down. The tip can be left in cash at the table, or added to the total if you are using a credit card.

DRESS CODES

As in most of California, restaurant owners in San Francisco take a fairly relaxed approach toward dress, and

Customers leaving a tip after a meal

most places will allow you in wearing a T-shirt and a pair of jeans. However, in the trendier establishments, which are design-conscious down to the last dinner plate, style is crucial and you are expected to dress the part. Otherwise, it is only in the grander dining rooms of the city center hotels that you are required to dress formally.

RESERVATIONS

It is always best to make a reservation in advance to avoid disappointment. Popular restaurants tend to be booked a week or more ahead for Friday and Saturday nights. Weekdays, however, you should be able to reserve a table if you phone only a day in advance. If you don't have a reservation, and sometimes even if you do, you may have to wait for a table. Pass the time nursing a cocktail or sampling one of the city's interesting beers.

SMOKING

Smoking in public is frowned on in San Francisco, and smoking indoors is prohibited in all cities throughout California, unless there is a separate air circulation system in places where the possibility of anyone breathing in unwanted secondary smoke is slim.

Some restaurants with outdoor eating areas may have a separate section reserved for smokers, and sometimes the bar area will have a separate section where you may be permitted to smoke.

CHILDREN

All restaurants in the city are happy to serve well-behaved children, although at some of the trendier ones you may feel uncomfortable bringing your offspring along.

At the more family-oriented establishments, such as North Beach Italian restaurants, or a Chinatown *dim sum* house on a Sunday morning, children are welcomed. They are also usually allowed in hotel dining rooms. Most places are happy to supply high chairs or booster seats and offer children's portions or alternative menus.

The minimum legal age of 21 for drinking beer and alcohol is strictly enforced throughout the city. Children are not allowed in any bar. However, if food is served on the premises, children can accompany adults to eat.

WHEELCHAIR ACCESS

Since 1992 all restaurants in San Francisco have been required by law to be accessible to those patrons who are wheelchair bound. There should be no steps into the restaurant or to the tables, and bathroom doors should be wide. Most established places comply fully with regulations and new places are designed with them in mind. Occasionally you may need to call ahead to find out about access facilities.

The forecourt of Mel's Drive-In diner *(see p228)*

The Flavors of San Francisco

If variety is the spice of life, then San Francisco's culinary scene is as red-hot as the tear-inducing salsa liberally dished out by the city's top-notch Mexican *taquerias*. You could find your way around San Francisco by scent alone: the sharp tang of espresso mingles with robust wafts of marinara sauce in the North Beach Italian sector, the sizzling *sabor de México* heats up the Mission district, and cacophonous Chinatown exudes the steamy fragrance of dim sum and crispy duck. For a sweet finale, indulge in San Francisco's very own Ghirardelli Chocolate, produced in the Bay Area for over 150 years.

Avocados

Celebrated chef, Yoshi Kojima, prepares a carp for cooking

CALIFORNIA CUISINE

The Bay Area is the birthplace of California cuisine. The sheer variety of fresh produce in Northern California results in a culinary style that's all about the "cult of the ingredient", rather than specific dishes, leaving ample room for creativity. Many of San Francisco's best chefs cultivate a close relationship with regional growers, so what arrives at the table may have been pulled from the earth only hours before, such as freshly-plucked arugula (rocket) leaves, just washed of their dirt clumps, and heirloom tomatoes so juicy you may have to ask for an extra napkin. With such agricultural riches, San Francisco's renowned chefs are inspired to work culinary magic, creating minimalist works of art that beg to be eaten, from baby artichokes ringed by vibrant lemon slices to wafer-thin slices of raw ahi tuna fanned atop a rainbow of grilled vegetables.

ASIAN FOOD

Explore Chinatown's web of bustling, pungent streets and you'll soon discover how the

Swordfish   Salmon   Lobster   Trout   Sole   Tuna

Clams   Scallop

A selection of ocean-fresh San Francisco fish and shellfish

SAN FRANCISCO DISHES AND SPECIALTIES

A true melting pot, San Francisco not only features authentic Mexican, Italian, and Oriental fare, but a creative commingling of them all. Each cuisine inspires the other, resulting in marvelous fusion dishes that have earned the city its gushing accolades as a foodie paradise. Feast on anything from wok-fried spicy greens to sautéed seafood with ginger salsa or baby vegetables with Vietnamese mint. Round out your meal with a warm hunk of the city's

Dim sum deservedly famous sourdough bread, widely considered among the best in the world. The bread's unique taste and texture stems from a yeast of wild micro-organisms, stumbled upon by gold-miners over a century ago, that thrive only in the Bay Area's unique climate.

Clam chowder *Restaurants on Fisherman's Wharf serve this dish of creamy soup in a hollowed-out sourdough roll.*

Colorful interior of a bustling Mexican *taqueria*

restaurants here turn out exquisite Asian fare fit for an emperor. Massive aquariums are home (temporarily, that is) to giant carp swimming in languid circles, and sinewy eels unfurling amid swaying seaweed. Bulging sacks overflow with aromatic spices, and wooden crates bloom with dew-sprinkled bok choy and scallions (spring onions). Peer into an open kitchen for a glimpse of skilled chefs, knives a-blur, transforming whole ducks into paper-thin slivers that will melt in your mouth. The secret to Chinatown's culinary prowess is that the neighborhood's chefs are cooking for the most discerning of diners – their own people. San Francisco's Chinatown boasts the second-largest Oriental population outside of China.

MEXICAN FARE

The urban fuel of San Francisco – and one of the best bargains around – is the city's fast, filling, and delicious Mexican fare. Dig into an

Crab and clams on a harborside seafood stall

epic burrito, filled to bursting with beans, rice and smoky chunks of beef, and you'll be satiated for the day. From saffron-scented rice and jumbo pinto beans to hand-rolled steamed tortillas infused with spinach and sun-dried tomato, the city's ubiquitous *taquerias* offer south-of-the-border pizzazz.

DUNGENESS CRAB

The Dungeness crab is famed for its delicate meat. When its season arrives, from mid-November to June, locals celebrate by eating it in as many ways as possible, or simply cracked with butter and crusty sourdough bread.

ON THE MENU

Cioppino A tomato-based stew made with chunks of fish and shellfish.

Dim sum A Chinese lunchtime specialty, these little dumplings, steamed or fried, are stuffed with fish, meat or vegetables.

Hangtown fry A hearty omelette filled with breaded oysters and bacon.

Petrale sole This delicate local fish is usually served lightly sautéed.

Tortilla A Mexican staple, this round, flat unleavened corn- or wheat-flour bread forms the basis of many other dishes, such as burritos, quesadillas, and tacos.

Spicy marinated steak *North Beach Italian restaurants often serve steak with garlic, anchovy and lemon butter.*

Seared ahi tuna with Asian salsa *The fusion salsa is made with shiitake mushrooms and Szechuan peppercorns.*

Ghirardelli tiramisu *A North Beach favorite of mascarpone cheese, Ghirardelli chocolate, cream, and coffee liqueur.*

What to Drink in San Francisco

California is now one of the world's largest and most exciting wine-producing areas, and the best vintages come from the wine country north of San Francisco, especially the Napa and Sonoma Valleys. Most California wines are made from the classic European grape varieties but, unlike European wines, are identified by grape rather than by wine-growing district. Locally brewed beers and mineral waters are also popular, and the usual range of beverages are available.

Northern Sonoma vineyards, the ideal local climate for growing the fussy Pinot Noir grape

RED WINE

Pinot Noir   Cabernet Sauvignon

Vines thrive in the mild climate of Northern California where cooling fogs help the grapes reach perfection. The main red wine varieties grown in the region are Cabernet Sauvignon, Pinot Noir, Merlot and Zinfandel. Cabernet Sauvignon is still the prime grape type, with excellent vintages produced in all major growing regions. Pinot Noir, used in the legendary French Burgundy wines, has become increasingly popular as wineries have mastered its temperamental nature, and the moist Anderson Valley in Sonoma and the Carneros in Napa Valley have emerged as prime growing regions. Merlot, used in many Bordeaux clarets, and Zinfandel, a bold and full-bodied grape popular in California, are grown all over the state.

Red Zinfandel wines can be light and fruity, but at their best are rich, dark and hearty.

Cabernet Sauvignon wines taste of black-currants with an acidic edge softened by oak.

Merlot, often used to provide more fruit in a blend, produces rich, soft wines on its own.

Pinot Noir, at its best, has a floral elegance and a delicate strawberry flavor.

WINE TYPE	GOOD VINTAGES	GOOD PRODUCERS
Red Wine		
Cabernet Sauvignon	04, 03, 02, 97, 96, 94, 93, 91, 90	Caymus Vineyards, Chateau Montelana, Jordan, Kistler Vineyards, Ridge, Robert Mondavi, Stags Leap, Swanson
Pinot Noir	03, 02, 01, 99, 97, 96, 95, 93, 92, 91	Au Bon Climat, Byron, Calera, Cuvaison, De Loach, Etude, Sanford, Saintsbury
Merlot	04, 02, 01, 99, 96, 95, 91, 90	Chateau St Jean, Duckhorn Vineyards, Newton, Pine Ridge, Robert Sinskey, Whitehall Lane Reserve
Zinfandel	03, 01, 96, 95, 91, 90	Clos du Val, Farrell, Fetzer, Frog's Leap, Kunde, Rabbit Ridge, Ravenswood, Ridge, Turley
White Wine		
Chardonnay	04, 03, 02, 01, 97, 96, 95, 94, 91, 90	Au Bon Climat, Beringer, Forman, De Loach, Far Niente, Kent Rasmussen, Kitzler, Peter Michael, Robert Sinskey, Sterling Vineyards
Semillon	06, 05, 03, 02, 96, 95, 94, 91, 90	Alban, Calera, Cline Cellars, Joseph Phelps, Niebaum-Coppola, Wild Horse
Sauvignon Blanc	06, 05, 03, 02, 99, 97, 96, 95, 94, 91, 90,	Cakebread, De Loach, Frogs Leap, Joseph Phelps, Robert Mondavi Winery, Spottswoode

WHITE WINE

Chardonnay   Organic
             Chardonnay

As with red, California's white wines are classified by grape variety, with Chardonnay by far the most popular of recent years. Grown throughout the West Coast region, this prestige grape produces wines varying in character from dry, light, lemon and vanilla-scented to the more headstrong and oaky. You can also find over 13 other white wine varieties and blends to try, as well as organically grown wines.

Sauvignon Blanc wines range from clean and zingy to soft and buttery.

Chardonnay is often fermented or aged in French oak barrels, lending it smooth vanilla tones.

White Zinfandel wines, often blushed pink, are light, sweetish and easy to drink.

Chenin Blanc, also used in blends, makes typically dry, quiet wines on its own.

THE 1976 BLIND TASTING

On May 24, 1976, at a blind tasting organized by the English wine consultant Steven Spurrier, French judges awarded California red (Stag's Leap Cabernet Sauvignon 1973, Napa Valley) and white (Chateau Montelana 1973 Chardonnay, Napa Valley) wines the top prizes in their respective categories. Six of the top ten in each category were also California wines, a result that sent shock waves through the wine world. Within a decade, a number of illustrious French producers such as Baron de Rothschild had invested in California wineries of their own.

SPARKLING WINE

If proof were needed that California is a prime spot for making sparkling wine, then look no farther than the fact that the finest French wine producers have huge investments in California. Moet & Chandon and Mumm, among others, have set up wineries in the Napa Valley and elsewhere. These companies, along with local producers Schramsberg and Korbel, have helped the West Coast establish an international reputation for excellent "Champagne" at the right price.

Sparkling wine

BEER

The resurgence in small breweries across the US can fairly be credited to the success of San Francisco's Anchor brewery, whose Steam Beer, Liberty Ale and other products show that American beer need not be bland and tasteless. Other tasty local brews include Mendocino County's rich Boont Amber and Red Tail Ale.

OTHER DRINKS

Coffee drinks of all kinds are available from kiosks, cafés and restaurants across the city; you can also find a great variety of herbal teas.

Espresso   Cappuccino   Latte

Red Tail   Liberty   Anchor
Ale   Ale   Steam Beer

WATER

Health-conscious San Franciscans avail themselves of locally produced mineral water, the best of which comes from Calistoga in Napa Valley. Many mineral waters come flavored with fresh fruit, and most are carbonated. The tap water is fresh and clean.

Calistoga bottled water

Choosing a Restaurant

These restaurants have been selected across a range of price categories for their exceptional food, good value, and interesting location. They are listed by area and within these by price, both for central San Francisco and the surrounding areas. Map references refer to the Street Finder, pages 302–312.

PRICE CATEGORIES
For a three-course meal for one, a glass of house wine, and all unavoidable extra charges including tax.

$ under $25
$$ $25–$35
$$$ $35–$50
$$$$ $50–$70
$$$$$ over $70

PRESIDIO

Good Luck Dim Sum $
736 Clement St, 94118 **Tel** (415) 386-3388   **Map** 3 5A

A local favorite, this joint is known to serve the freshest dim sum at rock-bottom prices. Those joining the long lines usually come for take-out. The Formica tables in the back provide a steady surface to eat from if not much else. Good Luck always sells out by early afternoon, so get there in the morning for the best selection.

King of Thai $
639 Clement St, 94118 **Tel** (415) 752-5198   **Map** 3 A5

The late-night hours and extremely inexpensive steaming noodle dishes make King of Thai a great hit. Many branches of this citywide chain are open late, and none take credit cards or checks. Spiciness can be adjusted according to each diner's preference. Vegetarian entrées are available.

The Warming Hut $
Marine Drive and Long Avenue, 94129 **Tel** (415) 561-3040   **Map** 2 F2

A great place to warm up on those cold San Francisco days with a cup of coffee and a sandwich. The real pull of this cozy shack is the view – a beautiful "only-in-San Francisco" vista surrounds you here. The perfect stop after a long walk across the Golden Gate Bridge.

Presidio Social Club $$$
563 Ruger Street, 94129 **Tel** (415) 885-1888   **Map** 3 C3

The retro vibe at this hip Presidio restaurant brings large crowds for dinner and lunch. Housed in an interesting refurbished Presidio building, the cool interior evokes a casual, rustic atmosphere. Brunch is less crowded and gets rave reviews. Not a huge menu, but lots of favorites, like macaroni cheese and hamburgers, that will certainly please.

Sociale $$$
3665 Sacramento Street, 94118 **Tel** (415) 921-3500   **Map** 3 B4

This is a hidden gem and local favorite. Sit outside on the heated patio for a truly romantic experience. The menu changes seasonally, yet always features local produce, organic meats and fish and homemade pastas. Known for its eclectic yet impressive wine list. Keep in mind that it is closed Sundays.

PACIFIC HEIGHTS AND THE MARINA

La Mediterranee $
2210 Fillmore St, 94115 **Tel** (415) 921-2956   **Map** 4 D4

Taking up only a narrow space, La Méditerranée serves delicious Mediterranean specialties, such as hummus and falafel, with the reasonably-priced house wine. This old neighborhood haunt still displays a flying dove and the name of the former tenants on the stained glass over the door. There is also a branch in Berkeley.

Liverpool Lil's $
2942 Lyon St, 94123 **Tel** (415) 921-6664   **Map** 3 C3

Liverpool Lil's fame as a preferred spot for lunch and dinner rests on its strong bar drinks, friendly service, and reliable pub menu featuring big salads, pepper steaks, and an outstanding hamburger. In warm weather, the outside tables look over the west boundary of the Presidio. It opens late and serves till after midnight.

Mel's Drive-In $
2165 Lombard St, 94123 **Tel** (415) 921-2867   **Map** 3 C3

This 1950s-style diner is not the real thing, but it comes close enough with period decor, tabletop jukeboxes, and brightly garbed waitresses. Perfect for hamburger-and-fries baskets with thick milkshakes, a latenight snack, or an early-morning breakfast of their country eggs and grilled potatoes.

Key to Symbols see back cover flap

Zao Noodle Bar

2406 California St, 94115 **Tel** *(415) 345-8088*

Map *4 D4*

Reliable, quick, cheap, and healthy noodle dishes, served up in large bowls, are the perfect alternative to greasy fast food. Though the preparation style is more home-cooking than *haute cuisine*, it's still one of the best deals in town. There are several branches in the city and beyond.

Balboa Café

319 Fillmore St, 94123 **Tel** *(415) 921-3944*

Map *4 D2*

Reliable lunches and brunches are the mainstay of Balboa Café, the elder statesman of the area known as "the Triangle" for its trendy bars. A must-try are the hamburgers here. After dinner, this restaurant becomes a meet-and-greet hotspot for 30-somethings.

Brazen Head

3166 Buchanan St, 94123 **Tel** *(415) 921-7600*

Map *4 D2*

This cash-only, dark, pub-like hideaway is the favored destination for those craving a traditional grilled steak, scotch on the rocks, and a quiet conversation late at night after the other local restaurants have closed. Visitors know the location by the address – there is no sign.

Fresca

2114 Fillmore, 94115 **Tel** *(415) 447-2668*

Map *4 D4*

This Peruvian restaurant has a country-feel interior with an open kitchen. There are plenty of great home-style meat and seafood dishes. Specialties include their ceviche dishes, based on halibut with ginger and *amarillo aji* (yellow Peruvian chili), and *parihuela*, a Peruvian bouillabaisse. The casual ambience adds to its appeal.

Pane e Vino

1715 Union St, 94123 **Tel** *(415) 346-2111*

Map *4 E2*

Pane e Vino is a good place to stop for lunch or dinner in the Union Street shopping area. During fine weather, diners may sit outside in a delightfully decorated patio to enjoy pastas and grilled Italian specialties along with the restaurant's delicious fresh-baked bread.

Rose's Café

2298 Union St, 94123 **Tel** *(415) 775-2200*

Map *4 D3*

At the Italian-inspired Rose's Café, the tables set outside look over the quiet end of Union Street, while the interior features a cheery yellow space with big windows. The restaurant's main draws are the weekday lunches (with good salads and pastas), as well as weekend brunches. Specialties include French toast, breakfast pizzas, and a good international wine list.

A16

2355 Chestnut Street, 94101 **Tel** *(415) 771-2216*

Map *3 C2*

Famous for its wood-burning oven that turns out delectable pizzas, this is the place to see and be seen in the Marina. The meatballs, house-cured salami and pastas are truly authentic and out of this world. Call ahead to get a reservation as the restaurant is very popular.

Betelnut

2030 Union St, 94123 **Tel** *(415) 929-8855*

Map *4 E2*

Serving contemporary Asian cuisine, Betelnut has been described as everything from "woodsey country Asian" to "sexy back alley." Great variety from salads, dumplings, noodles and larger plates of seafood, pork, beef and chicken can be found on the menu.

Clementine

126 Clement St, 94118 **Tel** *(415) 387-0408*

Map *3 5A*

It's best to arrive early at Clementine, a softly-lit corner of Paris in the inner Richmond area. The bargain prix-fixe menu fills up the small space quickly, especially on the weekends. French bistro classics, such as *cassoulet,* and lamb shank with white beans are some of the consistent favorites.

Elite Café

2049 Fillmore St, 94115 **Tel** *(415) 346-8668*

Map *4 D4*

In the middle of the Fillmore shopping area, Elite Café is an institution, with intimate booths and a hopping bar that serves fresh oysters along with stiff drinks. The New Orleans-style gumbos and jambalayas also feature on the weekend brunch menu.

Greens

Building A, Fort Mason Center, 94123 **Tel** *(415) 771-6222*

Map *4 E1*

Greens is considered by many as the city's most famous vegetarian restaurant. Its elegant, pale walls and views of the Golden Gate Bridge are the perfect setting for the imaginative meat-free delicacies that even a carnivore would love. The bread basket is always heaped with exceptional offerings from the in-house bakery.

Izzy's Steak and Chop House

3345 Steiner St, 94123 **Tel** *(415) 563-0487*

Map *4 D2*

Izzy's is all about meat – pork, steak, and chicken prepared in traditional ways, with side dishes such as scalloped potatoes and creamed spinach. There are a few fish specialties, particularly salmon, and the salads are exceptional. The interior is reminiscent of the dark wood-paneled men's clubs of the past.

PlumpJack Cafe

♣♣♣

3127 Fillmore St, 94123 **Tel** *(415) 563-4755*   **Map** *4 D2*

PlumpJack Café, a tiny, ultra-hip eatery, has remained a top destination since it opened in 1993. The Mediterranean menu is enhanced with fresh local produce and meats, and the wine list is well-chosen and reasonably priced. Reservations are a must.

FISHERMAN'S WHARF AND NORTH BEACH

Caffe Greco

♣

423 Columbus Ave, 94133 **Tel** *(415) 397-6261*   **Map** *5 B3*

When it's time for a rest, stop by this North Beach landmark for an espresso and some homemade tiramisù, or a cool gelato. The sidewalk seating and relaxed attitude about table turnover make this a great people-watching spot.

Capp's Corner

♣

1600 Powell St, 94133 **Tel** *(415) 989-2589*   **Map** *5 B3*

A lower-cost option popular with families, Capp's Corner serves up an Americanized version of Italian cooking. Don't expect fine cuisine, but generous portions of all the traditional favorites. Opened in 1960, the restaurant features a photographic gallery of famous former diners.

Brandy Hos

♣♣

217 Columbus Ave, 94133 **Tel** *(415) 788-7527*   **Map** *5 C3*

This hole-in-the-wall restaurant earned a fiery reputation for delicious, authentic Hunan dishes. Be forewarned – "medium spicy" means hot, while "hot" is alarming. Savvy diners know to quell the fire with rice, not water. Order a "mild" plate and enjoy.

Buena Vista Café

♣♣

2765 Hyde Street, 94109 **Tel** *(415) 474-5044*   **Map** *5 A1*

This is establishment is over 100 years old and is famous for its Irish coffee. The location in Fisherman's Wharf is great, with the cable cars going right by the window and the Golden Gate Bridge in full view. The food is good, hearty and satisfying but the café can get crowded and rowdy, so be warned.

Caffe Macaroni

♣♣

59 Columbus, 94111 **Tel** *(415) 956-9737*   **Map** *5 C3*

This densely packed, two-story eatery serves reliably good pastas (the creamy Alfredo is a favorite) and meat dishes to tourists and locals alike. The bustling café is known for its friendly, enthusiastic waiters and generous portions that satisfy the biggest appetite.

Caffe Sport

♣♣

574 Green St, 94133 **Tel** *(415) 981-1251*   **Map** *5 C3*

Big, family-style platters of garlic-infused vegetables, spaghetti Bolognese, *cioppino* seafood stew, and other Italian favorites, such as the superb *ziti* pasta in marinara sauce, are served by waiters known for their bossy attitude in this loud, busy eatery. They are happy to tell diners what to order – just ask.

Fog City Diner

♣♣

1300 Battery St, 94111 **Tel** *(415) 982-2000*   **Map** *5 C2*

Glorified comfort foods, such as garlic, leek, and basil loaf, cheddar biscuits, and mu shu pork burritos are on the menu, alongside burgers and fries at this chrome-trimmed diner lookalike. Weekend brunch features new twists on old favorites such as smoked chicken hash and eggs.

Il Fornaio

♣♣

1265 Battery St, 94111 **Tel** *(415) 986-0100*   **Map** *5 C2*

A chain that built its reputation on outstanding baked goods, Il Fornaio continues to attract diners with fresh breads, delicious pastas, and grilled meats and fish. The superb butternut squash ravioli in butter sauce is served as both an appetizer and entrée.

The House

♣♣

1230 Grant Avenue, 94133 **Tel** *(415) 986-8612*   **Map** *5 C3*

People rave about the melt-in-your-mouth sea bass at this understated restaurant in the heart of North Beach. If you're game for something other than Italian food, this is the place for intense Asian flavors and unique dishes. It's small, so reservations are strongly recommended.

The Stinking Rose

♣♣

325 Columbus Ave, 94133 **Tel** *(415) 781-7673*   **Map** *5 C3*

True to its name, The Stinking Rose uses garlic in every dish – including dessert. This Northern Italian-style pasta and pizza restaurant is often crowded with those curious about the unusual name, though service and quality can be uneven at times.

Key to Price Guide *see p228* **Key to Symbols** *see back cover flap*

Tre Fratelli $$
2801 Leavenworth St, 94133 **Tel** *(415) 474-8240*   **Map** *5 A2*

Since the move from its former Hyde Street location, this longstanding restaurant, opened in 1980, has added fresh fish to its excellent pastas and meat dishes. The alfredo (white-sauce pasta) is particularly creamy and delicious, and the service is friendly and efficient.

Zarzuela $$
2000 Hyde St, 94109 **Tel** *(415) 346-0800*   **Map** *5 A3*

A variety of tasty tapas, from succulent grilled prawns to hearty *albondigas* (meatballs), and strong sangria make Zarzuela a favorite for an authentic light meal or more. The best Spanish food in the city according to those who swear by the paella. Attentive staff and charming dining room. There may be a wait for a table in the evenings.

1550 Hyde Café $$$
1550 Hyde St, 94109 **Tel** *(415) 775-1550*   **Map** *5 A3*

The unadorned industrial look of this neighborhood café belies the rich, organic, sustainably-farmed ingredients used in the Mediterrean-inspired dishes. The wine bar features an exceptional list. This cafe is right on the Hyde Street cable car line.

Alioto's $$$
8 Fisherman's Wharf, 94133 **Tel** *(415) 673-0183*   **Map** *5 A1*

Lit by spectacular sunsets filtered through the Golden Gate, Alioto's has been serving well-prepared Sicilian-style seafood since 1925. The food is good, especially the bountiful shrimp or crab Louies (juicy seafood on a bed of crisp romaine lettuce).

Ana Mandara $$$
891 Beach Street, 94109 **Tel** *(415) 771-6800*   **Map** *4 F1*

Tasty and flavorful Asian fusion food is not easy to find in Fisherman's Wharf, but this establishment has it. The elegantly decorated space makes for a nice retreat from walking the Wharf. The restaurant comes alive at night with a hip bar scene and live music.

Moose's $$$
1652 Stockton St, 94133 **Tel** *(415) 989-7800*   **Map** *5 B2*

Perennially popular, Moose's is crowded with fashionable people around the bar, listening to live jazz in the evenings, and enjoying hearty plates of tasty grilled salmon, meatloaf, and other favorites. Regulars call it "style without attitude."

Scoma's $$$
Pier 47, 1 Al Scoma Way, 94133 **Tel** *(415) 771-4383*   **Map** *5 A1*

To have a street named after you means you've been here awhile, and Scoma's started out in 1965 as a coffee shop for local fishermen. A standard-bearer for well-cooked, big portions of fresh fish, this restaurant also features pretty views of the bay.

Sotto Mare $$$
552 Green Street, 94133 **Tel** *(415) 398-3181*   **Map** *5 B3*

Fresh fish, fabulous clam chowder and seafood pasta make this a favorite among tourists and locals. If you are looking for a quiet atmosphere, this isn't the place – the staff is lively and fun, and the dining room can get loud – but with a location right in North Beach, you can take a stroll from here after dinner to one of the many local cafés.

Gary Danko $$$$$
800 North Point St, 94109 **Tel** *(415) 749-2060*   **Map** *5 1A*

In spite of the exorbitant prices, Gary Danko has remained one of the favored restaurants in the city for its New American prix-fixes. Three-, four-, or five-course dinners provide hours of carefully choreographed courses, efficient service, and elegant surroundings. The selection of cheeses is a must-sample.

CHINATOWN AND NOB HILL

Golden Star Vietnamese Restaurant $
11 Walter U. Lum Place, 94108 **Tel** *(415) 398-1215*   **Map** *5 C3*

Situated across from the Transamerica Pyramid, the Golden Star is narrow and crowded, and the decor is as plain as a school cafeteria. Nonetheless, this little gem serves up big rice dishes and meat portions for very little money. The lunch specials are exceptional value.

Henry's Hunan $
674 Sacramento St, 94111 **Tel** *(415) 788-2234*   **Map** *5 C4*

Liberally using chunks of dried red chilies in its piquant food, this local chain lives up to its name. Though the decor is basic, making a functional use of Formica, the dishes are authentic and tasty, irrespective of the spiciness – the staff will tone it down on request. It is closed at weekends.

House of Nanking

🚹 ♿ Ⓢ

919 Kearny, 94133 **Tel** *(415) 421-1429*

Map *5 C3*

The good, traditional menu at the tiny House of Nanking attracts a loyal clientele. Even though the waiters here are a little unfriendly, food comes in generous portions and the prices are reasonably low. The menu offers favorites like sesame chicken and a good selection of vegetarian options. There is usually a wait, but it is well worth it.

Yuet Lee

🚹 ♿ Ⓢ

1300 Stockton St, 94133 **Tel** *(415) 982-6020*

Map *5 B3*

Yuet Lee's excellent fresh seafood menu and low prices are the reasons for locals flocking here. It has a live fish tank and the chef will cook a whole fish or crab to order. Specialties include steamed fish and seafood; shrimp and pork dumplings; salt-and-pepper squid; and an array of vegetables such as long bean, bokchoy, and asparagus. It opens until 3am.

Great Eastern

🚹 ♿ ⓈⓈ

649 Jackson St, 94133 **Tel** *(415) 986-2500*

Map *5 C3*

A longtime favorite in Chinatown, Great Eastern has a menu featuring reliable, if not inspired, Mandarin dishes. The real draw here is the fresh seafood swimming in the tanks – make sure to ask the waiter for the day's specials to sample the best that the restaurant has to offer.

Nob Hill Café

🚹 ♿ 🍴 ⓈⓈ

1152 Taylor St, 94108 **Tel** *(415) 776-6500*

Map *5 B4*

Nob Hill Café is a local favorite, frequently crowded to the rafters, as diners enjoy home-style Italian dishes. Visitors often spot "The Twins" – the delightful Brown sisters – here. The similarly dressed duo is as much a San Francisco institution as Nob Hill itself.

R&G Lounge

🚹 ♿ ⓈⓈ

631 Kearny St, 94108 **Tel** *(415) 982-7877*

Map *5 C4*

R&G Lounge features authentic Cantonese and seafood specialties. The decor is rather modest, but the food is always good and the prices are reasonable. Always ask for the specials of the day to sample the most unusual dishes they have on offer.

Street

🚹 ♿ ⓈⓈ

2141 Polk St, 94109 **Tel** *(415) 775-1055*

Map *5 A3*

Comfort food at its finest makes this neighborhood restaurant a favorite. Street is noisy and crowded, but the platters are ample. Try one of the best seafood entrées – big, juicy Gulf prawns served in a saffron-laced lobster broth over buttery homemade pasta. Round it up with the not-too-sweet pecan bread pudding.

Jai Yun

🚹 ♿ ⓈⓈⓈ

680 Clay St, 94111 **Tel** *(415) 981-7438*

Map *5 B3*

Set in a small space and simply decorated, Jai Yun is full of surprises. The daily prix-fixe includes a series of constantly-changing, small dishes containing fresh ingredients purchased the same morning from the markets. The excellent seafood menu features abalone, squid, and shrimp dishes.

Swan Oyster Depot

ⓈⓈⓈ

1517 Polk Street, 94109 **Tel** *(415) 673-1101*

Map *5 A4*

Lines can be long at this popular lunch destination as no reservations are accepted. The clam chowder is considered the best in the city by many, but all the seafood here is fresh. A small establishment but worth it for exquisite and plentiful seafood choices. Don't miss sampling the oysters. Cash only payments.

Venticello

♿ ⓈⓈⓈ

1257 Taylor St, 94108 **Tel** *(415) 922-2545*

Map *5 B3*

At Venticello, a *trattoria* serving fine Northern Italian cuisine, romance is not about holding hands by the fireplace – it's on the menu. The laidback ambience encourages one to linger with a decaffeinated espresso and port after enjoying a perfectly seasoned plate of scampi.

Acquerello

🚹 ♿ 🍷 ⓈⓈⓈⓈ

1722 Sacramento St, 94109 **Tel** *(415) 567-5432*

Map *5 A4*

An exquisite wine list, a knowledgable waitstaff happy to recommend food-and-wine pairings, carved glass decanters, and fine linen set the stage for a truly memorable experience in this former chapel. A rich, Venetian-themed menu makes for sumptuous dining.

Big Four

🚹 ♿ 🍷 ⓈⓈⓈⓈ

1075 California St, 94108 **Tel** *(415) 771-1140*

Map *5 B4*

Named after the enormously wealthy railroad barons, Big Four is the chosen place for the Nob Hill elite to hobnob. The dark polished-wood paneling and formal service are an appropriate setting for business people and financiers in particular. The top-quality menu includes rack of lamb, juicy chicken with artichokes, and a whiskey-marinated buffalo steak.

Fleur de Lys

🚹 ♿ 🍷 ⓈⓈⓈⓈⓈ

777 Sutter St, 94109 **Tel** *(415) 673-7779*

Map *5 B4*

The prix-fixes on the French *nouvelle cuisine* menu here are the ultimate in gourmet dining, and the waitstaff flawlessly guides diners from one dish to the next in a lovely tented room. Fleur de Lys also serves a spectacular vegetarian prix-fixe dinner.

Key to Price Guide *see p228* **Key to Symbols** *see back cover flap*

Masa's

🏃 ♿ 🍴 $$$$$

648 Bush St, 94108 **Tel** *(415) 989-7154*

Map *5 B4*

In Masa's stylish, urbane setting, diners are treated royally as they sample exquisite *nouvelle cuisine*. A celebrated local chef for several years, Masa continues to beguile diners by changing much of the menu every day, based on fresh market buys.

Ritz-Carlton Dining Room

🏃 ♿ 🍴 $$$$$

600 Stockton St, 94108 **Tel** *(415) 773-6198*

Map *5 C4*

Ranked number one in many city and travel magazine surveys, the elegant Dining Room is a perfect example of premium service in the grand European tradition. The highly praised menu exhibits an Asian influence, introducing ingredients found in local markets.

FINANCIAL DISTRICT AND UNION SQUARE

Café Bastille

🏃 ♿ 🔲 $$

22 Belden Place, 94104 **Tel** *(415) 986-5673*

Map *5 C4*

Tucked away in a traffic-free alley, this mini-Paris is often crowded with diners enjoying the fine weather at outside tables during the day or jazz in the evenings. Basic bistro soups, salads, beer and wine are served along with French specialties such as *moules marinière* with harissa (red chili) sauce and tripe sausage with caramelized onions.

Delancey Street Restaurant

🏃 ♿ 🔲 $$

600 Embarcadero, 94107 **Tel** *(415) 512-5179*

Map *6 E5*

A wonderful place for dining, Delancey Street Restaurant serves delicious comfort food, including the excellent meatloaf and ribs, and bourbon-glazed steaks as well as other American dishes. The service is beyond good. The restaurant supports a respected substance-abuse recovery program.

Gaylord India

🏃 ♿ $$

1 Embarcadero Center, 94111 **Tel** *(415) 397-7775*

Map *6 D3*

Gaylord turns out Indian standards – lamb curry, biriyanis, and vegetarian dishes – in pleasant surroundings. One of two branches in the city, this is the better of the two, and often crowded at lunchtime with local business people. The other branch is located at 900 Northpoint.

Yank Sing

🏃 ♿ $$

101 Spear St, 94105 **Tel** *(415) 957-9300*

Map *6 E4*

Much loved for its exquisite dim sum, Yank Sing allows diners to choose from over 100 different items, displayed on the constantly circulating carts. The upscale surroundings make this a cut above most dim sum parlors Reservations are available.

Canteen

🏃 ♿ $$$

817 Sutter Street, 94109 **Tel** *(415) 928-8870*

Map *5 B4*

Go for brunch and you won't be disappointed at this cozy, neighborhood-feel restaurant not far from Union Square. The eggs Benedict is heavenly, as is the French toast, but the star of the brunch is "The Big Pancake." Dinner wins equally rave reviews for its simplicity, real-sized portions and quiet atmosphere. Dinner menu changes weekly.

Chez Papa Resto

♿ 🔲 $$$

4 Mint Plaza, 94103 **Tel** *(415) 546-4134*

Map *11 A1*

This is a great place to come for a special celebration. The look and feel of the restaurant is uber chic but the staff is friendly and helpful. Dinner can be expensive, but its worth it for the mouth-watering kobe beef, fresh sea bass or scallop dishes. The fixed-price menu offers good value for money.

Globe

🏃 ♿ $$$

200 Pacific Avenue, 94111 **Tel** *(415) 391-4132*

Map *5 C3*

This sleek, modern bistro is located near the Transamerica Pyramid and offers tasty late-night cuisine and a buzzing bar scene. The steel bar next to the entrance is festooned with fresh flowers and the partly exposed kitchen lets the clientele peek at their food being prepared.

Kokkari Estiatorio

🏃 ♿ $$$

200 Jackson St, 94111 **Tel** *(415) 981-0983*

Map *6 D3*

The Kokkari serves stylish Greek food in a large, comfortable dining area with dark wood floors and a big, cozy fireplace. The signature moussaka and perfectly grilled lamb are top picks. The restaurant features an extensive list of Greek wines. The staff can guide your choices.

Kuleto's

🏃 ♿ $$$

221 Powell St, 94102 **Tel** *(415) 397-7720*

Map *5 B3*

The exceptionally pretty Kuleto's is primarily frequented by those looking for a people-watching spot. It has an interior salvaged from an elegant old San Francisco hotel. Standard, if not spectacular, Northern Italian dishes make up the menu, including a tasty prosciutto-wrapped pork tenderloin. Enjoy appetizers at the bar for the best view.

La Scene Café & Bar $$$
490 Geary St, 94102 **Tel** *(415) 292-6430*   **Map** *5 B5*

Simple French bistro-style food, such as cassoulet and lamb shank, makes this unpretentious restaurant a favorite with theatergoers. The prix-fixe menu is a bargain. The service is prompt, and the waitstaff are guaranteed to get you out of the door on time.

One Market $$$
1 Market St, 94105 **Tel** *(415) 777-5577*   **Map** *6 D3*

A dark-suited business crowd takes over this airy and sophisticated restaurant for lunch, and a well-dressed evening crowd moves in for dinner. Expect reliably fresh fish, meats with innovative side dishes, and crisp salads. "Chef's table" is reserved seating for four to seven diners who are treated to a special tasting menu ($85–$95 per person).

Palio d'Asti $$$
640 Sacramento St, 94111 **Tel** *(415) 395-9800*   **Map** *5 C4*

Palio d'Asti is another favorite of the midday lunch crowd looking for authentic Northern Italian pastas and veal and an excellent tiramisu. The happy hours bring them all back with a free wood-fired pizza for a two-drink minimum. Murals of the medieval Palio horse race decorate the walls.

Sam's Grill and Seafood Restaurant $$$
374 Bush St, 94104 **Tel** *(415) 421-0594*   **Map** *5 C4*

Founded in 1866, Sam's Grill is the oldest seafood restaurant in the city. It has been serving outstanding sand dabs and other fresh fish to generations of visitors. At midday, one can can hear the murmur of business people closing deals in the high-backed booths. It is closed at weekends.

Tadich Grill $$$
240 California St, 94111 **Tel** *(415) 391-1849*   **Map** *6 D4*

Founded during the Gold Rush, Tadich Grill is the oldest continuously operating restaurant in the state. It serves excellent *cioppino* and the fresh grilled fish is a tradition among seafood lovers. The wait for a table can be long in the evenings, but lunch is always a good bet.

Bix $$$$
56 Gold St, 94133 **Tel** *(415) 433-6300*   **Map** *5 C3*

The slick Art-Deco interior in this swanky supper club, named after jazz great Bix Beiderbecke, is a sophisticated setting for French-American dishes served impeccably to a tinkling jazz piano. Great martinis and a see-and-be-seen afterwork crowd.

Boulevard $$$$
1 Mission St, 94105 **Tel** *(415) 543-6084*   **Map** *6 E4*

The artistic creations of chef Nancy Oakes have earned fame for Boulevard, a Bay Area icon. The menu is a cross between American comfort food and French favorites. Try to be seated in the back section to take advantage of the wonderful Bay Bridge views.

Campton Place $$$$
340 Stockton St, 94108 **Tel** *(415) 955-5555*   **Map** *5 C4*

A serene room classically styled in the subtle colors of an Italian villa, Campton Place exudes elegance. Some of the best Provençal-Mediterranean fusion food in the area, accompanied by a top-notch wine list. This and the smooth service makes for a special night out.

Silks $$$$
222 Sansome St, 94104 **Tel** *(415) 986-2020*   **Map** *5 C4*

Dazzling with silken wall-hangings, floor coverings, and hand-painted silk chandeliers, Silks is a good spot for an intimate conversation and celebrity spotting. The efficient service underscores imaginative New Asian cuisine such as chicken and enoki mushroom spring rolls and spicy grilled shrimp.

Tommy Toy's $$$$
655 Montgomery St, 94111 **Tel** *(415) 397-4888*   **Map** *5 C3*

The tasting menu at Tommy Toy's is a great way to enjoy the elegant four-star Chinese cuisine here. There are also sophisticated dishes made with the freshest ingredients, like seafood bisque with fresh coconut. The *nouvelle cuisine*-inspired food is served in a dining room softened with tapestries, etched-glass, antique mirrors, and lamplight.

Aqua $$$$$
252 California St, 94111 **Tel** *(415) 956-9662*   **Map** *6 D4*

Chic and airy, decorated with gorgeous floral displays, Aqua is said by many to be the best seafood restaurant in the city. Its preparation of seafood with a French touch, such as fresh salmon with *foie gras*, has forged its reputation. The smoked swordfish is also exceptional.

Michael Minna $$$$$
335 Powell St, 94102 **Tel** *(415) 397-9222*   **Map** *5 B4*

Replacing the venerable Oak Room at St. Francis Hotel, this restaurant serves a new American prix-fixe menu built around a single ingredient prepared in three different styles. The eponymous chef, who was formerly at Aqua, also offers American classics along with 2,000 wines. The surroundings are ultra-luxurious.

Key to Price Guide *see p228* **Key to Symbols** *see back cover flap*

CIVIC CENTER

Mifune 🚶 ♿ ⑤

1737 Post St, 94115 **Tel** *(415) 922-0337* **Map** *4 E4*

Big steaming bowls of Japanese-style noodle soups delivered to your table within minutes of ordering make this Japantown hub a favorite for fans of fresh food and those with limited time. Mifune also serves bento boxes and other non-soup items.

Caffè Delle Stelle 🚶 ♿ ⑤⑤

395 Hayes St, 94102 **Tel** *(415) 252-1110* **Map** *4 F5*

Set in a modern, industrial space and serving hearty Tuscan specialties, this Hayes Valley institution has attracted a huge local following. Recalling a neighborhood grocery store in Italy, with its lively ambiance and rock-bottom pricing, it is easy to see why diners flock to this popular eatery.

Absinthe Brasserie and Bar ♿ 🛏 ⑤⑤⑤

398 Hayes Street, 94102 **Tel** *(415) 551-1590* **Map** *3 B5*

Recreating the 1940s era, this dark romantic setting is among the best European-style brasseries in town. Vintage cabaret music and cocktails are on the menu, along with an array of oysters, the best French onion soup, and hearty bistro food such as cassoulet, slow-cooked pork, and cinnamon-braised lamb. The wine list is excellent.

Citizen Cake ♿ ⑤⑤⑤

399 Grove St, 94102 **Tel** *(415) 861-2228* **Map** *4 F5*

Huge wraparound windows encase a spare, modern-industrial space frequented by a stylish Hayes Valley crowd. The menu changes every three to four months, and often includes sandwiches prepared with homemade breads and salads made from local, seasonal produce. The desserts are some of the best around.

Indigo 🚶 ♿ ⑤⑤⑤

687 McAllister St, 94102 **Tel** *(415) 673-9353* **Map** *4 F5*

With its cool, blue-themed interior, Indigo lives up to its name. The restaurant is celebrated for its phenomenal wine list and new American menu. The best bargain offered is the Wine Dinner after 8pm, with specially chosen wines and champagnes to accompany and enhance the chef's specialties.

Jardiniere ♿ 🍴 ⑤⑤⑤⑤⑤

300 Grove St, 94102 **Tel** *(415) 861-5555* **Map** *4 5F*

Thoughtful, efficient service, elegant atmosphere, and sumptuous California-inspired French food make the popular Jardinière a top choice for special occasions. The jazz duo plays quietly in the background while diners enjoy onion *tarte* and a Dubonnet from the mahogany and marble bar.

HAIGHT ASHBURY AND THE MISSION

Ali Baba's Cave 🚶 ♿ ⑤

531 Haight St, 94117 **Tel** *(415) 255-7820* **Map** *10 E9*

Don't be fooled by the low-key vibe at this counter service restaurant – one bite of the perfectly seasoned roasted lamb kebab, crispy falafel, creamy hummus, and other Middle Eastern delights, and you will be hooked. The cave-like interior, with low tables and floor pillows, is intimate and cozy.

Axum Café 🚶 ♿ ⑤

698 Haight St, 94117 **Tel** *(415) 252-7912* **Map** *10 D1*

Considered to be the best place in the city to sample Ethiopian food, Axum Café is also popular for its rock-bottom prices. Primarily a hole-in-the-wall, it serves spicy and abundant portions of meat and vegetable stews and pancake-like bread, *injera*.

Cha Cha Cha 🚶 ♿ ⑤

2727 Mission St, 94110 **Tel** *(415) 648-0504* **Map** *10 F3*

As much a lively nightlife scene as it is a restaurant, Cha Cha Cha serves small plates, from black mussels to fried calamari, and excellent sangria against a background of foot-tapping recorded Latin music. Reservations are advised, as it gets crowded on Friday and Saturday nights.

La Taqueria 🚶 ♿ ⑤

2889 Mission St, 94110 **Tel** *(415) 285-7117* **Map** *10 F4*

Flavorful marinated beef, pork or chicken layered with firm, tasty beans (rice on request), fresh lettuce, and tomato make for perfect burritos, at great prices. Another specialty at La Taqueria is the guacamole. The cafeteria-style line moves fast. Table seating is often filled during lunch, but the turnover is quick.

Memphis Minnie's BBQ Joint
🏃 ♿   Ⓢ

576 Haight St, 94117 **Tel** *(415) 864-7675*   **Map** *10 E1*

A takeout place and a sit-down restaurant, the Memphis Minnie is all about the slow-smoked southern-style fork-tender sausage, chicken, beef, ribs, and pork, dripping with barbecue sauce. Order a combo, and don't leave out the handcut fries and barbecued brisket chili. In true San-Francisco style, sake is served here.

Pork Store Café
🏃 ♿ 🍴   Ⓢ

3122 16th St, 94103 **Tel** *(415) 626-5523*   **Map** *10 E2*

Free coffee while standing in line during the weekends perks up diners and softens the wait at Pork Store Café. Big traditional American breakfasts feature the standard pancakes and bacon and eggs. This popular hangout has another branch at 1451 Haight Street.

Rosamunde Sausage Grill
🏃 ♿   Ⓢ

545 Haight St, 94117 **Tel** *(415) 437-6851*   **Map** *10 E1*

The menu at Rosamunde's specializes in one dish, and excels in it. Order a sausage – in the German, Italian, or Californian style – and layer on the condiments. Eat at the eight-stool counter, take your order to the bar next door, or have Rosamunde's deliver it there for you.

Zazie
🏃 ♿ 🍴   Ⓢ

941 Cole St, 94117 **Tel** *(415) 564-5332*   **Map** *9 B2*

The neighborhood's most popular brunch spot on the weekends, Zazie also serves bistro-style lunches and dinners daily. The bountiful plates are brought by an attentive staff, and the outdoor patio is a lovely place to enjoy a quiet conversation.

Andalu
🏃 ♿   ⓈⓈ

3198 16th St, 94103 **Tel** *(415) 621-2211*   **Map** *10 E2*

An international version of "small plates" (the Spanish tapas concept) using local, Asian-influenced ingredients is served at this popular restaurant. Andalu also boasts potent sangria and an expansive wine list. Public transport is the best way to get here.

Beretta
♿   ⓈⓈ

1199 Valencia Street, 94110 **Tel** *(415) 695-1199*   **Map** *10 F4*

The inventive cocktails will keep you happy while you wait for a table at this popular Mission hot spot. Exceptional pizzas and contemporary Italian food – like squid-ink risotto with calamari – keep people coming back time and again. The lively bar stays open until late.

Indian Oven
🏃 ♿   ⓈⓈ

233 Fillmore, 94117 **Tel** *(415) 626-1628*   **Map** *10 E1*

An upscale option in an area full of Indian eateries, Indian Oven is notable for its exceptional red and yellow curries, fresh-made *naan*, and flavorful vegetarian dishes. Attentive service performed by costumed waiters enhances the experience.

Pomelo
🏃 ♿ 🍴   ⓈⓈ

1793 Church St, 94131 **Tel** *(415) 285-2257*   **Map** *10 E5*

Noodles and rice plates from around the world – Chinese, Japanese, Indian, African, and European – are on the everchanging menu of Pomelo, a joint frequented by locals. Another location, with indoor seating only, is situated at 92 Judah Street.

Thep Phanom Thai Cuisine
🏃 ♿   ⓈⓈ

400 Waller St, 94117 **Tel** *(415) 431-2526*   **Map** *10 E1*

Dinner reservations are a must at this popular Thai restaurant, though lunch is more flexible. An accommodating staff serves well-seasoned Thai favorites, such as *yum pla muk* (spicy, crisp, cold calamari salad), in a comfortable, homely setting.

Chez Spencer
♿ 🍴   ⓈⓈⓈ

82 14th Street, 94103 **Tel** *(415) 864-2191*   **Map** *11 A3*

The sophisticated ambience of this French gem is meant to impress. Chez Spencer boasts delectable and authentic food served with an impressive wine list and artisanal cheeses. The heated patio is perfect for a romantic evening. Slightly off the beaten track but worth the effort.

Delfina
🏃 ♿ 🍴   ⓈⓈⓈ

3621 18th St, 94110 **Tel** *(415) 552-4055*   **Map** *10 E3*

Validated parking in a tough-to-park area makes this restaurant's simple, impeccably seasoned Northern Italian cuisine even better. Ingredients are ultra-fresh, from the morning markets. Delfina is popular, and dining space is at a premium, so get there early.

Zuni Café
♿   ⓈⓈⓈ

1658 Market St, 94102 **Tel** *(415) 552-2522*   **Map** *10 F1*

Perfect burgers and juicy roasted chicken, cooked over an open fire, complement a menu offering a variety of Mediterranean dishes. The glass walls overlook Market Street, giving a great view of the city's action until it slows down late at night. Brunch also served – don't pass up on their renowned Bloody Mary.

Key to Price Guide *see p228* **Key to Symbols** *see back cover flap*

GOLDEN GATE PARK AND LAND'S END

Khan Toke 👨 ♿ Ⓢ
5937 Geary Blvd, 94118 **Tel** *(415) 668-6654*   **Map** *8 E1*

A temple-like interior and colorfully-dressed staff transports diners to Thailand. Featuring both floor- and Western-style seating, this long-established restaurant serves Thai standards such as spicy, lemon calamari salad and grilled satay with peanut sauce. Top it off with the delicious fried banana and coconut ice cream.

Marnee Thai 👨 ♿ Ⓢ
2225 Irving St, 94122 **Tel** *(415) 665-9500*   **Map** *8 E3*

Large servings of consistently good Thai food have made this a dependable choice. Marnee Thai's green curries are quite good. The tight seating and sometimes-long waits for a table do not deter loyal fans. Another location at 1243 Ninth Avenue expands diners' choices.

Beach Chalet Brewery 👨 ♿ �ⓈⓈ
1000 Great Highway, 94122 **Tel** *(415) 386-8439*   **Map** *7 A2*

Craft brews, big hamburgers with side dishes of crispy fries, and a spectacular view of the Pacific make Beach Chalet Brewery a promising destination after a day in Golden Gate Park. The WPA murals on the first floor and carved stone stair-rails are a must-see.

Cajun Pacific Restaurant 👨 ♿ ⓈⓈ
4542 Irving St, 94122 **Tel** *(415) 504-6652*   **Map** *7 B3*

The food here is hot, and the decor just as zesty. The interiors are loaded with atmospheric baubles, from New Orleans-themed posters to funky idols and dolls, to Mardi Gras beads spilling color into the dusky room. Try the crawfish Monica, pasta with succulent curls of crawfish in a Creole-spiced cream sauce. Open Thursday–Saturday evenings only.

Cliff House 👨 ♿ ⓈⓈ
1090 Point Lobos Ave, 94121 **Tel** *(415) 386-3330*   **Map** *7 A1*

The original Cliff House, built in 1863, was where rich San Franciscans brunched. Twice destroyed by fire, the renovated fresh seafood place has the best views of the barking seals below on Seal Rocks. Enjoy cocktails at Zinc Bar. The formal restaurant is open for lunch and dinner, and the informal bistro for all meals daily.

Kabuto Sushi 👨 ♿ ⓈⓈ
5121 Geary Blvd, 94118 **Tel** *(415) 752-5652*   **Map** *8 F1*

Occasional long waits for tables are the only difficulty with this innovative sushi shop that creates artistic, unusual, and tasty combinations from fresh fish and sticky rice. Try the tempura halibut with their special curry sauce. New combinations are invented almost daily, so expect the unexpected.

La Vie 👨 ♿ ⓈⓈ
5830 Geary Blvd, 94121 **Tel** *(415) 668-8080*   **Map** *8 E1*

A wonderful neighborhood find in the outer Richmond area – a good stop before or after a visit to Golden Gate Park – La Vie gets consistently good reviews for its Vietnamese menu prepared and served with a French flair. The flaming beef and prawns are a favorite.

Pacific Café 👨 ♿ ⓈⓈ
7000 Geary Blvd, 94121 **Tel** *(415) 387-7091*   **Map** *7 C1*

Opened in the 1970s, Pacific Café is redolent of the era, down to the stained-glass windows. Good, reliable seafood is served to one's liking. Diners who have to wait for a table are often treated to a glass of wine. There are branches all over the Bay area; this was the original location.

Ton Kiang 👨 ♿ ⓈⓈ
5821 Geary Blvd, 94121 **Tel** *(415) 387-8273*   **Map** *8 E1*

Ton Kiang is one of the best and most popular dim sum restaurants in town – beware of the lines down the block on weekends. The huge variety of dishes is always fresh, and always rolling your way on cart after cart. Full plate dishes are also served.

Aziza ♿ ⓈⓈⓈ
5800 Geary Blvd, 94121 **Tel** *(415) 752-2222*   **Map** *8 E1*

At Aziza, guests are welcomed by sprinkling rosewater over their hands. Exotic Moroccan specialties, from a fragrant couscous to quail with huckleberry, are brought to the table, as diners lounge on luxurious cushioned seats. The meal is finished with sweet mint tea. On weekends, belly dancers perform while you dine.

Ebisu 👨 ♿ ⓈⓈⓈ
1283 Ninth Ave, 94122 **Tel** *(415) 566-1770*   **Map** *8 F3*

Often crowded, this sushi restaurant has visitors lined up to sample what some say is the best and freshest sushi in town, served by laughing, cleaver-flashing chefs at the bar. Ebisu is seafood-as-entertainment, and lines for table space are not uncommon.

The Moss Room   🚶 ♿ 🅿 $$$
55 Music Concourse Drive, 94118 **Tel** *(415) 876-6121*   **Map** *8 F2*

Elegant, modern and sleek, this dining space is befitting of its unique location inside the California Academy of Sciences. The restaurant has a dramatic living wall of fern, moss and stone and the food served is Californian-Mediterranean, inspired by local produce and seasonal ingredients.

SOUTH OF MARKET

Manora's Thai   🚶 ♿ $
1600 Folsom St, 94103 **Tel** *(415) 861-6224*   **Map** *11 A2*

Diners will find excellent value for money here as Manora's Thai serves generous portions of deliciously spiced soups such as a lemon-flavored shrimp and enoki mushroom combination, seafood plates, and rice-based dishes. The lunch menu offers well-priced specials.

AsiaSF   ♿ $$$
201 Ninth St, 94103 **Tel** *(415) 255-2742*   **Map** *11 A2*

The Asian-influenced small dishes served here take a back seat to the floor show, which features cross-dressing male performers in an hourly entertainment fest of songs and skits. Patience is required between courses if your waiter needs to be on stage, belting out a Judy Garland number.

Bizou   🚶 ♿ $$$
598 Fourth St, 94107 **Tel** *(415) 543-2222*   **Map** *11 C1*

Bizou serves hearty food with a French bistro feel in its airy, warm-toned dining room. Specialties include beef cheek Sainte-Menehould with mustard, watercress and new potatoes. Salads, such as pear-and-frisée, are top choices here. The prix-fixe lunches and dinners are a great bargain.

CoCo 500   ♿ $$$
500 Brannan Street, 94107 **Tel** *(415) 543-2222*   **Map** *11 C1*

A pleasant, trendy place to dine when you find yourself South of Market. The fried green beans are famous and worth a try. Save room after lunch or dinner as there is an extensive dessert menu. Since CoCo is located in a more commerical part of town, crowds flock here for lunch. Dinner can be a quieter, but pricier, experience.

Fringale   🚶 ♿ $$$
570 Fourth St, 94107 **Tel** *(415) 543-0573*   **Map** *11 C1*

Small, noisy, and festive, this lively bistro continues to be a popular choice for its good French-Basque cooking and friendly staff. The traditional menu features grilled meats, including succulent lamb-based dishes, with fresh breads and some seafood items.

South Park Café   🚶 ♿ 🍴 $$$
108 South Park, 94107 **Tel** *(415) 495-7275*   **Map** *11 C1*

Though South Park Café has lost some of its former sparkle, the bistro-style food in this simply decorated spot remains delicious. Its menu features soups and sandwiches as well as more complicated fare such as roast duck breast. The outdoor seating on sunny days looks out on South Park.

Bacar   ♿ 🍷 $$$$
448 Brannan St, 94107 **Tel** *(415) 904-4100*   **Map** *11 C1*

Industrial interiors and cool jazz in the background provide urban sleekness to this American-fusion restaurant-lounge. Seafood is a specialty here and includes such dishes as halibut with morel mushrooms. There is a three-story wine cellar that runs the length of the restaurant and boasts the most extensive international wine list in the city.

BERKELEY

The Cheese Board Pizza   🚶 ♿ 🍴 $
1512 Shattuck Avenue, 94709 **Tel** *(510) 549-3183*

Lines can be long at this cheap but fantastic pizza shop. Toppings vary daily and range from the classics like basil and mozzarella to potato, goat cheese and asparagus. In typical Berkely form, this is a co-op business so prices can be kept down. Don't miss their cheese shop and baked goods outpost next door for some take-home treats.

Vik's Chaat Corner   🚶 ♿ $
726 Allston Way, 94710 **Tel** *(510) 644-4412*

An exceptional, value-for-money place for incredibly delicious, authentic Indian food bursting with unique flavors. It's counter service only here but the food more than makes up for it. Be warned: the plates are small, so you will be tempted to over order.

Key to Price Guide *see p228* **Key to Symbols** *see back cover flap*

Corso Trattoria $$

*1788 Shattuck, 94709 **Tel** (510) 704-8004*

Parking spots can be tough to find at this popular Italian destination in Berkeley, but the rustic, authentic food is worth a few trips around the block. Fare includes large, delectable pizzas, pastas and risottos so make sure you don't fill up from the generous bread bowl.

Sea Salt $$

*2512 San Pablo Avenue, 94702 **Tel** (510) 883-1720*

It is well worth travelling over the Bay Bridge to this exciting, lively seafood restaurant for the seven-days-a-week Happy Hour menu featuring $1 oysters. The casual atmosphere makes you feel at home while you enjoy deliciously prepared seafood. Sit outside on the patio for an even more relaxed experience.

FARTHER AFIELD

Fenton's Creamery $

*4226 Piedmont Ave, 94611 **Tel** (510) 658-7000*

Mounds of homemade ice cream in a kaleidoscope of flavors, from peppermint stick to tin roof (vanilla with fudge sauce and peanuts), make their way into cones, banana splits big as your head, and other fountain favorites. Fenton's Creamery also has simple sandwiches, such as tuna and egg salad.

Jz Cool Eatery $

*827 Santa Cruz Ave, 94025 **Tel** (650) 325-3665*

This deli with casual seating and stripped-down decor has a special feature – the ingredients that make up the satisfying soups, sandwiches, and light desserts are all organic. The menu offers vegetarian specialties. Takeout is available.

Amber India $$

*377 Santana Row, Ste 1140, 95128 **Tel** (408) 248-5400*

The sleek outlet of an old Mountain View favorite, Amber India is popular for its lip-smacking butter chicken as well as exceptional – and bustling – lunch and weekend buffets. Table settings of fine china and swift and silent service complete the picture.

Dipsea Café $$

*200 Shoreline Hwy, 94941 **Tel** (415) 381-0298*

For those craving a plate-bending serving of blueberry pancakes with chicken-apple sausage, or a big juicy burger, Dipsea Café is where the search ends. On Richardson Bay, looking out on a wetland preserve, the setting could not be prettier. It is open for breakfast and lunch only.

O Chame $$

*1830 Fourth St, 94710 **Tel** (510) 841-8783*

One of the several restaurants among the shops on trendy Fourth Street, O Chame serves carefully prepared, artfully arranged traditional Japanese dishes such as teriyaki salmon and miso soup. The interior decor is simple, thoughtfully creating a refuge from the busy street outside.

Olema Inn $$$

*10,000 Sir Francis Drake Blvd, 94950 **Tel** (415) 663-9559*

An 1876 inn and former stagecoach stop along Highway 1, Olema Inn provides a dramatic setting for simple and elegant meals made from fresh local ingredients. Specialties such as Tomales Bay oysters are often featured on the menu. Ideal for a meal after sightseeing in Point Reyes National Seashore.

The Pelican Inn $$$

*10 Pacific Way, 94965 **Tel** (415) 383-6000*

In a setting that could have been airlifted from the Cotswolds, this stone-and-wood restaurant/inn serves the best in British cooking such as a superb shepherd's pie, along with warm Guinness on draft. Lunch and dinner are served daily in summer. The restaurant is closed in winter.

Lark Creek Inn $$$$

*234 Magnolia Ave, 94939 **Tel** (415) 924-7766*

Uber-chef Bradley Ogden's premier restaurant is tucked away in a lovely redwood grove in the charming town of Larkspur. The menu is a tribute to fresh local meats and produce, and elevates the concept of "home cooking" by several notches.

Chez Panisse $$$$$

*1517 Shattuck Ave, 94709 **Tel** (510) 548-5525*

Alice Waters, the grand mistress of California style fresh food cooking, has trained a multitude of chefs out of this kitchen. The food still reflects her insistence that the quality of the produce is what matters above all. You will not find overpowering sauces here – just lots of flavor. Advance reservations are required. For a more casual meal, try the café upstairs.

NORTHERN CALIFORNIA

CARMEL Duarte Tavern $
202 Stage Rd (Pescadero Rd), 94060 **Tel** *(650) 879-0464*

No scenic drive south along coastal Route 1 is complete without a stop at Duarte Tavern, an old roadhouse famed for typical American cuisine, including homemade soups. The house specialty is a pie made with olallieberries, a cross between a loganberry and a Texas dewberry (similar to blackberries) grown locally.

CARMEL Flying Fish Grill $$$
Carmel Plaza, Mission St **Tel** *(831) 625-1962*

Despite its location in the heart of a bustling shopping center, Flying Fish Grill remains the preference of those looking for fresh seafood in an informal setting. The small, underwater-themed restaurant, run by friendly owners, serves seafood grilled in a Japanese-influenced style.

CARMEL Anton & Michel $$$$
Mission St between Ocean & Sevent **Tel** *(831) 624-2406*

Carmel's "grand dame" since 1980, it has been serving a classic Continental menu and complementing it with an excellent wine list. Specialties include steaks and seafood paella. Diners may sit by a roaring fire or, during the summer, around a fountain in the picturesque courtyard.

CARMEL Marinus $$$$$
415 Carmel Valley Rd **Tel** *(831) 658-3500*

Elegant and rustic at the same time, the Bernardus Lodge dining room is set in the valley away from the ocean, and draws diners and those seeking a getaway. Delicious California-French *nouvelle cuisine* is backed by a wine list that includes Bernardus Winery bottlings.

LAKE TAHOE Alexander's $
High Camp, Squaw Valley, Olympic Valley, 96146 **Tel** *(530) 581-7278*

Getting to Alexander's is more than half the fun – diners must ride the Squaw Valley cable tram 2000 ft (610 m) over the valley floor to reach this restaurant above the valley. The food is ordinary, but there is a special menu for children. This is a fun place to perch after skiing all day.

LAKE TAHOE Fire Sign Café $
1785 West Lake Blvd, 96145 **Tel** *(530) 583-0871*

Reputed to have the best breakfasts on the lake (try the Eggs Benedict with smoked salmon and spinach), this cheerful café is open for breakfast and lunch seven days a week. A variety of fresh-baked muffins grace the menu every day, and chunky soups and fresh sandwiches appeal to the lunch crowd.

LAKE TAHOE Dory's Oar Restaurant $$
1041 Fremont Ave, 96150 **Tel** *(530) 541-6603* **Fax** *530 541-5332*

Set in a charming white clapboard house, Dory's formal dining room prepares fresh seafood and steaks such as pan-roasted red snapper and grilled New Zealand lamb loin. Upstairs, the informal Tudor Pub serves Guinness and a number of other beers on draft, plus plates and snacks at pub prices.

LAKE TAHOE Hunter William Bacchi's Inn $$$
2905 Lake Forest Rd, 96145 **Tel** *(530) 583-3324*

Opened in 1935, Hunter William Bacchi's Inn is Lake Tahoe's oldest restaurant. The menu features Italian classics, such as veal Parmigiana, as part of a belt-busting complete dinner, with soup, salad, antipasti, and a side of ravioli, spaghetti or tortellini. Wine is extra.

MENDOCINO Mendo Bistro $$
301 N Main St, 95437 **Tel** *(707) 964-4974*

The locally popular Mendo Bistro has a menu that changes with the seasons, making the most of local produce. Specialties include a salad made with warm walnut-crusted goats' cheese and citrus. An all-Mendocino wine list accompanies award-winning crabcakes and meats, cooked and sauced to your taste.

MENDOCINO Sharon's by the Sea $$
32096 N Harbor Dr, 95437 **Tel** *(707) 962-0680*

Considered the best for the least on the north coast, Sharon's presents the freshest seafood. You can watch your food being caught from the deck, outside under the bridge. Hidden away on a pier, the small clapboard structure also serves full breakfasts.

MENDOCINO Albion River Inn $$$
3790 North Hwy 1, 95410 **Tel** *(707) 937-1919*

The sun setting on the Pacific is a spectacular backdrop for relishing Albion River Inn's fresh and simple cuisine. The restaurant/inn offers lodging if you overindulge in tasting their large collection of scotch whiskies. Set on a cliff above the sea, it offers views of passing whales in winter.

Key to Price Guide *see p228* **Key to Symbols** *see back cover flap*

MENDOCINO The Moosse Café $$$
390 Kasten Street, 95460 **Tel** *(707) 937-4323*

Charming ambience, good food – much of it made with local, organic produce and seafood – and classic Mendocino vibes infuse this refuge of a restaurant. The dining room is cozy and quaint and occupies the ground floor of a popular B&B. Portions are very generous.

MENDOCINO Victorian Gardens $$$$$
14409 North Hwy 1, 95459 **Tel** *(707) 882-3606*

Set in an exclusive bed-and-breakfast inn on a 92-acre farm, the house itself is out of a fairytale; a mini-castle decked out in fine period decor. Prix-fixe dinners, based on fresh ingredients, are served nightly in the elegant 16-seat dining room at Victorian Gardens.

NAPA WINE COUNTRY Cook St Helena $$
1310 Main St, 94574 **Tel** *(707) 963-7088*

A casual eatery, Cook St Helena serves crisp and fresh classic salads, pasta and meat dishes. Good food, decent prices (especially for the area), and friendly service make it a regular stop for locals. The homemade lasagna and eggplant Parmigiana are much loved.

NAPA WINE COUNTRY Willow Wood Market Café $$
9020 Graton Rd, 95444 **Tel** *(707) 522-8372*

A combination café/shop, this hippie-inspired café in the small town of Graton is the antithesis of slick Wine Country restaurants. It serves hearty breakfasts, lovingly-prepared lattes, homemade soups, innovative sandwiches, and bakery items that will not put a dent in your wallet.

NAPA WINE COUNTRY Tra Vigne $$$
1050 Charter Oak Ave, 94574 **Tel** *(707) 823-0233*

Reminiscent of a Tuscan villa, this quintessential Wine Country eatery is reputed for its divine interpretations of Italian specialties with an inspired wine list. The bar is a hot spot for local vintners. Drive down to the end of Charter Oak Avenue to the old olive oil factory to pick up picnic items.

NAPA WINE COUNTRY Ubuntu $$$
1140 Main Street, 94559 **Tel** *(707) 251-5656*

Even die-hard meat-eaters are raving about this all-vegetarian restaurant in Napa Valley, known for its fresh local ingredients and yoga studio. The dishes are inventive, flavorful and unique. Show up in your best attire or yoga pants and you will be treated equally as well by the friendly, knowledgable staff.

NAPA WINE COUNTRY French Laundry $$$$$
6640 Washington St, 94599 **Tel** *(707) 944-2380*

French Laundry, the crème-de-la-crème of Wine Country restaurants, is hard to get in, unless a reservation is made well in advance. The impeccable interpretations of French *nouvelle cuisine*, flawless service, exquisite formal gardens, and an understated interior, all make it difficult to leave.

YOSEMITE Yosemite Lodge Food Court $
Rte 140, Yosemite Village, 95389 **Tel** *(559) 253-5635*

A low-cost alternative to the valley's upscale restaurants, the food court features hot breakfasts, pastries, pastas, pizzas as well as a grill with burgers, hot dogs, fries, and sandwiches. The menu also has vegetarian and meat entrées and a selection of desserts. Open year-round for breakfast, lunch and dinner.

YOSEMITE Columbia City Hotel $$
Columbia State Historic Park, 95310 **Tel** *(800) 532-1479*

A Wine Spectator Restaurant award-winner since 1986, Columbia City Hotel's kitchen prepares traditional favorites. The historic Gold Rush-era hotel is a training facility for future chefs. Special two-course dinners cost $14 per person. Open mid-Sep to mid-Nov, from Wednesday to Thursday. Student cookbook menus available.

YOSEMITE Ahwahnee $$$
One Ahwahnee Rd, Yosemite Village, 95389 **Tel** *(209) 372-1489*

Ahwahnee is the queen of the National Park lodges, with a stunning valley view, soaring beamed ceilings, and a sophisticated menu. Lunch might include a chili-rubbed chicken sandwich. For dinner, try the roast organic pork tenderloin with a pecan praline crust. Casual attire is allowed for breakfast and lunch.

YOSEMITE Wawona Lodge $$$
Rte 41, South Park, 95389 **Tel** *(209) 375-1425*

Victorian with a charming rustic flare, the lodge serves breakfast, lunch, and dinner when the hotel is open. The menu includes flatiron steak, and savory smoked trout chowder. Each Saturday in summer, diners gather for a pit-fired barbecue dinner. Open seven days a week.

YOSEMITE Erna's Elderberry House $$$$$
48688 Victoria Ln (Hwy 41), 93644 **Tel** *(559) 683-6800*

Part of the Château de Sureau inn, Erna's Elderberry House is a destination in itself. An extravagant fine-dining menu includes six courses of superb Continental cuisine, from *amusée bouche* (such as venison-chanterelle terrine) to *delice du patissier*. The menu changes daily.

San Francisco's Cafés

You need never search long for a place in which to quench your thirst in San Francisco. The city is known to be a paradise for coffee-lovers, as it teems with excellent cafés. Connoisseurs should head for those clustered in North Beach and the Mission District, to sample and enjoy the delights on offer.

CAFÉS

With so many cafés from which to choose, you could spend days sampling several and never visit the same place twice. One local purveyor, **Peet's Coffee & Tea**, has offered dark, strong coffee for four decades. **Emporio Rulli Il Caffè** is ensconced on Union Square. The **Caffè Trieste**, in North Beach, is an old bohemian haunt that serves excellent coffee. It also has a jukebox that plays songs from Italian opera, and family members who sing and play instruments on occasional weekend afternoons. Columbus Avenue's **Caffè Greco**, **Caffè Puccini**, and **Caffè Roma** are also well worth a visit. This neighborhood as well as SoMa is also a draw for many visitors because it is dotted with roasteries.

Beatniks frequented tiny **Mario's Bohemian Cigar Store Café** with Washington Square views; try a double latté with foccacia. **Vesuvio** (*see p270*) serves superb expresso. At **Stella Pasticceria e Caffè**, order cappuccino with the specialty rum, marsala, and sherry zabaglione sponge cake, *Sacripantina*.

In the Mission District try **Café La Bohème**, frequented by the San Franciscan literary set. The **Café Flore** on Market Street is very stylish, while **Firenze**, near the Civic Center, has terrific coffee and pastries. Francophiles will appreciate **Café Claude**, an attractive French café, with old furnishings rescued from a Paris bar that is tucked away in an alley near Union Square. **Café de la Presse**, across from the Chinatown Gateway, is the place to catch up with international periodicals. SoMa coffee and food choices range from the SFMOMA **Caffè Museo** and **Natoma Café** hidden at the back of the museum, to the combination café, entertainment venue and laundromat, **Brainwash**. The **Blue Danube Coffee House** and **Toy Boat Dessert Café** are situated on Clement Street. **Momi Toby's Revolution Café & Art Bar** combines Hayes Valley java and artwork and live music. At **Frjtz**, the crêpes lend a Belgian tone to coffee drinking. Check out the Inner Sunset District art and entertainment with your coffee at **The Canvas** or the heavenly aromas at the **Beanery**.

DIRECTORY

CAFÉS

Beanery
1307 9th Ave.
Map 8 F3.
Tel 661-1255.

Blue Danube Coffee House
306 Clement St.
Map 3 A5.
Tel 221-9041.

Brainwash
1122 Folsom St.
Map 11 A1.
Tel 861-3663.

Café La Bohème
3318 24th St.
Map 10 F4.
Tel 643-0481.

Café Claude
7 Claude La.
Map 5 C4.
Tel 392-3505.

Café Flore
2298 Market St.
Map 10 D2.
Tel 621-8579.

Caffè Greco
423 Columbus Ave.
Map 5 B3.
Tel 397-6261.

Caffè Museo
151 3rd St.
Map 6 D5.
Tel 357-4500.

Café de la Presse
352 Grant Ave.
Map 5 C4.
Tel 398-2680.

Caffè Puccini
411 Columbus Ave.
Map 5 B3.
Tel 989-7033.

Caffè Roma
526 Columbus Ave.
Map 5 B3.
Also: 885 Bryant St.
Map 11 B2.
Tel 296-7662.

Caffè Trieste
601 Vallejo St.
Map 5 C3.
Tel 392-6739.

The Canvas
1200 9th Ave.
Map 8 F3.
Tel 504-0060.

Emporio Rulli Il Caffè
at Union Square.
Map 5 C5.
Tel 433-1122.

Firenze
601 Van Ness Ave.
Map 4 F5.
Tel 771-5454.

Frjtz
579 Hayes St.
Map 4 E5.
Tel 864-7654.

Mario's Bohemian Cigar Store Café
566 Columbus Ave.
Map 5 B2.
Tel 362-0536.

Momi Toby's Revolution Café & Art Bar
528 Laguna St.
Map 10 E1.
Tel 626-1508.

Natoma Café
145 Natoma St.
Map 6 D5.
Tel 495-3289.

Peet's Coffee & Tea
22 Battery St.
Map 6 D4.
Tel 981-4550.

Stella Pasticceria e Caffè
446 Columbus Ave.
Map 5 B3.
Tel 986-2914.

Toy Boat Dessert Café
401 Clement St.
Map 3 A5.
Tel 751-7505.

Vesuvio
255 Columbus Ave.
Map 5 C3.
Tel 362-3370.

Light Meals and Snacks

If you do not have the time to sit down for a full meal, you can get a quick bite to eat almost anywhere in San Francisco. Many establishments serve good fast food at low prices, but if you look for them, you can find places that offer something a little special.

BREAKFAST

Coffee and pastries, or bacon and eggs are easy to find in San Francisco, or you can have a full American breakfast that will sustain you all day. **Sears Fine Foods** in Union Square is an institution, popular for its wonderful early morning meals. **Le Petit Café** serves great brunches on weekends. Hotel dining rooms offer good breakfasts, as do a few restaurants *(see pp228–41)*.

DELIS

If you want a perfect corned beef on rye sandwich try **David's**, the largest and most central delicatessen in San Francisco. **Tommy's Joint** in the Civic Center, **Pat O'Shea's**

Mad Hatter in the Richmond District and **Molinari's** in North Beach are also worth a visit. The **Real Food Deli/Grocery** in Russian Hill specializes in organic food.

HAMBURGER PLACES

While you can get a quick-hamburger and fries at all of the usual franchises, you would do better to try one of San Francisco's more unique places. The **Grubstake**, housed in a converted streetcar, is open late, **Mel's Drive-In** is a 1950s-style café, and **Louis'** has unbeatable views over the remains of the Sutro Baths *(see p157)*. **Bill's Place** in the Richmond District offers two dozen different burgers, all of which are named after local

celebrities while **Sparky's** near the Castro serves up juicy burgers 24 hours a day.

PIZZERIAS

San Francisco has many good pizzerias, mostly in North Beach. Choose between the traditional **Tommaso's**, the popular **North Beach Pizza** and the hectic, but excellent, **Golden Boy**. For a really exotic pizza, try **Pauline's** in the Mission District or the chain pizzeria **Extreme Pizza** in Pacific Heights.

MEXICAN FOOD

Mexican food, which is tasty and often extremely inexpensive, is sold by vendors all over the city. For a delicious snack, try **El Balazo, Pancho Villa, Roosevelt's Tamale Parlor**, or **Left Turn at Albuquerque**. For a treat before or after a movie, try **El Super Burrito** – great prices and large portions.

DIRECTORY

BREAKFAST

Le Petit Café
2164 Larkin St.
Map 5 A3.
Tel 951-8514.

Pork Store Café
1451 Haight St.
Map 9 B1.
Tel 864-6981.

Sears Fine Foods
493 Powell St.
Map 5 B4.
Tel 986-1160.

DELIS

David's
474 Geary St.
Map 5 B5.
Tel 276-5950.

Molinari's
373 Columbus Ave.
Map 5 C3. Tel 421-2337.

Pat O'Shea's Mad Hatter
3848 Geary Blvd.
Map 3 A5.
Tel 752-3148.

Real Food Deli/Grocery
2140 Polk St.
Map 5 A3.
Tel 673-7420.

Tommy's Joint
1101 Geary Blvd.
Map 5 A5.
Tel 775-4216.

HAMBURGER PLACES

Bill's Place
2315 Clement St.
Map 2 D5.
Tel 221-5262.

Grubstake
1525 Pine St.
Map 4 F4.
Tel 673-8268.

Louis'
902 Point Lobos Ave.
Map 7 A1.
Tel 387-6330.

Mel's Drive-In
3355 Geary Blvd.
Map 3 B5.
Tel 387-2244.

Sparky's
242 Church St.
Map 10 E2.
Tel 626-8666.

PIZZERIAS

Extreme Pizza
1908 Union St.
Map 4 D3.
Tel 929-8234.

Golden Boy
542 Green St.
Map 5 B3.
Tel 982-9738.

North Beach Pizza
1310 Grant Ave.
Map 5 B1.
Tel 433-1818.
Also:1499 Grant Ave.
Map 5 C2.
Tel 433-2444.

Pauline's
260 Valencia St.
Map 10 F2.
Tel 552-2050.

Tommaso's
1042 Kearny St at Broadway.

Map 5 C3.
Tel 398-9696.

MEXICAN FOOD

El Balazo
1654 Haight St.
Map 9 B1.
Tel 864-6981.

El Super Burrito
1200 Polk St.
Map 5 A5.
Tel 771-9700.

Left Turn at Albuquerque
2140 Union St.
Map 4 D3.
Tel 749-6700.

Pancho Villa
3071 16th St.
Map 10 F2.
Tel 864-8840.

Roosevelt Tamale Parlor
2817 24th St.
Map 10 F4.
Tel 550-9213.

SHOPPING IN SAN FRANCISCO

Shopping in San Francisco is much more than simply making a purchase, it's an experience that allows a glimpse into the city's culture. An enormous range of goods is available here, from the practical to the eccentric, and you can take your time in choosing, because browsers are generally welcome, particularly in the city's many small specialty shops and boutiques. If you want convenience, the shopping centers, malls and department stores are excellent. For those in search of local color, each neighborhood shopping district has a charm and personality of its own.

Clock over entrance to Tiffany's

Emporio Armani *(see p251)*

WHEN TO SHOP

Most shops in San Francisco are open between 10am and 6pm, Monday to Saturday. Many malls and department stores also remain open in the evening and on Sundays. On weekday mornings the shops are less crowded than in the afternoons, but lunch hours (noon–2pm), Saturdays, sales and holidays can be hectic.

HOW TO PAY

Major credit cards are accepted at most shops, although there will often be a minimum purchase price. Traveler's checks must be accompanied by identification, and foreign checks or foreign currency are rarely taken. Some smaller shops will allow only cash purchases.

CONSUMER RIGHTS AND SERVICES

Keep receipts for proof of purchase. Each shop sets and displays its own return and exchange policies. Shops cannot charge a fee to those using credit cards, but you may get a discount for cash. If you have a problem that shop management cannot solve, the Consumer Protection Unit or the California Department of Consumer Affairs may help.
Useful numbers Consumer Protection Unit **Tel** 551-9575.
California Department of Consumer Affairs **Tel** (916) 445-0660.

SALES

End-of-the-month, holiday and pre-season sales are common in many stores. Watch for advertisements in local newspapers where these are announced, especially mid-week and Sundays. Shop early for the best bargains, and beware of "Going out of business" signs – these can be left up for years. Some are legitimate sales; just ask at nearby shops.

TAXES

A sales tax of 8.5 percent is added to purchases made in San Francisco. This is not refundable to over-seas visitors, unlike the European Value Added Tax (VAT), but you are exempt if your purchases are forwarded to any destination outside California. Foreign visitors may have to pay duty at customs on arrival home.

SHOPPING TOURS

Serious shoppers who want to be guided to the best shops for their own particular needs, may want to go on a special tour. These are organized by companies such as A Simple Elegance Shopping Tour, or Shopper Stopper Shopping Tours. A guide takes you from shop to shop and knows where to find unusual items.
Useful numbers A Simple Elegance Shopping Tour **Tel** 661-0110.
Shopper Stopper Shopping Tours **Tel** (707) 829–1597.

MALLS AND SHOPPING CENTERS

In contrast with a great many suburban shopping malls, those of San Francisco have character, and one or two are of architectural interest. The Embarcadero Center *(see p110)* has over 125 shops, in an area covering eight blocks. Ghirardelli Square *(see p83)*

Flags and pagoda at the Japan Center

Flower stall on Union Square

was a chocolate factory from 1893 until early in the 1960s. It is now a mall that is popular with visitors, and houses over 70 restaurants and shops, overlooking San Francisco Bay.

The San Francisco Shopping Centre (see p117) has nine levels and contains more than 65 shops. Pier 39 (see p82) is a market place on the waterfront, with restaurants, a double-decker Venetian merry-go-round, a marina and many boutiques. In the Cannery (see p83), located at Fisherman's Wharf, you will find a variety of charming small shops, while the Crocker Galleria (see p116) is one of the city's most spectacular malls, with three floors under a high glass dome built around a central plaza.

The Japan Center (see p128), complete with pagoda, offers exotic foods, goods and art from the East, as well as a Japanese-style hotel and traditional baths. The Rincon Center (see p113), with a 90-ft (27-m) water column at its center, is an Art Deco haven for shopping and eating.

DEPARTMENT STORES

Most of San Francisco's major department stores are in or near Union Square. They are huge emporia that offer their customers an outstanding selection of goods and services. The frequent sales can get quite frantic as locals and visitors jostle for bargains. All sorts of extra services are available to make shoppers feel pampered, including cloakrooms where you can leave your belongings, assistants to guide you around the store, free gift wrapping or beauty salons offering treatments.

Macy's department store spans two city blocks. It stocks an enormous range of goods, all beautifully presented and sold by an enthusiastic sales force. It offers all sorts of extra facilities, including a currency exchange and an interpreting service. The men's department is particularly extensive.

Neiman Marcus is another stylish emporium, housed in a modern building that caused a furor when it was opened in 1982, replacing a popular store built in the 1890s. The huge stained-glass dome in its Rotunda Restaurant was part of the original building, and is well worth coming to see. **Nordstrom**, good for fashion and shoes, is known in the city as the "store-in-the-sky" as it is located on the top five floors of the innovative Westfield Shopping Centre.

Bloomingdales offers a huge range of coveted designer labels, luxury handbags, accessories, cosmetics, and shoes. For shoppers on a budget, go no further than **Mervyn's** department store. They stock women's, men's and children's clothes as well as a range of accessories. They also have housewares and a bed and bath department. There is something for everyone, including cosmetics, shoes, and lingerie.

BEST BUYS

Gourmet shoppers should look for seafood, one of the city's specialties. Wine from California is another good buy, particularly in the Napa Valley (see pp190–91). You will find blue jeans at competitive prices, also vintage clothing, ethnic art, books and records.

City Lights Bookstore (see p254), on Columbus Avenue

ADDRESSES

Bloomingdales
865 Market St. **Map** 5 C5.
Tel 856-5300.

Macy's
Stockton and O'Farrell Sts.
Map 5 C5.
Tel 397-3333.

Mervyn's
2675 Geary St.
Map 5 C5.
Tel 921-0888.

Neiman Marcus
150 Stockton St. **Map** 5 C5.
Tel 362-3900.

Nordstrom
Westfield Shopping Centre,
865 Market St. **Map** 5 C5.
Tel 243-8500.

Display of goods inside Gump's department store (see p249)

San Francisco's Best: Shopping

It is the diversity of San Francisco's stores that makes buying anything here such an adventure. Some of the best shopping areas are described below, each reflecting a different aspect of the city. Window shoppers will find glittering displays in Union Square, while bargain hunters should visit the South of Market outlets.

Street Fairs
Arts, crafts and specialty foods are sold from booths at neighborhood fairs like this one on Union Street, held in June.

Union Street
Clusters of boutiques in converted Victorian houses sell antiques, books and clothes on this busy street. (See p254.)

Haight Street
This is the best place in San Francisco for vintage clothes, record shops and books. (See p254.)

Presidio

Pacific Heights and the Marina

Golden Gate Park and Land's End

Civic Center

Haight Ashbury and the Mission

Japan Center
You can buy authentic food and goods from Japan here, and visit Japanese bars and galleries. (See p128.)

Jackson Square Antique Shops
Lovers of antiques will enjoy browsing in the shops in Jackson Square. (See p254.)

0 kilometers		2

0 miles	1

UN Plaza
*Named after the signing of the
United Nations Charter, this
is the site of the twice-weekly
Farmers' Market. (See p256.)*

Grant Avenue
*With its painted balconies,
souvenir shops and bars,
this is Chinatown's main
tourist street. (See p256.)*

Crocker Galleria
*Elegant shops fill the three floors of this
impressive modern mall, with daylight flooding in through the glass
roof. You can picnic in the rooftop
gardens on sunny days. (See p245.)*

Saks Fifth Avenue
*A department store
synonymous with
exclusive style and
elegance. (See p245.)*

Fisherman's
Wharf and
North Beach

Financial
District and
Union Square

Chinatown
and Nob Hill

Nordstrom
*This fashion store is located
in the gleaming Westfield
Centre, which has 400 shops
filling nine floors. (See p245.)*

SHOPPING AROUND UNION SQUARE

Serious shoppers should concentrate on the blocks bordered by
Geary, Powell and Post streets, and on the surrounding blocks
between market and Sutter streets. Here luxurious shops and
inexpensive boutiques sell everything from designer sheets to
pedigree dogs to souvenirs. Big hotels, splendid restaurants
and colorful flower stalls all add to the atmosphere.

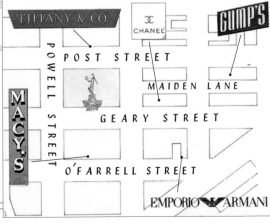

San Francisco Specials

Entrepreneurial spirit in San Francisco is strong and innovative. Owners of small shops, designers and buyers take much pride in bringing unusual and hand-crafted wares to their customers, and will often tell you the histories of these original items. From comic post-cards to fine handcrafted Florentine paper, and from Chinese herbal teas to high-tech electronic gadgets, all kinds of goods are available. Nestling in hidden corners or clustered with other tiny shops, these specialty outlets create an environment that makes shopping in San Francisco an exciting experience.

SPECIALTY SHOPS

If you want to laugh, go to **Smile–A Gallery with Tongue in Chic**, where humorous art to wear or display is sold, including many imaginative objects made by artists from the Bay Area.

Since Gold Rush days, **Malm Luggage**, a family-owned and operated shop for luggage, briefcases and small leather goods, has kept its reputation for excellence. At **Comix Experience** you can find a range of comic books and memorabilia from the newest offerings to antique, very expensive oldies.

Exquisite Italian ceramics (majolica) are on display at **Biordi Art Imports** in North Beach, where handpainted dishware, vases and platters of all sizes are for sale. Those who would like to experience the authentic atmosphere of Chinatown will find it at **Ten Ren Tea Company of San Francisco**. At **Golden Gate Fortune Cookies** descendants of Chinese immigrants allow customers to taste samples before buying the San Francisco fortune cookies which were a Chinatown invention. Sixty-year-old **Flax Art and Design** features a huge selection of handmade papers, customized stationery and artist's tools.

Precious gems, glittering gold and watches by some of the world's finest jewelers can be found at **Tiffany & Co** and **Bulgari**. **Jeanine Payer** creates jewelry that transcends the generations, fusing Old World craftsmanship with contemporary design.

SHOPS FOR A GOOD CAUSE

San Franciscans take great pleasure in shopping for a good cause: it assuages the conscience, and provides a temporary fix for the acquisitive urge. Here are a few establishments that cater to those shoppers who care enough to make a contribution. The **Planetweavers Treasure Store** is the official UNICEF shop, where crafts and clothes, which have been made in developing countries are sold, along with a choice of educational toys from around the world. UNICEF receives 25 percent of the net profits. The **Golden Gate National Park Store** is a not-for-profit shop offering park memorabilia, postcards, maps, and books. All the profits made at **Under One Roof** benefit various groups working to help combat AIDS.

SOUVENIRS

All sorts of souvenirs, such as T-shirts, keyrings, mugs and Christmas ornaments, are decorated with motifs symbol-izing San Francisco at **Only in San Francisco** and the **Cable Car Store**. Souvenir and novelty caps of every color, shape and size are available at **Krazy Kaps**, while shop entrances in Grant Avenue and Fisherman's Wharf are lined with baskets filled with inexpensive gifts.

ANTIQUES

Set in San Francisco's most sophisticated shopping area is the **Sacramento Street Antique Dealer's Association**,

a collection of stores offering an array of goods from furniture to small household items. This shoppers' paradise is great for browsing.

Fans of Art Deco should seek out Decorum on Market Street for its impressive selec-tion of elegant houseware and ornaments. A large selection of antique Japanese "Tansu" cabinetwork can be found at **Genji**, along with other Edo-period pieces made from unique woods such as elm.

TOYS, GAMES, AND GADGETS

One of the city's main toy shops, **Toys R Us** sells everything a child desires. Inside you will find a vast range of toys, video games and collectible toys, as well as a department with equip-ment and gifts for babies.

The **Academy Store** and the **Exploratorium Store** sell books, kits and games that make learning fun. At **Puppets on the Pier** new owners get puppetry lessons in the shop. **Gamescape** sells any type of game that doesn't require electricity, such as traditional game-boards, collectible cards and role-playing books.

The **Chinatown Kite Shop** takes shopping to new heights, displaying an extraordinary assortment of flying objects. These range from traditional to World Champion stunt kites, all making attractive souvenirs. In the **Sony Style** store even the adult who has everything is sure to be intrigued by the high-tech wizardry of the gadgets and electronic goods on sale. For more shops of interest to children (see p275).

MUSEUM SHOPS

Museum shopping is another option for visitors to San Francisco, and shops offer delightful and exquisite gifts to suit all budgets, ranging from science kits to reproduc-tion jewelry and sculpture. In San Francisco's Golden Gate Park, visit the **Academy Store** in the California Academy of Sciences (see pp150–51), one of the leading science and natural history museums in America. Here aspiring naturalists can buy dinosaur models, realistic rubber animals, and gifts that are environmentally friendly. Merchandise based on the Academy's Far Side Gallery, which displays the work of cartoonist Gary Larsen, is also for sale. Nearby, there is also a fine assortment of items at the **de Young Museum** shop. At Lincoln Park the **Legion of Honor Museum Store**

(see pp156–7) offers many beautiful selections based on current exhibitions.

The **Asian Art Museum** shop in the Civic Center is well stocked with books and objects that reflect the museum's area of interest.

There is a great deal to intrigue young scientists at the unique **Exploratorium Store** (see pp60–61). Here they will find all the equipment they need for scientific experiments, games based on topics ranging from astronomy to zoology, and how-to-do-it books and toys.

In the San Francisco Museum of Modern Art (see pp118–21) the expanded **San Francisco MOMA Museum-Store** sells a wide range of beautifully printed art books, posters, greetings cards and colorful T-shirts.

Gump's (see p116) is so splendid it could almost be mistaken for a museum. Many of the items are American or European antiques, limited editions or one of a kind. Well-heeled residents and visitors come here for furniture, fine art, china, crystal, jewelry and gifts.

DIRECTORY

SPECIALTY SHOPS

Biordi Art Imports
412 Columbus Ave.
Map 5 C3.
Tel 392-8096.

Bulgari
237 Post St.
Map 5 C5.
Tel 399-9141.

Comix Experience
305 Divisadero St.
Map 10 D1.
Tel 863-9258.

Flax Art and Design
1699 Market St.
Map 10 F1.
Tel 552-2355.

Golden Gate Fortune Cookies
56 Ross Alley.
Map 5 C3.
Tel 781-3956.

Jeanine Payer
672 Market St.
Map 5 C5.
Tel 788-2417.

Malm Luggage
222 Grant Ave.
Map 5 B1.
Tel 392-0417.

Smile–A Gallery with Tongue in Chic
500 Sutter St.
Map 5 D4.
Tel 362-3437.

Ten Ren Tea Company of San Francisco
949 Grant Ave.
Map 5 C3.
Tel 362-0656.

Tiffany & Co
350 Post St.
Map 5 C4.
Tel 781-7000.

SHOPS FOR A GOOD CAUSE

Golden Gate National Park Store
Embarcadero Center.
Map 6 D3.
Tel 984-0640.

Planetweavers Treasure Store
1573 Haight St.
Map 9 C1.
Tel 864-4415.

Under One Roof
549 Castro St.
Map 10 D1.
Tel 252-9430.

SOUVENIRS

Boudins Bakery
4 Embarcadero Center.
Map 6 D3.
Tel 362-3330.
One of several branches.

Cable Car Store
Pier 39.
Map 5 B1.
Tel 989-2040.

Krazy Kaps
Pier 39.
Map 5 B1.
Tel 296-8930.

Only in San Francisco
Pier 39.
Map 5 B1.
Tel 397-0122.

ANTIQUES

Decorum
1400 Vallejo St.
Map 5 B3.
Tel 474-6886.

Genji Antiques Inc.
22 Peace Plaza.
Japan Town
Map 4 E4.
Tel 931-1616.

Sacramento Street Antique Dealers Association
3419 Sacramento St.
Map 3 C4.
Tel 567-4094.

TOYS, GAMES, AND GADGETS

Chinatown Kite Shop
717 Grant Ave.
Map 5 C3.
Tel 391-8217.

Gamescape
333 Divisadero St.
Map 10 D1.
Tel 621-4263.

Puppets on the Pier
Pier 39. **Map** 5 B1.
Tel 781-4435.

Sony Style
101 4th St. **Map** 5 C5.
Tel 369-6053.

Toys R Us
2675 Geary Blvd.
Map 3 C5.
Tel 931-8896.

MUSEUM STORES

Academy Store
California Academy of Sciences, 875 Howard St (until 2008). **Map** 6 D5.
Tel 750-7330.

Asian Art Museum
200 Larkin St.
Map 4 F5.
www.asianart.org

de Young Museum
50 Tea Garden Dr, Golden Gate Park. **Map** 8 F2.
Tel 863-3330.

Exploratorium Store
Marina Blvd and Lyon St.
Map 3 C2.
Tel 561-0390.

Gump's
135 Post St. **Map** 5 C4.
Tel 982-1616.

Legion of Honor Museum Store
Legion of Honor, Lincoln Park.
Map 1 B5. **Tel** 750-3600.

San Francisco MOMA MuseumStore
Museum of Modern Art.
Map 6 D5.
Tel 357-4035.

Clothes and Accessories

San Francisco has a reputation for sophistication, which, judging from its clothing shops, is richly deserved. No matter what the occasion requires, from a designer outfit for a formal event to the comfort of a pair of jeans, you will find it in San Francisco.

August Fashion Week runway shows boost reputations of emerging designers from the San Francisco Bay Area, the West Coast, and New York. Unlike the department stores (see p245) that offer a wide selection, most of the shops listed below are small or medium-sized, and often focus on just one or two lines. Take time to see these true gems of the retail world.

SAN FRANCISCO AND OTHER US DESIGNERS

Lines by American designers are sold in boutiques within a department store or in exclusive shops under the designer's name. Retailers such as **Wilkes Bashford** feature up-and-coming designers with a bent for conservative clothing that would be a perfect option for current denizens of the Financial District.

San Francisco designer shops to discover include **Diana Slavin** for classic Italian styles, **Betsey Johnson** for outrageous women's fashions and accessories, and **Joanie Char's** for chic sportswear separates. **Emporio Armani Boutique** has an impressive selection of clothing and accessories, while **Jessica McClintock Boutique** is famous for her wedding gowns. Fashionable knits for women can be purchased at **Weston Wear** at rock-bottom prices.

Designer **Sunhee Moon** names each of her 1950s-influenced clothing items after friends. **MAC** or Modern Appealing Clothing, sources one-third of its menswear as well as womenswear from San Francisco designers.

DISCOUNT DESIGNER CLOTHES AND OUTLETS

For designer clothes at concessional rates, head to the SoMa (South of Market) area. Yerba Buena Square contains several kinds of outlets, including **Burlington Coat Factory**, which stocks more than 12,000 coats. Here you can find discounted lines

from many local designers. **Georgiou Outlet** showcases classic styles made from natural fibers. **Jeremy's** in SoMa's swish South Park area, discounts formal clothing and designerwear for both men and women.

BAY AREA MALL OUTLETS

Plan a drive to the Bay Area mall outlets, for a good bargain or take home major

designer brands at discounted prices. Though about an hour away from San Francisco, given the array of clothes on offer, the visit would certainly be a shoppers' delight.

Find fashion outlets for Liz Claiborne, Off 5th Saks Fifth Avenue, Brooks Brothers, as well as OshKosh and Gap for children's garments, and Bass and Nine West for shoes, at the large **Petaluma Village Premium Outlets**, 74 km (46 miles) north of the city.

Eighty km (50 miles) southeast of San Francisco in Milpitas, **Great Mall** outlets stock some of the best brands. The more popular names include Tommy Hilfiger, Eddie Bauer, Polo Jeans Factory Store, St. John Knits, and Chico's casual women's styles.

CASTRO DISTRICT

Clothing and accessories accent the dominant gay, lesbian, and transgendered lifestyles in this

---

SIZE CHART

For Australian sizes follow the British conversion.

Children's clothing

American	2–3	4–5	6–6x	7–8	10	12	14	16 (size)
British	2–3	4–5	6–7	8–9	10–11	12	14	14+ (years)
Continental	2–3	4–5	6–7	8–9	10–11	12	14	14+ (years)

Children's shoes

American	8½	9½	10½	11½	12½	13	1½	2½	2½
British	7	8	9	10	11	12	13	1	2
Continental	24	25½	27	28	29	30	32	33	34

Women's dresses coats and skirts

American	4	6	8	10	12	14	16	18
British	6	8	10	12	14	16	18	20
Continental	38	40	42	44	46	48	50	52

Women's blouses and sweaters

American	6	8	10	12	14	16	18
British	30	32	34	36	38	40	42
Continental	40	42	44	46	48	50	52

Women's shoes

American	5	6	7	8	9	10	11
British	3	4	5	6	7	8	9
Continental	36	37	38	39	40	41	44

Men's suits

American	34	36	38	40	42	44	46	48
British	34	36	38	40	42	44	46	48
Continental	44	46	48	50	52	54	56	58

Men's shirts

American	14	15	15½	16	16½	17	17½	18
British	14	15	15½	16	16½	17	17½	18
Continental	36	38	39	41	42	43	44	45

Men's shoes

American	7	7½	8	8½	9½	10½	11	11½
British	6	7	7½	8	9	10	11	12
Continental	39	40	41	42	43	44	45	46

neighborhood; shopping is amusing as well as intriguing. If a garment's function or how to wear it is unclear, don't hesitate to ask, Store names, like **InJeanious**, can be as clever as they are well stocked.

CHESTNUT STREET

Beautiful clothing carefully tweaked to suit a woman's lifestyle can be found at boutique **Rabat**, on this Marina District shopping street. Their shoes are stylish and comfortable and their handbags, well-designed and fashionable.

FILLMORE

Fillmore Street's Victorian buildings, and the creation of the Jazz Preservation District, lend hip history and ambience to this strolling strip. **Mrs. Dewson's Hats** gained fame as former mayor, Willie Brown's hatmaker.

HAIGHT-ASHBURY

Wandering along Haight Street, it is easy to spot tie-dye T-shirts and vintage clothing stores. **Piedmont Boutique's** landmark giantess legs adorned with fishnet stockings, mark one store where clothing patterns are still cut by hand.

HAYES VALLEY

Chain stores and big brands are opposed to in the vicinity of Hayes Valley. **Manifesto**'s name and independent attitude reflect the neighborhood's preference for hands-on design, such as the men's and women's clothing designed by the boutique's owners.

SOUTH OF MARKET

The SoMa area, once full of warehouses and flophouses, now has swanky studios and lofts aplenty. It still possesses a gritty, no-nonsense quality

that appeals to the younger set who patronize clubs that seem to blossom from nowhere at night. **Isda & Co** reflects its designer's preference for spare, and simple unisex clothing.

UNION SQUARE

European designers and importers have boutique out-posts around Union Square to provide San Franciscans with classic styles and designer label clothing. **David Stephen** purveys hand-made Italian men's shirts on the upscale Maiden Lane right across Union Square.

UNION STREET

It is a short walk from the nearby apartments and man-sions to this cheerful street of small boutiques. **Mimi's on Union** touts wearable art like hand-painted kimonos, scarves and jackets.

DIRECTORY

SAN FRANCISCO AND OTHER US DESIGNERS

Betsey Johnson
2031 Fillmore St.
Map 4 D4.
Tel 567-2726.

Diana Slavin
3 Claude Lane.
Map 5 C4.
Tel 677-9939.

Emporio Armani Boutique
1 Grant Ave.
Map 5 C5.
Tel 677-9400.

Jessica McClintock Boutique
180 Geary St.
Map 5 C5.
Tel 398-9008.

Joanie Char
527 Sutter St.
Map 5 B4.
Tel 399-9867.

MAC
387 Grove St.
Map 4 F5.
Tel 863-3011.

Sunhee Moon
3167 16th St.
Map 10 E2.
Tel 355-1800.

Weston Wear
584 Valencia St.
Map 10 F2.
Tel 621-1480.

Wilkes Bashford
375 Sutter St.
Map 5 C4.
Tel 986-4380.

DISCOUNT DESIGNER CLOTHES AND OUTLETS

Burlington Coat Factory
899 Howard St.
Map 11 B2.
Tel 495-7234.

Georgiou Outlet
925 Bryant St.
Map 11 B2.
Tel 554-0150.

Jeremy's
2 South Park St.
Map 11 C1.
Tel 882-4929.

BAY AREA MALL OUTLETS

Great Mall
447 Great Mall Dr.
Milpitas.
Tel 408-945-4022.

Petaluma Village Premium Outlets
2220 Petaluma Blvd.
North Petaluma
Tel 707-778-9300.

CASTRO DISTRICT

InJeanious
432 Castro St.
Map 10 D3.
Tel 864-1863.

CHESTNUT STREET

Rabat
2331 Chestnut St.
Map 3 C2. **Tel** 929-8868.

FILLMORE

Mrs Dewson's Hats
2050 Fillmore St.
Map 4 D4.
Tel 346-1600.

HAIGHT-ASHBURY

Piedmont Boutique
1452 Haight St.
Map 9 C1.
Tel 864-8075.

HAYES VALLEY

Manifesto
514 Octavia St.
Map 4 E5.
Tel 431-4778.

SOUTH OF MARKET

Isda & Co
19 South Park St.
Map 11 C1.
Tel 344-4891.

UNION SQUARE

David Stephen
50 Maiden Lane.
Map 5 C4.
Tel 982-1611.

UNION STREET

Mimi's on Union
2133 Union St.
Map 4 D3.
Tel 923-0454.

MEN'S CLOTHES

For men's designer brands, sportswear, shoes, and accessories with a European influence, try **Rolo**. **Brooks Brothers** was the first retailer of readymade clothes for men in the United States. They are now known for their smart suits and button-down shirts.

Rugged and fashionable outdoor clothing is available from **Eddie Bauer**. **The Gap** and **Old Navy** combine casual hipness with affordable prices. Men requiring larger sizes can buy travelwear and sweaters, and be fitted for both formal and business suits, at **Rochester Big and Tall**. **Body**, on Castro Street, is a mecca for form-fitting T-shirts, tops, under-wear, shoes, and more.

WOMEN'S CLOTHES

Many of the world's famous names in fashion are in San Francisco, including **Chanel** and **Gucci**. **Gianni Versace** is in the Crocker Galleria. **Prada** is famous for its extra-fine merino wool and cashmere clothes. **Jorja** stocks various designers and specializes in Nicole Miller. **Banana Republic** and **Guess** are well known for stylish, wearable clothes.

Hand-made sweaters from **Three Bags Full** have one-of-a-kind patterns and glorious colors. **Loehmann's** sells designer clothing from New York and Europe at a discount. **Ann Taylor** has well-made suits, blouses, evening dresses and sweaters. **Bebe** is for the chic and slim. **Harper Greer** puts sizes 12–26 in the height of sleek-line fashion. **Urban Outfitters** has chic second-hand and new clothes, and **American Rag** has stylish new and used European and American clothing.

CHILDREN'S CLOTHES

Colorful collections of cotton clothing, including tie-dyed and ethnic styles, as well as a large selection of hats, are on display at **Kids Only**. **Small Frys** is a local favorite for cotton attire. **Gap Kids** and **Baby Gap** are good on selection, size and color.

SHOES

Top-quality footwear is available at **Kenneth Cole**. Best names in comfort are at **Ria's**, including Clarks, Birkenstock, Timberland, Sebago and Rockport. **Nike Town** is a megastore for sneakers, and **DSW Shoe Warehouse** offers an enormous range of discounted shoes.

Shoe Biz II, one of three Shoe Biz stores on Haight Street, is easy to spot with its dinosaur mascot figure outside. The music and comfortable chairs in the store are an easy way to slide in and out of a large sneaker selection. **Shoe Biz I** has fashion-aware, value priced everyday shoes; and, **Super Shoe Biz** caters to more upscale fashionistas.

Foot Worship stocks women's sizes from 5–14, personally assisting a clientele that enjoys a precarious stiletto heel.

LINGERIE

San Francisco's playful side gets indulged, too. **Alla Prima Fine Lingerie** fits the finest European brand name underwear, silky gowns and camisoles. **Victoria's Secret** has San Francisco outposts, including Union Square. America's first topless dancer designs and sells at her store, **Carol Doda's Champagne & Lace Lingerie.**

LEATHER CLOTHING

In San Francisco, leatherwear is an antidote to fog effects as well as a lifestyle declaration. **Fog City Leather** custom-makes alligator jackets and purveys head-to-pants leather clothing. **Image Leather**, in the Castro District, carries a wide selection of motorcycle jackets and chaps. **A Taste of Leather**, in SoMa, is the place for men to get kitted out, from kilts and vest to briefs and thongs.

OUTDOOR OUTFITTERS

There is a lot of accessible outdoor space around the city and Northern California, with active adult clothing, gear, and equipment stores to provide for adventuring whims. **REI** bargain prices on the first Saturday-of-the-month and seasonal sales are a good bet for skiing, snowboarding, cycling, paddling and comfortable travelwear.

The **North Face** started in North Beach in 1966 and provides outerwear designed for sub-freezing temperatures. **Patagonia**'s mountain climbing roots developed organic cotton, and moisture and heat resistant clothing for activities ranging from climbing, surfing, running and mountain biking, to yoga.

SPORTSWEAR

Devoted baseball fans shop for logo caps to pants at **SF Giants Dugout** stores. A wide display of authorized NFL, and NBA team sweatshirts and sweatpants are available at the **NFL Shop** at Pier 39. San Francisco 49er jerseys and varsity jackets are popular buys at **Champs**.

Independent **Lombardi Sports** stocks lacrosse to lifestyle sportswear.

The **Adidas Store** has a great variety of classic shoes, sporty apparel, and genuine athletic wear for men and women. Specialty sportswear and gear shops include **Don Sherwood Golf & Tennis World** that meets or beats competitors' prices, and **KinderSport** that offers children's ski outwear all the year round.

For anyone shopping for name-embossed San Francisco T-shirts, hoodies, or sleepwear, **I Heart SF** at Fisherman's Wharf has one of the widest selection.

VINTAGE CLOTHING

Buffalo Exchange and **Crossroads Trading** offer secondhand clothing with something of a history. **Wasteland** in the Haight-Ashbury District is known for its vintage clothes. **Guys and Dolls Vintage** outfits flappers to swing dancers in hip styles, while **Clothes Contact** sells vintage clothes by the pound.

DIRECTORY

MEN'S CLOTHES

Body
450 Castro St.
Map 10 D3.
Tel 575-3562.

Brooks Brothers
150 Post St.
Map 5 C4.
Tel 397-4500.

Eddie Bauer
3521 20th Ave.
Map S. of 8 E5.
Tel 664-9262.

The Gap
100 Post St.
Map 5 C4.
Tel 421-2314.
Also: 890 Market St.
Map 5 C5.
Tel 788-5909.

Old Navy
801 Market St.
Map 5 C5.
Tel 344-0375.

Rochester Big and Tall
700 Mission St.
Map 5 C5.
Tel 982-6455.

Rolo
2351 Market St.
Map 10 D2.
Tel 431-4545.

WOMEN'S CLOTHES

American Rag
1305 Van Ness Ave.
Map 5 A5.
Tel 474-5214.

Ann Taylor
240 Post St.
Map 5 C4.
Tel 788-0716.

Banana Republic
256 Grant Ave.
Map 5 C4.
Tel 777-3087.

Bebe
San Francisco Centre.
Map 5 C5.
Tel 543-2323.

Chanel
155 Maiden Lane.
Map 5 C4.
Tel 981-1550.

Gianni Versace
60 Post St.
Map 5 C4
Tel 616-0604.

Gucci
200 Stockton St.
Map 5 C5.
Tel 392-2808.

Guess
90 Grant Ave.
Map 5 C5.
Tel 781-1589.

Harper Greer
580 4th St.
Map 11 C1.
Tel 543-4066.

Jorja
2015 Chestnut St.
Map 4 D2.
Tel 674-1131.

Loehmann's
222 Sutter St.
Map 5 C4.
Tel 982-3215.

Prada
140 Geary St.
Map 5 C5.
Tel 391-8844.

Three Bags Full
2181 Union St.
Map 4 D3.
Tel 567-5753.

Urban Outfitters
80 Powell St.
Map 5 B5.
Tel 989-1515.

CHILDREN'S CLOTHES

Gap Kids/Baby Gap
100 Post St.
Map 5 C4.
Tel 421-4906.

Kids Only
1608 Haight St.
Map 9 B1.
Tel 552-5445.

Small Frys
4066 24th St.
Map 10 D4.
Tel 648-3954.

SHOES

DSW Shoe Warehouse
111 Powell St.
Map 5 B5.
Tel 445-9511.

Foot Worship
1214 Sutter St.
Map 5 A5. *Tel 921-3668.*

Kenneth Cole
865 Market St.
Map 5 C5.
Tel 227-4536.

Nike Town
278 Post St. **Map** 5 C4.
Tel 392-6453.

Ria's
301 Grant Ave. **Map** 5 C4.
Tel 834-1420.

Shoe Biz I
1446 Haight St. **Map** 9 C1.
Tel 864-0990.

Shoe Biz II
1553 Haight St. **Map** 9 C1.
Tel 861-3933.

Super Shoe Biz
1420 Haight St.
Map 9 C1.
Tel 861-0313.

LINGERIE

Alla Prima Fine Lingerie
1420 Grant Ave.
Map 5 C2.
Tel 397-4077.

Carol Doda's Champagne & Lace Lingerie
1850 Union St.
Map 4 E2.
Tel 776-6900.

Victoria's Secret
335 Powell St.
Map 5 B5.
Tel 433-9671.

LEATHER CLOTHING

A Taste of Leather
1285 Folsom St.
Map 11 A2.
Tel 252-9166.

Fog City Leather
2060 Union St.
Map 4 D2.
Tel 567-1996.

Image Leather
2199 Market St.
Map 10 E2.
Tel 621-7551.

OUTDOOR OUTFITTERS

North Face
180 Post St.
Map 5 C4.
Tel 433-3223.

Patagonia
770 North Point St.
Map 5 A2.
Tel 771-2050.

REI
840 Brannan St.
Map 11 B2. *Tel 934-1938.*

SPORTSWEAR

Adidas Store
865 Market St, Suite 211.
Map 5 C5. *Tel 975-0934.*

Champs
San Francisco Centre.
Map 5 C5. *Tel 975-0883.*

Don Sherwood Golf & Tennis World
320 Grant Ave.
Map 5 C4. *Tel 989-5000.*

I Heart SF
2545 Powell St.
Map 5 B1. *Tel 392-2001.*

KinderSport
3655 Sacramento St.
Map 3 B4. *Tel 563-7778.*

Lombardi Sports
1600 Jackson St.
Map 4 F3. *Tel 771-0600.*

NFL Shop
Pier 39.
Map 5 B1. *Tel 397-2027.*

SF Giants Dugout
SBC Park.
Map 11 C1.
Tel 972-2453.

VINTAGE CLOTHING

Buffalo Exchange
1555 Haight St.
Map 9 C1. *Tel 431-7733.*
1210 Valencia St.
Map 10 F4.
Tel 647-8332.

Clothes Contact
473 Valencia St.
Map 10 F2.
Tel 621-3212.

Crossroads Trading
1901 Fillmore.
Map 4 D4.
Tel 771-8885.
2123 Market St.
Map 10 E2.
Tel 552-8740.

Guys and Dolls Vintage
3789 24th St.
Map 10 E4.
Tel 285-7174.

Wasteland
1660 Haight St
Map 9 B1.
Tel 863-3150.

Books, Music, Art and Antiques

Hundreds of shops cater to the many writers, artists and collectors living in and visiting San Francisco. Residents decorate their houses with items from local art and antiques galleries. Visitors who love shopping for fine and unusual objects – from that rare one-of-a-kind piece to distinctive contemporary ethnic arts – are sure to find a treasure in one of San Francisco's shops.

GENERAL INTEREST BOOKSTORES

Limelight Books is the West Coast's longest surviving resource for stageplays, screenplays, and books on writing and directing. Beats once gathered to talk about America's emerging 1960s social revolution at the **City Lights Bookstore** (see p88), a famous San Francisco institution. It stays open till late, making it a favorite hangout for students. **Green Apple Books** has new and used books, and is open until 10:30pm, or 11:30pm on Fridays and Saturdays. **Borders Books & Music** has just about everything, while **The Booksmith**, located in Haight Ashbury, is notable for its stock of foreign and political periodicals. **Cover to Cover** is a neighborhood bookshop with an excellent children's section and friendly staff, and both **Stacy's of San Francisco** and **Alexander Books** have good selections of children's and general interest books.

SPECIALTY BOOKSTORES

Books with an African-American perspective are available at **Marcus Books**. **The Complete Traveler** and **Rand McNally Map & Travel Store** stock a good selection of local and world-wide travel guides and maps. **Get Lost Travel Books, Maps & Gear** also has a very wide range of travel literature and maps.

RECORDS, TAPES AND COMPACT DISCS

A wide selection of music is available at branches of **Virgin**, which stocks all the platters that could ever matter, from Prince to Prokofiev and Blondie to Big Joe Turner. **Streetlight Records** offers a varied selection of new and used music as well as bargain DVDs, videos, and laser discs. Obscure sounds are available at **Recycled Records** on Haight Street, where new and used recordings are bought, sold and traded as eagerly as stocks in the financial district. **Open Mind Music** has friendly and knowledgeable staff, who sell a wide variety of old and new recordings and other music-related items. **Amoeba Music** has the largest selection of CDs and tapes in the country. It has 500,000 titles, both new and secondhand, including jazz, international blues and rock music. A music collector's paradise, this is *the* place to go if you are looking for hard-to-find music at low prices.

SHEET MUSIC

For the largest selection of classical music pay a visit to **Byron Hoyt Sheet Music Service**. All types of music and books of collections can be found at the **Music Center of San Francisco**.

ART GALLERIES

New enthusiasts as well as serious art lovers will find something to their liking in the hundreds of galleries. The **John Berggruen Gallery** (see p38) has the biggest collection in San Francisco of works by both emerging and well-established artists. **The Simmon's Gallery** sells limited edition graphics by such modern masters as Picasso, Matisse, and Miró. The **Fraenkel Gallery** is known for its collection of 19th- and 20th-century photography. The **Haines Gallery** in the same building stocks paintings, drawings, sculpture, and photography. **Compositions Gallery** is the place for glass art and works in wood. New works and those of American artists are hung at **Gallery Paule Anglim**. Realism is the theme at the **John Pence Gallery**. **Kertesz International Fine Art** has 19th- and 20th-century European oils.

For affordable art by local Bay Area artists, visit **Hang** gallery. At **Vista Point Studios Gallery** there are amazing photos of the Bay Area and beyond.

ETHNIC AND AMERICAN FOLK ART

Good collections of ethnic art are at several galleries. **Folk Art International, Xanadu, & Boretti** in the renovated Frank Lloyd Building has masks, textiles, sculptures and jewelry. Exhibitions at the **Albers Gallery of Inuit Art** express the culture and traditions of the Inuit tribe. Find beautiful handmade African masks, jewelry and textiles at **African Outlet**. Pottery and masks from Japan are hard to resist at **Ma-Shi'-Ko Folk Craft**. Traditional and contemporary works by local artists can be found at **Galaria de la Raza**.

INTERNATIONAL ANTIQUES

San Francisco's Barbary Coast area (see pp26–7) has been transformed into a shopping district for antiques, and is now called **Jackson Square** (see p110). Another collection of antique shops can be found at **Baker Hamilton Square**.

Ed Hardy San Francisco offers both English and French antiques and **Lang Antiques** has all kinds of items from the Victorian, Art Nouveau, Art Deco and Edwardian periods. **Dragon House** sells both Oriental antiques and pieces of fine art, while all sorts of antique books, prints and maps can be seen at **Prints Old & Rare** – although you will need to make an appointment.

DIRECTORY

GENERAL INTEREST BOOKSHOPS

Alexander Books
50 Second St.
Map 6 D4.
Tel 495-2992.

Borders
400 Post St.
Map 5 B4.
Tel 399-1633.

The Booksmith
1644 Haight St.
Map 9 B1.
Tel 863-8688.

City Lights Bookstore
261 Columbus Ave.
Map 5 C3.
Tel 362-8193.

Cover to Cover
3812 24th St.
Map 10 E4.
Tel 282-8080.

Green Apple Books
506 Clement St.
Map 3 A5.
Tel 387-2272.

Limelight Books
1803 Market St.
Map 10 E1.
Tel 864-2265.

Stacy's of San Francisco
581 Market St.
Map 5 C4.
Tel 421-4687.

SPECIALTY BOOKSHOPS

The Complete Traveler
3207 Fillmore St.
Map 4 D2.
Tel 923-1511.

Get Lost Travel Books, Maps & Gear
1825 Market St.
Map 10 E1.
Tel 437-0529.

Marcus Books
1712 Fillmore St.
Map 4 D4.
Tel 346-4222.

Rand McNally Map & Travel Store
595 Market St.
Map 5 C4.
Tel 777-3131.

RECORDS, TAPES AND COMPACT DISCS

Amoeba Music
1855 Haight St.
Map 9 B1.
Tel 831-1200.

Open Mind Music
342 Divisadero St.
Map 10 D1.
Tel 621-2244.

Recycled Records
1377 Haight St.
Map 9 C1.
Tel 626-4075.

Streetlight Records
2350 Market St.
Map 10 D2.
Tel 282-8000.

Virgin Megastore
Stockton St and Market St.
Map 5 C5.
Tel 397-4525.
One of several branches.

SHEET MUSIC

Byron Hoyt Sheet Music Service
360 Florida St.
Map 11 A3.
Tel 431-8055.

Music Center of San Francisco
207 Powell St.
Map 5 B1.
Tel 781-6023.

ART GALLERIES

Compositions Gallery
317 Sutter St.
Map 5 C4.
Tel 885-0402.

Fraenkel Gallery
49 Geary St.
Map 5 C5.
Tel 981-2661.

Gallery Paule Anglim
14 Geary St.
Map 5 C5.
Tel 433-2710.

Haines Gallery
5th Floor, 49 Geary St.
Map 5 C5.
Tel 397-8114.

Hang
556 Sutter St.
Map 3 C4.
Tel 434-4264.

John Berggruen Gallery
228 Grant Ave.
Map 5 C4.
Tel 781-4629.

John Pence Gallery
750 Post St.
Map 5 B5.
Tel 441-1138.

Kertesz International Fine Art
535 Sutter St.
Map 5 B4.
Tel 626-0376.

The Simmon's Gallery
565 Sutter St.
Map 5 B4.
Tel 986-2244.

Vista Point Studios Gallery
405 Florida St.
Map 11 A3.
Tel 215-9073.

ETHNIC AND AMERICAN FOLK ART

African Outlet
524 Octavia St.
Map 4 E5.
Tel 864-3576.

Albers Gallery of Inuit Art
760 Market St
Map 5 C5.
Tel 391-2111.

Folk Art International, Xanadu, & Boretti
Frank Lloyd Wright Bldg,
140 Maiden Lane.
Map 5 B5.
Tel 392-9999.

Galeria de la Raza
Studio 24, 2857 24th St.
Map 10 F4.
Tel 826-8009.

Images of the North
2036 Union St.
Map 4 E2.
Tel 673-1273.

Instinctiv Designs
3529 Mission St.
Tel 647-2131.

Japonesque
824 Montgomery St.
Map 5 C3.
Tel 391-8860.

Ma-Shi'-Ko Folk Craft
1581 Webster St,
Japan Center. **Map** 4 E4.
Tel 346-0748.

INTERNATIONAL ANTIQUES

Dragon House
455 Grant Ave.
Map 6 C4.
Tel 421-3693.

Ed Hardy San Francisco
188 Henry Adams St.
Map 10 D2.
Tel 626-6300.

Jackson Square Art & Antique Dealers Association
463 Jackson St (at Jackson Square.) **Map** 5 C3.
Tel 397-6999.

Lang Antiques
323 Sutter St.
Map 5 C4.
Tel 982-2213.

Prints Old & Rare
580 Mount Crespi Drive,
Pacifica, California.
Tel (650) 355-6325.

Food and Household Goods

San Francisco's "foodies"are a sophisticated breed, and they thrive on the city's reputation for fine food. When not dining out, they cook at home from well-stocked pantries in their ultra-equipped kitchens. Cravings for good wine, gourmet groceries and for the items that make cooking into an art form can easily be satisfied here. For the home, there are dozens of stores carrying the latest household goods, computers, and photographic and electronic equipment.

GOURMET GROCERIES

From abalone to zucchini (courgettes), and from fresh Californian produce to imported specialty foods, gourmet grocers such as **Whole Foods** carry a variety of items. **Williams-Sonoma** has jams, mustards and much more for gifts or as a special treat. **David's** is known for its lox (smoked salmon), bagels and New York cheesecake. For a quick takeout lunch or a choice of beautifully packaged foods, try one of the department store food sections such as **Macy's Cellar**. Most large chain grocery stores have good international sections.

In addition to fresh takeout items, Italian delicatessens stock olive oil, polenta and pasta from Italy. **Molinari Delicatessen** is famous for its ravioli and tortellini, ready to throw in the saucepan. **Lucca Ravioli** has a friendly staff, who makes their pasta on the premises. **Pasta Gina**, in lovely Noe Valley, sells pasta, prepared pesto and other sauces with ample meatballs.

It is worth going to the two Chinese quarters – Chinatown *(see pp94–99)* in the city center and Clement Street *(see p63)* – for Asian food products and produce. At **Casa Lucas Market** you will find Spanish and Latin American specialties.

SPECIALTY FOOD AND WINE SHOPS

Abaguette of fresh sourdough bread from **Boudins Bakery** is an addiction with locals and a tradition with visitors. **Boulangerie** brings Paris to San Francisco, with some of the best bread in the city. More Italian specialties come from **Il Fornaio** Bakery, a popular offshoot from their restaurant *(see p230)*. **La Nouvelle Patisserie** sells tasty and colorful desserts. Meat and fruit pies from **Bepple's Pie Shop** are delicious.

San Franciscans are coffee connoisseurs, and there are many specialty shops. **Caffè Trieste** sells custom-roasted and blended coffees and a variety of brewing equipment. **Caffè Roma Coffee Roasting Company** and the **Graffeo Coffee Roasting Company** both sell excellent beans. The locals are also loyal to **Peet's Coffee & Tea**, and **Tully's Coffee** company.

Chocoholics usually frequent **See's Candies, Confetti Le Chocolatier** and San Francisco's own **Ghirardelli**. Truffles beyond compare are created at **Joseph Schmidts**. Ice cream is good from **Ben & Jerry's** and **Hot Cookie Double Rainbow**. Head for **Bombay Bazzaar** for imported Indian spices.

The staff at the **California Wine Merchant** makes good recommendations and are very knowledgeable about their affordable wines. **Napa Valley Winery Exchange** features selections from California wineries, including smaller local producers.

FARMERS' MARKETS AND FLEA MARKETS

Locally grown produce arrives by the truckload at farmers' markets in the center of the city. Stalls are erected for the day, and farmers sell directly to the public. The **Heart of the City** is open from 7am to 5:30pm on Wednesdays and until 5pm on Sundays. The **Ferry Plaza** on Saturdays is from 9am to 2pm. Chinatown's produce stores have the feel of an exotic farmers' market and are open every day. All kinds of things are sold at the flea markets. The one in **Berkeley** is within easy reach. Be prepared to barter and to pay in cash. There may also be a nominal entrance fee.

HOUSEHOLD GOODS

Gourmet cooks dream of **Williams-Sonoma's** many kitchen gadgets and quality cookware. From practical pots and pans to beautiful serving plates, **Crate & Barrel** sells moderately priced items for your kitchen and patio. Chinese cooking gear is the specialty of the house at **The Wok Shop**. For bed, bath and table linens and general household goods visit **Bed, Bath & Beyond. Sue Fisher King** sells elegant, fashionable items for the home and bath. For a kaleidoscopic range of fabrics and accessories, from silks, woolens and cottons, to buttons, ribbons and laces, and even upholstery materials, look no farther than **Britex Fabrics**.

COMPUTERS, ELECTRONICS, AND PHOTOGRAPHIC EQUIPMENT

One of the best places to go for computers is **Central Computers**. For software and anything else electronic, try **Best Buy**. It's "one-stop shopping for the nerd population." **Video Only** competes with reasonably priced guarantees and a wide selection of equipment.

For new and second-hand camera gear, repairs and film, go to **Adolph Gasser** or **Brooks Camera**. Some of the discount camera shops along Market Street have shady reputations, so it is advisable to check with the Visitor Information Center *(see p117)* for the best and most reputable places to shop. If you just need film or other photographic supplies, **Photographer's Supply** offers very low prices along with good advice.

DIRECTORY

GOURMET GROCERIES

Casa Lucas Market
2934 24th St.
Map 9 C3.
Tel 826-4334.

David's
474 Geary St.
Map 5 A5.
Tel 276-5950.

Lucca Ravioli
1100 Valencia St.
Map 10 F3.
Tel 647-5581.

Macy's Cellar
Stockton St and
O'Farrell St.
Map 5 C1.
Tel 296-4436.

Molinari Delicatessen
373 Columbus Ave.
Map 5 C3.
Tel 421-2337.

Pasta Gina
741 Diamond St.
Map 10 D4.
Tel 282-0738.

Whole Foods
1765 California St.
Map 4 F4.
Tel 674-0500.

Williams-Sonoma
340 Post St. Map 5 C4.
Tel 362-9450. www.
williams-sonoma.com
One of several branches.

SPECIALTY FOOD AND WINE SHOPS

Ben & Jerry's Ice Cream
1480 Haight St. Map
9 C1. Tel 626-4143.
www.ben&jerrys.com

Bombay Bazaar
548 Valencia St.
Map 10 F2.
Tel 621-1717.

Boudins Bakery
4 Embarcadero Center.
Map 6 D3.
Tel 362-3330.
One of many branches.

Boulangerie
2325 Pine St. Map 4 D4.
Tel 440-0356.

Caffè Roma Coffee Roasting Company
526 Columbus Ave.
Map 5 B2.
Tel 296-7942.

Caffè Trieste
601 Vallejo St. Map 5 C3.
Tel 982-2605.

California Wine Merchant
3237 Pierce St.
Map 4 D2.
Tel 567-0646.

Confetti Le Chocolatier
525 Market St.
Map 5 D3.
Tel 543-2885.

Ghirardelli's
Ghirardelli Square.
Map 4 F1.
Tel 474-3938.

44 Stockton St.
Map 5 C1.
Tel 397-3030.

Graffeo Coffee Roasting Company
735 Columbus Ave.
Map 5 B2.
Tel 986-2420.

Hot Cookie Double Rainbow
407 Castro St.
Map 10 D2.
Tel 621-2350.
One of several branches.

Il Fornaio Bakery
1265 Battery St.
Map 5 C2.
Tel 986-0646.

Joseph Schmidt
3489 16th St.
Map 10 E2.
Tel 861-8682.

La Nouvelle Patisserie
2184 Union St.
Map 4 D2.
Tel 931-7655.

Napa Valley Winery Exchange
415 Taylor St. Map 5 B5.
Tel 771-2887. www.
napavalleywineryex.com

Peasant Pies
4108 24th St.
Map 10 D4.
Tel 642-1316.

Peet's Coffee & Tea
2156 Chestnut St.
Map 4 D2.
Tel 931-8302.
One of several branches.

See's Candies
3 Embarcadero Center.
Map 6 D3.
Tel 391-1622.
One of several branches.

Tango Gelato
2015 Fillmore St.
Map 4 D4.
Tel 346-3692.

The Stinking Rose
325 Columbus Ave.
Map 5 C3.
Tel 781-7673. www.
thestinkingrose.com

Tully's Coffee
2 Embarcadero Center.
Map 6 D3.
Tel 391-9447.
One of several branches.

FARMERS' MARKETS AND FLEA MARKETS

Berkeley Flea Market
1837 Ashby Ave,
Berkeley, CA 94703.
Tel (510) 644-0744.

Ferry Plaza Farmers' Market
Base of Market at the
Embarcadero. Map 6 D3.
Tel 291-3276. www.ferry
plazafarmersmarket.com

Heart of the City Farmers' Market
United Nations Plaza.
Map 11 A1.
Tel 558-9455.

HOUSEHOLD GOODS

Bed, Bath & Beyond
555 9th St.
Map 11 A4.
Tel 252-0490.

Britex Fabrics
146 Geary St.
Map 5 C5.
Tel 392-2910.

Crate & Barrel
55 Stockton St. Map 5 C5.
Tel 982-5200.
www.crateandbarrel.com

Sue Fisher King
3067 Sacramento St.
Map 3 C4.
Tel 922-7276.

The Wok Shop
718 Grant Ave.
Map 5 C4.
Tel 989-3797.

Williams-Sonoma
340 Post St.
Map 5 C4.
Tel 362-9450. www.
williams-sonoma.com
One of several branches.

COMPUTERS, ELECTRONICS & PHOTOGRAPHIC EQUIPMENT

Adolph Gasser, Inc
181 Second St.
Map 6 D5.
Tel 495-3852.

Best Buy
1717 Harrison St.
Map 11 A3.
Tel 626-9682.

Brooks Camera
125 Kearny St.
Map 5 C4.
Tel 362-4708.

Central Computers
837 Howard St.
Map 5 C5.
Tel 495-5888.

Photographer's Supply
436 Bryant St.
Map 11 C1.
Tel 495-8640.

Video Only
1199 Van Ness Ave.
Map 4 F4.
Tel 563-5200.
One of several branches.

ENTERTAINMENT IN SAN FRANCISCO

San Francisco has prided itself on being the cultural capital of the West Coast since the city first began to prosper in the 1850s, and here entertainment is generally of high quality. The performing arts complex of the Civic Center is the major location for the best classical music, opera and ballet. The latest addition to the cultural life here is the excellent Center for the Arts Theater at Yerba Buena Gardens. International touring shows can be seen here. Numerous repertory

Beach Blanket Babylon
(see p263)

movie theaters *(see pp262–3)*, offer filmgoers a wide range of choices, but theater, except for some independent productions is not the city's strongest suit. Popular music, especially jazz and blues, is where San Francisco excels, and you can hear good bands in intimate locales for the price of a drink, or at the street fairs and music festivals held during the summer months *(see pp48–51)*.
Facilities are also available around the city for all kinds of sports, from bicycling to golf or sailing.

INFORMATION

Complete listings of what's on and where are given in the *San Francisco Chronicle* and *Examiner* newspapers *(see p281)*. The Chronicle's Sunday edition is most useful, with a "Datebook" section (also called the "Pink Pages") that gives details of hundreds of events taking place each week. Other good sources are the free weekly newspapers, like the *San Francisco Bay Guardian* or the *San Francisco Weekly* (available at newsstands, kiosks, cafés and bars). These give both listings and reviews, especially of live music, films and nightclubs.

Visitors planning further in advance will find the *San Francisco Book* very helpful. This is published twice yearly by the San Francisco Convention and Visitors Bureau, and contains listings of both short and long-running cultural events. The book is available free if you go to the Visitors Information Center at Hallidie Plaza. You can also phone the bureau's events line for recorded information. Numerous free magazines for visitors are available, as

Banner for the Jazz Festival *(see p266)*

well as calendars of events. Among these are *Key This Week San Francisco* and *Where San Francisco*.

BUYING TICKETS

The main source for tickets to concerts, theater and sports events is **Ticketmaster.** This company has a virtual monopoly on ticket sales, running an extensive charge-by-phone operation in Tower Record shops all over northern California. They ask for a "convenience charge" of around $7 per ticket. The only alternative to Ticketmaster is to buy directly from the box offices, though many of these are open only just before the start of evening performances.

Many productions by the San Francisco Symphony and ballet and opera companies

Outdoor chess, popular in Portsmouth Plaza, Chinatown

are sold out in advance. So if you want to see one of these performances, advance planning is essential. All have subscription programs through which you can buy tickets for the season, useful if you are planning to stay in the city for a lengthy period of time.

There are only a few ticket agencies in San Francisco, mostly specializing in selling hard-to-get seats at marked-up prices. All are listed in the Yellow Pages of the telephone directory. "Scalpers," or ticket hawkers, can be found lurking outside most sold-out events, offering seats at extortionate prices. If you are willing to bargain (and miss the opening), you can sometimes get a good deal.

Shop front of San Francisco ticket agency

Playing the blues at the
Blues Festival *(see p267)*

DISCOUNT TICKETS

Discount tickets for selected
theater, dance and music
events are available from **TIX
Bay Area**, which offers half-
price seats from a booth on
the east side of Union Square.
Tickets are sold from 11am on
the day of the performance,
and can be purchased with
cash or travelers' checks.
There are also some half-price
tickets available on weekends
for events taking place on the
following Sunday and Monday.

TIX Bay Area is also a full-
service ticket outlet, and will
accept credit cards for advance
sales. It is open Tuesday to
Thursday 11am to 6pm, Friday
and Saturday 11am to 7pm,
and Sunday 11am to 3pm.

FREE EVENTS

In addition to San Francisco's
many ticket-only events, a
number of free concerts and
performances are staged all
over the city. Most of these
take place during the day. The
San Francisco Symphony gives
a late summer series of Sunday
concerts at Stern Grove, south
of the Sunset District, and is
occasionally used for ballets.

Cobbs Comedy Club,
Fisherman's Wharf, hosts the
San Francisco International
Comedy Competition for four
weeks in August/September.
Over 300 entertainers join in.

Performers from the San
Francisco Opera sing outdoors
in the Financial District, as part
of the "Brown Bag Operas"
series. They can also be heard
in Golden Gate Park in "Opera
in the Park" events. In the
summer the park is host to the
Shakespeare Festival, Comedy
Celebration Day and the San
Francisco Mime Troupe. A
series of concerts called "Music
in the Park" is held on summer Fridays at noon, behind
the Transamerica Pyramid *(see
p111)*, and at Old St. Mary's
Church *(see p98)* there are
sometimes lunchtime recitals
at 12:30pm during the week

FACILITIES FOR THE DISABLED

California is a national leader
in providing the handicapped
with access to facilities. Most
theaters and concert halls in
San Francisco are therefore
fully accessible, and have
special open-free areas set
aside for wheelchair-bound
patrons. A few of the smaller
houses may require you to use
special entrances, or elevators
to reach the upper tiers, but
in general access is free of
obstacles. Many movie
theaters also offer amplifying
headphones for the hearing
impaired. Contact the theaters
to be sure of their facilities,
and see *Practical Information*
on page 280.

The Presidio Cinema *(see p262)*

DIRECTORY

USEFUL NUMBERS

**San Francisco Conven-
tion and Visitors Bureau**
Suite 900, 201 3rd St.
San Francisco, CA 94103-9097.
***Tel** 974-6900*. www.sf.visitor.org
Visitor Info Center
Powell St at Market St, lower level
Hallidie Plaza.
***Tel** 391-2000*.

Events Line (24-hour)

391-2001 *(English)*
391-2003 *(French)*
391-2004 *(German)*
391-2122 *(Spanish)*

TICKET AGENCIES

Ticketmaster
Charge-by-phone. ***Tel** 421-8497*.
www.tickets.com

TIX Bay Area
East Side of Union Sq, Powell St
between Geary and Post sts.
***Tel** 433-7827*.
www.theatrebayarea.org

San Francisco's Best: Entertainment

With a huge variety of entertainment options, San Francisco is one of the most enjoyable cities in the world. Big names in every branch of the arts perform here, and many also make the city their home, attracted by the creative local community. In addition to the West Coast's best opera, ballet, and symphony orchestra, the city supports a wide range of jazz and rock music plus diverse theater and dance companies. For the sports-minded, there are numerous events to watch or take part in. And finally, the spectacular parks and recreation areas allow visitors to design their own outdoor activities, many of them costing nothing.

Fillmore Auditorium
Famous for acts such as Jefferson Airplane in the 1960s, the refurbished Auditorium is set so become a premier music spot again. (See p266.)

Presidio

Pacific
Heights a
the Marin

Golden Gate Park and Land's End

Civic Center

San Francisco Comedy Celebration Day

This annual festival in Golden Gate Park offers spectators a chance to see new talent that could, like Whoopi Goldberg, make it big. (See p259.)

Haight Ashbury and the Mission

| 0 kilometers | 2 |
| 0 miles | 1 |

Clay Theatre
For foreign films try the Clay Theatre on Fillmore Street, which was built in 1910 and is one of the city's oldest theaters. (See p262.)

Outdoor Ballet at Stern Grove
The natural outdoor amphitheater is a tranquil setting for ballet. (See p259.)

Street Entertainers on Fisherman's Wharf
A lively mix of street musicians, jugglers and various other impromptu performers entertain the crowds at Fisherman's Wharf. (See p259.)

The Saloon
Local blues bands perform nightly at this popular North Beach bar. Dating from 1861, the Saloon is an authentic Gold Rush survivor. (See p266.)

Fisherman's Wharf and North Beach

Financial District and Union Square

The Fairmont Hotel
Some of the best live music can be heard in piano bars at big hotels. The Tonga Room at the Fairmont is where Tony Bennett made "I Left My Heart in San Francisco" famous. (See p266.)

The Geary Theater
This landmark building, home of the renowned American Conservatory Theater, has been extensively renovated since the 1989 earthquake. (See p263.)

War Memorial Opera House
Book tickets in advance for the acclaimed San Francisco Opera Association. (See p264.)

Slim's

Slim's
One of the classiest of the SoMa nightclubs, Slim's offers a mixture of jazz, rock and blues. (See p266.)

Film and Theater

San Francisco has an avid film-going community, and newly released blockbusters often get shown at neighborhood theaters. In keeping with its reputation as a center of the arts, San Francisco really excels at film festivals. In addition to the well-known International and Mill Valley festivals, there are annual celebrations of the best of Native American, Asian-American, Women's and Gay and Lesbian film and video productions.

Theater offerings are much less varied and more expensive than films, and at any one time there may be only a handful of productions from which to choose. Mainstream theaters, which host a range of touring Broadway productions as well as those by local companies, are concentrated in the Theater District *(see p116)*, along Geary Street just west of Union Square. The Fort Mason Center *(see pp74–5)* is another theatrical nexus, with a more avant-garde reputation.

FIRST-RUN FILMS

The city's newest multimedia experience is the **Sony Metreon**, a 15-screen complex plus IMAX. There are also shops, restaurants, special programs, and other attractions. The **AMC Kabuki** Japan Center *(see p128)* and the modern **Embarcadero** and the **Presidio Theater** are other excellent movie houses for first-run films; the Embarcadero also excels at foreign and indie films. Prices for all first-run venues are roughly the same.

Other popular venues include the **AMC1000 Van Ness**, and **Loew's Theater at the Sony Metreon**. The **Century San Francisco Centre** is located in the Westfield Shopping Centre and has luxurious seats and a gourmet snack bar. Programs usually start around noon, with shows every two hours until around 10pm. On occasion, there are midnight shows on weekends. Half-price tickets may be available for at least the first showing, although this varies greatly from theater to theater. The Kabuki offers its best discounts every day from 4pm to 6pm.

FOREIGN FILMS AND ART HOUSES

Main venues for first-run foreign films are the **Clay** in Pacific Heights, the Civic Center's **Lumiere** and **Opera Plaza**, a four screen complex. All of these are owned and operated by the Landmark chain, which sells a discount card that gives five admissions for a saving of 30 percent.

The **Castro** *(see p136)*, San Francisco's finest older theater, shows Hollywood classics and other revivals, as well as unusual newer films, with programs changing daily. The chic **Roxie**, an independent rep house in the Mission District, and Haight Ashbury's tiny **Red Vic**, also screen forgotten classics and unusual new releases.

More obscure but intriguing fare is at **Cinematheque**, which has programs on Sunday nights at the San Francisco Art Institute, and on Thursday nights at the **Yerba Buena Center for the Arts**.

FILM FESTIVALS

Held at the Kabuki complex for two weeks in May, the **San Francisco International Film Festival** usually has some commercial hits. Generally, however, it shows independent and foreign releases that might not otherwise get shown. The tickets sell extremely fast, and you will need to book three or four days in advance. The **Mill Valley Film Festival**, held early in October, is also a mainstay of the circuit, as is the increasingly high-profile **Lesbian & Gay Film Festival** held each June at the **Castro**, **Roxie** and the **Yerba Buena Center for the Arts**.

MAINSTREAM THEATERS

Many residents of San Francisco show apparent disdain for the international

FILM RATINGS

Films in the US are graded as follows:
G General audiences, all ages admitted.
PG Parental guidance suggested. Some material unsuitable for children.
PG-13 Parents strongly cautioned. Some material inappropriate for children under age 13.
R Restricted. Children under 17 need to be accompanied by a parent or adult guardian.
NC-17 No children under 17 admitted.

ON LOCATION

Many places in and around San Francisco have played starring roles in films:

Alcatraz is the famous high security prison in *Bird Man of Alcatraz* and *Escape from Alcatraz*.
Alta Plaza Park is where Barbra Streisand drove a car down the steps in *What's Up Doc?*
Bodega Bay, on the coast just north of San Francisco, is the small town in Hitchcock's *The Birds*.
Chinatown as tourists don't usually see it is the setting for *Chan is Missing*, *The Dead Pool*, *Dim Sum* and *Hammett*.
Fillmore Auditorium's final week, with footage of the Grateful Dead, is the theme of *Fillmore*.
Mission District featured in the violent cop thriller *The Laughing Policeman*.
Presidio is where a brutal murder takes place in the crime thriller *The Presidio*.
Union Square is the scene for the key sequence of *The Conversation*.

commercial successes, which explains why theater has a lower profile here than in other large cities. There are likely to be at least a couple of major shows, however, playing at the main Theater District spots; three of the largest theaters are the **Golden Gate Theater**, the **Curran Theater** and the **Orpheum Theater**, all part of the Best of Broadway performance series. Others include the **New Conservatory Theatre Center** and the **Marines Memorial Theater**. The **Stage Door Theater** has a reputation for serious productions, while musicals, and comedy are staged at **The Marsh**.

The most respected major company is the **American Conservatory Theater (ACT)**. Its longtime home, the landmark Geary Theater, has now reopened after renovations following the 1989 earthquake *(see pp18–19)*. A variety of plays are performed during its October to May season.

ALTERNATIVE THEATER

With dozens of small theaters spread around the city, and many more in the Bay Area, San Francisco's off-Broadway scene is alive and well, if hard to find. **Fort Mason** is the most obvious center, home to the nationally known **Magic Theater** and diverse other groups, as well as the Playwrights Festival each August *(see p49)*.

The North Beach district is home to the **Actors Theater of San Francisco**, while the Mission District boasts the satirical **Theater Rhinoceros** and risk-taking **Theater Artaud**. The city's best-loved production, the uniquely San Franciscan revue *Beach Blanket Babylon*, plays at North Beach's **Club Fugazi**.

Other companies to look out for are **Intersection for the Arts**, the multimedia-oriented **Exit Theater**, and the highly regarded **Berkeley Repertory Theater** in the East Bay.

DIRECTORY

FIRST-RUN FILMS, FOREIGN FILMS AND ART HOUSES

AMC 1000 Van Ness
Map 4 F4.
Tel 922-4262.

AMC Kabuki
Map 4 E4.
Tel 346-3243.

Bridge
Map 3 B5.
Tel 267-4893.

Castro
Map 10 D2.
Tel 621-6120.

Century San Francisco Centre
Map 5 C5.
Tel 538-3456.

Cinematheque
Map 11 B3.
Tel 552-1990.

Clay
Map 4 D3.
Tel 267-4893.

Embarcadero
Map 6 C3.
Tel 267-4893.

Loew's Theater at the Sony Metreon
Map 5 C5.
Tel 369-6200.

Lumiere
Map 4 F3.
Tel 267-4893.

Opera Plaza
Map 4 F5.
Tel 267-4893.

Presidio Theater
Map 3 C2.
Tel 776-2388.

Red Vic
Map 9 B1.
Tel 668-3994.

Roxie
Map 10 F2.
Tel 863-1087.

Sony Metreon
Map 5 C5.
Tel 369-6000.

Yerba Buena Center
Map 5 C5.
Tel 978-2787.

FILM FESTIVALS

International Film Festival
Map 4 D5.
Tel 561-5000.
www.sffs.org

Lesbian & Gay Film Festival
Map 11 A2.
Tel 703-8650.
www.frameline.org

Mill Valley Film Festival
38 Miller Ave,
Mill Valley.
Tel 383-5256.

MAINSTREAM THEATERS

American Conservatory Theater (ACT)
Map 5 B5.
Tel 749-2ACT.

Curran Theater
Map 5 B5.
Tel 551-2000.

Golden Gate Theater
Map 5 B5.
Tel 551-2000.

Marines Memorial Theater
Map 5 B4.
Tel 771-6900.

New Conservatory Theatre Center
Map 10 F1.
Tel 861-8972.

Orpheum Theater
Map 11 A1.
Tel 551-2000.

Stage Door Theater
Map 5 B5.
Tel 749-2228.

The Marsh
Map 10 F3.
Tel 826-5750.

ALTERNATIVE THEATER

Actors Theater of San Francisco
Map 5 B4.
Tel 296-9179.

Berkeley Repertory Theater
2025 Addison St,
Berkeley.
Tel (510) 845-4700.

Club Fugazi
Map 5 B3.
Tel 421-4222.

Exit Theater
156 Eddy St
Map 5 B5.
Tel 673-3847.

Fort Mason Center
Map 4 E1.
Tel 441-3687.

Intersection for the Arts
Map 10 F2.
Tel 626-2787.

Magic Theater
Map 4 E1.
Tel 441-8001.

Theater Artaud
Map 11 A3.
Tel 626-4370.

Theater Rhinoceros
Map 10 F2.
Tel 861-5079.

Opera, Classical Music and Dance

Since the Gold Rush days of 1849, San Francisco has prided itself on the variety of its cultural institutions, and its ability to attract world-class performers. Black-tie fundraisers and the Hotel Tax Fund help support the performing arts, and there is great popular support as well, evidenced by the full houses. The main halls, including the War Memorial Opera House and the Louise M. Davies Symphony Hall, are in the Civic Center performing arts complex *(see pp126–7)*. The best times to see a performance are winter and spring, when the opera, symphony and ballet seasons are all in full swing. However, tickets can be hard to obtain, so it is sensible to book well in advance.

OPERA

Beginning well before 1932, when San Francisco built the first municipally owned opera house in the US, opera has been popular in the city. In recent years the San Francisco Opera has achieved international fame as one of the world's finest attracting such stars as Placido Domingo and Dame Kiri Te Kanawa, and artist David Hockney to design the sets. All performances feature English translations of the lyrics, which are projected as "supertitles" above the stage.

The main season runs from September to December, and the opening night is one of the principal social events on the West Coast. Summer special events are held in June and July, when tickets may be easier to obtain.

Ticket prices range from about $10 to $15 (for standing room, sold on day of performance) to more than $100. For advance information, contact the **San Francisco Opera Association**. To find out about ticket availability, contact the **War Memorial Opera House** box office.

Across the bay, the small but high caliber **Berkeley Opera** performs in April and May at the Julia Morgan Theatre.

CLASSICAL MUSIC

The most recent addition to the Civic Center performing arts complex, the **Louise M. Davies Symphony Hall**, was inaugurated on September 16, 1980. After a great deal of criticism about the acoustics, a decision was made to make alterations, and building work began in 1991. The hall reopened in 1992. It is now San Francisco's principal location for fine classical music performances, and home to the highly regarded **San Francisco Symphony Orchestra**.

The orchestra performs up to five concerts a week during its September to June season. Guest conductors, performers and various touring orchestras perform additional special concerts, and in July a "Symphony Pops" program is held at the Louise M. Davies Symphony Hall. Next door to the Opera House, the **Herbst Theatre** hosts recitals by prominent performers.

In addition to these big events, there are numerous less formal recitals and concerts in the Bay Area. The **Philharmonia Baroque Orchestra**, a period instrument ensemble, plays at various sites around the city, while the historic **Old First Presbyterian Church** has a series of chamber music and individual recitals on Friday nights and Sunday afternoons throughout the year. The **Florence Gould Theater** in the Legion of Honor *(see pp156–7)* is often used for classical small group performances, including quartets, and there are also demonstrations of classical or pre-classical musical instruments, such as the clavichord.

Across the bay, **Hertz Hall** on the UC Berkeley campus *(see pp176–7)* attracts rising stars of the classical world for its winter and spring seasons, while the innovative **Oakland East Bay Symphony** performs at the Art Deco landmark Paramount Theater.

CONTEMPORARY MUSIC

The completion of the **Yerba Buena Center for the Arts** has given a significant boost to contemporary music in San Francisco. Bay Area composers and performers, including John Adams and the internationally acclaimed **Kronos Quartet**, along with others from all over the world, give concerts in the Center's theater as well as in the much smaller Forum. Contemporary composers occasionally hold concerts in the Louise M.Davies Symphony Hall.

The other main spot for new music in the Bay Area is **Zellerbach Hall** on the UC Berkeley campus, while the **Cowell Theater** at Fort Mason also holds events approximately twice a month.

One of the more unusual musical adventures to be found in San Francisco is **Audium**. In this dynamic "sound sculpture," the audience sits through the performance in total darkness, surrounded by hundreds of speakers.

BALLET AND DANCE

Founded in 1933, the **San Francisco Ballet** is the oldest professional ballet company in the US. Under the direction of Helgi Tomasson it has proved itself to be among the best in the world. Starting off with an annual production of Tchaikovsky's Christmas classic *The Nutcracker*, the season runs from February to May. The schedule includes classic works choreographed by Balanchine and others, as well as premières by such leading artists as Mark Morris.

Performances by local talent take place at the intimate **Theater Artaud** and the **ODC Performance Gallery**, both located in the Mission District. The **Yerba Buena**

Center for the Arts is home to the **LINES Contemporary Ballet**, while **Zellerbach Hall** across the Bay attracts the best touring productions, with annual visits by Pilobolus, the Dance Theater of Harlem, and Merce Cunningham.

BACKSTAGE TOURS

Scheduled backstage tours are organized at the Louise M. Davies Symphony Hall and the War Memorial Opera House. You can tour both buildings on Mondays, every half hour from 10am to 2pm. Tours of the Davies Symphony Hall only can be arranged on Wednesdays and Saturdays, but reservations must be made a week ahead. All tours begin at the Grove Street entrance and offer an intriguing firsthand look behind the scene.

FREE EVENTS

In addition to the numerous ticketed events, free concerts and performances are staged all over the city. Most of these are outdoor daytime summer events. For example, the San Francisco Symphony Orchestra holds a late-summer series of Sunday concerts in a natural, wooded amphitheater at Stern Grove (see p259). Members of the San Francisco Opera Company sing a selection of favorite arias for lunchtime crowds in the Financial District on Bush Street as part of the "Brown Bag Operas" series, and in Sharon Meadow, Golden Gate Park (see pp143–55) during "Opera in the Park." Also free are the Tuesday lunchtime recitals at 12:30 at Old St. Mary's Church (see p98). On

Fridays at noon during the summer there is "Music in the Park" in the redwood grove behind the Transamerica Pyramid (see p111).

Grace Cathedral is a particularly striking setting for choral church music, performed by the Grace Cathedral Choir of men and boys, founded in 1913. The choir sings at Evensong on Thursdays at 5:15pm, while Choral Eucharist is celebrated on Sundays at 11am.

For details of free and other events, contact the SF Convention and Visitors Bureau (see p278), or call their 24-hour hotline for updates: 415-391-2001. You can also check the "Datebook" section of the Sunday *San Francisco Chronicle/ Examiner* or one of the weekly events papers.

DIRECTORY

OPERA

Berkeley Opera Box Office
2138 Cedar St. Berkeley.
Tel 510) 841-1903.

San Francisco Opera Association
301 Van Ness Ave.
Map 4 F5.
Tel 861-4008.

War Memorial Opera House Box Office
199 Grove St (day),
Map 4 E5;
301 Van Ness Ave (eve),
Map 4 F5.
Tel 864-3330.
www.sfopera.com

CLASSICAL MUSIC

Old First Presbyterian Church
1751 Sacramento St.
Map 4 F3.
Tel 474-1608.

Florence Gould Theater
Legion of Honor,
Lincoln Park.
Map 1 C5
Tel 863-3330.

Herbst Theatre
401 Van Ness Ave.
Map 4 F5.
Tel 621-6600.

Hertz Hall
UC Berkeley.
Tel (510) 642-9988.

Louise M. Davies Symphony Hall Box Office
201 Van Ness Ave.
Map 4 F5.
Tel 864-6000.

Oakland East Bay Symphony Box Office
2025 Broadway,
Oakland.
Tel (510) 444-0801.

Philharmonia Baroque Orchestra Box Office
180 Redwood St,
Suite 100.
Map 4 F5.
Tel 392-4400.

San Francisco Symphony Association Box Office
201 Van Ness Ave.
Map 4 F5.
Tel 864-6000.

CONTEMPORARY MUSIC

Audium
1616 Bush St.
Map 4 F4.
Tel 771-1616.

Cowell Theater
Fort Mason Center
Pier 2.
Map 4 E1.
Tel 441-3687.

Kronos Quartet
Tel 731-3533.

Yerba Buena Center
701 Mission St.
Map 5 C5.
Tel 978-2787.
www.ybca.org

Zellerbach Hall
UC Berkeley.
Tel (510) 642-9988.

BALLET AND DANCE

LINES Contemporary Ballet
Yerba Buena Center for the Arts
700 Howard St.
Map 5 C5.
Tel 978-2787.

ODC Performance Gallery
3153 17th St.
Map 10 E3.
Tel 863-9834.

San Francisco Ballet
455 Franklin St.
Map 4 F4.
Tel 861-5600.
www.sfballet.org

San Francisco Ballet Box Office
455 Franklin St.
Map 4 F4.
Tel 865-2000.

Theater Artaud
450 Florida St.
Map 11 A5.
Tel 626-4370.

BACKSTAGE TOURS

War Memorial Performing Arts Center
199 Grove St.
Map 4 E5.
Tel 552-8338.

FREE EVENTS

Grace Cathedral
1051 Taylor St. **Map** 5 B4,
Tel 749-6300.
www.gracecathedral.org

Rock, Jazz, Blues, and Country Music

You will find almost every genre of popular music played somewhere in San Francisco. It may be Dixieland jazz, country and western, Delta blues, urban rap, psychedelic rock or the latest sounds from West Africa or Eastern Europe. Good groups can be found in ordinary neighborhood bars, and there are a number of good small places with only a minimum charge.

The city's music scene has a long and varied tradition of excellence. It changes swiftly and there is no way to predict what you may find, but whatever it is, it's bound to be good.

MAJOR ARENAS

Big-name international performers are likely to be found at the large, municipal arenas around the Bay Area. In San Francisco itself one of the prime places is the small **Masonic Auditorium** on Nob Hill. Two larger venues, the **Cow Palace** and the outdoor **Shoreline Amphitheater**, are south of the city, while the main stadium-scale shows are held across the bay.

Berkeley's outdoor **Greek Theater** hosts a summerlong series of concerts by leading bands and artists. Concord's huge **Chronicle Pavilion** features such favorites as Bonnie Raitt, Dave Matthews, and Santana.

The best medium-scale spot in the city is the grand old **Warfield** on Market Street, which has dancing downstairs and seating in the balcony during its year-round, mostly rock season. Smaller clubs are throughout the city, with the densest concentration in the South of Market (SoMa) area around 11th and Folsom streets, where a handful of rock and jazz clubs are within walking distance of one another. Cover charges at clubs vary from $5 to $20, with the highest prices on weekends. Some places also impose a one- or two-drink minimum. Tickets for concerts cost from $15 to $25 and are available at the box office or through BASS or Ticketmaster, for a small service charge (*see p259*).

For listings and details of events in the city and the Bay Area as a whole, check the *SF Weekly, Bay Guardian* or other local newspapers (*see p281*); or pick up a free copy of *Bay Area Music* (*BAM*), which is readily found in record stores and clubs.

ROCK MUSIC

From Metallica and En Vogue to the more mainstream contemporary bands such as Counting Crows and Chris Isaak, San Francisco has a strong, if offbeat, rock music scene. The local bands tend to eschew the trappings of stardom, and most clubs are small, casual places. Bands and performers come from all over the US to give showcase performances at the radio industry's Gavin Convention every February. Events are generally cool, low-key and unpretentious, however, for the rest of the year.

Two of the best rock clubs to hear live music are **Slim's** and **Bimbo's 365 Club**. Bimbo's hosts rock, jazz, country and R&B – and attracts a similarly diverse crowd. Slim's, which is part-owned by musician Boz Scaggs, is a bit more upscale, tending to feature established performers in its comfortable, 436-seat room. Another popular place is the **Fillmore Auditorium**, which is the legendary birthplace of psychedelic rock during the Flower Power 1960s (*see p129*).

Smaller places to hear good rock music include the **Bottom of the Hill** club in Potrero Hill, the **Hotel Utah** under the I-80 freeway south of Market Street and **Great American Music Hall**. The Bay Area's punk rock world focuses on Berkeley's all-ages **924 Gilman Street** club.

JAZZ

In the late 1950s, the heyday of the Beat Generation (*see p32*), San Francisco enjoyed one of the liveliest jazz scenes in the country. Nightclubs like the legendary Blackhawk vied with the nation's hottest spots for performers like Miles Davis, John Coltrane, and Thelonius Monk. Things have quieted down considerably, but there is still a number of excellent places to hear live jazz. For traditional Dixieland in an informal (and free) setting, visit the amiable **Gold Dust Lounge**, just off Union Square.

If you prefer more modern sounds, choose from clubs such as **Jazz at Pearl's** in North Beach, or **Yoshi's** in Jack London Square. Many major jazz and blues artists, like B.B. King and Pat Metheny, perform here. Try also the piano bars located in downtown restaurants and hotels, the best of which is the beautiful **Carnelian Room** in the Bank of America building.

To catch major acts, you may have to head for the East Bay, where **Kimball's East** stands out as the Bay Area's best jazz club. The **SF Brewing Company** features jazz almost every night. Patrons at **Moose's** can enjoy listening to first-rate jazz pianists over lunch and dinner.

Many jazz fans plan trips to San Francisco to coincide with the world-famous **Monterey Jazz Festival**, which is held every September in Monterey (*see pp186–7*). Monterey is located two hours south of San Francisco.

BLUES

San Francisco probably has more blues clubs than anywhere else in the world, except Chicago. Good live blues is played somewhere in town every night of the week, from North Beach bars like **The Saloon** to **The Boom**

Boom Room, which is owned by musician John Lee Hooker. **Lou's Pier 47,** on Fisherman's Wharf, has live blues bands on the bill almost every day, with special shows on weekends. The award-winning **Biscuits and Blues** has local blues spotlights on weekdays and special shows on weekends.

The highlight of the calendar is the annual **San Francisco Blues Festival.** Held in late September on Great Meadow at Fort Mason (see pp74–5), it attracts dozens of blues bands from all over the US, some of which wail a mean tune.

FOLK, COUNTRY, AND WORLD MUSIC

Although Folk music's mass appeal has faded since the fervent days of the 1960s, when singers like Joan Baez and Pete Seeger appeared regularly, fans can find live performers playing in clubs and coffee-houses all around the bay. Berkeley's **Freight & Salvage Coffeehouse** hosts country and bluegrass bands as well as singer-songwriters, and it is probably the prime folk music club in the Bay Area. **Starry Plough** in Berkeley is also mostly folk oriented, although

many country/western music stars perform here. **Cafe Du Nord** has acoustic performers in its underground club, while the **Sweetwater** in Marin County attracts a diverse range of well-known singers and songwriters.

While down-home country music fans may have to search hard to find anything that suits their tastes, the Bay Area is rich in "World Music," which covers everything from reggae and soca to Taiko drumming and klezmer music. The cozy **Ashkenaz Music & Dance Café** hosts a wildly diverse range of performers.

DIRECTORY

MAJOR ARENAS

Chronicle Pavilion
2000 Kirker Pass Road, Concord.
Tel (925) 363-5701.

Cow Palace
Geneva Ave and Santos St.
Tel 404-4111.

Greek Theater
UC Berkeley.
Tel (510) 642-9988.

Masonic Auditorium
1111 California St.
Map 4 F3.
Tel 776-4702.
www.sfmasonic
center.com

Shoreline Amphitheater
1 Amphitheater Parkway, Mountain View.
Tel (650) 967-4040.

Warfield
982 Market St.
Map 5 C5.
Tel 775-7722.

ROCK MUSIC

Bimbo's 365 Club
1025 Columbus Ave.
Map 5 A2.
Tel 474-0365.
www.bimbo365clubs.
com

Bottom of the Hill
1233 17th St. **Map** 11 C3. *Tel 621-4455.*

Fillmore Auditorium
1805 Geary Blvd.
Map 4 D4.
Tel 346-6000.
www.thefillmore.com

Great American Music Hall
859 O'Farrell St.
Map 5 A5.
Tel 885-0750.

Hotel Utah
500 4th St.
Map 5 C5.
Tel 546-6300.

924 Gilman Street
924 Gilman St, Berkeley.
Tel (510) 525-9926.

Slim's
333 11th St.
Map 10 F1.
Tel 255-0333.
www.slims-sf.com

JAZZ

Carnelian Room
555 California St, 52nd Fl.
Map 5 C4.
Tel 433-7500.

Gold Dust Lounge
247 Powell St.
Map 5 B5.
Tel 397-1695.

Jazz at Pearl's
256 Columbus Ave.
Map 5 C3.
Tel 291-8255.

Kimball's East
5800 Shellmound St, Emeryville.
Tel (510) 658-2555.

Moose's
1652 Stockton St.
Map 5 B2.
Tel 989-7800.

SF Brewing Company
155 Columbus Ave.
Map 5 C3.
Tel 434-3344.

Yoshi's Nightspot
510 Embarcadero West.
Jack London Sq, Oakland
Tel (510) 238-9200.

BLUES

Biscuits and Blues
401 Mason St.
Map 5 B5.
Tel 292-2583.

The Boom Boom Room
1601 Fillmore St.
Map 10 F2.
Tel 673-8000.

Lou's Pier 47
300 Jefferson St.
Map 5 B1.
Tel 771-5687.

The Saloon
1232 Grant Ave.
Map 5 C3.
Tel 989-7666.

FOLK, COUNTRY, AND WORLD MUSIC

Ashkenaz Music & Dance Café
1317 San Pablo Ave, Berkeley.
Tel (510) 525-5054.

Cafe Du Nord
2170 Market St.
Map 10 E2.
Tel 861-5016.
www.cafedunord.com

Freight & Salvage Coffeehouse
1111 Addison St, Berkeley.
Tel (510) 548-1761.

Starry Plough
3101 Shattuck Ave. Berkeley.
Tel (510) 841-2082.

Sweetwater
153 Throckmorton Ave, Mill Valley. *Tel 388-2820.*

MUSIC FESTIVALS

Monterey Jazz Festival
2000 Fairgrounds Rd at Casa Verde, Monterey.
Tel (831) 373-3366.
www.montereyjazz
festival.com

San Francisco Blues Festival
Fort Mason. **Map** 4 E1.
Tel 826-6837.
www.sanfranciscoblues
festival.com

Nightclubs

Like almost everything else in San Francisco, the city's nightlife is fairly casual, friendly and low-key. There is little of the fashion consciousness of London, New York or Paris, and flashy discos are few and far between. Many of the trendy clubs are open only one or two nights a week, but cover charges and drink prices are generally low.

If you want to sample an aspect of nightlife that is "uniquely San Franciscan," try the stand-up comedy clubs. Although some of the once-vaunted places have closed in recent years, you can still find stand-up done with a special eccentric flair. In addition, San Francisco has many comfortable piano bars in luxurious hotels or restaurants, which are perfect for an entertaining, intimate night out. It is a good idea to rest up after the day so you can enjoy the city after hours, too.

WHERE AND WHEN

Names, times and locations of nightclubs change constantly, and even the most popular places may last no longer than a year. In many ways your best bet is to check the *SF Weekly, Bay Times* and *Bay Guardian (see p281)* and other magazines and newspapers to see what is happening. Most of the larger clubs are located in the industrial South of Market (SoMa) area, and run from around 9pm until 2am. A few stay open all night, especially on weekends, but all places stop serving alcohol at 2am. Always bring valid ID to prove you are over 21 or you will not be admitted.

DANCING

One of San Francisco's liveliest nightclubs is **Ruby Skye** on Mason Street, with its flashy decor, great sound system and fashionably mainstream clientele. R'n'B, hip-hop and jazz are played at **Nickie's BBQ** in Haight Ashbury; while **Factory 525** and **City Nights**, both on Harrison Street, feature alternative rock and modern dance music; take a cab home after club hours in this iffy neighborhood.

Bambuddha Lounge has some great dining and excellent DJs. **The Mexican Bus** is a real bus, which takes you to three different salsa dance clubs in one evening. **Suede** is the place to go if

you really like to boogie, with different indie music every night. **Ten 15** is another venue where the music is varied and the atmosphere electric. Also in this area is the after-hours **Cat Club**, which stays lively until dawn with acid jazz and alternative-industrial sounds, as well as a popular '80s night. Check out **330 Ritch Street**, where you can enjoy house music, goth, Brit pop, mod, indie, R'n'B and hip-hop.

Devotees of salsa should head straight for **Cafe Cocomo**, with the hottest live salsa and dance lessons most nights of the week from 8pm onwards.

GAY AND LESBIAN CLUBS

Some of San Francisco's most popular clubs are primarily, though rarely exclusively, homosexual. These include the ever-popular **Endup**, which is open around the clock from Friday night until Monday morning for nonstop dancing. Other gay and lesbian clubs include **El Rio** in the Mission District and the urban cowboy **Rawhide**, which has square dancing every night.

There are also a number of dance clubs on and around 18th Street in the Castro District, such as the **Midnight Sun** and **Detour**. In the East Bay, the **White Horse Inn** has been a popular bar and dance club since the early 1960s.

Gay and lesbian nightclubs tend to change even more quickly than their straight counterparts, so check listings and ads beforehand in local papers like *Bay Times* and *Bay Area Reporter*. Gay men in particular can check *Betty and Pansy's Severe Queer Review*.

PIANO BARS

The name "piano bar" does not really do justice to the variety of bars and nightclubs presented here. They all have nightly live music, usually jazz, to enjoy just for the price of a drink. Many of the most fabulous clubs in the city are in four-star hotels. A few blocks from the Theater District, **The Lush Lounge** offers stiff martinis in a funky setting. The Art Deco-style **Top of the Mark** sits high above Nob Hill at the top of the Mark Hopkins Hotel. Other good roof-top piano bars are **Grand View** on the 36th floor of Union Square's Grand Hyatt Hotel and the **Carnelian Room** at the Bank of America building, which offers great food, good music, and panoramic views.

Other piano bars are found in the better restaurants, where you can enjoy music before, during or after dinner. In North Beach, the **Washington Square Bar & Grill** offers nightly entertainment. It is popular with advertising and media types, as is **Moose's**, its arch rival near Washington Square, featuring more contemporary music. Both places offer better than average food and drink. Drop into **Lefty O'Doul's** for good piano bar music with an obvious Irish lilt and a fine selection of ales.

The Theater District west of Union Square has lively bars, and South of Market Street, **Julie's Supper Club** serves up good canned jazz and R'n'B along with Cajun food and great cocktails. **Harry Denton's Starlight Room** has nightly live music in a classy setting on the 21st floor at the Sir Francis

Drake Hotel. Just off Market Street, **Martuni's** offers stiff martinis and classic singalongs for a diverse crowd. Last but not least is the **Tonga Room** in the lower level of the Fairmont Hotel (see p213). In this elaborate Polynesian-style cocktail bar you can dance or just listen to jazz – interrupted every half-hour by a simulated rainstorm.

COMEDY CLUBS

The city's once-thriving live comedy scene brought the world the famous

comedian and movie actor Robin Williams, among many other talents. While the comedy scene has been cut back considerably in San Francisco, there is usually something happening somewhere in the city every night of the week at a bar or café. Check local newspapers for listings (see p281).

Some of the best shows take place at **Tommy T's Comedy House**, with such regular artists as Bobby Slayton, Will Durst, and Richard Stockton. Other clubs with stand-up comedy

acts and improvisation are **Marsh's Mock Cafe-Theater** in the Mission and **Cobb's Comedy Club** in North Beach, as well as **The Punchline** and **The Green Room Comedy Club**. Kimo's has been a Polk Street landmark for decades. It features drag, cabaret and comedy shows every week.

Shows usually start at 8pm, with late-night performances at weekends beginning at around 10pm. Most venues cost around $15 and can operate a one- or two-drink minimum policy.

DIRECTORY

DANCING

330 Ritch St
330 Ritch St.
Map 11 C1.
Tel 541-9574.

Bambuddha Lounge
Phoenix Hotel,
601 Eddy St. Map 5 A5.
Tel 885-5088.

Cafe Cocomo
650 Indiana (at Mariposa). Map 11 C3.
Tel 824-6910.
www.cafecocomo.com

Cat Club
1190 Folsom St.
Map 11 A2.
Tel 431-3332.
www.catclubsf.com

City Nights
715 Harrison St,
Map 5 D5.
Tel 339-8686
(SF Club hotline).

Factory 525
525 Harrison St.
Map 5 D5.
Tel 339-8686
(SF Club hotline).

The Mexican Bus
call for bus pick-up
Tel 546-3747.
www.mexicanbus.com

Nickie's BBQ
460 Haight St.
Map 10 E1.
Tel 621-6508.

Ruby Skye
420 Mason St. Map 5 B5.
Tel 693-0777.

Suede
383 Bay St.
Map 5 B2.
Tel 399-9555.

Ten 15
1015 Folsom St.
Map 11 B1.
Tel 431-1200.

GAY AND LESBIAN CLUBS

Detour
2348 Market St.
Map 10 D2.
Tel 861-6053.

El Rio
3158 Mission St.
Map 10 F4.
Tel 282-3325.
www.elriosf.com

Endup
401 6th St. Map 11 B1.
Tel 357-0827.

Midnight Sun
4067 18th St.
Map 10 D3.
Tel 861-4186.

Rawhide
280 7th St. Map 11 A1.
Tel 621-1197.

White Horse Inn
6551 Telegraph Ave.,
Oakland.
Tel (510) 652-3820.

PIANO BARS

Carnelian Room
555 California St, 52nd fl.
Map 5 C4.
Tel 433-7500.

Grand View
Grand Hyatt Hotel
24th floor
345 Stockton St.
Map 5 C4.
Tel 398-1234.

Harry Denton's Starlight Room
450 Powell St.
Map 5 B5.
Tel 395-8595.

Julie's Supper Club
1123 Folsom St.
Map 11 A1.
Tel 861-0707.

Lefty O'Doul's
333 Geary St.
Map 5 B5.
Tel 982-8900.

Lush Lounge
1092 Post St.
Map 5 A5.
Tel 771-2022.
www.lushlounge.com

Martuni's
4 Valencia St.
Map 10 F1.
Tel 241-0205.

Moose's
1652 Stockton St.
Map 5 B2.
Tel 989-7800.

Tonga Room
950 Mason St.
Map 5 B4.
Tel 772-5278.

Top of the Mark
Mark Hopkins Inter-Continental Hotel
1 Nob Hill.
Map 5 B4.
Tel 616-6916.

Washington Square Bar & Grill
1707 Powell St.
Map 5 B2.
Tel 982-8123.

COMEDY

Cobb's Comedy Club
915 Columbus Ave.
Map 5 B2.
Tel 928-4320.

The Green Room Comedy Club
2801 Leavenworth St.
Map 5 A1.
Tel 674-3540.

Kimo's
1351 Polk St. Map 4 F4.
Tel 885-4535.

Marsh's Mock Cafe-Theater
1074 Valencia.
Map 10 F3.
Tel 826-5750.

The Punchline
444 Battery St. Map 6 D3.
Tel 397-7573. www.punchlinecomedyclub.com

Tommy T's Comedy House
1655 Willow Pass Rd.
Concord.
Tel (925) 686-6809.
www.tommyts.com

San Francisco's Bars

San Francisco has been a drinkers' town ever since the heady days of the Gold Rush (see pp24–25), when there was a saloon for every 50 residents. The bawdy public houses of the mid-19th century no longer exist. Instead, today, you can drink with a view; grab a local brew; sip an elegant, sweet cocktail in a chic lounge; sample a fine local country vintage wine; mingle with cheering local fans at a sports bar; see satellite-broadcast matches from Europe and soak up charm and an occasional concert at an Irish Bar. Alternatively, you can observe how a notable segment of San Francisco's population parties at a gay bar.

ROOFTOP BARS

Those with a head for heights and a craving to be above the hills can visit the bars at the top of the towers in the city center. Grand Hyatt's **Grand View Lounge**, the **View Lounge** at Marriott Hotel, and **Top of the Mark** at the Mark Hopkins (see p102), all offer splendid views and evening jazz along with dance music. The highest of these rooftop bars is the ritzy, 52-story **Carnelian Room** (tie and reservations are required). The second in line, **Cityscape**, is on the 46th floor of the Hilton Hotel, with no pillars to obstruct the view.

BEER BARS

For a more down-to-earth experience, visit one of the city's many beer bars, popular gathering places for the after-work crowd and weekend revelers. The best of these specialize in beers brewed by West Coast breweries, including San Francisco's fine Anchor Steam and Liberty Ale.

One of the best, the English **Mad Dog in the Fog**, is situated on Haight Street. **Magnolia Pub & Brewery**, in a 1903 Haight Victorian, retains its original wooden bar and name from ex-dancer Magnolia Thunderpussy. **The Thirsty Bear**, known for tapas; the **SF Brewing Company** with a bargain happy hour; and the upscale **Gordon Biersch Brewery**, all make their own excellent beer on the premises. At the Pacific Ocean edge of Golden Gate Park, **Beach Chalet**'s brews combine with fine views.

COCKTAILS BARS

Traditional cocktail bars, with a chatty bartender holding court in front of rows of gleaming bottles, are great fun in San Francisco, and there are plenty of venues to choose from.

Singles often drink at **Harry Denton's Starlight Room**, and those in the need-to-be-seen crowd are in the Clift Hotel **Redwood Room**, with a backlit bar and upper tier cocktail prices. A lively bohemian crowd can be found along Columbus Avenue at **Specs'**, **Tosca**, and **Vesuvio** – a one-time beatnik hangout where a poular house drink is the Jack Kerouac (rum, tequila, orange/cranberry juice and lime). Banquettes, potent cocktail and Rat Pack-era decor mix with a relaxed North Beach crowd at **Tony Niks**.

Across town in the Mission District, **Elixir** is a neighborhood bar with darts, and a wooden back-bar in a Victorian building that once had a bootblack on the premises. **Buena Vista Café** is the 1952 birthplace of Irish Coffee and serves 2,000 glasses per day. **Minx** is as close as it gets to a classic, deep color cocktail lounge. Find a playful, imitation ethnic theme at Southeast Asian **Bambuddha Lounge**, or the Thai-style **Lingba Lounge** offers exotic drinks and fun music nights like "sexy karaoke" on Potrero Hill. Other bars, such as **Café du Nord**, in a former Prohibition speakeasy, and the award-winning **Biscuits and Blues**, have live jazz.

WINE BARS

With the proximity to Northern California Wine Country, the **Ferry Plaza Wine Merchant Bar**, surrounded by artisan cheesemakers, bakers and other gourmet outlets, is a fine spot to sample wines.

Champagne and candlelight create the atmosphere of the **Bubble Lounge**. On weekdays, the **London Wine Bar** caters to Financial District workers, craving a British atmosphere with their California vintages. **Diablo Grande Wine Gallery** features its own estate-bottled wines in SoMa's museum area. Across the street at **Vino Venue**, the ounce-at-a-time self-serve dispensing from an automated wine bar is a way to taste the 100 wines on offer before buying. Closer to AT&T Park in SoMa, **Bacar** caters to elegant drinkers as well as thirsty baseball fans with 1,400 wines each night.

THEMED BARS

One of the best spots to connect with local passion is **Knuckles Sports Bar**, with more than 24 televisions for live broadcasts. Bring your own food or snacks to the drinks-only **Greens Sports Bar**. **Pat O'Shea's Mad Hatter** combines the sports bar with another San Francisco tradition, the Irish Bar. Irish cheer and Guinness are quaffed at **The Irish Bank** and **The Chieftain**.

GAY BARS

Watering holes popular with the gay, lesbian, bisexual, and transgendered range from leather, biker, latex, and fetish-specialized to bars favored simply because the clientele is predominatly of one type. The Castro, SoMa and Mission Districts are magnet areas. **Daddy's**, in the Castro, draws a Levi's and leather crowd. **The Stud** and **EndUp** keep drinks flowing with the dancing. In a city where few lesbian bars have survived, **Cherry Bar** hosts live music-filled nights for ladies. **Divas** is a well-known transgendered spot.

DIRECTORY

ROOFTOP BARS

Carnelian Room
52nd floor,
555 California St.
Map 5 C4.
Tel 433-7500.

Cityscape
46th floor,
Hilton Hotel,
333 O'Farrell St.
Map 5 B5.
Tel 923-5002.

Grand View Lounge
36th floor,
Grand Hyatt Hotel,
345 Stockton St.
Map 5 C4.
Tel 398-1234.

Top of the Mark
19th floor,
Mark Hopkins
InterContinental Hotel,
999 California St.
Map 5 B4.
Tel 616-6560.

View Lounge
39th floor,
Marriott Hotel 55
4th St.
Map 5 C5.
Tel 896-1600.

BEER BARS

Beach Chalet
1000 Great Hwy.
Map 7 A2.
Tel 386-8439.

Gordon Biersch Brewery
2 Harrison St.
Map 6 E4.
Tel 243-8246.

Mad Dog in the Fog
530 Haight St.
Map 10 E1.
Tel 626-7279.

Magnolia Pub & Brewery
1398 Haight St.
Map 9 C1.
Tel 864-7468.

S F Brewing Company
155 Columbus Ave.
Map 5 C3.
Tel 434-3344.

The Thirsty Bear
661 Howard St.
Map 6 D5.
Tel 974-0905.

COCKTAIL BARS

Bambuddha Lounge
661 Eddy St.
Map 5 A5.
Tel 885-5088.

Biscuits and Blues
401 Mason St.
Map 5 B5.
Tel 292-2583.

Buena Vista Café
2765 Hyde St.
Map 4 F1.
Tel 747-5044.

Café du Nord
2170 Market St.
Map 10 D2.
Tel 861-5016.

Elixir
3200 16th St.
at Valencia St.
Map 10 F2.
Tel 552-1633.

Harry Denton's Starlight Room
450 Powell St.
Map 5 B4.
Tel 395-8595.

Lingba Lounge
1469 18th St.
Map 11 C3.
Tel 355-0001.

Minx
827 Sutter St.
Map 5 B4.
Tel 346-7666.

Redwood Room
495 Geary St.
Map 5 B5.
Tel 775-4700.

Specs'
12 Adler Place
(across Columbus Ave
from Vesuvio).
Map 5 C3.
Tel 421-4112.

Tony Niks
1534 Stockton St.
Map 5 B2.
Tel 693-0990.

Tosca
242 Columbus Ave.
Map 5 C3.
Tel 391-1244.

Vesuvio
255 Columbus Ave.
Map 5 C3.
Tel 362-3370.

WINE BARS

Bacar
448 Brannan St.
Map 11 C1.
Tel 904-4100.

Bubble Lounge
714 Montgomery St.
Map 5 C3.
Tel 434-4204.

Diablo Grande Wine Gallery
669 Mission St.
Map 5 C5.
Tel 543-4343.

Ferry Plaza Wine Merchant Bar
One Ferry Building,
Shop 23.
Map 6 E3.
Tel 391-9400.

London Wine Bar
415 Sansome St.
Map 5 C3.
Tel 788-4811.

Vino Venue
686 Mission St.
Map 5 C5.
Tel 341-1930.

THEMED BARS

Knuckles Sports Bar
555 North Point St.
Map 5 A1.
Tel 563-1234.

Greens Sports Bar
2339 Polk St.
Map 5 A3.
Tel 775-4287.

Pat O'Shea's Mad Hatter
3848 Geary Blvd.
Map 3 A5.
Tel 752-3148.

The Chieftain
195 5th St.
Map 11 B1.
Tel 615-0916.

The Irish Bank
10 Mark La
(off Bush St).
Map 5 B4.
Tel 788-7152.

GAY BARS

Cherry Bar
917 Folsom St.
Map 11 B1.
Tel 974-1585.

Daddy's
440 Castro St.
Map 10 D3.
Tel 621-8732.

Divas
1081 Post St.
Map 4 F4.
Tel 434-4204.

Endup
401 6th St.
Map 11 B2.
Tel 646-0999.

The Stud
399 9th St.
Map 11 A2.
Tel 252-7883.

Sports and Outdoor Activities

San Franciscans are sports enthusiasts, and there are plenty of activities to suit every taste. You can choose from a range of public and private health clubs, swimming pools, tennis courts and golf courses. Spectator sports are provided by two baseball teams, professional football, basketball and hockey, plus numerous Bay Area college games. Outdoor activities include cycling, skiing, boat trips and kayaking. Whale-watching adventures are also fun to try. Tickets are available through **Ticketmaster** *(see p258)* or other ticket agents *(see p273).*

FOOTBALL

The home ground of the **San Francisco 49ers** is Monster Park. The **Oakland Raiders** play at **Network Associates Coliseum**. Local colleges, including the **University of California** at Berkeley and **Stanford University** in Palo Alto, also have good football teams.

WHALE WATCHING

If you visit San Francisco in winter, don't miss the chance to experience one of nature's greatest shows, the annual migration of the California gray whale. These huge mammals are sometimes visible from headlands like Point Reyes *(see p160)*, but the best way to see them is to join an ocean-going charter trip, tickets for which are available from **Tickets.com** or Ticketmaster *(see p259)*.

The most informative trips are those offered by the **Oceanic Society Expeditions**. They sail west to the Farallon Islands, where you may also see rare birds and blue whales as well as migrating gray whales. Many whale-watching trips leave from Half Moon Bay *(see pp186–7)*, 20 miles (32 km) south of San Francisco.

Tickets.com
Tel (510) 762-2277.

Oceanic Society Expeditions
Fort Mason. **Map** 4 E1.
Tel 441-1106.

BASEBALL

Two professional baseball teams play in the Bay Area. The National League **San Francisco Giants** play their home games at the state-of-the-art stadium at AT&T Park. The American League **Oakland Athletics** play at the Network Associates Coliseum, just across the bay in Oakland.

BASKETBALL

The Bay Area's only NBA basketball team is the **Golden State Warriors**, who play at the Oakland Coliseum Arena. The Golden Bears of **UC Berkeley** also play some games there, but most of their home games take place on campus, as do all of **Stanford University's**.

ICE HOCKEY

Home games of the **San Jose Sharks**, the Bay Area's only professional ice hockey team, are played at the San Jose Arena in central San Jose, about one hour south of San Francisco.

GYMS AND HEALTH CLUBS

Large business hotels usually have health club facilities on the premises. Those that don't usually have an agreement with a private club that gives short-term membership to hotel guests. If neither of these options is available, choose from the upscale **Bay Club**, near the Financial District, the well-maintained **Crunch Fitness**, or the basic **24-Hour Nautilus Fitness Center**.

BOATING

Unless you are fortunate to know someone willing to take you out on their yacht, the only way to sail around the bay is to rent a boat from **Cass' Marina** in Sausalito, where lessons and piloted charters are also available. For more limited water trips, rent a kayak from the **Sea Trek Ocean Kayak Center** or a rowboat, pedal boat or motorboat from the **Stow Lake Boathouse** in Golden Gate Park.

GOLF COURSES

Golfers have a wide range of courses to choose from, including municipal links in **Lincoln Park** and **Golden Gate Park** and the beautiful **Presidio Golf Club**. Farther away, some of the world's most famous courses line the Pacific Ocean in Carmel *(see pp186–7)*, where for about $275–$300 you can test your skills and play a round or two at the renowned **Pebble Beach Golf Links**.

SKIING

For skiing, San Franciscans head east to the mountains of Lake Tahoe *(see pp196–9)*, where resorts like **Heavenly** and **Alpine Meadows** provide excellent slopes for all levels of ability, amid gorgeous alpine vistas. The biggest resort, **Squaw Valley**, is just north of the lake and was the site of the 1960 Winter Olympics. Also within reach of the Bay Area are **Badger Pass**, in Yosemite National Park *(see pp200–201)*, and cross-country oriented **Kirkwood Ski Resort**. Skiing equipment can be rented at all these resorts, and lessons are also available.

SWIMMING

Most public swimming pools are out in the suburban fringes, so for times and fees contact **City of San Francisco Recreation and Parks Department** swimming information line. To swim in the chilly ocean, head to China Beach, the only safe beach in the city. Join the "Polar Bear Club" and swim in the bay. There are also two swimming clubs at Aquatic Park (see pp172–3), the **Dolphin Club** and the **South End Rowing Club**. If you are in San Francisco over the New Year, watch the New Year's Day sponsored swim organized by these two clubs for their members (see p51).

BICYCLING

Cycling up and down San Francisco's steep hills may not seem like a sensible idea, but if you plan your route well a bike can be the best way to appreciate the city. Particularly on weekends, when the traffic is comparatively quiet, riding along the Embarcadero and the Golden Gate Promenade gives great views of the bay. The Presidio and Golden Gate Park area is also ideal for cycling, and where most rental shops are, including **Stow Lake Bike Rentals**. In North Beach, **Blazing Saddles** rents bikes.

In the Wine Country (see pp190–93), you can take advantage of the tours organized by **Backroads Bicycle Tours**. Many are multi-day tours through Napa and Sonoma counties as well as through Alexander Valley.

TENNIS

There are good tennis courts in almost all of the city's public parks, with the largest group in Golden Gate Park. All city courts have been renovated, and many have lights for night games. They are all operated by the **City of San Francisco Recreation and Parks Department**. For details, phone their information line. The **San Francisco Tennis Club** has 24 indoor and outdoor courts and offers private and group lessons. Guests staying at the famed **Claremont Resort, Spa and Tennis Club** (see p163) can have lessons and play tennis to their heart's content.

DIRECTORY

TICKETS

Golden State Warriors
Oakland Coliseum Arena.
Tel (1) (888) 479-4667.

Oakland Athletics
Tel (510) 638-0500.

Oakland Raiders
Tel (1) (800) 949-2626.

San Francisco 49ers
Monster Park.
Tel 656-4900.

San Francisco Giants
AT&T Park.
Tel 972-2000.
www.sfgiants.com

San Jose Sharks
San Jose Arena.
Tel (408) 287-7070.

Stanford University Athletics
Stanford University.
Tel (1) (800) STANFORD.

Tickets.com
Tel (510) 762-2277.

UC Berkeley Intercollegiate Athletics
UC Berkeley.
Tel (1) (800) 462-3277.

HEALTH CLUBS

Bay Club
150 Greenwich St.
Map 5 C2.
Tel 433-2550.

Crunch Fitness
1000 Van Ness Ave.
Map 5 A5. *Tel* 931-1100.
www.crunch.com

24-Hour Nautilus Fitness Center
1200 Van Ness St. **Map** 4 F4. *Tel* 776-2200.
www.24hourfitness.com
One of several branches.

BOATING

Cass' Marina
1702 Bridgeway, Sausalito.
Tel 332-6789.

Sea Trek Ocean Kayak Center
Schoonmaker Point Marina, Sausalito.
Tel 488-1000.

Stow Lake Boathouse
Golden Gate Park.
Map 8 E2.
Tel 752-0347.

GOLF COURSES

Golden Gate Park
(Municipal 9 hole).
Map 7 B2.
Tel 751-8987.

Lincoln Park
(Municipal 18 hole).
Map 1 C5.
Tel 221-9911.

Pebble Beach Golf Links
Pebble Beach.
Tel (831) 624 3811.

Presidio Golf Club
300 Finley Rd. **Map** 3 A3.
Tel 561-4653.

SKIING

Alpine Meadows
Tahoe City.
Tel (530) 583-4232.

Badger Pass
Yosemite National Park.
Tel (209) 372-1001.

Heavenly Ski Resort
Stateline, Nevada.
Tel (775) 586-7000.

Kirkwood Ski Resort
Kirkwood.
Tel (209) 258-6000.

Squaw Valley USA
Squaw Valley.
Tel (530) 583-6985.

SWIMMING

Dolphin Club
502 Jefferson St. **Map** 4 F1. *Tel* 441-9329.
www.dolphinclub.com

City of San Francisco Recreation and Parks Department
Swimming information.
Tel 831-2747.
Tennis information.
Tel 831-6302.
www.parks.sf.gov.org

South End Rowing Club
500 Jefferson St.
Map 4 F1. *Tel* 776-7372.
www.southend.org

CYCLING

Backroads Bicycle Tours
1516 Fifth St, Berkeley.
Tel (510) 527-1555.
www.backroads.com

Blazing Saddles
1095 Columbus Ave.
Map 5 A2.
Tel 202-8888.
One of two branches.
www.blazingsaddles.com

Stow Lake Bike Rentals
Golden Gate Park.
Map 8 E2.
Tel 752-0347.

TENNIS

Claremont Resort, Spa & Tennis Club
41 Tunnel Rd, Oakland.
Tel (510) 843-3000.
www.claremont resort.com

San Francisco Tennis Club
645 5th St.
Map 11 B1.
Tel 777-9000.

CHILDREN'S SAN FRANCISCO

San Francisco is full of attractions that can satisfy children's curiosity and never-ending quest for adventure and fun. Many museums tailor their exhibits to spark a child's imagination and occupy busy little hands. Colorful street fairs run from spring to fall. And year-round, the days of the Gold Rush, the Wild West and gangsters imprisoned on Alcatraz come alive with a visit to historic sites. Children can see exotic animals up close at the zoo, or enjoy the varied attractions of Golden Gate Park. This is a city for families, and many places offer free or discounted admission for children.

PRACTICAL ADVICE

Families are well provided for in San Francisco. Family discounts at most hotels allow children to stay in their parents' room free of charge, and cots and cribs are usually available. Most hotels will arrange babysitters, or licensed agencies such as the **American Child Care Services, Inc**. will provide experienced childcare.

Parking is costly, but public transportation is excellent. Plan your trip, using the map on the inside back cover of this book, to include an exciting combination of buses, streetcars and cable cars; each is an adventure in itself. Under-fives travel free on public transportation. There are reduced fares for children aged 5 to 17, and 1, 3 and 7-day Muni Passports for all age groups *(see p294)*.

Use the pay public toilets *(see p280)* or rest rooms in large hotels and stores; they are usually well kept. Medications are available 24 hours a day at Walgreen's Drugstore *(see p283)*.

Current activities that are recommended for families are listed in the quarterly *San Francisco Book* and *Arts Monthly* calendar *(see p281)*.

Crazy Castle at San Francisco Zoo

WILDLIFE

Animal lovers will find a wealth of wildlife in the Bay Area. Drive or take the ferry to **Six Flags Marine World** in Vallejo and spend the day riding an elephant or coming nose-to-nose with a dolphin. At the Marine Mammal Center in the Marin Headlands *(see pp174–5)* you can get close to rescued sea lions. San Francisco Zoo *(see p160)* makes a good day or half-day trip. Here you can see a rare, white Siberian tiger, watch the antics of a lowland gorilla family in Gorilla World and feed penguin chicks in the world's most successful breeding colony. The

Meeting a Barbados sheep at San Francisco Children's Zoo

Josephine D. Randall Junior Museum has a petting zoo and nature walks. Oceanic Society Expeditions *(see p299)* sail 25 miles (40 km) into the Pacific to the Farallones National Marine Sanctuary. Trips run all through the year, but gray whales are best seen from December to April.

MUSEUMS

Many museums are action-packed for children. At the California Academy of Sciences *(see pp150–51)* you can ride out an earthquake in the Earthquake! Theater. The Academy is also home to the Morrison Planetarium and the huge Steinhart Aquarium's 8,000 marine specimens. **Zeum** at the Rooftop in Yerba Buena Gardens, is an interactive facility where kids can explore the media arts. The Rooftop includes an ice-skating rink and a 1906 carousel.

The **Bay Area Discovery Museum** is for 2 to 12-year-olds, offering a activities to encourage budding imaginations. The **Exploratorium** *(see pp60–61)* is acclaimed for its 700-plus hands-on exhibits. Adventurous children visiting its Tactile Dome have to rely on their sense of touch to find a way out of the complete darkness. Don't miss the Wells Fargo History Museum *(see p110)*, where

A welcoming face for children

your children can relive the Gold Rush days, hopping aboard a stagecoach, tapping out a telegraph message and discovering gold. Admission is free, and also at the Maritime Historical Park *(see p83)*, a nautical treasure-house of ship models and relics. Three of the museum's restored historic ships can be explored at Hyde Street Pier.

Museums at Fisherman's Wharf are designed to amuse, mystify, horrify and fascinate youngsters. Sample the delights of Ripley's Believe It Or Not! *(see p82)*, and the Wax Museum *(see p82)*. Everyone can enjoy the restored marshland, dunes, and beach at Crissy Field in the Presidio.

OUTDOOR FUN

The most exciting way to take children around town is on the cable cars *(see pp296–7)*. For a thrilling descent, ride the last leg of the Powell–Hyde line to Aquatic Park *(see pp172–3)*, then take the nearby ferry to Alcatraz Island *(see pp84–7)*.

In Golden Gate Park *(see pp142–57)* there are riding stables, bike trails, boating lakes, a carousel in the Children's Playground and even a herd of bison. At **Make*A*Circus** in Fort Mason, young spectators can become clowns or jugglers at the workshops following every show. **Paramount's Great America** is a theme park with 100 acres of rides and shows.

SHOPPING

The sheer abundance of toys at **Toys R Us** is sure to enthral any child. At **Basic Brown Bear** shoppers can tour the factory

Riding stables in Golden Gate Park

Children on the beach at Crissy Field *(see pp58–9)*

and buy and stuff their own huggable bear. **Gamescape** sells all kinds of non-electric games, or watch chocolate being made at the Ghirardelli Chocolate Manufactory *(see p83)*, and then buy candy to eat or to take home as presents and souvenirs.

INDOOR FUN

Slightly older children can burn off their excess energy at **Mission Cliffs**, an enormous indoor rock-climbing gym. For creative fun, try the Exploratium for interesting, hands-on exhibits. Zeum and Sony Metreon are musts for children of all ages.

EATING OUT

Fast food is available all over the city, from take-out *dim sum* in Chinatown to burgers in Union Square. For a more relaxed meal, most restaurants welcome children and provide high chairs and special menus for them. **California Pizza Kitchen** and **The Night Kitchen** at Metreon serve tasty pizzas with unique toppings, sandwiches and salads. Surrounded by animated wild-life and other special effects, eating out at the **Rainforest Café** is a really wonderful experience.

SURVIVAL
GUIDE

PRACTICAL INFORMATION

San Francisco proclaims itself as "Everybody's Favorite City." This is endorsed by many travel magazines, which have heaped awards on its facilities. The everyday needs of visitors are well taken care of. All travelers, from the economy-minded to the extravagant, will find a wide range of hotels (see pp206–21), restaurants serving many kinds of food (pp222–43),

Badge on State Building

shops (pp244–57), entertainment (pp258–73), and guided tours (p279) to suit their budget. Getting around the city is easy and usually safe if you use common sense (pp282–3). The following practical information will help you locate banks (pp284–5) and medical resources (pp282–3). There are various tips, from making long-distance calls to taking a cable car trip (pp286–7).

Traffic in Chinatown

SIGHTSEEING TIPS

If you want to avoid long lines and crowds, visit the major attractions (Alcatraz, Pier 39, Fisherman's Wharf and cable car rides) in the morning and leave the more unstructured explorations (Bay cruises, the Golden Gate Bridge, Golden Gate Park, museums and shopping) until after lunch. Plan to visit a group of sights in the same vicinity on the same day to save time and transportation costs – see the *Street-by-Street* plans of each area for suggested routes. Weekends are usually much more crowded than weekdays. Rush hours are Monday to Friday, from 7am to 9am and 4pm to 6:30pm, when all forms of transportation (including cable cars) and streets in the city center will be full. See page 282 for information on visitor safety whilst travelling around the city.

ETIQUETTE AND TIPPING

It is illegal to smoke in all workplaces, stores, and restaurants and in the seating areas at 3Com Park. Smoking is allowed in bars and bar areas of some restaurants. Hotels must designate 35 percent of their rooms and 75 percent of the lobby as non-smoking zones though many are now adopting a complete non-smoking policy. Inquire about smoking policies when booking a hotel or restaurant.

In restaurants, tip around 15 to 20 percent of the total bill. Allow for an average tip of 15 percent for taxi drivers, bar staff and hair stylists. Hotel and airport baggage handlers expect $1 to $1.50 per bag. Leave hotel chambermaids $1 to $2 for each day of your stay.

OPENING HOURS

Most businesses are open on weekdays from 9am to 5pm and do not close for lunch.

Bankers' hours vary, but all operate a core time from 10am to 3pm Monday to Friday. Some banks open as early as 7:30am, close at 6pm or have Saturday morning hours. Many have round-the-clock cash machines. Some museums are closed on Mondays and/or Tuesdays and major public holidays, but some occasionally stay open in the evening (phone for details).

TOURIST INFORMATION

Maps, guides, events' listings, and discount passes for public transportation and attractions are available at the Convention and Visitors Bureau (see p117).
Useful information San Francisco Convention and Visitors Bureau, Lower Level of Hallidie Plaza, Powell St and Market St. **Map** 5 B5. **Tel** 391-2000. **Mailing address**: PO Box 4299097, San Francisco, CA 94142-9097. ◻ *9am–5:00pm Mon–Fri, 9am–3pm Sat. Send $3 for a visitor's kit.* **www**.sfvisitor.org

Visitor Information Center, Hallidie Plaza

◁ **Cable car passing a mock-Tudor building**

MUSEUM ADMISSION CHARGES

San Francisco's museums have been revitalized by moves to new locations. Major museums have entry fees ranging from $5 to $10, with discounts for senior citizens, children and students. Smaller museums are either free or request a donation. At most large institutions entrance is free once a month (phone for details) and free guided tours, demonstrations and lectures are offered. In Fort Mason (see pp74–5), Yerba Buena Gardens (see pp114–15) and Golden Gate Park (see pp143–55), several museums are grouped together. Golden Gate Park's Culture Pass allows the holder entrance to three museums and two attractions,

saving 30 percent on the admission charge. City Pass is available from the Visitor Information Center (see p278) and gives a similar percentage reduction on the entrance fees to all the city's museums.

ENTERTAINMENT LISTINGS

Two free guides are available at the Visitor Information Center (see p278): The San Francisco Book details the city's concerts, shows, nightclubs and restaurants; Arts Monthly has film, theater, visual arts, music and dance listings. Key This Week in San Francisco and Where Magazine (monthly) are free from hotels and stores. The "Datebook" section of Sunday's San Francisco

San Francisco listings magazines

Chronicle/Examiner lists the major arts and entertainment events. Friday's San Francisco Examiner "Weekend" section and The Bay Guardian's and San Francisco Weekly's listings are also good sources.

GUIDED TOURS

Bus coach tours cover the main city sights in an informative half day, while walking tours may be dramatic and have more "personality." "Flightseeing" is a thrill, as cable cars whisk you around the city in about an hour. Horse-drawn carriages go anywhere on request, or you can set your own pace with a prerecorded tour. City Segway Tours cover the waterfront.

Boat Trips
See p299.

Bus Tours
Agentours, Inc
126 West Portal Ave.
Tel 661-5200.
www.agentours.com

California Parlor Car Tours
1253 Post St, # 1011
Map 4 F4.
Tel 474-7500 or
(1 800) 227-4250.
Minibus tours.
www.calpartours.com

Gray Line of San
Francisco
Pier 43½. **Map** 5 B1.
also at: Transbay Terminal.
Map 6 D4.
Tel 558-9400.
Double-decker and luxury
buses. **www**.grayline
sanfrancisco.com

Lucky Tours
1111 Mission St.
Map 11 A1.
Tel 864-3855.
www.luckytours.com

The Mexican Bus
3rd and Howard sts.
Map 6D5. **Tel** 546-3747.
Mission District murals
www.mexicanbus.com

Helicopter and Air Tours
San Francisco Helicopter
Tours **Tel** (1 800) 400-
2404. **www**.sfhelicopter
tours.com

Red and White Fleet
Helicopter Tours
Pier 43½.
Tel 673-2900.
www.redandwhite.com

Motorized Cable Car
Cable Car Charters
Tel 922-2425.

Horse and Carriage Tours
Waterfront Horse/Carriage
Rides. **Tel** 771-8687. Rides
start and finish at Pier 41.

Prerecorded Audio Tours
Amninav Inc. Cassettes and
CDs available.
Tel (1) (650) 219-8029.

Walking Tours
Chinatown Tours with the
"Wok Wiz." 660 California
St. **Map** 5 C4. **Tel** 982-
8839. *Award-winning tour
and dim sum lunch.* **www**.
allaboutchinatown.com

City Guides
Friends of the San Francisco
Public Library. **Tel** 557-4266.
Free history, architecture
and cultural tours.

Cruisin' the Castro from
an Historical Perspective
375 Lexington St,
94110. **Map** 10 F3. **Tel**
550-8110. Explores gay
and lesbian community.
www.webcastro.com
/castrotour

Heritage Walks 2007
Franklin St. **Map** 4 E3.
Tel 441-3000.
Architectural tours.
www.sfheritage.org

Roger's Highpoints
Chartered Tours
2640 Ridgeway Ave,
San Bruno, 94066.
Tel (650) 742-9611.

San Francisco Parks Trust
McLaren Lodge, Golden
Gate Park. **Map** 9 B1.
Tel 750-5105 or 263-
0991. Free guided walks
in Golden Gate Park Sat
and Sun, May–Oct only.

Victorian Home Walk Tour
Map 5 B5. **Tel** 252-9485.
www.victorianwalk.com

Walking Tours San
Francisco
925 Sutter St, Suite 101.
Map 5 C4.
Tel 317-8687. **www**.
walkingtourssf.com

Waterfront Tours
City Segway Tours
Tel 409-0672. **www**.
citysegwaytours.com

Guided motorized cable car tour around the city

DISABLED TRAVELERS

Nearly all attractions, buildings and public transportation are equipped for easy access in San Francisco. To comply with the American Disabilities Act, direction signs, toilets and entrances are specially adapted for blind and disabled visitors. Theaters and movie theaters may offer special audio equipment for hearing-impaired patrons. TDD and TTD/TTY are phone systems that allow hearing-impaired users to communicate by a keyboard and screen. Parking spaces reserved for vehicles with disabled permits are marked by a blue and white sign, and a blue curb. Often a wheelchair outline is painted on the pavement.

Parking bay for the disabled

CUSTOMS AND IMMIGRATION

Holders of a valid EU, Australian or a New Zealand passport and a return ticket are not required to have visas if staying 90 days or less in the US. However, visitors must register online via the Electronic System for Authorization (https://esta.cbp.dhs.gov). Applications must be made at least 72 hours before travel. Canadians and returning Americans must have a passport or other accepted form of official ID. Sometimes foreign visitors must prove they carry sufficient funds. Ask your travel agent or contact the US Embassy for current requirements and stipulations.
  Customs allowances for

SAN FRANCISCO TIME

San Francisco is in the Pacific Time Zone. Daylight Saving Time begins on the first Sunday in April (at 2am) when clocks are set ahead one hour. It ends on the last Sunday in October (at 2am) when clocks are set back one hour.

City and Country	Hours + or - PT	City and Country	Hours + or - PT
Amsterdam (Netherlands)	+ 9	Nairobi (Kenya)	+ 11
Athens (Greece)	+ 10	New York (US)	+ 3
Auckland (New Zealand)	+ 20	Paris (France)	+ 9
Beijing (China)	+ 16	Perth (Australia)	+ 16
Berlin (Germany)	+ 9	Prague (Czech Republic)	+ 9
Brussels (Belgium)	+ 9	Rome (Italy)	+ 9
Chicago (US)	+ 2	Singapore (Singapore)	+ 16
Istanbul (Turkey)	+ 10	Sydney (Australia)	+ 18
Kowloon (Hong Kong)	+ 16	Tokyo (Japan)	+ 17
London (UK)	+ 8	Toronto (Canada)	+ 3
Madrid (Spain)	+ 9	Vienna (Austria)	+ 9
Moscow (Russia)	+ 11	Washington, DC (US)	+ 3

---

visitors over 21 years of age entering the US are: 200 cigarettes; 50 cigars (not from Cuba) or 1.4 kilograms (3 lbs) of tobacco; no more than 1 liter (2 pints) of alcohol; gifts that are worth no more than $100. Not allowed: meat or meat products (even in cans), illegal drugs, cheese, seeds, live plants, or fresh fruit. Foreign tourists to the United States may bring in or take out up to $10,000 in US or foreign currency.
  Upon arrival at San Francisco International Airport *(see pp288–9)* follow the signs that read "other than American passports" to immigration counters for passport inspection and stamping. After claiming your luggage, proceed to customs where an officer will review the declaration filled in by you on your flight. You will be directed either to the exit or to another officer who may search your luggage. It takes on average 30 minutes to an hour including the wait to complete the formalities.

STUDENT TRAVELERS

Students receive discounts at many museums and theaters if they can produce proof of student status. The most accepted

proof is an International Student Identity Card. Apply for one at your local student center, youth hostel organization or student travel association. Once on the road, it may be difficult to get validated documentation from your college. Working vacations for students from other countries may be arranged through **Student Travel Association**. STA Travel has two offices in the Bay Area, 10 in the US and over 100 offices worldwide.

International Student ID Card

PUBLIC BATH-ROOMS/TOILETS

In bus depots and underground BART stations, public facilities are often frequented by the city's homeless and can attract drug users. However, the new, automatic, self-cleaning, pay toilets that may be found on street corners in tourist areas offer a cleaner and safer alternative. These can be recognized easily by their distinctive dark green color and oval shape. They display a yellow circle surrounding a blue triangle – and a blue and white disabled access sign. As an alternative, major hotel lobby and department store facilities are free and usually well maintained.

CONVERSION CHART

Bear in mind that 1 US pint (0.5 liter) is a smaller measure than 1 UK pint (0.6 liter).

Imperial system
1 inch = 2.5 centimeters
1 foot = 30 centimeters
1 mile = 1.6 kilometers
1 ounce = 28 grams
1 pound = 454 grams
1 US pint = 0.5 liter
1 US gallon = 3.8 liters

Metric system
1 millimeter = 0.04 inch
1 centimeter = 0.4 inch
1 meter = 3 feet 3 inches
1 kilometer = 0.6 mile
1 gram = 0.04 ounce

NEWSPAPERS, TELEVISION AND RADIO

Foreign newspapers and magazines are for sale at several shops and newsstands, including **Café de la Presse** and **Galleria Newsstand**. TV schedules can be found in the weekly

A selection of newspapers available in San Francisco

TV Guide magazine and also in the television section of the *Chronicle*'s Sunday edition. Four television networks operate in San Francisco: CBS is on channel 5 (KPIX), ABC on channel 7 (KGO), NBC on channel 11 (KNTV) and FOX on channel 2 (KTVU). The local PBS station is Channel 9 (KQED). This broadcasts educational and cultural programs, and some classic BBC shows. Cable offerings include CNN, ESPN and pay channels. Some hotels have a free channel for tourist information, but may charge

for cable or movie channels. AM radio stations include: KCBS (740 Hz) for news; KNBR (680 Hz) sport; KOIT (1050 Hz) soft rock. FM stations include: KLLC Alice (97.3 M) pop; KBLX (102.9 M) jazz; KDFC (102.1 M) classical.

ELECTRICAL APPLIANCES

All electric current flows at a standard 110–120 volts AC (alternating current) in the US. In Europe the standard is 220 volts, so to operate 220-volt appliances, you will need a voltage converter and an electrical adaptor plug with two flat parallel prongs to plug into US outlets. Rooms are equipped with special plugs just for electric shavers that carry either 110- or 220-volt current. Many modern hotels have hair dryers

Standard US 2-pin plug

mounted on the bathroom walls. Some hotels provide coffee makers in the room, and irons can usually be requested from your hotel's room service.

DIRECTORY

RELIGIOUS SERVICES

Most hotels have lists of service times and locations. Among the places of worship are:

Catholic
St Mary's Cathedral
1111 Gough St.
Map 4 E4. **Tel** 567-2020.

Episcopal
Grace Cathedral
1100 California St
at Taylor. **Map** 5 B4.
Tel 749-6300.

Jewish
Conservative
Congregation B'Nai
Emunah, 3595 Taraval.
Tel 664-7373.

Orthodox
Adath Israel
1851 Noriega St.
Map 8 D4. **Tel** 564-5665.

Lutheran
St. Mark's
1111 O'Farrell St.
Map 5 A5.
Tel 928-7770.

Methodist
Glide Memorial United
330 Ellis St. **Map** 5 B5.
Tel 771-6300.

Presbyterian
Calvary
2515 Fillmore St.
Map 4 D3. **Tel** 346-3832.

DISABLED TRAVELERS

Muni Access Guide
Muni Accessible Services
Programs,
949 Presidio Ave.
Map 3 C4.
Tel 923-6142 weekdays
or 673-MUNI.

San Francisco Convention and Visitors Bureau
Tel 391-2000.

EMBASSIES AND CONSULATES

Australian Consulate General
625 Market St, Suite 200.
Map 5 C4.
Tel 536-1970.

British Consulate General
Suite 850,
1 Sansome St.
Map 6 D4
Tel 617-1300.

Canadian Consulate General
550 S Hope St.
9th Floor,
Los Angeles.
Tel (213) 346-2700.

Consulate General of Ireland
100 Pine St,
33rd Floor.
Map 6 D4.
Tel 392-4214.

New Zealand Consulate General
1 Maritime Plaza,
Map 6 D3.
Tel 399-1255.

STUDENT INFORMATION

STA Travel
36 Geary St.
Map 5 C5.
Tel 391-8407.

INTERNATIONAL NEWSSTANDS

Café de la Presse
352 Grant Ave.
Map 5 C4.
Tel 398-2680.

Galleria Newsstand
50 Post St, Ste 44.
Map 5 C4.
Tel 398-4847.

Personal Security and Health

According to the FBI's crime reports, San Francisco is one of the safest large cities in the US. Very few visitors are victims of any form of street crime because police officers patrol tourist areas regularly. Community groups in the Civic Center, Tenderloin, Western Addition and Mission Districts are also taking positive steps to improve their locale and image.

A San Francisco Police badge

During the late afternoon and after dark, however, it is advisable to take a taxi to and from these districts since tourist sights often border sleazy theaters and vacant buildings. Follow the guidelines below, set by the Police Department, and use common sense and your stay should be safe and healthy.

Powell Street police *koban*

LAW ENFORCEMENT

The San Francisco Police Department provides foot, horse, motorcycle and car patrols day and night. Major community and cultural events are overseen by police, especially at night in the Tenderloin area. Five police station kiosks, called *kobans*, are located in Chinatown, Japantown, Union Square, the Mission District and at Hallidie Plaza (hours vary). Traffic and parking enforcement officers make their rounds on foot or in small three-wheeled vehicles. Airports, stores, hotels and the transit system have their own uniformed and plain-clothes security staff who also provide safety services.

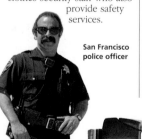

San Francisco police officer

GUIDELINES ON SAFETY

Most of San Francisco's street people are not dangerous, but some are compulsive law breakers, so treat them with caution. Do not advertise that you are a visitor; plan your route in your hotel room or look at maps and brochures discreetly. If you look lost, you may also be an easy target for crime. Be aware of your surroundings: if an area appears unsafe, leave. Ask directions only from hotel, shop or office staff, or police officers, and avoid talking to strangers on the street.

Use your ATM card to take out limited amounts of cash or use travelers' checks. Never display cash; money belts concealed under clothing are better than bags and wallets. If you must carry bags, hold them securely under your arm, and keep wallets in the inside front pocket of your pants or jacket. Carry some cash and credit cards in a concealed secondary wallet. Be alert in crowds, especially in stores, at bus stops or on public transportation. Copy all your travel documents and carry them separately.

In your hotel, guard your luggage while you check in and check out, and do not broadcast your name and room number. Ask about the hotel's key-control policy, room cleaning schedules and staff identification badges. Verify the identity of room service and repair personnel with reception before you let them in, especially if you did not call for them. Keep an inventory of items that you deposit in the hotel safe. Do not leave cash or valuables in your room and keep your luggage locked. Know how to double lock your hotel room door, and use the door viewer

Motorcycle patrolman

before you let anyone in. Report suspicious activity, and keep the key with you until you check out.

If you have a car, lock it and keep the keys with you; always check the interior before you get in. Park in well-lit, busy areas, and remove all luggage and valuables.

Police car

LOST PROPERTY

Although the chances of retrieving property lost on the street are few, phone the **Police Non-Emergency Line**. The **Muni** transportation system has a **Lost-and-Found** office.

Note the company name, the color and the number of any taxi you take. If you lose an item, you will need this information when calling the cab company to report your loss.

Fire engine

TRAVEL INSURANCE

Travel insurance is essential for foreign travelers; medical care is good, but costly, in the US. Every traveler should check that their coverage includes emergency medical and dental care, lost or stolen baggage and travel documents, accidental death and trip cancellation fees.

Ambulance

MEDICAL MATTERS

If you do not have medical insurance, a visit to a doctor, hospital or clinic can be expensive. Even with medical insurance you may have to pay for the services yourself, then claim reimbursement from your insurance company. Many doctors, dentists and hospitals accept credit cards, but traveler's checks and cash are sometimes the only form of payment allowed for visitors.

If you get a prescription from a doctor, ask that it be called in to a pharmacy that will deliver it to you. Pharmacies that deliver include **Four-Fifty Sutter** and **Saint Francis Medical Center**. Some **Walgreen's Drugstores** stay open late or 24 hours. If you take medication, it is a good idea to bring a back-up prescription with you.

EMERGENCIES

For emergencies that require medical, police or fire services, phone 911. Hospital emergency rooms and city hospitals are listed in the Blue Pages of the telephone book. These can be crowded, but are less expensive than private hospitals. Private hospitals are listed in the Yellow Pages of the telephone book.

Hotels may be able to arrange for a doctor or dentist to visit you in your room. The local office of **The Salvation Army** can also provide assistance in many kinds of emergencies.

DIRECTORY

CRISIS INFORMATION

All Emergencies
Tel 911. Alerts police, fire and medical services.

Crime Victims Hot Line
Tel (1) (800) 842-8467.

Pharmacies
Four-Fifty Sutter Pharmacy, 450 Sutter St, 7th Floor.
Map 5 B4. *Tel* 392-4137. (Will deliver)

Saint Francis Medical Center 901 Hyde St.
Map 5 A4.
Tel 776-4650. (Will deliver)

Walgreen's Drug Stores
135 Powell St.
Map 5 B5.
Tel 391-4433
498 Castro St.
Map 10 D3.
Tel 861-3136 (24 hour).
3201 Divisadero St.
Map 3 C2.
Tel 931-6417 (24 hour).

Red Cross
Tel 427-8000.

San Francisco Dental Society Referral Service
Tel 421-1435.

Salvation Army
Tel 553-3500.

Suicide Prevention
Tel 781-0500.

Walk-In Clinics
University of California, San Francisco Clinic, 400 Parnassus Ave.
Map 9 B2.
Tel 353-2602.

Physician Access Center, 26 California St.
Map 6 D4.
Tel 397-2881.

Wall Medical Group 2001 Union St.
Map 4 E3.
Tel (415) 447-6800.

LOST PROPERTY

Local Police Non-Emergency Line
Tel 553-0123.

Muni Lost-and-Found
Tel 923-6168.

Lost or Stolen Credit Cards (Toll free)
American Express
Tel (1) (800) 528-4800.
Diners Club
Tel (1) (800) 234-6377.
MasterCard (Access)
Tel (1) (800) 627-8372.
VISA
Tel (1) (800) 336-8472.

Banking and Currency

San Francisco's financial district *(see pp106–21)* is the banking center of the West Coast. The imposing corporate headquarters of major US banks, and foreign branches of some of the world's leading financial institutions, can be found in this prestigious area. For the convenience of residents and visitors alike, hundreds of cash machines (ATM's) throughout the city allow automatic transactions 24 hours a day.

One of San Francisco's local banks

BANKING

Banks are generally open Monday to Friday from 10am to 3pm in San Francisco. There are some, however, that open as early as 7:30am, close as late as 6pm and are open on Saturday mornings.

Always ask if any special fees apply before you make your transaction. Generally, at most banks, US dollar traveler's checks can be cashed, if you have a recognized form of photographic identification (for example, a passport, a driver's license that carries your photograph, or an international student identity card). Foreign currency exchange is available at the main branches of large banks. You may not have to wait in the general service line if you see a sign designating a teller

An automated teller machine in the external wall of a bank

window specifically for foreign exchange. Credit unions will serve only their members, so look for banks that offer services to the general public. Bank of America and Wells Fargo Bank have headquarters in the city. You will see many local branches in the Financial District and in neighborhood shopping areas.

AUTOMATED TELLER MACHINES

Automated Teller Machines (ATM) are found in most bank lobbies or on an outside wall near the bank's entrance. US currency, usually in $20 bills, can be electronically withdrawn from your bank or credit card account in seconds. Ask your own bank which ATM systems your card can access in San Francisco and how much each transaction will cost. Popular systems include Cirrus, Plus, and Star, and they accept various US bank cards, in addition to MasterCard (Access), VISA and others.

Robberies can occur at ATM machines, so it is wise to use them only in daylight or when there are plenty of people nearby. Withdrawals from ATMs may provide a better foreign currency exchange rate than cash transactions.

CREDIT CARDS

Credit cards allow you to carry minimal cash and sometimes offer merchandise guarantees or other benefits. American Express, Diners Club, JCB, MasterCard (Access) and VISA are widely accepted. Credit cards can be used in the US to book hotel rooms or rent cars. Most hotels ask for a credit card imprint on check-in. Car rental agencies penalize patrons without credit cards by asking for large cash deposits.

Credit cards are very helpful in emergencies, when you may have to fly home at short notice, or if you need medical treatment during your stay. Hospitals will accept most credit cards in payment.

FOREIGN CURRENCY EXCHANGE

Fees and commissions are charged by foreign currency exchanges, and offices are generally open on weekdays from 9am to 5pm. One of the best known firms is **Thomas Cook Currency Services**. The **Bank of America** operates a foreign exchange service at San Francisco International Airport from 7am to 11pm daily. Otherwise, try the main branch of any major bank.

Foreign currency exchange sign

CASHING TRAVELER'S CHECKS

Traveler's checks issued by American Express and Thomas Cook in US dollars are widely accepted without a fee by most shops, restaurants and hotels. Foreign currency traveler's checks may be cashed at a bank or by the cashier at a major hotel.

Exchange rates are printed in the daily newspapers and posted at banks in branches where currency exchange services are offered. American Express offices cash their own checks without a fee. Personal checks from foreign banks are rarely accepted at business establishments or by check-cashing services.

Coins

American coins come in $1, 50-, 25-, 10-, 5-, and 1-cent pieces. The gold-tone $1 coins are in circulation, as are the State quarters, which feature an historical scene on one side. Each coin has a popular name: 1-cent pieces are called pennies, 5-cent pieces are nickels, 10-cent pieces are dimes and 25-cent pieces are quarters.

**25- cent coin
(a quarter)**

**10- cent coin
(a dime)**

**5- cent coin
(a nickel)**

**1- cent coin
(a penny)**

**One dollar coin
(a buck)**

Bank Notes (Bills)

Units of currency in the United States are dollars and cents. There are 100 cents to a dollar. Notes come in $1, $5, $10, $20, $50 and $100 denominations and all are the same color. The $20 and $50 bills with extra security features are now in circulation. Paper bills were first issued in 1862, when coins were in short supply and the Civil War needed financing.

DIRECTORY

FOREIGN CURRENCY EXCHANGE ADDRESSES

American Express Card Services
Tel 536-2600; (800) 528-4800 for card information; (800) 221-7282 for traveler's check information.

Bank of America
2835 Geary St.
Map 3 C4
Tel (650) 615-4700.
⬜ 9am–6pm Mon–Fri, 9am–2pm Sat.

345 Montgomery St.
Map 5 C4
Tel (650) 615-4700.
⬜ 9am–6pm Mon–Fri.

Thomas Cook Currency Services
75 Geary St.
Map 5 C5
Tel 362-3452.

San Francisco International Airport, Level 3.
Tel 362-3452.

1-dollar bill ($1)

5-dollar bill ($5)

10-dollar bill ($50)

20-dollar bill ($20)

50-dollar bill ($50)

100-dollar bill ($100)

Using San Francisco's Phones

Coin-operated public pay phones are usually in good working order. They are easy to find at many street corners, restaurants, bars, theaters, department stores, hotels and offices. Credit card phones allow you to make a call without using change. Hotels set their own rates, so calls from your room can be more expensive than from the pay phone in the lobby.

PUBLIC TELEPHONES

Modern pay phones have a hand receiver and 12-button key pad. Pacific Bell (PacBell) operates most of the pay phones in the city. These are designated by a blue and white sign with a receiver and the word "phone" or a bell with a circle around it. They are mounted on walls, on poles or in a booth.

Independent companies operate some pay phones, but they are not as reliable and may be more expensive to use. Charges must be posted by law, as well as toll-free numbers, how to make calls using other long-distance service carriers and the phone's exact street location. Telephone directories are often found at pay phones. Pre-paid phonecards are widely available and an inexpensive option for long-distance calls. To complain about service, call the operator (0).

PAY PHONE CHARGES

Within the city area, the standard charge of 50 cents buys three minutes' time. If you talk for longer than that, additional payment may be requested by the operator. The only local prefix (area code) serving the city is **415**. The prefixes **650** and **408** serve the southern suburbs; **510** is for Oakland, Berkeley and the East Bay. These and other numbers called from San Francisco (or vice versa) are long-distance. When you call a number outside the city, but within the same area code, a recorded message will tell you how much more to deposit. Long-distance calls are less expensive if you dial without the help of an operator. In fact, operator assistance is usually unnecessary unless you want to reverse the charges. Many international calls can be dialed direct. Savings on long-distance direct-dial calls are available during the night and weekends within the US. The white pages of the telephone book offer current rate and long-distance calling information in the *Customer Guide* section. The times of day when discounted rates apply for calls to foreign countries vary; the international operator can tell you the least expensive time to phone.

Chinatown phone box

USING A COIN-OPERATED PHONE

1 Lift the receiver and listen for the dial tone.

3 Dial or press the number.

Coins
Make sure you have plenty of these coins available.

5 cents

10 cents

25 cents

2 Insert the required coin or coins. The coin drops as soon as you insert it.

4 If you want to cancel the call before it is answered, or if the call does not connect, press the coin-release lever and take the coins from the coin return.

5 If the call is answered and you talk longer than three minutes, the operator will interrupt and tell you how much more to deposit. Pay phones do not give change.

Fax machine at the airport

FAX SERVICES

Worldwide fax services are available throughout the city. San Francisco International Airport has fax machines in the business center (*see p289*). Many city center mail and copy services charge for sending faxes by the destination and the number of pages being faxed. These same services can receive documents faxed to you and will charge only per-page fees. Look under *Facsimile Transmission Services* in the telephone book Yellow Pages for details. For telegrams, telex and fax, you can also contact **Western Union.**

REACHING THE RIGHT NUMBER

• Long-distance direct-dial call outside your local area code, but within the US and Canada: dial **1**.
• International direct-dial call: dial **011**, followed by country code (Australia: 61; New Zealand: 64; UK: 44), then the city or area code (omit the first 0) and then the local number.
• International call via the operator: dial **01**, followed by the country code, then the city code (without the first 0) and then the local number.
• International directory inquiries: dial **00**.
• International operator assistance: dial **01**.
• Local operator assistance: dial **0**.
• An **800**, **888**, or **887** prefix indicates that the call is free. Dial **1** before the 800.
• Local directory inquiries dial **411**. There may be a charge for this service.
• **Emergencies: dial 911.**

USEFUL NUMBERS

California Public Utilities Commission
Tel (1) (800) 649-7570.

Directory Inquiries within the US
Tel 411.

National Weather Service
Tel (831) 656-1725. *Recorded forecast for the Bay Area.*

Speaking Clock
Tel 767-8900.

Western Union
Tel (1) (800) 325-6000.

Sending a Letter

Stamps can be purchased at post offices, hotel reception desks or from vending machines. Other outlets selling stamps may charge extra. Check current domestic and international postal rates at the post office. Letters can be mailed in post offices, at your hotel, at the airport and in mailboxes on the street. Weekend pickups may be limited or nonexistent.

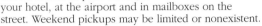
US mail logo

POSTAL SERVICES

Post offices also sell money orders, recommended packaging materials and collectors' stamps. Main post offices are marked on the *Street Finder* maps (*see pp302–11*).

All domestic mail is first class and will usually arrive within 1 to 5 days. Letters without zip codes will be delayed. International air mail to Australia, Canada, Ireland, New Zealand and the UK takes 5 to 10 business days. Packages sent overseas by surface parcel rate may take 4 to 6 weeks for delivery. The federal post office offers two special services. **Priority Mail** promises delivery faster than first class mail.

Standard mailbox

Mailboxes
Collection times are printed on the inside of the pull-down door on each mailbox. Express Mail and Priority Mailboxes look the same but are clearly marked.

The more expensive **Express Mail** delivers next-day within the US, and within 2 to 3 days to many international destinations. Private express mail can be arranged through the Delivery Services listed in the Yellow Pages of the telephone directory. Two international companies are **DHL** and **Fed Ex.**

Colorful US stamps

GENERAL DELIVERY

Letters and parcels will be held for 30 days for collection at the General Post Office. Address mail with: Name, General Delivery, Civic Center, 101 Hyde Street, San Francisco, CA 94142. Be prepared to show proof of identity bearing a photograph when collecting mail sent to General Delivery.

POSTAL SERVICES

San Francisco Post Office Answer Line (24 hours)
Tel (1) (800) 275-8777.

General Mail Facility
1300 Evans Ave.
Tel 550-5134.
☐ 7am–8:30pm Mon–Fri,
8am–2pm Sat. **www**.usps.com

Express and Priority Mail
Tel (1) (800) 222-1811.

DHL
Tel (1) (800) 225-5345.

Fed Ex
Tel (1) (800) 463-3339.

GETTING TO SAN FRANCISCO

Several international airlines operate direct flights to San Francisco, and charter and domestic services are numerous. Competition between airlines has reduced prices and makes flying a feasible alternative to traveling by bus or train. Amtrak trains run from all parts of the United States to nearby Oakland, and bus shuttles operate from the station into San Francisco. Long-distance luxury bus services offer a less frenetic and often cheaper way to travel for those arriving from North American cities. Several cruise lines dock at Pier 35 on their way to Alaska or south to the Mexican Riviera. Check with your travel agent or the operators for the best deals. For visitors arriving by car or bus, there can be little to beat the great views of the city and its surroundings when driving over the Golden Gate and Bay Bridges.

A passenger jet

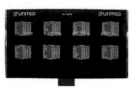

Airport arrivals screens

ARRIVING BY AIR

San Francisco International Airport (SFO) is one of the busiest airports in the world. Its ongoing expansion program will make SFO not only the largest domestic airport but one of the most user friendly. The major carriers there include: **Air Canada, American Airlines, British Airways, Delta Airlines, Northwest/KLM Airlines, Qantas Airways, United Airlines, USAirways** and **Virgin Atlantic.**

SAN FRANCISCO INTERNATIONAL AIRPORT

Located south of the city, 14 miles (23 km) from the center of town, SFO's main runways are right next to San Francisco Bay. SFO serves the Greater San Francisco and metro Bay areas and Silicon Valley with international connections to and from the Pacific Rim, Europe, and Latin America. The arrival and departure gates are arranged around each of three terminals (North, South, International). Walkways connect the three terminals, which surround a short-term parking area. New long-term parking garages, an updated Global Communications Center, and a consolidated car-rental center are planned for the next stage of SFO expansion. All international airlines are now located in the new state-of-the-art International Terminal. Flights to and from Canada are located in other terminals, so be sure to check the airport directory.

Bank of America branches and currency exchange services are available in North and International terminals, and there are Wells Fargo ATMs in all areas.

For travelers with an extra hour, there is no better place to spend it than in the new "History of Aviation" Museum in the International Terminal. Modeled on the old Passenger Waiting Room from the 1937 airport, the museum offers a library, archive, and galleries dedicated to the rise of commercial air transportation. South Terminal has an entire aquarium featuring the Underwater Planet exhibit; Kids' Spot II in North Terminal offers interactive exhibits from the Exploratorium. Throughout the airport, designated galleries display changing exhibits on subjects from Japanese Parasols to Native American art, music, and crafts.

Rental car shuttle

Door-to-door minibus shuttle

SAN FRANCISCO AIRPORT FACILITIES

Visitors arriving at San Francisco International Airport will find customs, baggage claim, sightseeing information, car rental booths and ground transportation into the city on the lower level. The top level has services for those departing from San Francisco, including baggage handlers, ticket and insurance counters, restaurants, bars, shops and security checkpoints. All car rental and parking shuttles, public buses, and door-to-door shuttle minibus services deliver (and pick-up) their passengers at this level.

The airport's 24-hour shuttle, which operates between terminals and long-term parking, picks up on the center

One of the duty-free shops in the International Terminal

island near the ticket counters every 5 to 20 minutes.

Bank of America's foreign exchange office in the international terminal is open from 7am to 11pm daily. **Global Communications Center** has special telephone and teleconferencing equipment, a conference room and fax machine for travelers' use. Each terminal has snack bars, restaurants and cocktail lounges, banks and ATMs, newsstands, and other shops.

Other services provided include baby changing facilities, nurseries, mailboxes and postage stamp vending machines. There are also pay TVs, showers and a clinic for those with medical problems. Wheelchairs, TDD terminals for the hearing-impaired *(see p280)* and an airport shuttle service for the disabled are readily available. You can also use the white courtesy phones that allow you to contact all airport services and facilities free of charge.

limousines will drop you at a specific address. You share the cost of the trip with other passengers for an average cost of $10 to $25.

The average fare for a metered taxicab ride into San Francisco will cost $35. This non-stop trip between the airport and the city center can take 25 minutes or stretch to 40 minutes or more during rush hours (7am to 9am and 4pm to 7pm).

AIRPORT LOCATIONS AROUND SAN FRANCISCO AND THE BAY AREA

New access escalators between levels in the new International Terminal

GETTING INTO THE CITY

Information booths on the lower level offer advice on ground transportation, fares and boarding locations. Follow the arrows marked "Ground Transportation." Luxury buses operated by **SFO Airporter** depart every 20 minutes from 5am to 11pm, serving three city center areas with drop-offs at major hotels. Door-to-door minibus shuttles or shared

Travelers on a budget, with only one bag and plenty of time (to allow for frequent stops), can take a **SamTrans** public bus to the Transbay Terminal *(see p291)*. A light rail system (the AirTrain) links San Francisco International Airport with a designated BART station, which then connects directly with San Francisco, the East Bay and with **CalTrain** rail services *(see p290)* and SamTrans buses.

OTHER AIRPORTS SERVING THE CITY

While most flights arrive at San Francisco International (SFO), **Oakland International** and **San Jose International** airports are less congested. Both offer good ground transportation into San Francisco by door-to-door bus shuttle and limousine. **BART** *(see p298)* serves SFO and Oakland International in conjunction with a shuttle, and a Sam Trans/CalTrain connection serves San Jose.

Glittering glass and steel façade of the new San Francisco International Airport

ARRIVING BY TRAIN

The national passenger rail network, **Amtrak**, links most major US cities. It connects with bus, ferry and air carriers and also operates a joint service across the border with Rail Canada. Noted for their comfort and luxury, all long-distance trains have sleeping accommodations and full refreshment facilities. Often there is a sightseeing lounge.

Passengers are required to reserve seats in advance on many services; in any case, advance booking is advised for all travel during peak periods. Amtrak offers a varied program of special discounts and packages, including 15- and 30-day passes that allow unlimited travel within specified zones. Ask your travel agent for details. Visitors traveling to San Francisco by train will arrive at Amtrak's station in Emeryville to the north of Oakland. The station is in an industrial area, so most passengers reclaim their luggage and continue to their final destination as soon as possible. Amtrak runs a free shuttle to the city center. The ride takes approximately 45 minutes to cross Oakland and the Bay Bridge and ends at the Ferry Building (see p112). From here, ferries, buses, **BART** and Muni Metro streetcars will take you right across the city. Amtrak passengers

CalTrain ticket

Market Street, looking toward the bay

arriving at San Jose Station can transfer via the **CalTrain** commuter rail system to San Francisco. A separate ticket is required for this trip, which can be purchased on the train.

Most Oakland shuttle buses stop at San Francisco's CalTrain station, which is located on the corner of Fourth Street and Townsend Street.

ARRIVING BY CAR

You will get a spectacular introduction to the city by driving over the Golden Gate Bridge or the Bay Bridge. Both are toll bridges, but toll is charged only one way. If your route is from the north via US 101, the Golden Gate Bridge toll will be collected as you enter the city. There is no toll on the return crossing into Marin County. To get into the city center from Golden Gate Bridge, follow the US 101 signs to Lombard Street and Van Ness Avenue.

Approaching the city from the east via I-80 through Oakland, the Bay Bridge toll is collected on the approach to San Francisco. This bridge has two main sections (see pp164–5), divided by Treasure Island, and its highway runs alongside the skyscrapers of the city's Financial District. The first two exits take you to the city center. Arriving from the south via the peninsula, you can choose to follow US 101, 280 or Highway 1. All of these primary routes into the city are well marked, and there are no tolls on the roads.

Driving in the states is on the right-hand side of the road. Red stop lights and stop signs are compulsory stops. Useful tips for driving in San Francisco are given on page 300.

ARRIVING BY LONG-DISTANCE BUS

Regular services are operated by **Greyhound Bus Line** to almost all parts of the United States. The buses are modern and clean. Ask at the Greyhound ticket counter about current discounts or any special rates that may be on offer. If you are planning to interrupt your trip several times along the way or if you want to tour the country on an extended trip, there may be a package designed to suit your requirements. The **Adventure Travel Network (ATN)** is a highly flexible service, which runs down the West Coast to Los Angeles on to Las Vegas. Riders may get on and off at any point, and can use the service as frequently as they wish for the duration of their ticket's validity.

The **Green Tortoise** bus line is an inexpensive, unconventional and sometimes adventurous way to travel by bus, but it is not for everyone. Facilities and stops are very

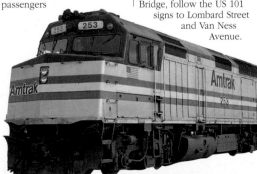

Amtrak trains run to most parts of the US from Emeryville

limited, so passengers have to prepare and share meals among the group. On some routes buses do stop to let riders freshen up in a natural hot spring. Journeys are slow, so if you need to reach your destination at a precise time, take the Greyhound or a train. Green Tortoise routes include Los Angeles, Yosemite National Park, the Grand Canyon, Death Valley and Seattle.

The Transbay Terminal at First and Mission streets is the terminal for long-distance, regional and local public transit bus lines, as well as a few sightseeing tour companies. It does attract petty criminals, so watch your belongings.

Long-distance Greyhound bus

ARRIVING BY SEA

Sailing under Golden Gate Bridge into San Francisco Bay is a highlight of arriving at the Port of San Francisco. Luxury cruise ships dock near Fisherman's Wharf at Pier 35. The city is the embarkation and debarkation point of many operators' Alaskan or Mexican Riviera itineraries. Taxis and public transportation such as BART (see p298), buses and Muni Metro Streetcars (see pp294–5) are readily available at the dock; the city center is only a few minutes' ride away.

DIRECTORY

SAN FRANCISCO AIRPORT (SFO) INFORMATION

Airport Information
Tel (650) 876-2377.
Listen to the voice mail menu and choose the service you need.

Airport Paging
Tel (650) 876-2377.

Airport Police
Tel (650) 876-2424.

Foreign Currency Exchange
Tel (650) 876-2377.

Global Communications Center
Tel (650) 876-2377.

Parking Garage
Tel (650) 821-7900.

Traveler's Aid
Tel (650) 821-2730.

SFO AIRLINE CARRIERS

Air Canada
Tel 1-(888) 247-2262.
American Airlines
Tel 1-(800) 433-7300.
British Airways
Tel 1-(800) 247-9297.
Delta Airlines
Tel 1-(800) 221-1212.

Northwest KLM Airlines
Tel 1-(800) 225-2525.

Qantas Airways
Tel 1-(800) 227-4500.

United Airlines
Tel 1-(800) 241-6522.

USAirways
Tel 1-(800) 428-4322.

Virgin Atlantic Airways
Tel 1-(800) 862-8621.

BUS SERVICE

SFO Airporter
Tel (650) 624-0500.

SFO AIRPORT HOTELS

Best Western El Rancho Inn
1100 El Camino Real
Millbrae.
Tel (650) 588-8500.

La Quinta Inn
20 Airport Blvd
South San Francisco.
Tel (650) 583-2223.

Travel Lodge Airport West
1330 El Camino Real
South San Francisco.
Tel (650) 589-8875.

OAKLAND INTERNATIONAL AIRPORT

Airport Information
Tel (510) 577-4000.

Hotels
Clarion
500 Hegenberger Rd
Oakland.
Tel (510) 562-5311.

La Quinta Inn
8465 Enterprise Way
Oakland.
Tel (510) 632-8900.

SAN JOSE INTERNATIONAL AIRPORT

Airport Information
Tel (408) 277-4759.

Hotels
Executive Inn Airport
1310 N 1st St, San Jose.
Tel (408) 453-1100.
Hyatt Hotel
1740 N 1st St, San Jose.
Tel (408) 993-1234.

DOOR-TO-DOOR SHUTTLE (24-HOUR)

American Airporter Shuttle
Tel 202-0733. Reservations recommended.

Bayporter Express
Tel 467-1800.
Scheduled service operates between SFO and Oakland airports.

SuperShuttle
Tel 558-8500.
www.supershuttle.com

TRAIN INFORMATION

Amtrak
Tel 1-(800) 872-7245.
www.amtrak.com

BART
Tel (650) 992-2278.
www.bart.gov

CalTrain
Tel 1-(800) 660-4287.
www.caltrain.com

SamTrans
Tel 1-(800) 660-4287.
www.samtrans.com

LONG-DISTANCE BUS SERVICES

Adventure Travel Network (ATN)
Tel 247-1800.

Green Tortoise
Tel 956-7500.
www.greentortoise.com

Greyhound Bus Line
Tel 1-(800) 231-2222.
www.greyhound.com

GETTING AROUND SAN FRANCISCO

San Francisco occupies a compact area, making it a sightseer's dream. Many of the sights that feature prominently in visitors' itineraries are only a short walk from each other. The city's public transportation is also very easy to use and efficient. Few visitors can resist a cable car ride. Bus routes crisscross town and pass many attractions.

The pedicab, popular transportation in good weather

Muni Metro streetcars and BART lines serve the suburbs and the outlying neighborhoods. Taxis are affordable but are often difficult to find. They are recommended if you have to make a trip after dark or even during the day through certain parts of the city. Passenger ferries and boat trips run regularly east and north across the bay.

Walking San Francisco's streets

PLANNING YOUR JOURNEY

All public transportation and taxis run at capacity during the rush hours, which are Monday to Friday, 7am to 9am and 4pm to 7pm. The entire city is busy at these times, and it is easier to face the crowds on the sidewalks than to board a bus, cable car or train full of commuters, or to sit in a traffic jam. South of Market Street, city center roads are particularly busy at the end of the day, when cars line up to take their turn on the Bay Bridge and head for

the southbound freeway. Parades and special events can often jam up an area. Ask at your hotel's reception desk and check their calendar of events to avoid getting caught in the middle of a particular celebration (see pp148–51). Protests at City Hall are fairly common, and police escort these planned, peaceful demonstrations into the city center, maintaining crowd control. Look in newspapers and local publications and check with the San Francisco Convention and Visitors Bureau (see p278) or your hotel for the day's events.

STREET LAYOUT AND NUMBERING

Most of San Francisco's streets are based on a grid system. Market Street crosses the city from southwest to northeast. This divides the northern and southern sections. With few exceptions, each block is designated a number by hundreds, starting at zero. So, the first block from Market Street has addresses between 1 and 99. The second block has addresses between 100 and 199, and so on.

House numbers on east – west streets increase as they move west. Numbers on north–south streets increase going north of Market Street, but also increase as they move south of Market Street. When asking for an address, make sure you also get the

name of the nearest cross street and the neighborhood of your destination.

Local residents refer to the numerically named *avenues* in the Richmond District as "The Avenues." Numerically named *streets* begin on the

south side of Market Street, in the city center, and end in the Mission District. The *Street Finder* on pages 302–11 provides a comprehensive map with details of the city.

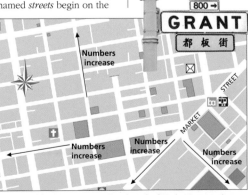

Street numbering increases north and south of Market Street and west from San Francisco Bay

WALKING IN SAN FRANCISCO

The best way to explore San Francisco is on foot. The main tourist areas are within 15 to 20 minutes of each other if you walk at average speed. The hills, particularly Nob Hill (see pp101–3) and Telegraph

Pedestrian crosswalk

Hill (see pp90–93), can be a struggle, but the views from the top over the city and the bay make them well worth the strenuous climb.

Most road intersections are marked with a green and white sign bearing the name of the cross street. These signs are posted high on utility poles. This can be especially confusing along Market Street where the street names are different on each side of the thoroughfare. Street names are often imprinted in the concrete pavement at corners.

Traffic lights signal red (stop), green (go) and yellow (prepare to stop or caution)

Do not cross the street

You may cross the street

for vehicles. For pedestrians, electronic "Walk" signs show an illuminated white human figure. Orange lights flash the words for a few seconds. This is a warning for pedestrians to get out of the street before the signs change to a solid "Don't Walk" signal.

Vehicles are driven on the right-hand side of the road in the US, except on the many one-way streets. Make sure you look both ways before you cross. Vehicles are allowed to turn right on a red light if the way is clear, so be careful when crossing at traffic lights. Never rely solely on a pedestrian signal to protect you from oncoming traffic or those who drive through red lights.

Jaywalking is common but illegal. Crossing in the middle of a block or using a crosswalk when the "Don't Walk" signal is showing can result in a minimum $50 fine.

MOTORCYCLES AND MOPEDS

Motorcycles and mopeds are in the minority compared with private cars on San Francisco's streets. The adventurous visitor can track down a few places where motorcycles and mopeds are available for rent. These tend to be close to beaches and university campuses. Helmets, a valid US or international motorcycle license, security deposit, and prior riding experience are required.

BICYCLING

Bicycling is very popular in San Francisco, and it is possible to find routes that avoid hills, especially along the waterfront. Bicycles can be rented for around $25 a day or $130 a week. There are bicycle lanes in parts of the city and the Bay Area, and some buses are equipped to carry bikes strapped to the outside. There are two marked scenic bicycle routes. One goes from Golden Gate Park (see pp142–57) south to Lake Merced; the other starts at the southern end of Golden Gate Bridge (see pp64–7) and crosses to Marin

County in the north. Bicycles and equipment, repairs, rentals and details of tours are available from **Bay City Bike** and **Blazing Saddles**.

Cycling in Golden Gate Park

OTHER WAYS TO GET AROUND

Pedicabs can be found along The Embarcadero, especially near Fisherman's Wharf (see pp80–81). A fleet of motorized cable cars dashes around the city giving a set guided tour. Passengers can get on or off where they choose. Sight-seeing bus tours can be half- or full-day excursions (see p279). To travel in real style, you can

rent a limousine with driver and guide. A water taxi service is planned to run along the waterfront.

DIRECTORY

MOTORCYCLE AND MOPED RENTAL

Eagle Rider Motorcycle Sales & Rentals
1060 Bryant St. **Map** 11 B2.
Tel 503-1900.
www.eaglerider.com

BICYCLE RENTAL

Bay City Bike
2661 Taylor Street, at Fisherman's Wharf. **Map** 5 A1.
Tel 346-2453.
www.baycitybike.com

Blazing Saddles
1095 Columbus Ave.
Map 5 A2.
Tel 202-8888.
Pier 41. **Map** 5 B1.
Tel 202-8888.
www.blazingsaddles.com

Call **CityBike Hotline** for routes, maps, and information on bikes on Muni/Bart.
Tel 585-2453.

Traveling by Bus and Muni Metro Streetcar

San Francisco Municipal Railway, or Muni as it is commonly called, is the organization that runs the city's public transportation system. You can use one interchangeable pass – Muni Passport – to travel on Muni buses, Muni Metro streetcars (electric trams) and the three cable car lines, which are mainly used by tourists. Buses and streetcars serve most tourist attractions and all neighborhoods. Armed with the bus and streetcar map on the inside back cover, and a Muni Passport, you can use the city's public transportation all day at a fraction of the cost of private rentals and parking fees.

Muni bus shelter with glass walls and public pay phones

FARES AND TICKETS

Buses and streetcars both cost $2 per ride. When paying your fare, you can request a free transfer, which will allow you to change to another bus or streetcar without paying an additional fare. The transfer is valid for 90 minutes. Reduced fares are available for senior citizens aged over 65 and children (five to 17 years). There is no extra charge for express or limited-stop services.

If you are planning to make a number of trips by Muni, a Muni Passport, valid for one, three or seven days, allows unlimited travel on buses, streetcars and cable cars for the duration specified. Muni Passports are available from the information booths near the baggage reclaim areas at San Francisco International Airport. They can also be purchased from the information kiosk at the **Visitor Information Center** outside the Powell Street BART/Metro station, and at the cable car ticket booths at Powell & Market streets and Hyde & Beach streets.

You can also buy tokens that offer a saving of 20 percent off the standard fare.

USING BUSES

Buses stop only at designated bus stops, every two or three blocks. On boarding, put the exact change or tokens in the fare box, or show your Muni Passport to the driver. Ask your driver to let you know when you are near your destination. Senior citizens and disabled passengers have priority at the front of the bus, so be prepared to give up your seat.

Smoking, drinking, eating, and playing music are prohibited on buses. Guide dogs for the blind can ride for free at any time; other animals may be allowed to ride on Muni vehicles at certain times of day, at the driver's discretion.

To indicate that you want to get off at the next stop, pull the cord that runs along the windows. The "Stop Requested" sign above the front window will light up. Instructions about how to open the doors are posted near the exit. Look carefully for oncoming traffic

Route numbers shown on the front and side of the bus

when alighting from the bus; some stops are located at islands in the middle of the street so be particularly cautious at these stops.

The route number and name of the destination are shown on the front and side of every bus, near the front door. Route numbers that are followed by a letter (L, X, AX, BX, etc.) are either express services or make limited stops. Ask the driver if you are not sure where the bus stops. Several lines offer a Night Owl Service from midnight to 6am, but taxis are considered the safest means of getting around town after dark.

BUS STOPS

Bus stops are indicated by signs displaying the Muni logo or by yellow bands on poles. Bus shelters are usually three-sided with glass walls. Route numbers of buses that stop there are listed below the sign and on the exterior wall of the shelter. Route maps and service frequency guides are posted inside most bus shelters, and many are equipped with pay phones.

Muni Passports

DIRECTORY

MUNI INFORMATION

Tel *673-6864*, TTY: *923-6373*.
www.sfmta.com

MUNI PASSPORTS

Visitor Information Center
Lower level, Hallidie Plaza, Market and Powell Sts.
Map 5 C5. **Tel** *391-2000*.
www.transitinfo.org

Powell Street Kiosk
Hallidie Plaza, Market and Powell Sts. **Map** 5 C5.

USING STREETCARS

In the city center, streetcars operate both above and below ground, whereas in outer neighborhoods, they run at street level only.

Streetcar lines J (Church), K (Ingleside), L (Taraval), M (Ocean View), N (Judah), and T (Third) all share the same tracks, which run beneath Market Street. So if you intend to catch a streetcar at a Market Street station, it is a good idea to check the letter and name of the one you are about to board to avoid taking the wrong line.

Along Market Street, four of the seven underground stations are shared by both Muni Metro streetcars and BART (see p298). Orange, yellow and white illuminated signs mark the entrances.

Muni Metro streetcar with its distinctive red and silver cars

In the station, look for the separate "Muni" entrance.

Pay or show a Muni Passport, then proceed downstairs to the platform. To go west, choose "Outbound," to go east, choose "Downtown." Electronic signs show which streetcar is about to arrive. Doors open automatically to allow passengers to enter. In the event they don't open at a street-level or low-level platform stop, push on the low bar beside the exit.

Stops above ground are indicated by an orange-and-brown metal flag, or by a yellow band around a pole, marked "Muni" or "Car Stop."

Lines J, K, L, M, N, and T all use new Breda cars, which have distinctive silver and red cars. Streetcars are also known as Light Rail Vehicles (LRVs).

SIGHTSEEING BY BUS/STREETCAR

Popular routes for visitors include 30, 38, 39, 45 47, Market and Wharves historic streetcar line. Route 38 runs to the hills above Ocean Beach, and Golden Gate Park is on route No. 21. More information is available from Muni or the city's **Visitor Information Center**. For more bus and streetcar routes see the map on the inside back cover.

Historic streetcar near Fisherman's Wharf

KEY

— Route 10
— Route 21
— Route 30
— Route 38
— Route 39
— Route 41
— Route 45
— Route 47
— Route 76
— F line
— N line
🚇 BART station
🚆 Caltrain station
⚓ Ferry jetty

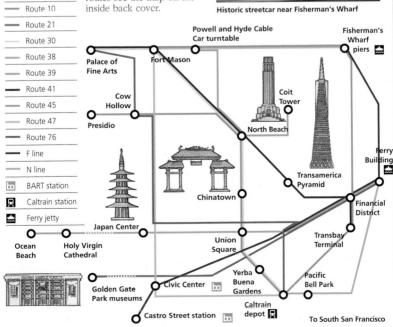

Traveling by Cable Car

San Francisco's cable cars are world famous *(see pp104–5)* and every visitor will want to ride one at least once. The cable car service runs from 6:30am to 12:30am daily. There is a flat fare of $5 for each journey, with a discount for seniors and the disabled between 9pm and 7am. Although this is a great way to see the sights, buses *(see pp294–5)* are a more practical option.

USING THE CABLE CARS

Cable cars run along three routes. The Powell–Hyde line is the most popular. Starting at the Powell and Market turntable *(see p117)*, it skirts Union Square and climbs Nob Hill providing good views of Chinatown. It continues past the Cable Car Museum *(see p103)*, crosses Lombard Street *(see p88)* then descends Hyde Street to the turntable near Aquatic Park *(see p172)*. The Powell–Mason line also begins at Powell and Market streets and follows the same route to the Cable Car Barn. From there, it passes by North Beach and ends at Bay Street. Sit facing east on the Powell lines, and you will see the

**Cable car
signal box**

best sights as you travel about. The California line runs from the base of Market Street along California Street. It passes through part of the Financial District and Chinatown. At Nob Hill the Powell lines cross the California line, so passengers can transfer between lines, but they have to pay again if they have one-way ticket. The California line then continues over Nob Hill, ending at Van Ness Avenue. For each of the three lines, the return trip follows the outward route, so riders are able to catch views from the other side of the car.

Commuters like to use cable cars too, so avoid traveling during rush hours if possible *(see p278)*. Whatever time you travel though,

you are much more likely to get a seat if you board the cable car at the end of the line you have chosen.

TICKETS

If you have not already purchased a Muni Passport *(see p294)*, you can buy a ticket or a one-day pass from the conductor. Tickets are collected once you board. Muni passes, souvenir tickets, and maps are available at kiosks at Powell and Market streets and at Hyde and Beach streets, or at the city Visitor Information Center *(see p294)*.

CABLE CAR STOPS

To catch a cable car you can line up at either end of a line or wait at a stop. Stand on the sidewalk and wave to alert the gripman. Do not board until the car has come to a complete stop and be prepared to jump on quickly. Stops are marked by maroon signs that display the outline of a cable car in white, or by a yellow line painted on the road.

RECOGNIZING YOUR CABLE CAR

Currently 40 cable cars operate on the city's three lines. Each car seats 29 to 34 passengers and, depending on the type of car, can accommodate an additional 20 to 40 people standing.

On the front, back and sides of every cable car is the name of the line: Powell–Hyde, Powell–Mason or California Street. The number of the cable car is also displayed. California Street cars are easy to identify because they have a driver's cab at both ends. Cars on the two Powell lines have only one cab.

The conductor and gripman are generally friendly and helpful, so ask one of them if you are not sure which line to take to reach your destination.

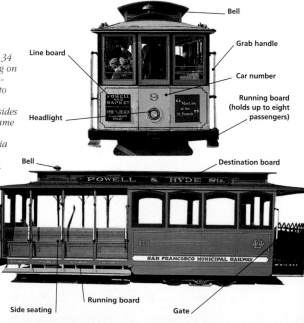

Bell

Grab handle

Line board

Car number

Running board
(holds up to eight
passengers)

Headlight

Bell

Destination board

Side seating

Running board

Gate

SIGHTSEEING BY CABLE CAR

The city's hills present no problem to cable cars. They tackle precipitous slopes effortlessly, passing sights and areas popular with tourists. The most thrilling descent is the final stretch of the Powell–Hyde line.

KEY

══	California line
━━	Powell–Hyde line
──	Powell–Mason line
◖	Turntable/crossing
◯	Terminus
🚃	Cable Car Barn

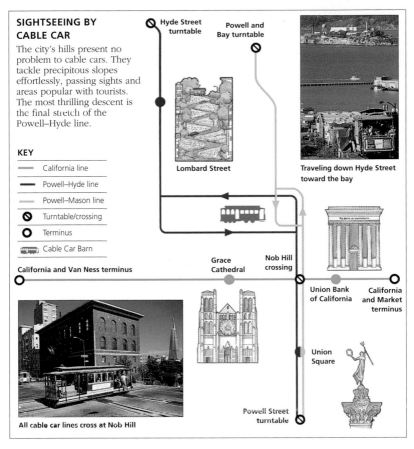

Hyde Street turntable

Powell and Bay turntable

Lombard Street

Traveling down Hyde Street toward the bay

California and Van Ness terminus

Grace Cathedral

Nob Hill crossing

Union Bank of California

California and Market terminus

Union Square

Powell Street turntable

All cable car lines cross at Nob Hill

TRAVELING SAFELY IN A CABLE CAR

If there is not a crowd, you can choose whether to sit or stand inside, sit outside on a bench or stand on an end. More adventurous passengers may prefer to hang onto a pole while standing on a side running board. Wherever you find a place, hold on tight.

Try not to get in the way of the gripman; he needs a lot of room to operate the grip lever. This off-limits area is marked by yellow lines on the floor.

Use caution while on board. Passing other cable cars is exciting, but be careful not to lean out too far because they get very close to one another. Be very careful when boarding or getting off. Often cable cars stop at an intersection so that you have to get on or off between the car

and other vehicles, and this can be dangerous. All passengers must get off at the end of the line. If you wish to make a return trip, you must wait for the car to be turned around on the turntable, or switched to the return line, before boarding again.

USEFUL NUMBERS

Cable Car Barn
1201 Mason St. **Map** 5 B3.
Museum Tel *(415) 474-1887.*

Muni Information
Tel 673-6864. Cable car information, fares, Muni Passports.

Passengers riding on a cable car's running board

Traveling by BART

San Francisco Peninsula and the East Bay are linked by BART (Bay Area Rapid Transit). This is a 103-mile (165-km) rapid transit system with a highspeed fleet of trains, all wheelchair-accessible. In 2003 a new station opened in the San Francisco International airport.

The BART logo

TAKING A TRIP BY BART

1 BART trains operate daily until midnight. BART stops at five stations beneath Market Street – Civic Center, Powell, Montgomery and Embarcadero – and above ground in most outer areas. All trains from Daly City stop at city center stations before heading for the East Bay through a 4-mile (6-km) underwater tunnel. Transfers in the East Bay are possible at only two stations: MacArthur and Oakland City.

KEY

—	Richmond–Daly City
—	Milbrae–Bay Point
—	Fremont–Daly City
—	Fremont– Richmond
—	Pleasanton–SF Airport
—	Millbrae–SF Airport

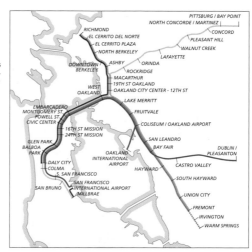

2 All BART tickets are issued by dispensing machines. To calculate your fare, look for the rates posted near the machines inside the BART stations.

3 Insert coins or bills here. Machines will accept coins and notes, and some will accept debit/credit cards with a $20 minimum purchase.

4 The value inserted is shown here. To buy a round trip ticket, insert twice the amount for one-way fare.

5 Tickets are magnetically coded with the value, which is then printed on the ticket.

6 Your ticket is issued here. Each person traveling should have his or her own ticket.

Ticket value

Magnetic strip   **Insert ticket into barrier this way**

7 To gain access to the platforms, you must run your ticket through a turnstile. The fare for your trip is automatically deducted from the ticket value. Before you leave the station you must also insert your ticket in the turnstile. If any value remains, your ticket will be returned as the turnstile opens.

8 All trains display their final destination: westbound to San Francisco/Daly City for example; east-bound to Oakland, Richmond, Bay Point or Fremont. Train doors open automatically. Platforms are marked with the end of the line in the direction in which the train is traveling.

9 Fortunately, BART stations have personnel on hand to answer questions and assist passengers with the machines. If you just want to explore the BART system without breaking your trip, inquire about an excursion fare. For information telephone 788-BART (788-2278) or visit www.bart.gov.

Ferries and Bay Trips

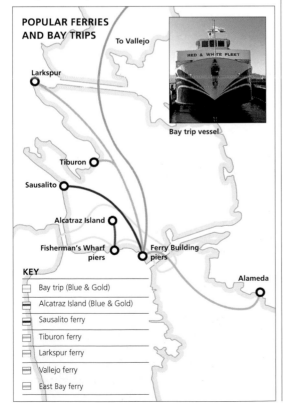

Sign for bay sightseeing cruise tickets

Before the Golden Gate and Oakland bridges spanned the bay, hundreds of ferries shuttled from shore to shore, carrying commuters and goods from the northern counties and East Bay. Although they are no longer a necessity, boats and ferries are still a favorite way to see the city's shoreline and get around. The coastline of San Francisco Bay encompasses the cities of San Francisco and Oakland *(see pp164–7)* as well as the smaller towns of Tiburon and Sausalito *(see p161)*.

FERRY SERVICES

Residents of the Bay Area adore their ferries. During the week commuters pack them to avoid rush-hour traffic on the bridges, and on weekends suburban families leave their cars behind for jaunts to the city.

Ferries do not have audio tours to identify and describe the sights, but they are less expensive than sightseeing cruises. Food and drink are available onboard. Ferries carry only foot passengers and bicycles, not motor vehicles.

The Ferry Building, on the Embarcadero *(see p112)*, is the terminal for **Golden Gate Ferries**. Another service, **Blue & Gold**, docks at nearby Fisherman's Wharf *(see pp80–81)*. Contact ferry companies for fares and timetables.

BAY TRIPS

Bay sightseeing cruises from Fisherman's Wharf are operated by **Blue & Gold Fleet and Red & White Fleet**. Trips offered include Angel Island, Alcatraz *(see pp84–7)* and towns on the north shore of the bay *(see pp160–61)*. There are also combined boat and bus tours to visit Six Flags Marine World *(see p274)* and Muir Woods *(see p160)*.

You can dine and dance aboard one of several cruisers that ply the bay's waters. **Hornblower Dining Yachts** offer lunch on Friday, brunch on weekends, and dinner daily on their charter tours. Meals are also served at bayside tables that offer diners spectacular views of the waterfront.

The **Oceanic Society** offers nautical environmental safaris with an onboard naturalist to the Farallon Islands, 25 miles (40 km) offshore.

There are also whale-watching expeditions off San Francisco's west coast *(see p272)*. Check with individual operators for seasonal details.

DIRECTORY

FERRIES

Blue & Gold Fleet
Pier 39, 41. **Map** 5 B1.
Tel 773-1188. 75-minute tour.
www.blueandgoldfleet.com

Golden Gate Ferries
Tel 923-2000. **www**.
goldengateferry.com

BAY TRIPS

Hornblower Dining Yachts
Pier 33. **Map** 5 C1. *Tel 394-8900, ext. 7.* **www**.hornblower.
com. *Dinner and dancing cruises.*

Oceanic Society Expeditions
Tel 441-1104.
www.oceanicsociety.org

Red & White Fleet
Pier 431/2. **Map** 5 B1.
Tel 447-0597.
www.redandwhite.com

POPULAR FERRIES AND BAY TRIPS

To Vallejo

Larkspur

Bay trip vessel

Tiburon

Sausalito

Alcatraz Island

Fisherman's Wharf piers

Ferry Building piers

Alameda

KEY

	Bay trip (Blue & Gold)
	Alcatraz Island (Blue & Gold)
	Sausalito ferry
	Tiburon ferry
	Larkspur ferry
	Vallejo ferry
	East Bay ferry

Driving in San Francisco

Congestion, a shortage of parking areas (and their high prices), and strictly enforced parking laws discourage many visitors from driving in San Francisco. Seat belts are required by law. Speed limits vary, but the maximum is 35 mph (56 km/h). Many streets are one-way, with traffic lights at most corners in the city center.

CAR RENTAL

You must be at least 21 years old with a valid driving license (a US or International Driver's License is best) to rent a car. All agencies require a major credit card or a large cash deposit. Damage and liability insurance is recommended. Always return the car with a full tank of gas to avoid the inflated gas prices charged by the rental agency. It is less expensive to rent a car at the airport: rental taxes are $2 a day more in the city.

TRAFFIC SIGNS

Colorful signs and symbols point the way to the main tourist areas, such as Chinatown (a lantern); Fisherman's Wharf (a crab); North Beach (outline of Italy). "Stop" and "Do Not Enter" signs are red and white. "Caution" and "Yield" signs are yellow and black. "One Way" signs are black and white. If

Tourist area direction sign

there is no oncoming traffic, drivers may turn right at a red light. Otherwise, red and amber lights mean stop.

PENALTIES

If you park your car at an out-of-order meter, expect to get a parking ticket. Blocking bus stops, fire hydrants, driveways, garages, and wheelchair ramps will also incur a fine, as will running a red light. For details of traffic regulations, contact the **Parking and Traffic Department**. If you receive a ticket, you are expected to pay the fine or appear in court. After five parking tickets, a "Denver Boot" may be clamped to the wheel,

immobilizing the car. This is removed when the fines are paid. If your car has been towed away, call the **Police Department Towed Vehicle Information** line. Obtain a release permit from the nearest police station, then go to **City Tow**. You will have to pay a towing and storage fee. If it is a rental car, you will need to produce the contract before the car will be released.

DIRECTORY

CAR RENTAL AGENCIES

Avis
Tel (1) (800) 831-2847.
www.avis.com

Hertz
Tel (1) (800) 654-3131.
www.hertz.com

USEFUL NUMBERS

City Tow
850 Bryant St. **Map** 11 B2.
Tel 621-8605.

Parking and Traffic Department
Tel 554-7275.

Police Department Towed Vehicle Information
Tel 553-1235.

PARKING

Parking meters operate from 8am to 6pm Monday to Saturday, and occasionally on Sundays too. Most meters have short time limits, usually of one hour. City center parking garages cost $9 to $20 a

day, and many accept only cash. Curbs are color coded: red mean stopping is prohibited; yellow are loading zones; green allow 10 minutes parking, while white permit 5 minutes during business hours. Blue curbs are reserved for the disabled. Some parking spaces are tow-away zones from 7am to 9am and after 3 or 4pm.

By law you must curb your wheels when parking on steep hills. Turn wheels into the road when facing uphill and toward the curb when facing downhill.

Time elapsed shown here

Insert coins here

Turn handle to register coins

Curbing the wheels of a car – the curb acts as a block

PREVENT RUNAWAYS
CURB WHEELS
PARK IN GEAR
SET BRAKE

PARK AT
90 DEGREES

Curbside parking information signs, to prevent runaway cars

San Francisco's Taxis

Taxis in San Francisco operate 24 hours a day. Taxis can be hard to find, especially in the outer areas, but the drivers are generally helpful and friendly. Many drivers are veterans eager to share their knowledge of the streets. Taxis are licensed and regulated, so you can always expect courtesy, efficient service and a set price. The guidelines below will make sure that you do not get "taken for a ride" when you take a taxi.

Heavy traffic in Chinatown

TAKING A TAXI

Cabs have a rooftop sign that is illuminated when the vehicle is vacant. The various company liveries are red, white and blue; yellow; yellow and orange; and green. All taxis display the company name and telephone number, plus the cab number.

To catch a cab, wait at a taxi stand, call and request a pick-up, or try to hail a vacant cab. When you request a pick-up, give your exact address and name. You are expected to meet the cab on the street. If you wait more than 15 minutes, call again. Requests for cabs to the airport usually get a quick

response. Passengers ride in the back seat, which may or may not have seat belts. The meter is on the dashboard. Note the company and cab number or the driver's name and number. Tell the driver your destination and the cross street, if possible. The driver should get you there in the shortest amount of time. Traffic congestion can slow the best drivers down, so it may be better to pay the fare, get out and walk the final few blocks.

Taxi drivers do not carry much cash. Pay with bills of $20 or smaller. Add a 10 to 15 percent tip and hand it to the driver before you get out of the cab. The driver will write a receipt on request. Check you have all your belongings before you get out. If you have left something in a cab, call the cab company and give them the cab number or driver's name.

FARES

Fares are posted inside the cab. There is a flat fee (around $3.35) for the first mile (1.6 km). This increases by about $2.25 for each additional mile (1.6 km) or 40 cents a minute while waiting outside an address or in traffic delays. The average fare from San Francisco airport to the city center is $35. Fares from the Ferry Building to the west

coast ocean beaches are about $20 to $24. These estimates do not include any additional charges such as time spent waiting in heavy traffic, or a tip for the driver.

Fare meter inside a taxi

REGULATIONS

Taxi drivers must carry with them photographic identification and a permit to drive a taxi, called a medallion. The driver can designate the cab a smoking or nonsmoking vehicle. If you need to complain about a taxi driver, call the **Police Department Taxicab Complaint Line**.

DIRECTORY

TAXI COMPANIES

City Cab
Tel 920-0700.

De Soto Cab
Tel 970-1300.

Luxor Cab
Tel 282-4141.

Veteran's Cab
Tel 552-1300.

Yellow Cab
Tel 626-2345.

INFORMATION

Police Department Taxicab Complaint Line
Tel 553-1447.

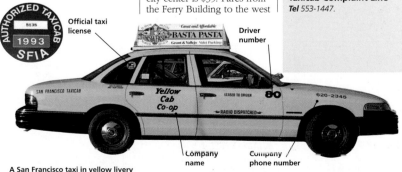

Official taxi license

Driver number

Company name

Company phone number

A San Francisco taxi in yellow livery

STREET FINDER

Map references given with sights, restaurants, hotels, shops and entertainment sites refer to the maps in this section. A complete index of the street names and places of interest marked on the maps follows on pages 313–320. The key map below shows the area of San Francisco covered by the *Street* *Finder*. This includes the sightseeing areas (which are color-coded) as well as the whole of central San Francisco, with the main districts where restaurants, hotels and entertainment sites are located. Because the city center is so packed with sights, there is a large-scale map of this area on pages 5 and 6.

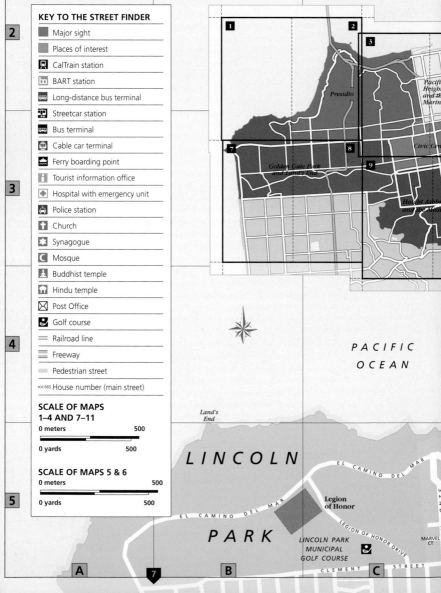

KEY TO THE STREET FINDER

■	Major sight
	Places of interest
🚆	CalTrain station
🚇	BART station
🚌	Long-distance bus terminal
🚋	Streetcar station
🚍	Bus terminal
🚡	Cable car terminal
⛴	Ferry boarding point
ℹ	Tourist information office
✚	Hospital with emergency unit
🚓	Police station
✝	Church
✡	Synagogue
☪	Mosque
卍	Buddhist temple
🛕	Hindu temple
⊠	Post Office
⛳	Golf course
=	Railroad line
≡	Freeway
—	Pedestrian street
<<665	House number (main street)

SCALE OF MAPS 1–4 AND 7–11

0 meters	500

0 yards	500

SCALE OF MAPS 5 & 6

0 meters	500

0 yards	500

PIER 27

PIER 23

PIER 19

PIER 17

PIER 15

PIER 9

Pier 7

PIER 5

PIER 3

PIER 1

Alcatraz Island

San Francisco Bay

FRONT STREET

DAVIS STREET

THE EMBARCADERO

JACKSON STREET

WASHINGTON STREET

DRUMM STREET

MARITIME PLAZA

EMBARCADERO PLAZA PARK

Embarcadero Center

JUSTIN HERMAN PLAZA

Hyatt Regency Hotel

BATTERY

SACRAMENTO STREET

FRONT STREET

DAVIS ST.

<< 200 STREET

World Trade Center

PIER 2

Ferry Building

Embarcadero Station

STEUART STREET

SPEAR STREET

Rincon Center

cific Coast ck Exchange

Amtrak Terminal Ticket Office

MISSION STREET

BEALE STREET

MAIN STREET

TREMONT STREET

Folsom Station

PIER 24

Greyhound Bus Depot

HOWARD STREET

Transbay Terminal

1ST STREET

ntgomery Station

STEVENSON ST

2ND STREET

MINNA STREET

<< 333

FREMONT STREET

FOLSOM STREET

ZERO STREET

ELKHART ST

PIER 26

PIER 28

artoon rt Museum

Pacific Telephone Building

Museum of Modern Art

TEHAMA STREET

MALDEN AL

CLEMENTINA ST

GUY PL.

ESSEX ST.

LANSING ST

PIER 30

PIER 32

THE EMBARCADERO

HAWTHORNE STREET

DOW PL

HAMPTON PL

VEROKICA PL

HARRISON STREET

Brannan Station

BRYANT STREET

RINCON ST

1ST STREET

PIER 34

PIER 36

Moscone nvention Center

FOLSOM STREET

STILLMAN ST

DE BOOM ST

BRANNAN STREET

PIER 38

<< 665

SAN FRANCISCO OAKLAND BAY BRIDGE

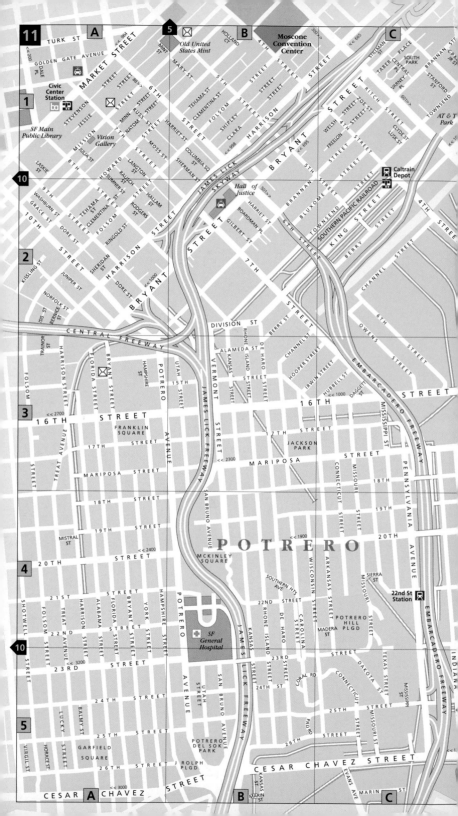

Street Finder Index

General Index

Acknowledgments

Dorling Kindersley would like to thank the many people whose help and assistance contributed to the preparation of this book.

Main Contributors
Jamie Jensen grew up in Los Angeles and moved to San Francisco to study architecture at the University of California at Berkeley, where he still has his home. His other credits include *Built to Last*, an authorized biography of the Grateful Dead, and numerous travel guides including the *Rough Guide to California*. His most recent project is *Road Trip: USA*, a practical travel guide to the "old roads" across America.

Barry Parr was born in the San Francisco Bay Area, and studied English literature at the University of California at Berkeley, and at Cambridge University. He has written and edited travel guides, and writes for many magazines.

Additional Photography
John Heseltine, Trevor Hill, Andrew McKinney, Ian O'Leary, Robert Vente.

Additional Illustrations
James A. Allington, Annabelle Brend, Craig Draper, Steve Gyapay, Kevin Jones Associates, Simon Roulston, Sue Sharples, Paul Williams, Ann Winterbotham.

Design and Editorial
Pardoe Blacker Publishing Limited
MANAGING EDITOR Alan Ross
MANAGING ART EDITOR Simon Blacker
PROJECT SECRETARY Cindy Edler
Dorling Kindersley Limited
MANAGING EDITORS Douglas Amrine, Carolyn Ryden
MANAGING ART EDITOR Stephen Knowlden
US EDITOR Mary Ann Lynch
MAP COORDINATORS Simon Farbrother, David Pugh
PRODUCTION Hilary Stephens
MAPS Lovell Johns Ltd., Oxford UK
Street Finder Maps based upon digital data, adapted with permission from original survey by ETAK INC 1984–1994.

Michael Blacker, Dawn Brend, Laaren Brown, Maxine Cass, Aaron Chamberlin, Kelly Chamberlin, Peter Cieply, Sherry Collins, Melissa Corrigan, Jo Gardner, Emily Green, Fay Franklin, Sally Hibbard, Paul Hines, Katie Hogg, Rose Hudson, Claire Jones, Heather Jones, Esther Labi, Maite Lantaron, Nicola Malone, Joanne Miller, Karen Misuraca, Sonal Modha, Adam Moore, Mary Ormandy, Catherine Palmi, Marianne Petrou, Mani Ramaswamy, Steve Rowling, Dan Rubin, Mary Sutherland, Ros Walford, Hugo Wilkinson.

Cartography
Jennifer Skelley, Jane Hugill, Phil Rose, Rachel Hawtin.

Index
Indexing Specialists, 202 Church Road, Hove, East Sussex, UK.

Special Assistance
Marcia Eymann and Abby Wasserman at The Oakland Museum of California, Stacia Fink at the Foundation for San Francisco's Architectural Heritage, Richard Fishman, Debbie Freedon at the Legion of Honor, Michael Lampen at Grace Cathedral, Dan Mohn, Chief Engineer of Golden Gate Bridge, Dr. John R. Nudds at Manchester University Museum, Richard Ogar at Bancroft Library, Peppers, Riggio Café, Royal Thai Restaurant, Scott Sack at the Golden Gate National Recreation Area, Sandra Farish Sloan and Jennifer Small at the San Francisco Museum of Modern Art, Stella Pastry and Cafe, Stephen Marcos Landscapes, Dawn Stranne at the San Francisco Convention and Visitors Bureau, The Little Cafe, Carl Wilmington.

Research Assistance
Christine Bartholomew, Jennifer Bermon, Cathy Elliott, Kirsten Whatley, Jon Williams, Michael Wrenn.

Photography Permissions
Dorling Kindersley would like to thank the following for their kind permission to photograph at their establishments:
Asian Art Museum, Cable Car Barn Museum, California Academy of Sciences, Cha Cha Cha, Chinese Historical Society, City Hall, Coit Tower, Columbarium, Crocker Galleria, Ernie's, The Exploratorium, Fort Mason Center, Fortune Cookie Factory, Foundation for San Francisco's Architectural Heritage (Haas-Lilienthal House), Golden Gate National Recreation Area (Alcatraz), Gump's, Hyatt Regency Hotel, Kong Chow Temple, Kuleto's, MH de Young Memorial Museum, Mission Dolores, Nordstrom, The Oakland Museum of California, Presidio Museum, Rincon Annexe, Saints Peter and Paul Church, San Francisco History Room, San Francisco Main Library, San Francisco National Historical Park, Sheraton Palace Hotel, Sherman House, St. Mary's Cathedral, Temple Emanu-El, Tosca, USS *Pampanito*, Veteran's Building, Wells Fargo History Room.

Picture credits
t = top; tc = top center; tr = top right; cla = center left above; ca = center above; cra = center right above; cl = center left; c = center; cr = center right; clb = center left below; cb = center below; crb = center right below; bl = bottom left; bc = bottom center; br = bottom right.

Works of art have been reproduced with the permission of the following copyright holders:
© ADAGP, Paris and DACS, London 2006: 108tl, 118tl; © ARS, NY and DACS, London 2006 38bc; By permission of DARA BIRNBAUM:

118bl; © DACS, London/VAGA, 2006 188clb;
New York Five Sacred Colors of Corn © Susan
Kelk Cervantes 1996. All rights reserved: 140tl;
Creativity Explored © Creativity Explored
1993. All rights reserved: 141t; © Succession
Picasso/DACS, London 2006: 120t; © Man Ray
Trust/ ADAGP, Paris and DACS, London
2006: 119cra; © Kate Rothko Prizel &
Christopher Rothko ARS, NY and DACS
London 2006 118c; *Carnival* © David Galvez
1983. All rights reserved: 138b; By permission
of Jeff Koons: 121t; By permission of the
Estate of Philip Guston: 37crb; *8 Immortals
(Bok-Sen) & 3 Wisdoms* © Josie Grant 1979. All
rights reserved: 141br; By permission of
Charles O. Perry (Montana), sculptor: 104
(*Eclipse*, 1973, anodized aluminum); *Untitled*
© Michael Rios 1978. All rights reserved: 140tr;
By permission of Wendy Ross, Ross Studio:
173b.

The Publishers are grateful to the following
museums, companies and picture libraries for
permission to reproduce their photographs:

Alamy Images: Douglas Peebles
Photography, 207c; Robert Harding Picture
Library Ltd. 207tl; Roberto Soncin Gerometta
206cla; Allsport: Otto Greule, 50cl; Tony
Duffy, 33br; Archive Photos: 32cb, 102bl;
Armstrong Redwoods State Reserve: 182c; J.
Allan Cash Limited: 178/179; Roger Allen Lee:
186c; The arts and Crafts Museum, Fort Mason:
38t; Bancroft Library, University of California,
Berkeley: 22br, 22cla, 22/23c, 23br, 23cla,
24br, 24clb, 27crb, 60bl, 146c; Morton Beebe:
11br, 179tr; Berkeley Convention and Visitors
Bureau: 162t; Bridgeman Art Library: *The
Thinker (Le Penseur)*, by Auguste Rodin
(1840–1917), Musée Rodin, Paris/Bridgeman
Art Library, London, 156tr; Marilyn Blaisdell
Collection: 27cr.

California Academy of Sciences: 150bc, 151bl,
151cra, 151tc; Caroline Kopp 145c; Dong Lin
36br, 150tr; Susan Middleton 35tl; California
Historical Society, San Francisco: 27b, 28cla,
29crb, 46c, 146b; Camera Press: Gary Freed-
man 32tr; Carolyn Cassady: 32tl, 88b; Center
for the Arts Galleries: 37br; Ken Friedman,
114t; Center of the Arts Theater/Margaret
Jenkins Dance Company: 115tl; Cephas Picture
Library: Mick Rock, 191bl, 193br; Colorific!:
Chuck Nacke, 49b; Corbis: Morton Beebe
148-9, 179b; Bettman 42bl, 43b, 198tr; Jan
Butchofsky-Houser 127b, 178t; Richard
Cummins 10cla, 178b; Kevin Fleming 10b
Gerald French 199t; Lowell Georgia 10t;
125cr; Robert Holmes 38b, 89tc, 192b, 193t,
244br, 261cra; Catherine Karnow 181t; Craig
Lovell 45br; Charles O'Rear 192cl, 193cl;
Reuters Newmedia Inc 259b; Tony Roberts
154-155; Royalty Free 180t; San Francisco
Chronicle/Deanne Fitzmaurice 43t; Phil
Schermeister 11t Michael T Sedam 75br;
Culver Pictures, Inc: 31tl. De Young Museum:

Mark Darley 143t; Bernard Diamond: 60br;
Embarcadero Center: 108tr; Donna Ewald/ Peter
Clute/Vic Reyna/Ed Rogers: 72br; Explor-
atorium: 36tr, 61b, 61cr, 61tl; Fairmont Hotel:
207t; Fort Ross State Historic Park: Daniel F.
Murley, 188t; The Fine Arts Museums of San
Francisco. *Sailboat on the Seine*, c.1874, by
Claude Monet, gift of Bruno and Sadie
Adrian, 36cla; *Saint John the Baptist*, by Matti
Preti, 38cl; High chest, museum purchase, gift
of Mr. and Mrs. Robert A. Magowan, 144tr;
Saint Wenceslaus, Patron Saint of Bohemia,
after a model by Johann Gottlieb Kirchner
(b.1706), hard-paste porcelain, museum
purchase, Roscoe and Margaret Oakes
Income Fund, 156b; *Waterlilies*, c.1914–17, by
Claude Monet, oil on canvas, Mildred Anna
Williams Collection, 156c; *Camille Claudel*,
1880s, by Auguste Rodin, plaster with plaster
base, 154tl; *Old Woman*, c.1618, by Georges
de la Tour, Roscoe and Margaret Oakes Collection, 157cla; *The Impresario, (Pierre Duc-
arre)*, c.1877, by Edgar Degas, oil on paper
board, 157clb; The Flight Collection: 288t.

Steven Gerlick: 105bl; Getty Images: News
/Justin Sullivan 42cr; Stone 2/3, 48b, Roy
Giles 78c; Taxi 11br; Golden Gate Bridge
Highway and Transportation District: 64 all
pictures, 65 all pictures, 66bl, 66tl, 66/67tc,
67tr; Golden Gate National Recreation Area:
Don Denevi Collection: 86clb, 86tl, 87bl, 87br,
87crb, 87tr; Fischetti Collection, 84bl; Stephen
D. Gross, G-WIZ G&P: 188b. © The Henry
Moore Foundation: 123t; Robert Holmes
Photography: Markham Johnson 37bl, 49cr;
Hulton Getty: 33br, 33 bc; Ine Tours: 247cr;
Mark Hopkins Inter-Continental Hotel 102t; The
Image Works: Lisa Law, 129c; Kelley/ Mooney
Photography: 209bl; Courtesy of Landmark
Theatres: 260br; Lawrence Hall of Science,
University of California: Peg Skorpinskin,
162b; Courtesy Levi Strauss & Co., San
Francisco: 135c, 135t; Neil Lukas: 200br, 200cl.

Andrew McKinney Photography: 72bl, 109c;
Alain McLaughlan 289c, 289b; Magnes Museum
Permanent Collections: 19th-century blue
velvet embroidery brocade robe, 163t;
Magnum Photos: Michael K. Nichols, 33bl;
Mark Hopkins Inter-Continental Hotel: 206bl;
Museo ItaloAmericano: *Muto*, 1985, by Mimmo
Paladino, aquatint and sugarlift etching, gift of
Pasquale Iannetti, Museo ItaloAmericano, 39tl;
Meta III, 1985, by Italo Scanga, oil and
lacquer on wood, Museo ItaloAmericano, gift
of Alan Shepp, 75bl; Museum of the City of
San Francisco: Richard Hansen, 19br, 21t,
28clb, 28/29c, 29clb, 29t; Names Project *AIDS
Memorial Quilt*: Mark Theissen, 136b; Napa
Valley Visitors Bureau: 190b, 190tl; Peter
Newark's American Pict-ures: 6t, 9 (inset), 23bl,
25bl, 25br, 25cra, 25crb, 25tl, 26b, 26tl, 86bl,
105crb, 205 (inset), 277 (inset); N.H.P.A.:
David Middle-ton 194bl; John Shaw 203cr;
Bob von Normann: 189t;

OAKLAND CONVENTION BUREAU: 165t. COURTESY
THE OAKLAND MUSEUM HISTORY DEPARTMENT: 19bl,
22tl, 23cra, 24clb, 25cra, 26cla, 27tr, 29cra, 30c,
31cr, 166bl, 166tl, 166tr, 167tl; OAKLAND MUSEUM
OF CALIFORNIA: Phyllis Diebenkorn, Trustee,
Ocean Park No.107, 1978, Richard
Diebenkorn 166cl; PACIFIC UNION RAILROAD
COMPANY: 27tl; PICTORIAL PRESS LIMITED: J.
Cummings/SF, 32ca, 129b, 134c, 260tr; WWW.
PHOTOGRAPHERSDIRECT.COM: Justin Bailie198tl,
199br; Ann Purcell Travel Journalism, 198b;
Nancy Warner 180b, 181b; PICTUREPOINT: 87tl;
PRECITA EYES MURAL ARTS AND VISITORS CENTRE:
Balloon Journey © 2008 Precita Eyes
Muralists, by Kristen Foskett 140crb; Hillcrest
Elementary School © 2007 Precita Eyes
Muralists 140 cb; *Oakland, Stop the Violence* ©
2007 Precita Eyes Muralists. Directed by
Joshua Stevenson. Designed and painted by
AYPAL youth (Asian Pacific Islander Youth
Promoting Advocacy and Leadership)
including Recy, Marcus and many others.
Acrylic paint on Tyvek 140b; PRESIDIO OF SAN
FRANCISCO: NPS staff 59tl.

REX FEATURES: B. Ward, 33tl; SAN FRANCISCO ARTS
COMMISSION GALLERY: 126t; SAN FRANCISCO BLUES
FESTIVAL: 259t; SAN FRANCISCO CABLE CAR MUSEUM:
26br, 105tl; SAN FRANCISCO CONVENTION AND
VISITORS BUREAU: 40b, 48bl, 48c, 49c, 50cr, 51c,
104c, 161b, 258t; SAN FRANCISCO EXAMINER: 48br;
SAN FRANCISCO MUSEUM OF MODERN ART: *Back
View*, 1977, by Philip Guston, oil on canvas,
gift of the artist, 37crb; *Orange Sweater*, 1955,
by Elmer Bischoff, oil on canvas, gift of Mr.
and Mrs. Mark Schorer, 115c; *Les Valeurs
Personnelles*, 1952, by Rene Magritte, purchased through a gift of Phyllis Wattis 118tr; *No
14*, 1960, by Mark Rothko, 118c; *Zip-Light*,
1990, by Sigmar Willnauer, leather, polyester,
zipper, San Francisco Museum of Modern Art
purchase, 118tl; *The Nest*, 1944, by Louise
Bourgeois, steel, 118bl; *Country Dog
Gentlemen*, 1972, by Roy De Forest, polymer
on canvas, gift of the Hamilton-Wells
Collection, 119br; *Koret Visitor Education
Center*, photo © Richard Barnes 119crb;
Lesende (Reading) (1994) © Gerhard Richter
119cr; by R for Richter; *Melodious Double Stops*,
1980, by Richard Shaw, porcelain with decal
overglaze, purchased with funds from the

National Endowment for the Arts and Frank
O. Hamilton, Byron Meyer and Mrs. Peter
Schlesinger, 119tl; '*92 Chaise*, 1985–92, by
Holt, Hinshaw, Pfau, Jones Architecture, steel,
plastic, rubber and ponyhide, Accessions
Committee Fund, 120b; *Les Femmes D'Alger
(Woman of Algiers)*, 1955, by Pablo Picasso, oil
on canvas, Albert M. Bender Collection, gift of
Albert M. Bender in memory of Caroline
Walter, 120t; *Cave, Tsankawee, New Mexico*,
1988, by Linda Connor, gelatin silver print,
fractional gift of Thomas and Shirley Ross
Davis, 121b; *Graphite To Taste*, 1989, by Gail
Fredell, steel, gift of Shirley Ross Davis, 121c;
Michael Jackson and Bubbles, 1988, by Jeff
Koons, porcelain, purchased through the
Marian and Bernard Messenger Fund, 121t;
SAN FRANCISCO OPERA: 124clb; SAN FRANCISCO
PUBLIC LIBRARY, San Francisco HISTORY CENTER:
22clb, 28bl, 28br, 28tl, 31bl, 31cl, 32bl, 32cra,
33cla, 42cl, 84c, 87clb, 102br, 146tl, 146tr,
299bl; SAN FRANCISCO ZOO: 160t; SAN JOSE
CONVENTION AND VISITORS BUREAU: 168c, 168t,
169t; SANTA CRUZ SEASIDE COMPANY:
186t; SCIENCE PHOTO LIBRARY: Peter Menzel, 18t;
David Parker, 18c, 19c, 19t; MARK SNYDER
PHOTOGRAPHY: 246tl; SONOMA VALLEY VISITORS
BUREAU: Bob Nixon, 226tr, 195cr; SPECTRUM
COLOR LIBRARY: 187b, 282br.

TAHOE NORTH VISITORS AND CONVENTION
BUREAU: 196tl 196tr; Deacon Chapin, 197tr;
UNIVERSITY OF CALIFORNIA, BERKELEY: *Within*,
1969, by Alexander Lieberman, gift of the
artist, University Art Museum, 177b; VISION
BANK: Michael Freeman, 191c, WELLS FARGO
BANK HISTORY ROOM: 21b, 24/25c, 25tr, 110b;
PAUL WILLIAMS: Chinese dish, front cover; VAL
WILMER: 30br; YOSEMITE COLLECTIONS; NATIONAL
PARK SERVICE: 200tl; ZEUM: 114clb.

JACKET
Front – DK IMAGES: bl; GETTY IMAGES: Photo-
grapher's Choice/Mitchell Funk main image.
Back – DK IMAGES: John Heseltine tl; Neil
Lukas cla, bl; Andrew McKinney clb. Spine –
DK IMAGES: Neil Lukas b; GETTY IMAGES:
Photographer's Choice/Mitchell Funk t.

All other pictures Dorling Kindersley. See
www.dkimages.com for further information.

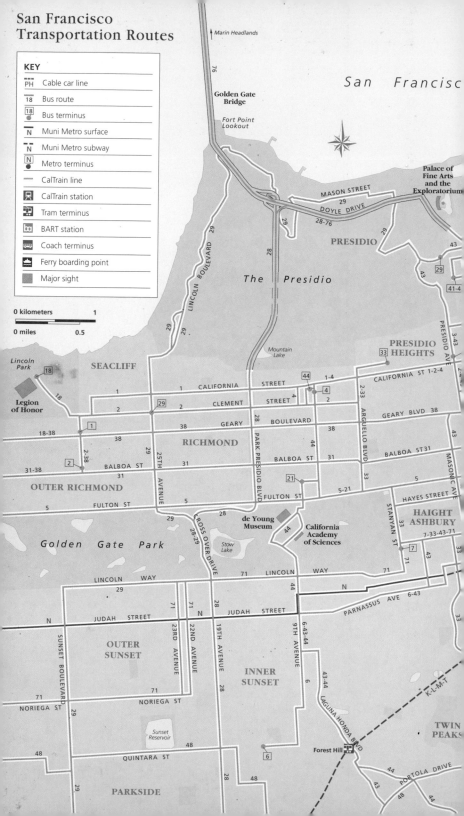